QUALITY ASSURANCE IN HIGHER EDUCATION

HIGHER EDUCATION DYNAMICS

VOLUME 20

SCOPE OF THE SERIES

Higher Education Dynamics is a bookseries intending to study adaptation processes and their outcomes in higher education at all relevant levels. In addition it wants to examine the way interactions between these levels affect adaptation processes. It aims at applying general social science concepts and theories as well as testing theories in the field of higher education research. It wants to do so in a manner that is of relevance to all those professionally involved in higher education, be it as ministers, policy-makers, politicians, institutional leaders or administrators, higher education researchers, members of the academic staff of universities and colleges, or students. It will include both mature and developing systems of higher education, covering public as well as private institutions.

The titles published in this series are listed at the end of this volume.

QUALITY ASSURANCE IN HIGHER EDUCATION
Trends in Regulation, Translation and Transformation

edited by

DON F. WESTERHEIJDEN

University of Twente,
The Netherlands

BJØRN STENSAKER

NIFU-STEP
Oslo, Norway

and

MARIA JOÃO ROSA

CIPES and University of Aveiro,
Portugal

 Springer

A C.I.P. Catalogue record for this book is available from the Library of Congress.

ISBN-13 978-1-4020-6011-3 (HB)
ISBN-13 978-1-4020-6012-0 (e-book)

Published by Springer,
P.O. Box 17, 3300 AA Dordrecht, The Netherlands.

www.springer.com

Printed on acid-free paper

TABLE OF CONTENTS

LIST OF CONTRIBUTORS

ALBERTO AMARAL is professor at the University of Porto and director of CIPES. He is a former rector of the Universidade do Porto (1986–1998), vice-chair of EUA's steering committee on institutional evaluation, and a member of the EUA Board. He is chair of the Board of CHER, life member of IAUP, and a member of EAIR and IMHE. Recent publications include articles in *Quality Assurance in Education*, *Higher Education Quarterly*, *Higher Education Policy*, *Higher Education in Europe*, and *European Journal of Education* and *Higher Education*. He is a member of the editorial board of *Quality Assurance in Education* and of the Springer book series, *Higher Education Dynamics*. He is editor and co-editor of several books, including *Governing Higher Education: National Perspectives on Institutional Governance* (2002), *The Higher Education Managerial Revolution?* (2003), *Markets in Higher Education: Rhetoric or Reality?* (2004), and *Reform and Change in Higher Education: Analysing Policy Implementation* (2005), all in Springer/Kluwer.

DOUGLAS BLACKMUR holds the Standard Bank Chair in Management at the University of the Western Cape in South Africa. He has published in several disciplines including higher education quality assurance, the economics of vertical integration, public sector reform, and industrial relations history. His book, *Strikes: Causes, Conduct and Consequences*, has been commended as a seminal contribution to the international literature on strikes. Douglas is also the senior independent non-executive director of DRDGOLD Limited, chairman of its Remuneration and Nominations Committee, and a member of its Audit and Risk Committee. Other corporate governance appointments have included non-executive director with the Port's Corporation of Queensland and The National Centre for Vocational Education Research Ltd in Australia. Between 1997 and 1999, Douglas was the chief executive officer of the New Zealand Qualifications Authority (NZQA). He has also held positions which include deputy chief executive officer, Canberra Institute of Technology; head, School of Management, Human Resources and Industrial Relations, Queensland University of Technology; and economist, Planning and Supply Division, Shell Australia. He has also served in various other capacities including membership of the Minister of Education's Chairs and Chief Executives' Forum, New Zealand; Australian Qualifications Framework Advisory Board; Australian Curriculum, Assessment and Certification Authorities Chief Executives; Independent Review Panel, National Competition Policy, Office of Fair Trading, Queensland; Joint Consultative Committee, NZQA and New Zealand Vice Chancellors' Committee; Queen Elizabeth II Technicians' Study Awards Selection Committee, New Zealand; and as international advisor, National Accreditation Board of Malaysia, and advisor to the Namibian Government and Namibian Qualifications Authority.

VANEETA-MARIE D'ANDREA is currently director of Academic Affairs and Operations and professor of Higher Educational Development at Central Saint Martins College of Art and Design, University of the Arts London. She has held secondments as co-director of the Teaching Quality Enhancement Fund, National Coordination Team for the Higher Education Funding Council for England, fellow of Kellogg College, lecturer in the Department of Educational Studies at Oxford University, and assistant director of Quality Enhancement at the Quality Assurance Agency for Higher Education (United Kingdom), the former Higher Education Quality Council. She has been a Dana Faculty Fellow while at Guilford College (United States) and was a Fulbright Scholar in India. She has received numerous awards for her work as an educator, and was selected as a Carnegie Scholar. Her primary research and teaching interests include quality enhancement of teaching and learning, scholarship of teaching and learning, higher education policy, educational development, and issues of gender and ethnicity. She has published widely on a range of higher education issues and is a consultant to universities and governments on her research and teaching interests in Europe, Africa, and North America. Her most recent book, co-authored with David Gosling, is entitled *Improving Teaching and Learning in Higher Education: A Whole Institution Approach* (McGraw-Hill).

DAVID D. DILL is professor of Public Policy at the University of North Carolina at Chapel Hill where he is director of the Research Program on Public Policy for Academic Quality, a cross-national study of quality assurance policies in higher education supported by the Ford Foundation. He has been a visiting research fellow at the University of Manchester Business School, a visiting fellow at Wolfson College, Cambridge University, and a visiting professor at the Center for Higher Education Policy Studies (CHEPS) at the University of Twente in the Netherlands. He has conducted research in academic and industrial settings, has consulted with academic and government organisations and agencies in the United States, Europe, and Asia, and has written numerous articles, chapters, and books. His research interests include public policy analysis, higher education policy, and research policy.

PETER EWELL is vice president of the National Center for Higher Education Management Systems (NCHEMS), an independent research and policy organisation in the United States where he has worked since 1981. His research and policy interests related to this volume centre on quality assurance in higher education and he has worked extensively with individual states in the United States on issues related to accountability, as well as with accreditation and quality assurance agencies worldwide. He is also engaged in policy work related to student learning outcomes including the design of state and national assessment systems in higher education and has written extensively on these topics.

LEE HARVEY is a professor and the director of the Centre for Research and Evaluation at Sheffield Hallam University. He has been involved in researching higher education policy since the late 1980s and is an acknowledged expert, inter alia, on issues of quality, employability, and student feedback. He has been a quality advisor to institutions across the world. Lee has wide experience of social research as a research methodologist and social philosopher. He has a teaching qualification alongside his masters in information technology and a doctorate in sociology. He is the editor of the international journals *Quality in Higher Education* and *Higher*

Education Quarterly. Lee is currently chair of EAIR, a member of the Council of SRHE, an ex-officio member of the Board of INQAAHE, an evaluator for ESMU, and an EAU reviewer and member of the latest EAU conference steering committee. Lee is frequently invited as a keynote speaker at international conferences. He is widely published.

JETHRO NEWTON is dean of Learning and Teaching, and professor of Higher Education, at the University of Chester. His research interests and publications are in the areas of quality improvement and enhancement, the management of change in higher education, and policy implementation issues in 'quality' and 'learning and teaching'. He is an executive editor of the international journal *Quality in Higher Education*, and also convenor of the European Association for Institutional Research (EAIR) special interest group 'Quality in Higher Education'.

JUAN F. PERELLON is scientific deputy at the General Directorate for Higher Education of the Department of Training and Youth of the Canton de Vaud (Switzerland). He holds a PhD in Higher Education Policy from the Institute of Education, University of London, and has worked as a researcher on this subject at the Federal Institute of Technology Lausanne and the University of Lausanne. His areas of investigation include the governance, funding, and steering of higher education institutions and their mechanisms for quality assurance and accreditation on which he has published a book and several chapters in edited books as well as articles and reports in English, French, and Spanish. In his current position, he attempts to translate his knowledge and understanding of higher education institutions into advice for policy making at the regional and national levels.

MARIA JOÃO ROSA is assistant professor at the Department of Economics, Management and Industrial Engineering at the University of Aveiro and a researcher at CIPES. She was awarded a PhD by the University of Aveiro, Portugal, in December 2003, with a thesis entitled *Defining Strategic and Excellence Bases for the Development of Portuguese Higher Education*. Her main research topics are quality management and quality assessment in higher education institutions. Recent publications include articles in journals such as *Total Quality Management, Higher Education Quarterly, European Journal of Education,* and *Quality in Higher Education*. She is co-editor of *Cost-sharing and Accessibility in Higher Education: A Fairer Deal?* (2006) in this series.

BJØRN STENSAKER is working at NIFU STEP in Oslo as programme director for studies in higher education. He holds a doctoral degree from the School of Business, Technology and Public Administration at the University of Twente in the Netherlands, and has a special interest in studies of quality, leadership, and organisational change in higher education. Stensaker is the editor-in-chief of *Tertiary Education and Management*, one of the editors of *Quality in Higher Education*, and a former member of the Executive Board of EAIR, the European Higher Education Society.

DON F. WESTERHEIJDEN is a senior researcher at the Center for Higher Education Policy Studies (CHEPS), University of Twente. Since joining CHEPS in 1988 his research has concentrated on the themes around quality and quality assurance of higher education. He has written extensively on external quality assessment and accreditation schemes, and internal quality management of higher education institutions. Besides this, he has published on transitions in Central and Eastern European higher education, and on scenarios for higher education's development. He was a founding member of the Steering Group of the European University Association's Institutional Evaluation Programme and was involved in evaluation agencies in Hungary and Hong Kong. As a staff member of CHEPS, he has been involved in commissioned research projects, training seminars, and consultancies in the area of higher education policy and institutional management.

PREFACE

The Douro seminars on higher education studies that take place every October on the banks of the river Douro in the heart of the Port wine region, are now an established tradition well known by the higher education research community. The seminars are the result of an initiative by *Hedda*, a European consortium of nine centres and institutes devoted to research on higher education, and CIPES, its Portuguese associated centre.

At the seminars, each member of a small group of invited researchers presents and discusses an original research-based paper that is revised afterwards taking into account the comments of the participating colleagues. The revised papers form the basis for the annual thematic book published by Springer in the book series called Higher Education Dynamics (HEDY). Paying tribute to the regularity of the seminars it was decided that the volumes originating from the initiative will be collected in a 'series in the series' called the Douro Series.

The first seminar (2001) was dedicated to the *Governance Structures of Higher Education Institutions*. The second seminar (2002) discussed the *Emergence of Managerialism in Higher Education Institutions*, and the third seminar (2003) focused on *Markets in Higher Education*. The 2004 seminar was dedicated to the topic *Cost Sharing and Accessibility in Higher Education*, while the fifth seminar (October 2005) focused on the *Dynamics and Effects of Quality Assurance in Higher Education*.

The present volume contains the edited versions of the papers presented at the fifth Douro seminar. This volume is dedicated to quality, a theme that pervades the life of higher education institutions all over the world. With massification of higher education, quality has come to the forefront of the debates on higher education being used as a tool for a number of diversified actions, ranging from quality management to compliance and control. The developments of the Bologna process and the proposals concerning a European system of quality assurance and accreditation are additional reasons for the interest in the theme underlying the present book.

By using the marketplace more directly as a coordination mechanism for higher education, governments have been forced to strengthen the autonomy of higher education institutions. The rules of the marketplace demand that producers have decision-making freedom to compete and adapt to the competitive environment. However, this has created challenges with respect to governments' steering capacity and policy effectiveness, as institutions have acquired freedom to define their own strategies under conditions of market-like competition. Quality assessment might be seen as a government tool to regain some degree of control over institutions.

On the other hand, new public management approaches have reduced the power of the academic professionals; and one may argue that the use of quality assurance in new public management has led to micromanagement techniques that have been used at the local level (faculty and/or department) to control the behaviour of academics in an intrusive way. Recently, the European Commission has promoted the implementation of a European accreditation system that may result in a highly stratified European Higher Education Area.

Being initially an almost exclusive concern of academics, quality assurance has become progressively a matter of public concern in the 1980s and 1990s with an emphasis on quality improvement and accountability. The balance between these potentially conflicting objectives shifts towards improvement when academics have a strong voice, and towards accountability when the will of the government predominates.

This book shows that assuring quality, albeit in a number of different forms (quality assessment, programme review, accreditation, licencing, etc.), is nowadays an (intrusive) reality in each national higher education system and will remain an important regulation and steering tool for many governments. The book also analyses some recent trends and developments, such as the increasing internationalisation of quality assurance mechanisms as part of a more globalised higher education sector; the recent focus on accreditation mechanisms in Europe, with the support of the European Commission; the relevance of efficiency and effectiveness in the new quality assurance modes; and the emergence of the marketplace or quasi-market solutions of quality assurance problems. We are convinced that the present book will contribute to a better-informed discussion about the choices and options on the future of quality assurance in higher education.

We are grateful to all who have made the fifth Douro seminar and book possible, namely Amélia Veiga at CIPES and Therese Marie Uppstrøm at *Hedda*, the perfect organisers of the Douro seminars. We are also grateful to Di Davies for her editorial work. We have appreciated the diligence of all our colleagues who have contributed to this book with their papers, comments, and editorial suggestions, and we certainly noticed their forbearance in replying to our tedious editorial demands.

We want to acknowledge the financial support from *Fundação para a Ciência e Tecnologia*, of the Portuguese Ministry for Science, Technology, and Higher Education, making the organisation of the fifth Douro seminar possible. We also want to acknowledge the financial support of the Luso-American Foundation with the participation of our American colleagues. And last but not least, we register once more the superb environment provided by the management of the Vintage House Hotel on the banks of the Douro River.

Alberto Amaral
Matosinhos

and

Peter Maassen
Oslo

December 2006

DON F. WESTERHEIJDEN, BJØRN STENSAKER,
AND MARIA JOÃO ROSA

INTRODUCTION

1. TRANSFORMATION AND CONTINUITY:
ANOTHER BOOK ON QUALITY?

'Quality is here to stay' may be one of the worst platitudes in the discourse about quality assurance in higher education – and still it may be a useful statement. It is a platitude, because as Guy Neave stated: "quality is not 'here to stay', if only for the self-evident reason that across the centuries of the university's existence in Europe, it never departed" (Neave 1994: 116). Indeed, quality, especially if taken in its meaning of something exceptional, of excellence (Harvey and Green 1993), is and must be the core value in higher education – it is what makes higher education 'higher'. Without striving for excellence, there is no way to distinguish higher education from skills training. How much of higher education has already succumbed to demands for providing skills training instead of giving students a higher education?[1] The quality debate is not used just to further the traditional understanding of quality as excellence, but simultaneously as 'fitness for purpose', the new purpose being to make higher education institutions more responsive to societal demands for graduates with readily usable knowledge and skills in the job market. In such debates much depends on who uses the term 'quality'. The new aspect, making our opening platitude still worth repeating, may be that the ambiguity of the term has increasingly come to the fore.

Another reason why we repeat it is that quality has become a central theme in the ways that higher education operates: we have 'quality management' in thousands of higher education institutions, we have 'assessments', 'audits', and 'accreditation' as policy instruments in many states[2] around the world. Apparently, the quality of higher education is no longer seen as self-evident, but as a value about which different actors in higher education systems have different views – and thus it requires special attention. Different actors may have different reasons why they want to give special attention to quality – we will come back to that later – but the general point is that nowadays they do. And there are no signs that this is a fad that will soon wither away. On the contrary, quality assurance schemes are being developed in many states and higher education systems as one of the necessary instruments to adapt higher education institutions to the increasing demands put upon them within the states' economy and society, and equally to prepare or adapt the states' systems for the increasing impacts of globalisation on higher education (Vlk 2006). Higher education has to 'produce' ever-larger numbers of increasingly relevant graduates; it has to focus its research on areas and projects with economic impact; and it has to

1

D.F. Westerheijden et al. (eds.), Quality Assurance in Higher Education: Trends in Regulation, Translation and Transformation, 1–11.
© 2007 *Springer*.

attract increasing numbers of foreign students, whether in the continuing project of, for example, European cooperation or in the global competition for short-term income generation (Van Vught, Van der Wende, and Westerheijden 2002) and for long-term development of a workforce that can realise the knowledge-based economy.

Given this continuing and perhaps still growing interest in quality assurance schemes, the aim of this volume is to step back for a moment from the bustle of day-to-day assuring of quality, adapting or changing schemes to new demands and turbulent environments, and reflect on some fundamental questions. The overarching goal of the whole 'Douro Series' is to give an overview of the (theoretical and empirical) state-of-the-art research on certain topics in higher education. We wish to reflect, therefore, from an academic perspective on the dynamics and effects of quality assurance as a policy instrument and management tool in higher education. We look at different institutional arrangements for regulating quality and quality assurance, at how these are 'translated' to the level of higher education institutions, how the higher education institutions respond to the challenges set before them, and we want to sketch some principles of what may be consequences of this reflection for alternative quality assurance schemes in the future. The perspectives that we collected were varied on purpose. This volume is to aid thinking about quality assurance and to extend knowledge about it through critical analysis. Criticism is essential for scientific progress in all areas of knowledge as Lakatos and Musgrave (1974) claim.

2. PRINCIPLES UNDERLYING THE STRUCTURE OF THE BOOK

We will look at the content and main statements of each chapter in the conclusion (Chapter 11), so we will limit ourselves here to indicating the main flow of the argument, noting at the same time that across the chapters different and sometimes contradictory arguments are made.

Quality assurance as a separate area of attention in the steering of higher education can trace its roots back over more than a century, to the end of the 19th century, when in the United States the first accreditation organisations arose. Yet for a long time, this remained an exceptional approach to quality in higher education and even in the United States accreditation was an issue of limited interest. Only when the effects of the transition from 'elite' to 'mass' higher education emerged as a focal area for decision makers ('early warning' was given by Trow 1974) did quality assurance move out of what Ewell in Chapter 6 calls the 'pre-quality' era – he gave 1982 as the time of transition in the United States. European countries caught up quickly, as the first formal quality assurance schemes there were introduced in 1984 (Schwarz and Westerheijden 2004). By the way, the move to mass higher education was certainly not a fad, as mass – or even universal – higher education is here to stay. Consequently, the size and variety of higher education institutions and higher education systems demanded more formal management than what was needed in the small, socially homogeneous elite institutions. There is no need to look to further causes than the size of higher education systems to realise that quality assurance is here to stay. But there are other reasons as well: limits (or reductions) to public budgets, increasing demands for transparency in general, governmental approaches that favour ex post evaluation over ex ante regulation, often – rightly or wrongly – labelled neo-liberalism or new public management (Van Vught and Westerheijden 1994).

2.1. Framing Quality Assurance: Governmental Tools and Theoretical Perspectives

Quality assurance may in other words be seen in a context of the regulation of higher education. Given the fact that, at least on the surface, there seems to have developed what one could call a 'general model' with respect to quality assurance (Van Vught and Westerheijden 1994), one could run the risk of overlooking the options and tools available if quality assurance is conceived as a regulatory problem. As Hood (1983) has pointed out, there are in principle at least four different tools available: economic resources, laws and other regulations, organisation, and signals/information. In many states, the debate on quality assurance is often an indirect result of the choice of instruments: Should quality be economically rewarded? Should new laws on the rights and duties of higher education institutions be clarified? Should an intermediate body be established to control or enhance quality? Should governments limit themselves to informing the general public about the importance of having a focus on quality? Hence, we start our book with the topic of regulation, and how this mix of instruments can and is combined in various states.

In Part I of the book, various public policy perspectives are used to shed light on the choosing and functioning of various governmental policy mixes. Within this broader public policy perspective, several approaches can be identified. Hence, the chapters by Blackmur, Dill, and Westerheijden use and combine various theoretical perspectives from welfare economics, human capital theory, public choice, and neo-institutional theory. Their common denominator is not in the theoretical perspectives as such, but in their search for a better understanding of the quality problem, and how both 'market failure' and 'government failure' can occur as a result of ill-combined mixes of governmental tools.

Against the backdrop of these analyses, an observer could be surprised by how quality assurance, in practice, was implemented in higher education. After initial, sometimes vehement, discussion on the meaning of 'quality', leading to exasperated reactions like "What the Hell is Quality?" (Ball 1985), a rather pragmatic consensus in practice was reached that quality means 'fitness for purpose' as well as 'fitness of purpose'. Hence, as the introductory part illustrates, many higher education systems started working on quality assurance, perhaps without a proper analysis of the policy problem(s) quality assurance was to solve. This point can be empirically illustrated by the fact that 'fitness for purpose' and 'fitness of purpose' are empirically empty terms: they can mean anything, depending on what is given as purpose.

Consequently, 'quality higher education' often remains undefined in operational terms, because there is no single understanding of what the purpose (or multiple purposes) of higher education in current society is: Is it maximising graduate completion whatever the level of qualification? Providing society with a fitting number of competent workers? Advancing scientific knowledge to gain Nobel

Prizes etc.? Or all of the above and more, perhaps in different parts (sectors, institutions, degree levels) of a higher education system? It is to shed light on these issues that other theoretical perspectives are introduced in Parts II and III of the book, acknowledging that the more structural perspectives need to be accompanied by perspectives with greater emphasis on the cultural and political dimensions of higher education? As the chapters by Stensaker as well as Rosa and Amaral illustrate, higher education is also a sector open to policy copying from other sectors, or as the chapters by Perellon and Ewell show, higher education is open to various forms of institutionalisation in which actors, structures, and events form certain political outcomes. Hence, views may differ about what quality is, and how it should best be obtained: politicians, academics, students, employers, and other stakeholders may have different views; each of these groups of stakeholders among themselves may have different views. The variety seems boundless and leads back to Ball's exasperated reaction.

Still, for all those possible purposes, student learning is a necessary condition, but then again there is no well-established 'production theory' detailing how to turn all available inputs (students, staff, facilities, curriculum) into the desired student learning. And who are the students? They seem to become evermore heterogeneous in age, time available for study, study modes (from on-campus to Internet-only), learning styles, gender, ethnicity, previous knowledge, experience and competencies, reasons for studying, etc. Again, we do not see a way out of the vexed definition question by focusing on student learning, although we do emphasise the need to be better informed about the often overlooked microprocesses quality assurance is supposed to improve. As the chapters by Harvey and Newton as well as D'Andrea illustrate, there is a need to improve our theoretical knowledge about the microprocesses of higher education, and to be more open to the possible contributions from theories of learning when designing quality assurance schemes in higher education.

Hence, for our purposes, it is more important to highlight the debates and processes to arrive at a common understanding of the terms in use than to emphasise what are exactly the perspectives of quality in use, or the exact standards and criteria in use. We can, therefore, go forward in this volume without a detailed definition of quality from the outset. In the contributions to follow, there will accordingly not be extensive attention to defining the term. It is noteworthy, however, that Blackmur in Chapter 2 took the observation very seriously that one of us once made, to the effect that there are as many views on quality as there are dimensions distinguished by stakeholders; he consequently writes about 'qualities' in the plural. In a way, this goes back to the literal meaning of the roots of the word, because 'qualitas' in Latin was derived from the interrogative adverb 'qualis', meaning 'how'. 'Qualitas' then would literally mean 'howness', and would point to the different characteristics of higher education for different users rather than to excellence. But that was 20 centuries ago, and language has changed over that long period of time. Yet, even our not choosing an explicit definition of quality has consequences, as will be apparent in the following chapters.

The renewed interest in quality of higher education since the 1980s centred on two questions: Were graduates learning the knowledge and skills necessary for a changing economy in the context of improved study programmes to achieve more and better learning? Were higher education institutions spending tax money in the right way? In the United States, both questions culminated in the single issue of loan defaults; in Europe and many other more state-dominated higher education systems, the two were seen as separate questions. The tension between the two extremes of improvement and accountability ever since has remained the Scylla and Charybdis (Vroeijenstijn 1995) between which quality assurance schemes had to be steered. While both extremes had an external, societal, and internal, institutional aspect to them – the former was emphasised in the previous sentence – quite often the improvement issue became associated with institutional actors, and the accountability issue was more often the external view on quality assurance schemes. From the outset, therefore, it was clear to us that we would have to include in our book academic perspectives at the institutional level as well as at the level of society and the state, each taking both improvement and accountability aspects into account. Thinking only one step further took us to the buzzwords – and the realities – of a multilevel and multi-actor approach. Taking the mixed public and private system of higher education as a multi-actor system, embedded in a multilevel governance situation (especially if we look at Europe or at federal systems like the United States), instruments such as quality assessment need to be assessed from multiple actors' viewpoints and at different system levels. Also for that reason, we are happy to be able to include comparative perspectives on issues in quality assurance. Sometimes, the comparison is cross-institutional, sometimes cross-national, depending on the level of the issue addressed – Parts I and II are more about cross-national comparison (including multilevel states), while the institutional perspectives dominate Part III. Sometimes the comparisons are across chapters and sometimes it is found within single chapters (as in Dill's Chapter 3 and Perellon's Chapter 7).

The multi-actor perspective was already implicit in the notion of quality as fitness for purpose. The multilevel idea of governance should come naturally to anyone living in a federal state (like the United States) or in the complex international and supranational governance constellation of the European Union and the European Economic Area, which together include almost all our co-authors in this volume. In governance relationships, as well as in multilevel systems, funding may be the main driver and the most direct way of influencing behaviour, since "what gets rewarded, gets done" (as Westerheijden states in Chapter 4). In contrast to such direct steering, quality assurance is a major vehicle in a communication view of steering: the way quality is assessed, and the consequences (sanctions) of positive and negative assessments in a certain quality assurance scheme, carry important strategic messages to all concerned, higher education institutions and stakeholders alike.

2.2. Sensitising Concepts and Foci

In section 2.1, we moved from quality to quality assurance. We venture the statement that quality assurance is here to stay – or maybe that too is a platitude. However that may be, it seems that this new instrument for policy makers and for managers in higher education institutions has gained a secure place among the other modes of management. As Harvey and Newton point out in Chapter 10, there are four basic methods associated with quality assurance: accreditation, audit, assessment, and external examination. In the literature on quality assurance, much has been written about these methods, and on the pros and cons associated with each. In our discussion of quality assurance, we want to move beyond a focus on the method per se, towards a stronger focus on what we see as the main issues, concepts, and questions surrounding this area: What is the use of quality assurance? Can quality assurance be more than a ritual of filling out forms for student feedback or to record publications? Can it achieve its main goals of accountability and improvement? For whom can it achieve these aims?

To answer these and related questions there are a number of sensitising concepts and foci that can be of assistance to improve our understanding of quality assurance. As such, a key focus in Part I is exactly on these *cost/benefit* relationships in quality assurance, since one of the lessons learned in the practice of quality assurance in higher education has been that, whatever the official balance between quality improvement and accountability, quality improvement is not easily achieved through external quality assurance. As Dill (1995) stated, we cannot achieve higher quality by inspecting; quality has to be 'made' painstakingly in the interaction between educators and students at the work-floor level. Accordingly, there is a crucial role for quality management within the higher education institution and even more so for the professional teachers and researchers at the 'chalk-face' level. Parts II and III address questions relevant to this. Stensaker in Chapter 5 introduces the concept of *translation*, which we used as the title of Part II, for the process that goes with the move from the governmental, external outlook on quality assurance to the internal, management view. Translation suggests a more complicated process than the more traditional term of 'implementation'. Implementation suggests a linear, mechanical process of making commands happen, while translation has the image of an active process performed by an interpreter – and much may be lost in translation, as the 2003 movie of that name showed. Successful translation is not just a matter of replacing a word from one language with a word from another, but also must take account of different grammar, syntax, and cultural nuances.

The latter term takes us from the design focus related to regulatory issues to how policies are translated into practice with increased attention paid to policy networks, policy communities, and policy styles. Hence, in Part II, it is not the design, but the *dynamics* of the policy translation process that is emphasised. As Perellon argues in Chapter 7, politicians in various states view problems in various ways: the role of government and their agencies might differ from state to state leading to differently constructed debates on quality and distinct policy styles across states. In a similar vein, though using other words, Ewell in Chapter 6 characterises the history of quality assurance in the United States as a 'quality game' with a number of 'players', forming a particular, informal, policy community. In this chapter, as well as in the one by Perellon, we can also find examples of the dynamics of the past in the form of the establishment of 'path dependency' where new developments can often be explained as reactions and continuations of former decisions and outcomes. Hence, quality assurance that focuses on accountability has to do with knowing about what is done in higher education, and how it affects students and external stakeholders such as employers and society at large.

A lesson learned in the practice of quality assurance in higher education in this perspective is that quality assessment does not automatically lead to quality assurance (Stensaker 2003). That too might need a translation process. Yet the aim of the translation is a different one than in the previous paragraph, as is the target. The aim of accountability is to re-establish a situation where *trust* characterises higher education, as was the case when higher education was still an elite system, both in quantitative terms and in terms of educating the elite classes of society (Trow 1996). Trust is visible in the provision of support, by either public or private bodies, without the requirement that institutions either provide specific goods and services in return for that support or account specifically and in detail for the use of those funds. When trust is weakened, accountability is enforced, since they represent two alternative modes of linking institutions to their surroundings (Trow 1996). Quality assessment in this context can be seen as a substitute for trust (Amaral, Rosa, and Tavares 2006). Accordingly, the target in this case is society at large or more narrowly the political world, not the professional in the higher education institution. With a focus on trust comes also the introduction of the more symbolic aspects of quality assurance. In general, quality assessment has not been very successful in re-establishing trust, because if it had, external quality assessment would have become superfluous. Currently, it seems that subsequent generations of quality assurance schemes have, if anything, become stricter – witness the spread of accreditation across Europe (Schwarz and Westerheijden 2004). However, one should be open to the possibility that this new development also has some elements of symbolic adjustments to it, with the promise of accreditation as a 'hard' form of quality assurance although this image might be questioned in practice (Stensaker and Harvey 2006). The intention is, nevertheless, that the introduction of accreditation will increase the level of trust in the sector, an ambition that Ewell questions in Chapter 6.

An interesting exception to this view nowadays seems to be the United Kingdom, where programme assessments were replaced with institutional audits in 2001 (Brennan and Williams 2004). It remains a question, though, whether that was a move to re-establish trust in the higher education institutions. Hence, the penultimate chapter by two British authors, Harvey and Newton, proposes 'moving on' by giving more weight to empirical evidence and by blurring the boundaries between institutional enhancement and external evaluation.

In this way, Harvey and Newton address a theme missing in much of the popular discussions and publications: the question of what higher education does to students. We want to pay attention to this aspect of *transformation* (as put forward forcibly in Harvey and Knight 1996), also because it implies that for an important category of 'consumers' there is no fixed purpose against which they can assess higher education's fitness. The aim of education, and especially of students' first experience of higher education, is to assist students to be transformed from adolescents with school-type knowledge into adults ready to enter society and the labour market at the highest levels of competencies available. From this, two consequences follow. First, at a superficial level, we chose 'transformation' as the title of Part III. Second, and much more importantly, it means that standard models of quality assurance in which customers' needs are taken as exogenous and immutable cannot be applied to the bulk of higher education (in short training courses, especially for post-bachelor participants, this may be different). Quality assurance models, for example, developed in the business world may be useful, but only after smart adaptation, not simple adoption[3]; a first approximation of such an approach is described in Chapter 8 by Rosa and Amaral.

The contribution by Rosa and Amaral simultaneously helps to illustrate the final point we want to make in this section about the themes in this book – that a 'one size fits all' approach is not suitable for successful quality assurance in higher education. The contrast between their chapter and the one following, by D'Andrea (Chapter 9), shows that while in a Portuguese university a business and management-oriented approach to introducing quality assurance may be useful, in other situations improving the quality in higher education institutions would be better served by looking to the nature of the 'primary process' – education and the theories underlying it.

3. BEYOND STATE CONTEXTS – QUALMS FACING THE FUTURE

A careful reader of the 'Douro Series' will notice that this volume is different from previous books in that it is less occupied by country-specific experiences and chronicles of changes in higher education, emphasising more the basic challenges facing quality assurance regardless of geography, and some of the universal lessons that research on this topic has disclosed. This is not an attempt to override the conclusion in section 2.2 – our scepticism towards the 'one size fits all' approach is still present, and many of the chapters draw their empirical evidence from specific states – but a recognition of some general tendencies with respect to how quality assurance seems to develop in different parts of the world. Even though this volume can be said to have a European touch to it, we do not think that that is a disadvantage, because an understanding of the situation in Europe can be of relevance to a number of other regions and contexts as well. The European touch in this volume does not go so far as to give a detailed account of, for example, the Bologna process; that international policy development is mentioned mainly in the final part of Westerheijden's chapter. He stresses that the Bologna process is primarily an international lever for national reform agendas, but it is developing its own dynamic, thereby influencing the national agendas of the participating states' higher education systems to some extent (very slightly in some states, and considerably in others). This is the perspective from which we want to view the European situation and the Bologna process in it: as cases of the general class of influences on quality assurance in higher education systems coming from beyond the national context.

What is first and foremost in our mind is the tendency that quality assurance issues are to a growing extent internationalised and fast becoming an inherent part of a more globalised higher education sector (Van Vught, Van der Wende, and Westerheijden 2002). What this internationalisation and globalisation of higher education mean for quality assurance is still unknown, but we do have some indications where the chapters in this book might be of assistance in improving our knowledge on how to better understand the current developments.

The increasing focus on accreditation is one such tendency (Schwarz and Westerheijden 2004) which can be seen with the use of quality assurance as a tool for the implementation of supranational policies such as in the case of the Bologna process (Amaral, Rosa, and Tavares 2006). Nevertheless, for those predicting that internationalisation and globalisation in a more deterministic fashion will lead to harmonisation and less diversity, the chapters by Westerheijden (Chapter 4) and Ewell (Chapter 6) provide some counter-arguments pointing to the importance of the inherent dynamics of policy processes, sometimes leading to quite unexpected outcomes.

If one perceives internationalisation to include policy copying between different states, Stensaker (Chapter 5), Perellon (Chapter 7), and Rosa and Amaral (Chapter 8) should also provide interesting examples of how global ideas and practices might be interpreted quite differently in various contexts. We do know that quality assurance is a phenomenon that is 'travelling' between countries, creating a field where one can identify both adopters and latecomers (Neave 1994), and where the latter sometimes looks to the former for inspiration and experience. There is a tendency to overestimate what can be learned from one setting to another, as we can see from the adoption of the European Union 'open method of coordination' as a way to induce policy borrowing between states, based on the use of indicators and benchmarks. Therefore, we would argue that perhaps the most important lesson to be learned is acknowledging the complexities surrounding the spread of ideas in higher education. These complexities derive from the fact that higher education is embedded in contexts of regulation, funding, and other policy instruments, in economic circumstances and in specific societies and cultures. Accordingly, the ideas have to be made to fit all those contexts as well as the particular policy problems they are supposed to solve.

Another tendency that can be identified internationally is the issue of efficiency and effectiveness of the current quality assurance modes. This is a theme that is high on the agenda in some of the most experienced states with long-established quality assurance schemes, and which is a common starting point also for the chapters by Blackmur (Chapter 2), Dill (Chapter 3), D'Andrea (Chapter 9), and Harvey and Newton (Chapter 10), although their answers differ with respect to means and ways to address such issues. Although one probably cannot relate the emergence of 'lighter touch' arrangements of quality assurance in some states to the issues of the lack of efficiency and effectiveness of existing schemes alone, one should not overlook the possibility that concerns about the costs and increasing bureaucracy surrounding many existing systems will increase in strength in years to come – both from the higher education institution and the government.

That leads us to the final point we want to make on the increasing internationalisation of quality assurance, i.e. the increasing weight given to quasi-market and market solutions of quality assurance problems. As illustrated by Dill in Chapter 3, and partly also by Ewell in Chapter 6, quality assurance in the governmental mode has a new competitor in the growing numbers of ranking systems that are being established (Dill and Soo 2005; Van Dyke 2005). With the increasing interest in such alternative ways of accountability in many parts of the world, we should also be open to the possibility that the current governmentally initiated or governmentally owned quality assurance schemes actually face a competitive arrangement that could diminish their influence, and maybe even threaten their existence (Stensaker and Harvey 2006). On the other hand, rankings may – like quality assurance schemes have done over the past decades – be added to the higher education policy toolbox without replacing any previously existing instrument. Overall then, agreeing with Dill (1998: 362) that the state not only decides "the effectiveness of government provision of higher education" but also the "effective functioning of markets and professional control", our hope is that the present volume contributes to a better-informed discussion about the choices and options concerning the future of quality and of quality assurance in higher education.

NOTES

1   At the same time, the mistaken belief that 'excellence' must mean 'academic excellence' has led to the widespread phenomenon of academic drift, especially among 'colleges', i.e. mainly teaching-only, polytechnic types of higher education institutions. This tendency threatens to pervert excellent higher education institutions aimed at educating highly skilled but also reflective 'practitioners' (Schön 1987).

2   The connection between nation states and higher education systems seems to have been loosened in recent years. Ever since its Constitution was written, the United States has had higher education systems within the federal states, but in large European countries the devolvement of authority over, amongst other things, higher education from nation states to regional entities, as in the United Kingdom, Spain, or Germany, means that we have to be increasingly careful about words. In our text, we will use 'state' as a neutral term denoting any public authority with a say over higher education, from federal states to nation states and up to supranational authorities like the European Union. Since there is no easy adjective for 'state', we will often use 'national' where one should read 'of the state'.

3   Using a different metaphor, we return here to the implementation–translation divide.

REFERENCES

Amaral, A., M.J. Rosa, and D. Tavares. "Assessment as a Tool for Different Kinds of Action: From Quality Management to Compliance and Control." Paper presented at the conference Quality Assessment in Institutions of Higher Education in Europe: Problems, Practices and Solutions, University of Pavia, Italy, 23–25 March, 2006.

Ball, C. *Fitness for Purpose*. Guildford: SRHE and NFER-Nelson, 1985.

Brennan, J. and R. Williams. "Accreditation and Related Regulatory Matters in the United Kingdom." In Schwarz, S. and D.F. Westerheijden (eds). *Accreditation and Evaluation in the European Higher Education Area*. Dordrecht: Kluwer Academic Publishers, 2004, 465–490.

Dill, D.D. "Through Deming's Eyes: A Cross-national Analysis of Quality Assurance Policies in Higher Education." Paper presented at the INQAAHE 3rd meeting, Utrecht, 1995.

Dill, D.D. "Evaluating the 'Evaluative State': Implications for Research in Higher Education." *European Journal of Education* 33.3 (1998): 361–377.

Dill, D.D. and M. Soo. "Academic Quality, League Tables, and Public Policy: A Cross-national Analysis of University Ranking Systems." *Higher Education* 49.4 (2005): 495–533.

Harvey, L. and D. Green. "Defining Quality." *Assessment & Evaluation in Higher Education* 18.1 (1993): 9–34.

Harvey, L. and P.T. Knight. *Transforming Higher Education*. Buckingham: Society for Research into Higher Education and Open University Press, 1996.

Hood, C. *The Tools of Government*. London: Macmillan, 1983.

Lakatos, I. and A. Musgrave. *Criticism and the Growth of Knowledge*. Cambridge: Cambridge University Press, 1974.

Neave, G. "The Politics of Quality: Developments in Higher Education in Western Europe 1992–1994." *European Journal of Education* 29.2 (1994): 115–133.

Schön, D.A. *Educating the Reflective Practitioner*. San Francisco: Jossey-Bass, 1987.

Schwarz, S. and D.F. Westerheijden. "Accreditation in the Framework of Evaluation Activities: A Comparative Study in the European Higher Education Area." In Schwarz, S. and D.F. Westerheijden (eds). *Accreditation and Evaluation in the European Higher Education Area*. Dordrecht: Kluwer Academic Publishers, 2004, 1–41.

Stensaker, B. "Trance, Transparency and Transformation: The Impact of External Quality Monitoring on Higher Education." *Quality in Higher Education* 9.2 (2003): 151–159.

Stensaker, B. and L. Harvey. "Old Wines in New Bottles? A Comparison of Public and Private Accreditation Schemes in Higher Education." *Higher Education Policy* 19.1 (2006): 65–85.

Trow, M. "Problems in the Transition from Elite to Mass Higher Education." In OECD (ed.). *Policies for Higher Education*. Paris: OECD, 1974, 51–101.

Trow, M. "Trust, Markets and Accountability in Higher Education: A Comparative Perspective." *Higher Education Policy* 9.4 (1996): 309–324.

Van Dyke, N. "Twenty Years of University Report Cards." *Higher Education in Europe* 30.2 (2005): 103–125.

Van Vught, F.A., M.C. van der Wende, and D.F. Westerheijden. "Globalization and Internationalization: Policy Agendas Compared." In Fulton, O. and J. Enders (eds). *Higher Education in a Globalizing World. International Trends and Mutual Observations*. Dordrecht: Kluwer, 2002, 103–120.

Van Vught, F.A. and D.F. Westerheijden. "Towards a General Model of Quality Assessment in Higher Education." *Higher Education* 28.3 (1994): 355–371.

Vlk, A. *Higher Education and GATS: Regulatory Consequences and Stakeholders' Responses*. Enschede: CHEPS, University of Twente, 2006.

Vroeijenstijn, A.I. *Improvement and Accountability: Navigating Between Scylla and Charybdis: Guide for External Quality Assessment in Higher Education*. London: Jessica Kingsley, 1995.

PART I: REGULATION

DOUGLAS BLACKMUR

THE PUBLIC REGULATION OF HIGHER EDUCATION QUALITIES: RATIONALE, PROCESSES, AND OUTCOMES

1. INTRODUCTION

This chapter[1] examines the rationale, processes, and outcomes of the public regulation of higher education qualities. At one extreme, all higher education relationships could, in principle, be governed by the state; at the other, by private negotiation between the principal parties such as universities and their students, although this latter would take place under the relevant general law of contract, arbitration law, and so on. All governance arrangements in practice will have consequences (some intended, others unintended) for the nature of the relationships which define higher education including termination of relationships as occurred recently, for example, in South Africa when state registration of certain MBAs was withdrawn. From a general equilibrium perspective, these consequences may impact significantly on the dimensions of many other relationships outside the higher education industry. In public policy terms, a government selects which higher education relationships it will regulate, and how such regulation will be effected. The reasons for such choices, as well as their consequences, all of which can differ across place and time, occupy a prominent position on the agenda of research into the public regulation of higher education attributes and standards.

The notion of standards necessarily underpins measures of quality such as perfection; excellence; value for money; fitness for, and of, purpose; and trans-formation (these are the Harvey and Green (1993) measures). These (and other) quality measures can, in principle, be applied to each quality of higher education. This can be illustrated by a hypothetical example whereby a government announces that it will take steps to assure itself that the quality it requires (say, perfection: 100% of exam questions are answered correctly by each candidate) has been achieved in university calculus education (a characteristic, an attribute, or a quality of higher education). In this case, analysis of the quality of one of the qualities of a higher education system is the object of the exercise.

Two examples from recent experience in the United Kingdom and Australia are also illustrative. One of the qualities of higher education has to do with the publicly available information about systemic, and/or institutional, activities and performance. Since 2004, public policy in the United Kingdom has defined the standards (quality) of information availability (a quality of the system) in higher education. In the final analysis, the UK government also requires assurance that these standards have been

D.F. Westerheijden et al. (eds.), Quality Assurance in Higher Education: Trends in Regulation,
Translation and Transformation, 15–45.
© 2007 *Springer.*

met (Quality Assurance Agency for Higher Education 2005). The essential qualities of all universities since World War II furthermore include a 'teaching' and a 'research' quality. Recent debates in Australia suggest that government is, however, giving serious thought to altering these fundamental characteristics by regulating the public higher education system in a way that will create 'teaching-only' universities. In this case, the 'research' quality would be removed from certain institutions.

This chapter argues that when governments regulate any aspect of higher education, a process of qualities' assurance is necessarily involved. When governments, in other words, regulate matters of higher education, they are, explicitly or implicitly, thinking in terms of standards with respect to some or all characteristics of the system (or its components) against which assurance of adequate performance is subsequently sought. It is this process of identifying characteristics (qualities), defining required performance standards (desired quality) for each, and monitoring of performance (actual quality) which can be conceptualised as 'qualities' assurance'. This chapter uses both 'qualities' assurance' and 'quality assurance' to denote this process[2] (for an assessment of the utility of the term 'quality assurance', see Westerheijden 1999: 235). Given the definition of both these terms employed in this chapter, it is argued that public policy with respect to this process in higher education can be fruitfully analysed in terms of the economics of public regulation.

The terms qualities' assurance and quality assurance are employed here in a value-neutral sense. They can describe a process whereby, for example, a government sets a very high standard for university teaching and seeks assurance that it had been met. They can, by the same token, also describe a process whereby a government reduces a prevailing standard of, say, academic freedom and seeks similar assurance. This latter would occur, for example, if a diminution of an existing freedom of individual universities to design their own academic programmes occurred as a result of steps taken by a government to ensure that a higher education system exhibited a certain level of responsiveness to community demands with respect to its course offerings.

Governments in the final analysis regulate, in higher education and elsewhere, in pursuit of objectives which they accept as appropriate. Positive, inductive analyses may reveal significant regularities in, for example, the nature of the higher education relationships which are selected for public regulation; in the methods and/or instruments employed; in the reasons advanced for such choices; and in their effects (see e.g. Crozier, Curvale, and Henard 2005). A note of methodological caution may be appropriate here. The fact that a government has required, for example, universities to provide nominated information on their websites is not, by itself, sufficient evidence that such regulation was motivated by, in this case, considerations of market failure arising out of incomplete and/or asymmetric information. There may have been other reasons (e.g. assisting the information technology industry and/or subsidising low income students) which could be discovered only by a thorough analysis of the primary sources relevant to the particular case. Failure to conduct such research could result in an improper attribution of motives to governments.

This chapter does not claim to be comprehensive. It does not examine all of the reasons advanced for, and all of the methods and instruments used in, all of the processes by which governments conduct qualities' assurance in higher education. Rather it provides examples and suggests some directions for further research. The chapter consists of three sections: section 2 asks why governments engage in the public regulation of higher education qualities; section 3 discusses some of the methods and instruments which governments can employ in public higher education quality assurance; and section 4 reviews some possible and, very briefly, actual consequences of the public regulation of higher education qualities. Concluding remarks follow.

2. WHY MIGHT GOVERNMENTS IMPOSE CERTAIN CHARACTERISTICS ON A HIGHER EDUCATION SYSTEM AND REQUIRE ASSURANCE THAT EACH IS IN EVIDENCE TO THE REQUIRED EXTENT?

The quality of each and every conceivable characteristic of higher education is, in principle, potentially subject to some form of public determination in terms of the development and application of explicit and/or implicit minimum performance standards (the reality is, of course, much more complicated). Thus, for example, student fees may be governed in part by reference to certain standards of equity; the costs of university operation may be subsidised by tax relief and/or public funding of certain types of research which enjoy national priority (determined against certain criteria); enrolment limits in some courses may be decided against national labour supply benchmarks; legislated ethical standards may constrain certain research activities; the size and structure of, for example, a bachelor's degree may be determined nationally against certain standards; certification may be regulated against technical minimum standards associated with the ease of document forgery; teaching of some courses may be restricted to people who possess at least certain nominated qualifications; principles of universality and/or economies of scope may inform standards which regulate the use of the term 'university'; and the size of university governing bodies may be determined in terms of principles derived from the sociology and economics of committees (or, perhaps, on the basis of some rough and ready notions of 'what works' based on experience; even this, however, involves thinking in terms of some standards).

Governments typically conceptualise quality in whatever they mean by higher education (this meaning varies internationally) in terms of the extent to which minimum performance standards are met in respect of each characteristic of the system (and/or its components) that is of interest to them. The characteristics of interest to the government, for example, in the 1990 reforms to higher education in New Zealand included institutional autonomy, accountability, resource use, responsiveness to the community; governing councils; credit transfer; the structure of the higher education system; and relationships between qualifications. The government set broad expectations in respect of each of these but left the detail of standards' setting, and the monitoring and reporting of outcomes, to the Ministry of Education and the New Zealand Qualifications Authority (Minister of Education, New Zealand 1990). Ko Scheele, furthermore, has discussed public policy in Europe towards accreditation as a form of public regulation of higher education qualities: the defining feature, for example, of the east European approach "is the achievement of the minimum quality standard" (Scheele 2004: 19).

In this context, it is important to ask why governments might wish to influence the pace and direction of change, through a process of establishing minimum standards and monitoring or enforcing compliance, in some or all of the qualities and characteristics of higher education. Motive and method clearly cannot be separated analytically, but the emphasis in this section will be squarely on motives. Methods that may be used to regulate higher education qualities will be discussed in more detail in section 3.

The dynamics of electoral politics largely explains why governments in most countries seek to regulate higher education attributes and performance. From a more disaggregated perspective, governments may decide to influence the quality of certain characteristics of higher education for reasons concerning, say, economic development, equity, accountability, public opinion, market failure, and the activities of interest groups. These are not, of course, mutually exclusive categories. Public opinion, for example, on matters regarding market failures in higher education may stimulate government interest in system performance. Selected issues with respect to each of these categories are analysed seriatim.

2.1. Economic Development and Equity

Since World War II a consensus has arisen in most countries that improvements in human welfare depend in no small measure on the rate of growth of real, per capita national product and its distribution within communities. This consensus includes the view that government policies can have a major bearing on growth rates and on the pattern of income distribution. The last quarter of a century or so has also seen significant changes in the composition of output in many countries in favour of the production of a relatively greater proportion of services, as opposed to tangible commodities, and the associated increases in the demand for, and supply of, various types of information and knowledge. The relative economic importance of the 'knowledge production' industries, including higher education, has grown under these circumstances to the point where variations in their performance can have significant macroeconomic consequences. In certain countries, moreover, these consequences can, in part, be transmitted through the mechanisms of international trade. Income from the export of higher education services has a major impact on, for example, Australia's balance of payments and on the rate of growth in Australia's national income.

In this context, governments are typically not indifferent to the nature and performance of national higher education systems. A recent study of higher education 'quality convergence' in several European countries drew attention to "the State's strategic interest in developing a 'knowledge economy' which would be favourable in terms of employment, economic development and international recognition" (Crozier, Curvale, and Henard 2005: 17–18). The characteristics of higher education systems favoured by public policy under these circumstances would obviously include those of adding value to economic development and to internationalisation.

This study also provided insights into the character of the equity foundations of government interest in the characteristics of higher education. In Norway, for example, there is evidence of "the State's growing interest in maintaining the employability of its students" (Crozier, Curvale, and Henard 2005: 19). Equity considerations played a major role, moreover, in explaining, for example, the African National Congress government's interest in reshaping South African higher education: "to serve our new social order, transformation of higher education must meet pressing national needs and respond to new realties and opportunities, but importantly it must also redress past inequalities" (Minister of Education, South Africa 1997: 5559). One of the qualities the South African government required of the higher education system after 1994 was that its previous apartheid attributes yielded totally to the non-racial, non-sexist, democratic values of the new dispensation. The government, moreover, established processes designed to provide assurance that this new quality was, in fact, embedded appropriately in the new system. Politicians, furthermore, may also be persuaded that it is 'unfair' for students to pay some or all of the costs of their higher education. Governments may thus believe that this justifies a public policy (usually financial) response, in which case redistributive taxpayer-funded fee subsidies will become a characteristic of the higher education system. Assurance that this quality was present to the desired extent would typically be provided by an auditor-general.

2.2. Accountability

Accountability considerations may motivate government interest in the characteristics and performance standards of higher education systems. The New Zealand government, for example, introduced significant changes in public policy towards higher education in 1990. It stressed:

> the need for accountability by institutions and ... the proper use by institutions of resources allocated to them. Accountability is essential. No institution ... should be beyond review of its integrity, and the efficiency and effectiveness with which it uses public resources. (Minister of Education, New Zealand 1990)

More generally, governments may simply lose political support if they provide, for example, taxpayer-funded subsidies to students and/or universities unconditionally and in the absence of any external accountability processes, the results of which are publicly available. In some countries, adequate performance (determined through audits) is a precondition for universities to receive public funds (Crozier, Curvale, and Henard 2005: 18; for recent developments in Japan, see Hara 2005).

2.3. Public Opinion

Public opinion may be a powerful force in motivating governments to seek to shape a variety of production and consumption systems including higher education systems. Historically, public concerns over issues related to the adulteration, safety, and effectiveness of food and drugs, road safety, and environmental pollution, for example, have stimulated government interest (Gruenspecht and Lave 1989: 1509–1510). Recently, public disquiet, for example, over certification fraud and grade inflation in higher education has produced a similar response in the sphere of higher education

(Buscall 2005a; Maslen 2005). Governments may also seek assurance that the potential for conflicts of interest in the production of qualifications, especially at the delivery/assessment interface, is not realised to the extent that it compromises system performance unduly. Such conflicts may arise if the same people who deliver the curriculum also assess student performance – they are, in a sense, pronouncing judgments on themselves. Public concern, and perhaps a political response, over assessment (and certification) processes may arise on this account.

2.4. Market Failure

Governments may be persuaded that market failure provides grounds for public policy with respect to the performance of higher education systems. Market failure is a concept associated in the first instance largely with welfare economics. Broadly speaking, this theory postulated that consumer preferences could be satisfied to the greatest extent, given a relative scarcity of resources and a given pattern of income distribution, by means of a perfectly competitive market economy operating in the absence of increasing returns to scale. The marginal conditions for optimal outcomes in production and consumption were satisfied under such conditions. Any deviations from the composition of output determined under these conditions were concept-ualised as efficiency losses and explained in terms of the absence of at least one of the optimality requirements. Such failures, collectively known as market failures, could arise on account of the existence of a degree of monopoly (in production and/or consumption); public goods, externalities, and impaired information. This is a very broad outline: some refinements to the concept of market failure will be discussed at appropriate points in the following analysis.

2.4.1. Monopoly

Market failures[3] can arise in higher education. In many countries, for example, a largely unorganised and rapidly changing student body enters into educational and other contracts with single universities some of which possess regional and/or other types of monopoly power. For certain purposes, moreover, universities as a whole may be organised in cartel-like groups. Governments may not necessarily always be indifferent to the consequences of such arrangements which may relate, for example, to the level of tuition fees, and to protective behaviour in matters such as credit transfer (close parallels can be found in the strategic manipulation of interconnection quality (analogous to credit transfer) in various network industries; see Sappington 2005: 129–130).

2.4.2. Public Goods

Pure public goods are commodities or services which, once provided, can be consumed by people in equal measure, and with respect to their consumption it is too expensive to exclude those who refuse to pay for them. Voluntary exchange through private markets cannot organise the production and consumption of such goods and services. Private markets must necessarily operate in terms of the exclusion principle whereby those who do not pay for a commodity or service can be excluded from owning it. If public goods are to be produced at all, such provision necessarily must be financed by means of taxation. It is, however, difficult enough to offer practical examples of public goods in general, and extremely difficult to identify examples in higher education since the exclusion principle can be applied across the board in this case.

2.4.3. External Effects

There may, by the same token, be various external effects associated with the production and/or consumption of higher education services which have a public goods' dimension to them and which may be of interest to governments. The reputation of a national higher education system may provide a relevant instance. Thus, the contributions which one university makes to enhancing its reputation will, at the same time, increase the reputation of the system to which it belongs, and of the other individual universities, students, and graduates that constitute this system: the 'reflected glory' effect. The reputation-enhancing university cannot, however, require the others who gain from its action to pay for these benefits. It *may*, on this account, be tempted to reduce its investments in reputation (a somewhat analogous situation can be found in network industries such as telecommunications; see Sappington 2005: 129). The other side of this coin is, however, perhaps of greater analytical interest.

A university may engage in actions which reduce its reputation. The effects of this will, however, extend to the other universities, to their students and graduates, and to the reputation of the system. The affected universities, students, and graduates, however, are unlikely to be able to extract voluntary compensation from the offending institution. Such uncompensated damages reduce, *ceteris paribus*, the resources available to each university, its students, and its graduates and may, furthermore, encourage the original institution to continue, at least to an extent, with its reputation-damaging activities.

It may be argued that no university would act in a way that reduces its reputation. A counterargument suggests that students may attend universities in a given system because of perceptions that the *system* is of high quality and enjoys a high reputation. What might be called a demand externality arises in this way. There may, under these circumstances, be an incentive for a university to 'freeride' on this system reputation by underinvesting in internal quality assurance processes. The other universities, assuming that they can identify such threats to system reputation (information costs will be a key variable), will have an incentive to devise a correction lest the value of the system's reputation deteriorates to individual and collective disadvantage. Such a private response may not, however, be feasible for a multitude of reasons concerning incomplete and/or asymmetric information, credibility,[4] and deficiencies in enforcement powers. Given these conditions, universities may collectively approach government to address the matter by deploying its superior information-gathering and enforcement powers (government may become independently aware of this matter and may act accordingly). A variation on this theme occurs if a government discovers that universities "oscillate quality in cycles of building and milking a reputation" (Gruenspecht and Lave 1989: 1528).

External effects of a cultural nature may also excite government interest in higher education. Especially controversial curriculum content may produce a widespread and politically significant community reaction. The cultural components and assumptions in, say, degree programmes exported from one country to another may attract the attention of the government in the importing country if, for example, the language preferences of many in the receiving community are offended (this observation was stimulated by some brief comments made by Williamson 1985: 293). Communities, or at least influential sections, may furthermore wonder about the wisdom of public subsidies that are made available to support the production of, for example, some of the extreme versions of postmodernism, especially those which inform societies that there is no such thing as reality but only 'fictional discourse' (in which case taxpayers might well ask why they should pay for something which does not exist: their taxes seem real enough!; see Wheen 2004: ch. 4).

2.4.4. Information Asymmetry: Consumer Protection

In very broad terms, a government may develop an interest in higher education because it becomes concerned that the information available to some or all of the participants is somehow impaired to the extent that inappropriate decisions are taken (on information asymmetries in higher education, see Dill 2001: 3, 11, 15, 18, 19). Considerations of transparency can arise here: 'truth in advertising' is one of them (Gruenspecht and Lave 1989: 1527). In this regard, governments may become concerned that various claims made, for example, by universities about the qualities and standards of their qualifications are, at the very least, contestable. Governments in this instance may not be prepared to allow caveat emptor to govern choices about appropriate courses of study.

Government interest may be aroused if it discovers that significant problems of adverse selection – the 'lemon effect' – are encountered in a higher education system. In his famous paper, George Akerloff (1970) demonstrated the possibility that "the consumers' inability to distinguish 'lemons' from good cars drives good cars out of the used-car market" (cited in Gruenspecht and Lave 1989: 1527). David Sappington (2005: 129) has expressed the point more formally:

> If consumers are completely unable to distinguish high quality products from low quality products, and only purchase the product in question once, the equilibrium price for the product may not vary with quality and may reflect the average quality of products sold in the market. In this case ... producers of high quality products may withdraw their products from the market altogether.

A report in the *Times Higher Education Supplement* News Round-up (2003) to the effect that "a fifth of company finance directors [in a survey] ... said that 'dumbed down' degrees in less traditional subjects could harm the market value of university qualifications" provides a partial illustration of the adverse selection issue.

Governments may, on this account, remove certain qualifications (referred to as 'basket weaving' courses in some political cultures) completely from those available to students, thereby altering the nature of the 'product range' characteristic of the system in question.

Consumer protection considerations may draw government attention to the performance of a higher education system (Williamson 1985: 205). Students and/or employers may experience severe problems in obtaining and/or processing information about, for example, graduation rates, postgraduation earnings and employment opportunities associated with certain qualifications, the pattern of student complaints about aspects of provider performance, the 'true' bundle of qualities which characterises each qualification, the authenticity of degree certificates, graduate and employer opinions on the worth of certain degrees, and so on. Broadly speaking,

> the nature of the provision of services and the direct contact involved between producer and consumer generate significant problems and risks, as well as consequences that are not easily reversible for consumers who lack information about the skill of their service provider. (Findlay 2000: 10)

These problems and risks may be magnified to the extent that any of the parties are given to opportunism. Potential consumers of higher education, for example, may suffer if graduates of a particular programme do not reveal, frankly and completely, information about it when asked, say, in surveys of graduates' opinions. But graduates who had grave reservations about any aspects of their higher education experience and/or knowledge that employers had concerns over the value of their qualifications would have an incentive to conceal this information (or to make different, favourable representations about it) to protect their investment. Matters of moral hazard arise in this way (Williamson 1985: 47–51; Blackmur 2004: 106). More generally, as Williamson showed in his work on transaction costs economics, contracting difficulties can arise under certain combinations of small numbers bargaining, uncertainty, incomplete information, and opportunism (see e.g. Williamson 1985; Menard and Shirley 2005).[5] Some form of government response may be forthcoming to address the sources of these difficulties if the government wishes to act in the interests of securing the maximum possible gains from trade, or if appropriate political pressures are brought to bear. Paternalism may also play a role in explaining government interest in the character of higher education. Individuals may be thought to lack relevant information for whatever reasons and/or the capacity to interpret it meaningfully. Governments may simply claim that they are "concerned with overriding private decisions in order to protect individuals from themselves" (Gruenspecht and Lave 1989: 1512).

2.4.5. Socially Suboptimal Range of Qualifications and other Higher Education Outputs

A higher education system may, under certain conditions "offer [a] socially suboptimal selection of products and qualities" (Laffont and Tirole 1993: 537). This type of market failure may invite government concern, especially if it were convinced that, say, national economic development required a particular qualification which the system was not providing. In 1997, the South African government was determined that the academic programmes of higher education institutions would be "transformed so that the human resource, economic and developmental needs of [South Africa] ... are met" (Minister of Education, South Africa 1997: 5564).

2.4.6. Slow Adjustment to Changing Conditions

Markets can also fail in the sense that the time taken for them to adjust to changed conditions does not satisfy the expectations of governments, consumers, and/or producers. In a somewhat exasperated turn of phrase, Gruenspecht and Lave (1989: 1512) have opined that "almost all people, except economists and some 'Chicago' lawyers ... fail to see how economic incentives will call forth desired behaviour as quickly and comprehensively as command-style regulation". This is a contestable position: there is an argument to the effect that such extra speed and comprehension may be purchased too dearly. Be that as it may, it is unlikely that community preferences regarding the pace of change in higher education (as well as elsewhere) would always remain unnoticed by governments. Alterations to the 'responsiveness' characteristic of a higher education system and its component institutions might thus occur through public intervention in existing bilateral arrangements.

2.4.7. Non-existent Markets

Markets may also fail in the sense that they simply do not exist for certain activities. Students, for example, invest in obtaining qualifications, but they cannot insure themselves against the risk that the labour market may ultimately discount the value of the qualification in some way, or that a university may offer substandard teaching and/or research facilities. Insurance markets for these forms of higher education risk simply do not exist, largely for reasons associated with informational inadequacies and costs, moral hazard, and associated difficulties in setting premiums (Joskow and Noll 1981: 26).[6] Under these circumstances, political considerations may motivate governments to assume a de facto role as an insurer (the insurance would be provided largely by regulation).

2.5. Interest Groups: Public Choice

Governments internationally may seek to determine the pace and direction of change in higher education systems because various interested parties may be able to convince them that some or all existing attributes and standards in higher education are undesirable (such as, say, market failure or the allocation of national research grants by means of open competition and peer review), and that better outcomes can be secured through the use of certain nominated regulatory instruments (Rowley and Elgin 1988: 286–288; Laffont and Tirole 1993: 1–6, 596).

2.5.1. Lobbying over Attributes and Standards

Existing students, for example, who cannot get satisfactory responses from universities to their complaints over contract execution will not necessarily rely on exit as a strategy (or on the courts) but may, rather, approach government to devote taxpayer funds to alleviate their concerns. Potential students, furthermore, have a selection problem: How can they predict at acceptable cost the performance of universities? What screening devices are feasible?[7] Students, aware that they lack access to certain information pertinent to their educational choices, may lobby governments success-fully to finance the provision of this information through taxpayer funds (rather than pay for it out of their own pockets). Employers may act in a similar fashion: in 1997, UK employers, argued the case for public (taxpayer) provision of information on qualifications before the National Committee of Inquiry into Higher Education (Quality Assurance Agency for Higher Education 2005). And, as already noted, students are typically able to convince governments in many countries that the taxpayer (rich and poor alike) should subsidise, either partially or completely, the costs of their university education. Any such interventions involve government in altering the characteristics and performance expectations of a higher education system.

2.5.2. Rent-seeking and Higher Education Quality

The public choice literature, arising out of Chicago and Virginia traditions of political economy, argues that industries in particular, far from having public regulation imposed on them, may actively seek it (brief but useful summaries can be found in Braeutigam 1989; and Gruenspecht and Lave 1989: 1530–1531). The theories emanating from both Chicago and Virginia reject the assumptions of the new welfare economics that government is essentially benevolent and acts to secure 'the public interest' or, in other words, to maximise social welfare. Welfare economics posits that governments would necessarily address the inefficiencies attendant upon monopoly, public goods, externalities, and information incompleteness and asymmetries by the most efficacious measures and instruments. In his seminal article on regulation, George Stigler (1971: 3) disputed this analysis, and argued that "regulation may be actively sought by an industry, or it may be thrust upon it. ... As a rule, regulation is acquired by the industry and is designed and operated primarily for its benefit". Stigler (1971: 4) amplified this proposition:

> The state has ... the power to coerce. The state can seize money ... by taxation. The state can ordain the physical movements of resources and the economic decisions of households and firms without their consent. These powers provide the possibilities for the utilization of the state by an industry to increase its profitability.

The Virginia School sees the state largely as a creator and defender of a class of special privileges which has negative consequences for economic development:

> The opportunity to effect wealth transfers, through the machinery of government, on at least a partially coercive basis, encourages lobbying and counter-lobbying of a negative sum nature as individuals and groups invest resources in attempting to obtain a transfer or to resist a transfer away from themselves. (Rowley 1988: 18)

Stigler (1971: 4–5) argued that an industry (or an occupation) would seek some or all of four broad categories of policies from the state: price controls; the suppression of substitutes and the encouragement of complements; control over entry by new rivals (and/or retardation of the growth of new firms which had managed to enter the industry); and financial subsidies. On this last point, Stigler (1971: 4) observed that "the education industry has long shown a masterful skill in obtaining public funds" (contemporary vice chancellors in many countries may wish that these days would return). On the matter of barriers to entry, some of the literature on regulation suggests that the existing members of an industry may seek entry restrictions because they wish to prevent or slow down innovation (Tullock 1988: 61), and/or to prevent 'cream skimming' whereby new entrants, say private postgraduate business education providers, compete with existing institutions for high-demand customers (Laffont and Tirole 1993: 273). Universities may, moreover, lobby governments to empower some form of third-party governance in the interests of assisting them to identify and contain self-serving actions and arrangements – 'informal contracts' – jointly entered into by various internal university managers in pursuit of their personal goals (Faith, Higgins, and Tollison 1988: 317–319). Lobbying of governments may also occur in order to secure public funding of measures to police various franchising agreements which universities sometimes make with organisations in other countries.

A significant insight of the rent-seeking public choice theory of public policy is that governments will not, as a matter of course, address market failures. Whether, and how, this may occur depends significantly on the net impact of the pressures which groups interested in market failures can bring to bear on the political process. Market failures, for example, could persist, in higher education and elsewhere, if interested parties could persuade governments to this course of action. Market failures of one sort or another could thus constitute a potentially permanent characteristic of a higher education system as a deliberate matter of public choice for reasons over and above the possibility that to address them beyond a certain point may be inefficient (see notes 2, 4, and 7).

The theory of rent-seeking has its critics. Laffont and Tirole, for example, have criticised the Chicago and Virginia models for a failure to include 'informational asymmetries' in the analytical framework, and for an overemphasis on the demand for regulation as opposed to the supply: "all the action takes place on the side of interest groups" (Laffont and Tirole 1993: 476). Douglass North (1986) had earlier criticised the models for implicitly assuming that transaction costs were zero (for a response, see Rowley 1988: 21–24). And it could be argued that existing universities may lobby governments to prevent the entry of certain new qualifications into the higher education market on the grounds that the proposed qualifications were significantly deficient in certain respects. 'Altruistic', public interest considerations may motivate such lobbying, not the narrow, self-seeking motives typically attributed in the public choice literature. It is not, however, the purpose of this chapter to delve into these debates. There is no need to do this since this chapter is only concerned with suggesting a range of possible motives for government interest in regulating higher education qualities. Research into the specifics of particular cases could, by the same token, be guided fruitfully by these findings.

3. HOW DO GOVERNMENTS INFLUENCE THE CHARACTERISTICS OF HIGHER EDUCATION AND THEIR QUALITY?

This section discusses methods of public higher education qualities' regulation, although the 'what, why, and how' issues are clearly interrelated. These inter-relationships are emphasised in all branches of regulatory scholarship. The public choice literature suggests that parties with something to gain from government intervention in the form of 'rents' will be especially interested in drawing government attention to certain higher education issues and, moreover, in proposing how government ought to respond to them through the imposition of particular qualities and standards. Existing universities may be one such party. Minimum quality standards (MQS), for example, constitute a regulatory instrument used widely in higher education. It can, however, preclude or inhibit

> the operation of firms that could provide meaningful discipline on incumbent suppliers. To limit such discipline, incumbent suppliers in regulated industries may lobby for the imposition of stringent MQS, particularly when the stringent standards raise the operating costs of potential rivals more than they raise the incumbents' costs. (Sappington 2005: 133)

The public interest or efficiency approach, furthermore, has been captured in David Dill's (2001: 18) argument that many of the regulatory initiatives which governments have taken in higher education since the 1980s implicitly assume

> that the transaction costs involved in student selection of an academic programme warrant an intermediary body ... supposedly acting on behalf of the public interest, to formally contract with universities ... for academic programmes of a given quality, and to monitor academic quality through assessment of academic processes or outcomes. (For a detailed analysis of the efficiency perspective on regulation, see Spulber 1989)[8]

It is, however, not obvious from an efficiency perspective why taxpayer resources ought to be devoted to economising on the higher education transaction (and other) costs of actual and potential students, many of whom, moreover, may currently (or will likely) enjoy relatively affluent circumstances.

There are, moreover, some international differences in which qualities and standards of higher education are regulated publicly. Third-party intervention in the recruitment of university teachers, for example, seems to obtain in France. In the United Kingdom, on the other hand, market-determined, bilateral arrangements prevail. In one case, a degree of public regulation is deemed necessary; in the other, private negotiations are regarded as adequate for the achievement of precisely the same objective in both cases of attracting "the most qualified, motivated and dedicated staff possible" (Crozier, Curvale, and Henard 2005: 15).

There is a significant literature on how governments choose (and should choose)[9] between various regulatory options. It is not, however, the purpose of this chapter to consider explanations of the regulatory choices made by governments with regard to higher education qualities.[10] Rather, aspects of some of the actual choices and some of the theoretical possibilities are discussed.

Public regulation of higher education attributes and standards can occur in a variety of ways which may complement, or substitute for, each other. Over time, furthermore, an objective may be pursued in different ways if governments become dissatisfied with the outcomes of a particular process. Governments may issue advisory guidelines with respect to, say, the provision of information by universities to students. These may yield to more prescriptive declarations if the degree of voluntary compliance fails to meet government expectations.

3.1. Broad Legal Institutions and Frameworks

National constitutions may make explicit reference to higher education. The Constitution of the Republic of South Africa, for example, protects academic freedom. Unless specifically excluded,[11] higher education internationally is subject to a wide body of general law which includes criminal, labour, administrative, and commercial law. The law courts and other institutions such as the ombudsman, the auditor general, the competition authorities, and so on may play a central role in the regulation of higher education qualities. If the law courts become involved, this usually occurs on an *ex post* basis and in response to matters brought before them by parties (including governments) with appropriate standing. Students, for example, may sue a university on the grounds that it failed to execute teaching contracts satisfactorily. Governments may grant students access to legal aid funds to pursue such cases (see e.g. Buscall 2005b). The outcomes of such cases may well lead to changes in the characteristics and standards of a higher education system.

Institutions, furthermore, may seek court judgments with respect to government higher education policies as occurred recently in New Zealand where government efforts to regulate the structure of the New Zealand university system were challenged in the courts (Dye 2005). This serves as a useful reminder that government efforts to determine higher education qualities (in this case, the structural qualities of the higher education system) may sometimes be contested. In certain countries, furthermore, attempts by universities to amalgamate may be scrutinised and determined by the competition authorities, and student complaints may fall within the jurisdiction of the ombudsman. In the United Kingdom, a specialist ombudsman, the Office for the Independent Adjudicator for Higher Education, deals with student complaints. In these ways the shape (attributes and standards) of higher education systems can also be determined.

Certain state institutions may have the power to initiate enquiries into university performance on their own initiative, and to recommend or require changes. In 2002 the auditor general in the Australian state of Queensland decided to evaluate university governance and risk management processes (Illing 2002; for other examples, see Blackmur 2004: 105). This is obviously a form of public quality assurance. Recently, the Information Commissioner in the United Kingdom, exercising powers under the Freedom of Information Act, decided that universities must release the contents of certain secret reports when to do so would serve the public interest (Baty 2005). Governments may also provide other dispute complaints' handling mechanisms which can regulate higher education qualities. Voluntary or compulsory mediation, conciliation, and binding arbitration are possibilities. Moral suasion may also be used as a public regulatory device whereby governments define and broadcast the nature of the values, ethics, and behaviour which they expect all the participants in higher education to adopt.

3.2. Specific Higher Education Statutes

Higher education is governed by specific statutes at both systemic and institutional levels.[12] This legislation typically regulates institutional governance by defining the structure and powers of university councils (and other internal bodies on occasions such as a university academic board). It may provide current and past consumers of higher education with a significant voice as a means of facilitating an exchange of information. Alumni representation may be of particular importance given that the university 'product' has delayed effects. Government interests may be represented directly by ministerial appointments to governing bodies, and legislation may also require universities to demonstrate that they are responsive to criticisms raised by parliamentary committees.

The structural features of a higher education system may be statutorily determined (in whole or in part), apart from rules regulating mergers, by legislative barriers to entry, definitions of a degree, and by public ownership of some or all universities. Governments may regulate franchising agreements which a domestic university has with international partners, possibly by requiring that the contract include provisions for 'hostages' to reduce the risk of adverse reputation effects (on hostage theories of exchange, see Williamson 1985: chs 7 and 8). Higher education regulation may, moreover, be imported by one country from another (others) in the form of arrangements which facilitate mutual recognition of qualifications.

3.3. Public Finance Methods of Determining Higher Education Qualities

Fiscal incentives are an obvious, and important, means by which the qualities of any higher education system are regulated and assured. The composition of a student body will be determined, in part, by the nature and extent of public subsidies (regulation of 'access' characteristics) which may, in turn, only be available for, say, study in programmes, the dimensions of which have met certain publicly mandated standards. Australian universities, moreover, are eligible for public funding from the Learning and Teaching Performance Fund to the extent that their teaching is adequately transformative (a Harvey and Green quality measure) in ways which include improving students' generic skills (Illing 2005). Public funding for university research internationally rarely comes with no strings attached. A government which is concerned that universities were not offering certain degree programmes could enter the higher education market directly as a purchaser. It could, in order to change the 'product range' characteristic, allocate taxpayer funds to the delivery, assessment, and certification of programmes which met its design requirements (in the 1990s, for example, purchaser/provider models were used in some public education systems to address what was argued were provider-dominated processes at the expense of student and national priorities).

3.4. Higher Education Regulatory Agencies

A government's efforts to determine the qualities of a higher education system typically require that it rely on public and/or private sector agents. Many characteristics and standards can be specified in legislation (e.g. the definition of a degree; the age of retirement for academic staff; codes of good teaching practice) but they need to be written, amended from time to time, and enforced. Third-party involvement which relies on some form of agency in all of these activities would seem to be unavoidable. Private professional bodies may be mandated by government to set regulatory objectives and/or methods within a framework of very broad enabling legislation (for European variations on this theme, see Schwarz and Westerheijden 2004: 34–35). Many attributes and standards of accounting, medical, and engineering tertiary education may be governed in this way. Occupational licensing may be delegated to private bodies, although state regulatory agencies perform such functions in many countries. In the field of higher education, third-party involvement in the regulatory process is frequently conducted by means of public monopolies[13] such as the New Zealand Qualifications Authority (NZQA), and the South African Qualifications Authority (SAQA) and Council on Higher Education, although other options are found in private accreditation bodies; student satisfaction surveys and/or audits conducted by private firms; and in the case of the Quality Assurance Agency of the United Kingdom (a private charity).

Examples of public regulatory monopolies abound. In the early 1990s, the New Zealand government maintained "that there are clear arguments in support of an across the board approach to maintaining high standards in the delivery of education of all kinds and in qualifications". It established a public regulatory body to determine and administer the relevant standards, and "to exert strong public pressure when grounds exist for believing that standards are not being maintained" (Minister of Education, New Zealand 1990). Recently, in parts of Europe, governments have "opted for a statutory system with a public quality mark that shows that education satisfies the criteria of basic quality" (Scheele 2004: 19; see also ENQA 2003; and Schwarz and Westerheijden 2004).

Subject to the provisions of enabling legislation, higher education regulatory agencies typically have significant discretion in determining and monitoring the qualities of higher education (restraints on the discretion available to regulatory bodies in an American context are discussed in Baron 1989: 1351; see also Laffont and Tirole 1993: 4–6). In the early 1990s, NZQA decided that one of the qualities which post-compulsory education had to have was that design, delivery, assessment, and certification be determined in terms of the 'unit standards' competency outcomes model. This was not required by the enabling legislation; rather it was an exercise of NZQA's considerable regulatory discretion. Regulation is, of course, a dynamic process and the extent of such discretion is ultimately negotiable given, amongst other things, systemic and/or community responses to the choices made by agencies. In the New Zealand case, these were strongly and bitterly contested over more than a decade, and the debate continues to this day to the extent that the survival of NZQA as an organisation is on the public policy agenda (for some of the NZQA policy issues, see Blackmur 2003; for some of the recent issues surrounding NZQA, see State Services Commissioner, New Zealand 2005).

The responsibilities of agencies include determining certain qualities and their required levels, advising governments on higher education policy, the dissemination of information, and, in some cases, occupational licensing and complaints management. A wide variety of techniques are available to discharge these functions. It is not, however, the purpose of this chapter to discuss the detail of these arrangements. This is a major undertaking in its own right which has been skilfully conducted in recent publications that include the research findings contained in Schwarz and Westerheijden (2004) and in "Quality Procedures in European Higher Education" (ENQA 2003). Comment on some selected themes is, by the same token, offered in the rest of this section.

3.5. Examples of Specific Regulatory Techniques

3.5.1. Quality Standards

Regulatory techniques include the specification of desired characteristics and associated minimum standards, and financial and/or other rewards/penalties for acceptable/substandard performance. The efficacy of minimum quality standards relies, amongst other things, on qualities and performance being verifiable, and requires "substantial knowledge of the costs of supplying quality and the benefits that consumers derive from quality" (Sappington 2005: 133–134). These requirements place an especially heavy burden on the investigative, information-processing, and time capacities of the expert peer panels, which are an integral element of various state-approved higher education qualities' assurance models. It is, indeed, debatable whether the expert panel component of these models can bear the weight placed upon them, especially in view of the fact that, in some cases, the duration of site visits may not be more than 2 days (for a South African example, and a brief expansion of this argument, see Blackmur 2005: 97–98). Regardless of how eminent, distinguished, and important the members of expert panels may be, data gathering, information processing, and strategic considerations could for a priori reasons constitute the Achilles heel of these models (the deficiencies, however, in this case may not be fatal: a 'failed' four-stage process, like a 'failed' market, may produce net benefits). Qualities and standards of performance may simply not be capable of being verified, regardless of the extent of the resources devoted to the exercise, in the ways assumed in, for example, the four-stage models. If significant public faith is placed in the outcomes of such processes, it may for these reasons need to be alert to their limitations.

There are further noteworthy features of a standards-based approach to the regulation of the attributes of higher education. Joskow and Noll (1981: 27) have argued that

> [t]he regulation of product quality (including the banning of certain products) requires
> us to know not only that a public authority can collect and evaluate the relevant
> information more efficiently than can individual agents in the market, but also that the
> more efficient use of these results is to set a standard or ban rather than to provide the
> information directly to consumers. This is a difficult case to make.

Reservations such as this have not, however, deterred some regulators. The South African Council on Higher Education recently banned certain MBAs on the basis of performance against prescribed characteristics which were bureaucratically determined and which paid scant regard to student, graduate, and/or employer preferences (Blackmur 2005). Johnson (1989: 195) has argued that "the standard-setting approach to regulatory policy is not based on the principle of respect for [individual] autonomy, but on the principle of beneficence" (see also Gruenspecht and Lave 1989: 1523). Even where information is provided directly to consumers of higher education, say in the United Kingdom by means of the Teaching Quality Information site (http://www.tqi.ac.uk), the amount and type of information are presumably limited to that which has met the standard of having gained public regulatory approval.[14]

3.5.2. Risk Communication Strategies

An approach more consistent with the autonomy principle involves the notion of hazard warnings and other risk communication strategies. Viscusi (1989: 84) has argued that

> [f]rom a theoretical standpoint, hazard warning programs have much to recommend
> them. One of the major sources of market failure ... has been a lack of information in
> situations in which individuals are making decisions under uncertainty. Because of this
> ... individuals may buy goods for which they are not fully cognizant of the risks. ...
> Hazard warning efforts can eliminate this source of market failure directly by
> eliminating the information gap.

In the higher education context, public agencies could issue hazard warnings, based on complaints and/or analysis against criteria and standards, in respect of, say, certain qualifications, research activity, and so on. Potential and current students, graduates, universities, and employers could respond to this information as they saw fit. Public information on the nature and pattern of the complaints, and the criteria and standards which underpinned these warnings, could assist interested parties to judge the integrity of the models and the analysis on which the warnings were based.

3.5.3. Barriers to Entry

Another instrument which is available to higher education regulators is to restrict entry of various parties to the system. NZQA, for example, has a statutory power to award the 'university' title in certain instances and to advise the Minister of Education on applications for university status. In South Africa, the use of the term 'university' is restricted to public, domestic institutions. Thus, a university such as Monash, despite the fact that it is a public university in Australia and has considerable international standing, is not allowed to use the 'university' title in respect of its South African operations. The South African university system includes universities which cannot be called universities! A system of occupational licensing of, for example, university teachers, and restrictions on student access to universities, are other examples of barriers to entry in higher education which may be erected by public agencies in an effort to determine the characteristics of the system. A key requirement of licensing, designed presumably to protect students against the consequences of incompetent university teaching, is that lecturers be subjected to periodic examinations of their competence (Joskow and Noll 1981: 33).

3.5.4. Some Other Regulatory Methods

In principle, qualities' assurance agencies might be granted seats on university governing councils and/or academic boards as a representative of consumer interests and to monitor certain externalities. Their corporate memory, and information-gathering and information-processing capabilities, may attenuate the usual problems which can arise with consumer participation in governance (Williamson 1985: 308–311). A variation on this theme can be found in private sector practice whereby customers demand the right to have their own qualities' assurance staff located within a supplier which is able to exercise authority over matters of attributes and standards, as a condition of purchase.

3.6. Multiple Regulators

The analysis in this section shows that multiple regulators will almost certainly be involved in determining and assuring higher education qualities (for some issues regarding multiple regulators, see Baron 1989: 1434–1435; and Laffont and Tirole 1993: 655–668). The complexity, uncertainty, and costs of higher education regulation may be magnified considerably on this account. Even if only one regulator were involved, these considerations would be unlikely to be trivial. These and some other possible effects of the regulation of higher education qualities are discussed in Section 4.

4. POSSIBLE AND ACTUAL CONSEQUENCES OF THE PUBLIC REGULATION OF HIGHER EDUCATION QUALITIES

The effects of higher education qualities' regulation may be either those which were sought by government (for whatever reasons: a search for efficiency, the pursuit of personal agendas by politicians, paternalism, or a response to pressure groups)[15] and/or those which were not. Regulatory efforts to attenuate, say, market failure characteristics of a higher education system need to be considered in terms of Becker's (1989: 16) caveat: "Governments do not automatically solve the problems created by selfish behaviour in the marketplace primarily because bureaucrats, legislators, and voters also tend to be selfish, and seek to promote their own interests." Baron (1989: 1349) has noted that "incomplete information and limited observability create opportunities for strategic behaviour on the part of both the regulator and the regulated".

4.1. Principal/Agent: General Issues

The issues involved in exploring the effects of regulation can be understood to a significant degree within the principal/agent analytical framework. Broadly speaking, a responsible cabinet minister (the principal) may empower a public agency(ies) and/or use a private body(ies) (the agents) to effect the government's decisions regarding what ought to be the characteristics, and minimum acceptable standards for each, in a higher education system.[16] The agency may be required to pursue the government's objectives in the spirit of cost minimisation. The agency will, however, have discretion to decide the degree to which it meets the minister's objectives. The extent of this discretion is largely defined by the costs which the principal would have to incur in order to determine the degree of agency compliance and to correct detected deviations. The agent may thus pursue the government's mandate always, on some occasions, or never. From the government's perspective, the latter two possibilities will almost certainly be problematic.

4.2. Principal/Agent: Agent Capture

An agency may pursue these latter options for a variety of reasons. There may be, for example, difficulties in communication between government and agency, and/or the agency's budget may be inadequate to meet the government's expectations. The regulatory literature suggests a further explanation to the effect that the agenda and methods of the agency may be subject to some type of capture. This can take the form of capture by external interests which are able to pressure the agency to adopt their preferred objectives and/or methods, and/or by dominant coalitions within the agency's staff. Capture may involve the trading of favours (e.g. high-profile public support for the agency, promises of future employment for agency staff, financial and/or other rewards) for desired policies. Existing universities may, for example, use various means to convince a higher education regulatory authority to adopt measures which increased the compliance costs of potential new entrants to a greater degree than they increased the incumbents' costs. This may have the effect of deterring new entry and maintaining current structural characteristics which confer a range of advantages on the existing institutions. A form of collusion thus arises and a cartel is sustained through which rents are captured even though this outcome may not have been favoured or sought by government (Laffont and Tirole 1993: 538). In this regard, it has been argued that one of the effects of standards-based higher education regulation may be that the process is susceptible to capture. Joskow and Noll (1981: 28), in comparing this approach and that of information provision, have maintained that

> the standard-setting process is likely to be more easily captured by some particular interest group, whether a consumer group ... or a producer group that can use the standards as a means to help cartelize an industry by making entry and product differentiation difficult.

The space created by information asymmetries, and the principal's monitoring and enforcement costs, could enable agency staff to pursue ideological preferences as to the nature and performance requirements of a higher education system which are inconsistent with those of their principals. This is arguably also a form of rent-seeking and appropriation (of the non-pecuniary variety).

Capture may occur through agency governance processes. In some countries higher education regulatory agencies are governed by government-appointed boards. The membership of these boards is typically drawn from stakeholders. Capture can occur under these circumstances to the extent that individual board members act as representatives of the stakeholder interests from which they were drawn, as opposed to representing their principals' interests. A misunderstanding of corporate governance principles and best practice, or a deliberate pursuit of sectional interests, may explain such behaviour. Such attempts at capture may not necessarily succeed – this depends, amongst other things, on the motives and power of other board members. Efforts to sidestep this constraint may be made by individual board members by means of privately cultivating the support of a senior manager(s) within the regulatory body. Specific policy favours may not always be sought; rather, privileged access to information and/or an insight into the drift of organisational thinking on certain matters may be the objective. Regulatory agencies are particularly vulnerable to such capture when the ethical constraints on conflicts of interest and self-seeking on the part of board members are weak. For all these reasons, the objectives sought by government through higher education regulation (certain attributes and standards) are unlikely to be completely achieved in practice.

4.3. University Responses to Public Regulation of Higher Education Qualities

The reactions of regulators in the area of higher education may also contribute to this outcome and may take several forms. In the case of the 'fitness of and for purpose' regulation of MBAs in South Africa, potential students who prefer a different type of MBA, and thus seek to escape the effects of domestic qualities' regulation, may seek alternatives delivered by means of the Internet.[17] To the extent that this strategy is successful, this may perhaps provoke a further regulatory response whereby regulators seek, for example, to hinder Internet access to such degree programmes, to prevent students using public subsidies to pay for such programmes, and to declare that holders of such degrees are not eligible for private and/or public sector employment and/or to be involved in tenders for government contracts. The 'product range' characteristic of a higher education system would be significantly altered under such circumstances.

Public regulation of attributes and standards may encourage universities to develop means of resistance and avoidance. Universities may seek to lobby and dominate the regulatory agenda, and they may be partially successful in several respects,[18] but where such efforts do not succeed, resistance to unacceptable regulation becomes an option. The costs of complying with certain regulations, for example, are unlikely to be trivial and, especially in a context in which regulation extends to fee and funding levels (qualities of a higher education system), could possibly be met in part through sacrifices of investments in teaching and research – sacrifices which are bitterly resented in university communities, and in efforts to conceal the outcomes of such activities from the regulators.[19] Resources may be directed to searching for evermore sophisticated methods of evading the compliance costs and other impacts of regulation (Becker 1989: 21).

If universities have some flexibility with regard to fee levels, these may be increased on account of the need to meet regulatory compliance costs.[20] This may reduce student access to higher education in a way which compromises government equity policies. In general, compliance games may be played, and universities may concentrate their efforts on complying with, say, regulatory standards at the cost of ignoring other, perhaps more difficult-to-measure, dimensions of higher education. This outcome, of course, may be precisely what regulators wish to achieve.

4.4. Public Regulation of Higher Education Qualities: Implications for Innovation

Some scholars of regulation have maintained that it can have dire consequences for innovation:

> Design standards are enacted to control quality but serve to impede innovation; the temptation is great to write standards that eliminate competition. ... Regulation also pose[s] barriers to innovation, since innovators must persuade regulators ... that their product is ... desirable. Regulation might be thought of as imposing a vast amount of inertia. (Gruenspecht and Lave 1989: 1537)

The significance of this particular source of inertia can be multiplied if innovation has multinational origins. An international network of scholars in corporate governance may design a postgraduate diploma to be delivered online as well as in each partner institution. There is a real risk, however, that such an enterprise would founder (or be inhibited in some way) to the extent that it encountered inconsistent and/or significantly different requirements in the national regulatory systems from which approval of the qualification had to be sought.

One of the risks in the four-stage models of higher education qualities' assurance used in South Africa and parts of Europe is that the process of peer review may identify innovations in one university which reviewers subsequently apply in their own institutions. In the short term, and from a systemic perspective, such diffusion of innovation may be desirable. But the incentives to innovate in component parts of the system may be seriously compromised under such 'externalisation' (theoretical reflection on related points can be found in Williamson 1985: 143). Commercial-in-confidence rules may attenuate opportunism in this context to an appropriate extent, but this is by no means certain. The peer review process may thus have the effect (if not the intent) of creating an externality, a somewhat paradoxical situation in the sense that the process may well have been designed in the first place as a means of eliminating certain systemic characteristics which were associated with market failure including externalities. Managing market failure in a way which may create market failure is an interesting state of affairs.

The pursuit of allocative efficiency by reducing those characteristics of a higher education system associated with market failures may also compromise what Douglass North has called 'adaptive efficiency', which, amongst other things, is concerned with "the willingness of a society to acquire knowledge and learning, to induce innovation, to undertake risk and creative activity of all sorts, as well as to resolve problems and bottlenecks of the society through time" (North 1990: 80). North goes on to argue that

> [a]llocatively efficient rules would make today's firms and decisions secure – but frequently at the expense of the creative ... process. ... Moreover, the very nature of the political process encourages the growth of constraints that favour today's influential bargaining groups. (1990: 81–82)

Universities may have further grounds for selectively displaying their innovations in teaching, managerial systems, and so on over the above avoiding the risks of expropriation. Quality improvement is a favourite catch phrase of many higher education regulators (uttered often in total disregard of the possibility that the costs of supplying qualities' improvements may, at some point, have to be included in the regulatory and university decision-making processes). Minimum standards in respect of those characteristics of higher education which are of interest to governments and/or their agents will thus rise over time. Universities may have an incentive to slow down this process by deflating regulator expectations by, amongst other things, concealing the true state of the qualities' improvements (new attributes and/or higher actual performance standards) which they have adopted. Avoiding what the regulatory literature refers to as the 'ratchet effect' may become a priority (Laffont and Tirole 1993: 664).

4.5. Moral Hazard

An effect of the public regulation of qualities and standards may be to increase the extent of moral hazard inefficiencies in a higher education system. Students, for example, may be less vigilant, less critical, less discerning over matters of higher education qualities relying instead as a matter of faith on the activities of the public regulator(s). They may take greater risks in course selection, given that they think they have been afforded a form of taxpayer-funded insurance against the deleterious effects of any poor decision making on their part (the relationship between moral hazard and regulation is discussed in Spulber 1989: 61–62, 611–617). The value of such insurance, however, depends, amongst other things, on the performance of the regulatory agency. A possible effect of an agency's regulatory behaviour might be that regulators and/or the general public lose respect for it. The agency may provide incorrect or misleading information (Joskow and Noll 1981: 27); it may perform in an administratively inefficient manner; and/or it may impose poorly considered policies and/or ineffective implementation requirements (for material relevant to some of these issues, see Blackmur 2003, 2005; and State Services Commissioner, New Zealand 2005).

4.6. Too Much Information?

The effect of risk communication/hazard warning methods of regulation (which are based on respect for the principle of consumer sovereignty) may be, perhaps paradoxically, that 'too much' information is made available to students and others in a higher education market. The amount of information which is of value in any decision-making context will depend, amongst other things, on the cognitive limits of these involved: "a limit exists beyond which additional information does not improve decisions. ... Increasing the amount of risk information creates an information processing trade-off" (Shogren 1989: 6). Despite their shortcomings, standards-setting approaches may thus augment the effective exercise of consumer choices under relatively severe conditions of risk, opportunism, and bounded rationality. Joskow and Noll (1981: 28) have acknowledged that "standard setting makes sense only in those situations in which a strong case can be made that the dissemination of information is extremely costly, or that consumers will find it difficult to use the information effectively".[21]

4.7. Multiple Agencies

The higher education sector in any country may have some or all of its characteristics and standards defined and assured by several agencies. Contradictory regulation may be the result (Gruenspecht and Lave 1989: 1512–1513). One agency, for example, may seek to maximise access to higher education by people without formal entry requirements; another may regulate recognition of prior learning in ways which inhibit such access. Each may optimise in terms of its own goals, but such a process fails to account for interaction effects and any necessary trade-offs. Clearly, the greater the number of agencies which exercise regulatory authority in higher education, the greater is the risk of this type of suboptimisation. When added to the suboptimisation, which can occur if single agencies fail to establish trade-off ratios between multiple dimensions and standards (Gruenspecht and Lave 1989: 1514), and which occurs if agencies are subject to various forms of capture, there are substantial a priori reasons for suggesting that the goals of government and the performance of regulators may not always coincide.

4.8. Wider Effects

The likely effects of higher education qualities' regulation in particular, and regulation in general, can also be examined from more holistic perspectives. Regulation can have both intended and unintended effects on the distribution of income. Relatively poor taxpayers may subsidise relatively rich (or soon to become so) university students through the means whereby higher education funding characteristics are determined.[22] Other outcomes are, of course, possible: funding arrangements may assist the poor to gain access to higher education. Again, funding devoted to higher education regulation is not available to be spent on providing, say, basic services to the poor, a matter of deep significance in developing countries.[23] The Chicago school of regulatory theory is especially interested in distributional issues: "The theory predicts that regulators will use their power to transfer income from those with less political power to those with more" (Joskow and Noll 1981: 36).

Discussions of the effects of higher education regulation on variables such as employment, inflation, interest and exchange rates, and economic growth do not occupy a prominent place in research on the impact of higher education qualities' assurance. Matters such as these arguably should be added to the research agenda. Another candidate is the magnitude of the impact of higher education regulation on the regulatory reputation of a country. A reputation for, say, 'excessive' command and control regulation in this sphere, especially if such an approach is applied more widely across the economy, may damage a country's attractiveness to foreign investors, which can produce deleterious consequences for, say, employment and growth (*Economist* 2005).

4.9. Actual Outcomes: Examples

There are many judgements concerning the impact of higher education qualities' regulation in particular cases. Alan Ryan, the Warden of New College, Oxford, has maintained that the Quality Assurance Agency "has been unable to do anything beyond reducing what was already a pretty minimal amount of really spectacular incompetence in the management of teaching" (Ryan 2005). John Mullarvey (2005), the Chief Executive Officer of the Australian Vice Chancellors' Committee, has argued that

> [u]niversities operate in an increasingly legislated and regulated environment, requiring an unprecedented level of reporting to ... governments that impinge on their ability to fulfil their academic missions. The increasing redirection of resources away from teaching and research to meet government reporting requirements is having an impact on our universities.

There are, furthermore, many clearly demonstrated outcomes such as the recent decision by the Council on Higher Education to remove certain MBAs from the South African market in the name of quality assurance. It will be important to assess the longer-term impact of this and similar decisions (Blackmur 2005). What is also needed is further comparative international research which can inform inductive theories of the impact of public efforts to regulate higher education characteristics and performance. The techniques of the econometricians may be of particular assistance in parts of this enterprise.

5. CONCLUSION

Higher education has many characteristics. Public policy may seek to determine some of these and to define certain performance expectations. A government may thus decide that universities must, for example, undertake research. It may also specify minimum standards against which the actual quality of the research characteristic will be measured. Qualities' assurance, or quality assurance, involves a process whereby interested parties seek confidence that desired qualities are, in fact, present to at least the required extent. There will, of course, be often formidable problems of definition and standards' setting in the regulation of higher education quality, regardless of whether this is conducted by the state or by individual universities or, as typically happens, by some combination of the two. These problems, amongst others, suggest that there are limits to regulation in general, and to certain types of regulation in particular. In respect of the latter, governments may discover that public regulatory processes are incapable of replicating (at any acceptable cost, or at all) important tacit knowledge held by academics in certain significant areas, and that, on this account, many matters of attribute selection and/or their quality assurance are best decided within universities including at the level of the individual academic (universities may come to the same conclusion). There may be considerable space for various forms and levels of self-regulation in matters of higher education quality. Having said that, even individual academics will, in the final analysis, necessarily think about higher education qualities, and make judgements about them, in terms of some (often personal) standards, expectations, preferences, and so on.

The economics of regulation can enrich our understanding of the motives, processes, and effects associated with government intervention in the nature of higher education relationships. Much of the scholarly literature on higher education qualities' assurance, however, has a strange characteristic (to the economist's eye) in that there are but rare references to the costs of regulating qualities and their quality (the 'value for money' perspective may be an exception). It is as if, once the market has been rejected as the arbiter of qualities, matters of price and cost can be safely left out of the analysis. Exhortations, furthermore, which assert the desirability of 'quality improvement' are often made and in the complete absence of any references to the possibility that, at some point, such improvements may not justify the costs of securing them. The implication is that quality improvements should be pursued regardless of cost. A general equilibrium dimension is also lacking in much of this literature. All of the costs, for example, associated with higher education qualities' regulation clearly must be properly accounted for in terms of their systemic and institutional impacts, but they also represent foregone opportunities in parts of a society other than the higher education sector. They may, moreover, have important consequences for employment, inflation, investment reputation, and growth.

Public choice perspectives remind scholars of higher education public regulation that government/bureaucratic failure needs to be considered alongside market failure, and that governments/agencies may act for reasons which have nothing to do with, or are actively opposed to, efficiency. Attention has also been drawn in this chapter, amongst other things, to the possibility that, whether higher education regulatory agencies pursue efficiency and/or other goals, they may perform so poorly that they lose client and/or public respect. It may not be too far-fetched to suggest that in the future the fact that a degree has been favourably accredited by a particular agency will not necessarily be to the advantage of those who hold that degree!

The fact that governments internationally are vitally concerned with determining various higher education qualities is a commonplace. The various theoretical insights which have been discussed in this chapter help to define the range of possible motives for this. A series of case studies, guided in part by these theories, may be able to identify the precise reasons for government regulation of certain higher education relationships and structures. Such studies, furthermore, perhaps ought to give consideration to the relevant empirical magnitudes. Are there estimates of the losses incurred, and by whom, as a result of, say, market failures in higher education? Are the costs of addressing these, if governments so decide, far greater than the benefits? Answers to such questions may assist communities to determine which, if any, of the 'problems' that public higher education qualities' assurance processes allegedly seek to address are really worth worrying about and, where they are not, why they might nevertheless remain on the public policy agenda.

NOTES

1   I gratefully acknowledge critical comment on an earlier version of this chapter which was offered by the participants in the Douro 5 Seminar "Dynamics and Effects of Quality Assurance in Higher Education" convened by CIPES and HEDDA in Portugal in October 2005. Special thanks are due to Don Westerheijden for encouraging me to think differently about parts of the argument, and to Glyn Davis of the University of Melbourne for valuable comments. I am also indebted to Gina Verberne's for discussing with me many of the issues raised in this chapter and for assisting with matters of format and style. Responsibility for all errors is entirely mine.

2   This is in the spirit of Kelvin Lancaster's research on the properties of goods and services and of the implications of such an approach for theories of consumption (the foundation article is Lancaster 1966). Consider the case of potential buyers of air-conditioning machines. One of the many characteristics of these machines of interest to these buyers would almost certainly be the noise associated with their operation. In terms of this characteristic, a very quiet machine would be of very high quality (assuming people do not enjoy noise, at least beyond a certain level). Another desired characteristic might be the efficiency of the machine. The higher the cooling effect per unit of energy input, the higher would be the quality of this characteristic of the machine. Another example, which includes the role of the state, can be taken from the production and sale of cigarettes. Cigarettes and their packaging will have characteristics decided by the manufacturers, but they will also have characteristics decided by the state. The nature of the cigarettes themselves, for example, has to conform to defined public standards: certain ingredients may be prohibited. The packets must display health warnings that must comply with government standards, which include the requirement that a warning be displayed on the external part of the packet. Public checking (assurance) at the point of sale (and elsewhere) assures all interested parties that the characteristic of displaying a health warning is, in fact, in evidence to the required extent. This chapter uses an analogous approach to the public regulation of higher education quality (for a discussion of this perspective, see Klein and Leffler 1989: 618; and Spulber 1989: 386–387).

3   'Failures' has an unfortunate pejorative ring to it. The outcomes of a 'failed market' may, in an imperfect world, be the best that can be achieved. A government *may* decline to exhibit an interest in addressing market failure(s) in higher education on the grounds that corrective action would produce an improvement of lesser magnitude than the costs of securing it.

4   A university-established body charged with policing quality and devising penalties for malfeasance may nevertheless appear, or could be represented, as nothing but a servant of self-interested universities concerned largely with cosmetic adjustments and/or responses.

5   To anticipate the argument, from a public choice perspective, government action may not be motivated by efficiency considerations at all but by lobbying by special interest groups which have an interest in the maintenance, not the elimination, of certain sources of inefficiency. This challenges assumptions to the effect that "inefficiency invites relief" (Williamson 2000: 603). The public choice literature suggests that situations of inefficiency will be deliberately created and, at times, successfully defended. Those seeking relief from the consequences of the 'rent-seeking and obtaining' behaviour of others may never prevail. Williamson's assumption is also debatable on other grounds. In a world of bounded rationality and costly information, inefficiencies may persist undetected in the form of habits and routines.

6   If such markets were viable, insurance companies would act as qualities' assurance institutions. Banks can also be thought of as performing a qualities' assurance function if they make loans to, say, students and/or universities for higher education purposes.

7   Universities also may have a selection problem, but this is of relatively less magnitude than that faced by students given the range of selection instruments which are available to universities and their capacity to take advantage of economies of scale and scope in selection processes.

8   Such an assumption, however, may not be justified in particular cases: any efficiency gains attributable to public regulation may be smaller than the associated costs. It is for this reason, in general terms, from an efficiency perspective, that market failure is a necessary but not sufficient condition for public intervention. Adam Smith, perhaps not surprisingly, enunciated this principle in 1776. In discussing the behaviour of sellers in a competitive market, he noted that "some of them, perhaps, may sometimes decoy a weak customer to buy what he has no occasion for. This evil, however, is of too little importance to deserve the public attention" (Smith 1776: 460).

9   This chapter does not explicitly address normative issues. One of the many normative theories on how governments should implement decisions to change relationships in a market economy has been developed by Ayres and Braithwaite (1992).

10 Principal and agent theory, and theories of own as opposed to market-mediated production, (especially transaction costs theories of vertical integration), could be particularly useful in this regard. McCubbins (1985: 722) has drawn attention to American instances of the Congress choosing to deal directly with the detail of regulation as opposed to delegating this to administrative agencies. He poses a central question in this context: "under what conditions do legislators prefer to delegate legislative authority to administrative entities?" (1985: 722). Analysis of this matter is based on considerations which include the "technical complexity of modern society" and a desire "on the part of legislators to escape the costs, political and otherwise, of regulating directly" (McCubbins 1985: 722–723; see also Laffont and Tirole 1993: 501). Public choice theorists would argue that the choice of regulatory means would turn significantly on its relevance to the identification and extraction of rents: "there may also be gains from specialization in identifying industries with appropriable producers' surplus and in determining how best to extract it. If so, legislators predictably would delegate cost-imposing functions to specialized bureaucratic agencies" (McChesney 1988: 187). Consideration might also be given to the possibility that delegation of authority to an agency may be chosen on the grounds that it is important to have a corporate memory, especially with regard to 'consumption' issues, in those areas of the economy and society where exchange is often 'one off' and the advantages of repeat dealing as a (market-based) regulatory device are thus unavailable. Many aspects of higher education would seem to qualify in this respect given the rapid turnover of students and the fact that they typically only obtain one degree from any given university. Survivability considerations would suggest that an agency serving a corporate memory purpose may be a public authority rather than a private firm, although other matters may also impact on this choice.

11 Universities may, for example, be excluded from the ambit of product liability laws and from general consumer protection law.

12 Much of the New Institutional Economics uses the word 'institution' to refer to norms, customs, practices, values, and so on. This chapter does not follow this convention. The words 'institution' and 'organisation' and their derivatives are used interchangeably.

13 It is interesting to note that governments in many countries have established competition (anti-monopoly) authorities but at the same time they have established public monopolies to regulate higher education (and other industries and occupations). Under these circumstances, the issue of 'who regulates the regulators' takes on special relevance. Possible changes to the system of monopoly regulators are foreshadowed in a recent draft of a European Commission proposal to allow universities to select from accreditation agencies (Baty 2004). It would seem, however, that, under the proposals, these agencies would have to be accredited by a single authority.

14 I am not sure if there is a statutory requirement for universities to provide information to the Teaching Quality Information site, which provides details of the National Student Survey of UK higher education.

15 These are not necessarily mutually exclusive categories. Certain pressure groups, for example, may lobby governments to introduce efficiency-enhancing regulation.

16 The chain of principal/agent relationships can be complex. The analysis in this chapter oversimplifies it in this respect.

17 Students may seek to substitute unregulated (or differently regulated) services for regulated ones (Menard and Shirley 2005: 14).

18 It could be hypothesised, for example, that the enormous political pressure exerted by New Zealand universities in the 1990s to escape the jurisdiction of NZQA was motivated, in part, by concerns over compliance costs, notions of academic freedom and institutional autonomy, a sense of status, and especially by a rejection of the philosophical underpinnings of NZQA's regulatory model. The

universities may, of course, have also been very afraid of what an external agency may have discovered and disclosed about their performance.

19   A more likely possibility is that such economising would occur in relatively unregulated university activities.

20   There are costs which arise out of regulation over and above compliance costs. The resources devoted by universities to lobbying governments on regulatory matters (which could include drawing attention to the impact of compliance costs) provide an example (Laffont and Tirole 1993: 505–506). On the other hand, fees may also be increased by universities as a result of their successful lobbying, or as a result of independent, but favourable, decisions of regulators. Thus, universities which receive regulatory protection against competition in certain degree markets may be able to increase the fees charged for these degrees and to use the proceeds to finance competition against rivals elsewhere (Baseman 1981: 329).

21   These considerations are, of course, largely irrelevant if regulation is explicitly designed to suppress the exercise of consumer preferences.

22   The notion of a 'funding' characteristic may cause some discomfort. The argument is that a government may decide to regulate a higher education system in such a way that students are charged less than full cost fees and the shortfall is made up from general taxation revenue. This system thus exhibits a 'less than full cost fees' funding characteristic.

23   In terms of my own personal prejudices, I wonder at the wisdom of countries such as South Africa, encouraged by, for example, the European Union and UNESCO, establishing extremely expensive systems of post-compulsory educational regulation (of arguably doubtful net benefit) while at the same time millions of their citizens lack even basic services such as clean water, electricity, and primary health care.

REFERENCES

Akerloff, G. "The Market for 'Lemons': Qualitative Uncertainty and the Market Mechanism." *Quarterly Journal of Economics* 84.3 (1970): 488–500.

Ayres, I. and J. Braithwaite. *Responsive Regulation*. Oxford: Oxford University Press, 1992.

Baron, D.P. "Design of Regulatory Mechanisms and Institutions." In Schmalensee, R. and R.D. Willig (eds). *Handbook of Industrial Organization*, vol. 2. Amsterdam: North-Holland, 1989, 1347–1447.

Baseman, K.C. "Open Entry and Cross-subsidisation in Regulated Markets." In Fromm, G. (ed.). *Studies in Public Regulation*. Cambridge, MA: MIT Press, 1981, 329–360.

Baty, P. "QAA Could Face EU Market." *Times Higher Education Supplement*, 10 December, 2004.

Baty, P. "Public Right Trumps University Secrecy." *Times Higher Education Supplement*, 12 August, 2005.

Becker, G.S. "Political Competition Amongst Interest Groups." In Shogren, J.F. (ed.). *The Political Economy of Government Regulation*. Boston: Kluwer, 1989, 13–27.

Blackmur, D. "Policy Challenges in Educational Quality Assurance: The New Zealand Qualifications Authority, 1997–1999." In *Qualifications and Standards: Harmonisation and Articulation Initiatives*. Proceedings and Resources, SAQA Seminar, Pretoria, South Africa, 2003, 111–121.

Blackmur, D. "Issues in Higher Education Quality Assurance." *Australian Journal of Public Administration* 63.2 (2004): 105–116.

Blackmur, D. "An Evaluation of the South African Model of MBA Accreditation." *Quality in Higher Education* 11.2 (2005): 87–102.

Braeutigam, R.R. "Optimal Policies for Natural Monopolies." In Schmalensee, R. and R.D. Willig (eds). *Handbook of Industrial Organization*, vol. 2. Amsterdam: North-Holland, 1989, 1289–1346.

Buscall, J. "Sweden Faces Surge in Bogus Degrees." *Times Higher Education Supplement*, 3 June, 2005a.

Buscall, J. "Business School Sued Over 'Masters'." *Times Higher Education Supplement*, 14 January, 2005b.

Crozier, F., B. Curvale, and F. Henard. "Quality Convergence Study." ENQA Occasional Papers 7, Helsinki: European Network for Quality Assurance in Higher Education, 2005.

Dill, D.D. "An Institutional Perspective on Higher Education Policy: The Case of Academic Quality Assurance." Seminar on the Application of Neo-institutional Approaches in Higher Education, Centre for Higher Education Policy Studies, University of Twente, 2001.

Dye, S. "Government Action Unlawful in UNITEC Case." *New Zealand Herald*, 15 August, 2005.

Economist. "Special Report: Higher Education." 26 February, 2005.

ENQA. "Quality Procedures in European Higher Education: An ENQA Survey." ENQA Occasional Papers 5, Helsinki: European Network for Quality Assurance in Higher Education, 2003.

Faith, R.L., R.S. Higgins, and R.D. Tollison. "Managerial Rents and Outside Recruitment in the Coasian Firm." In Rowley, C.K., R.D. Tollison, and G. Tullock (eds). *The Political Economy of Rent-seeking.* Boston: Kluwer, 1988, 315–335.

Findlay, C. "Introduction to the Regulation of Services." Paper presented at the Productivity Commission and Australian National University Conference Achieving Better Regulation of Services, Canberra, Australia, 26–27 June, 2000.

Gruenspecht, H.K. and L.B. Lave. "The Economics of Health, Safety, and Environmental Regulation." In Schmalensee, R. and R.D. Willig (eds). *Handbook of Industrial Organization,* vol. 2. Amsterdam: North-Holland, 1989, 1507–1550.

Hara, N. "Concern as Japan Links Efficiencies to Subsidies." *Times Higher Education Supplement,* 8 July, 2005.

Harvey, L. and D. Green. "Defining Quality." *Assessment and Evaluation in Higher Education* 18.1 (1993): 9–34.

Illing, D. "Governance under Scrutiny." *Australian,* 11 September, 2002.

Illing, D. "Shock Teacher Rating for Unis." *Australian,* 12 August, 2005.

Johnson, F.R. "Disclosure, Consent, and Environmental Risk Regulation." In Shogren, J.F. (ed.). *The Political Economy of Government Regulation.* Boston: Kluwer, 1989, 191–208.

Joskow, P.L. and R.C. Noll. "Regulation in Theory and Practice: An Overview." In Fromm, G. (ed.). *Studies in Public Regulation.* Cambridge, MA: MIT Press, 1981, 1–65.

Klein, B. and K.B. Leffler. "The Role of Market Forces in Assuring Contractual Performance." *Journal of Political Economy* 89.4 (1989): 615–641.

Laffont, J.-J. and J. Tirole. *A Theory of Incentives in Procurement and Regulation.* Cambridge, MA: MIT Press, 1993.

Lancaster, K.J. "A New Approach to Consumer Theory." *Journal of Political Economy* 74.2 (1966): 132–157.

Maslen, G. "Trade in Fake Papers Soars." *Times Higher Education Supplement,* 3 June, 2005.

McChesney, F.S. "Rent Extraction and Rent Creation in the Economic Theory of Regulation." In Rowley, C.K., R.D. Tollison, and G. Tullock (eds). *The Political Economy of Rent-seeking.* Boston: Kluwer, 1988, 179–196.

McCubbins, M.D. "The Legislative Design of Regulatory Structure." *American Journal of Political Science* 29.4 (1985): 721–748.

Menard C. and M.M. Shirley (eds). *Handbook of New Institutional Economics.* Dordrecht, The Netherlands: Springer, 2005.

Minister of Education, New Zealand. *Education Amendment Bill, Second Reading Speech.* New Zealand Parliamentary Debates, Wellington, 1990.

Minister of Education, South Africa. *Higher Education Bill, Second Reading Speech.* South African Parliamentary Debates, Cape Town, 1997.

Mullarvey, J. "Are Our Universities Losing Their Autonomy?" *Age,* 16 June, 2005.

North, D.C. "The New Institutional Economics." *Journal of Institutional and Theoretical Economics* 142.1 (1986): 230–237.

North, D.C. *Institutions, Institutional Change and Economic Performance.* Cambridge: Cambridge University Press, 1990.

Quality Assurance Agency for Higher Education. "A Brief Guide to Quality Assurance in UK Higher Education." 2005, http://www.qaa.org.uk.

Rowley, C.K. "Rent-seeking Versus Directly Unproductive Profit-seeking Activities." In Rowley, C.K., R.D. Tollison, and G. Tullock (eds). *The Political Economy of Rent-seeking.* Boston: Kluwer, 1988, 15–25.

Rowley, C.K. and R. Elgin. "Government and its Bureaucracy: A Bilateral Bargaining Versus a Principal-Agent Approach." In Rowley, C.K., R.D. Tollison, and G. Tullock (eds). *The Political Economy of Rent-seeking.* Boston: Kluwer, 1988, 267–290.

Ryan, A. "Alan Ryan." *Times Higher Education Supplement,* 12 August, 2005.

Sappington, D.E.M. "Regulating Service Quality: A Survey." *Journal of Regulatory Economics* 27.2 (2005): 123–154.

Scheele, K. "Licence to Kill: About Accreditation Issues and James Bond." In Di Nauta, P., P.-L. Omar, A. Schade, and J.P. Scheele (eds). *Accreditation Models in Higher Education Experiences and Perspectives.* ENQA Workshop Reports 3, Helsinki: European Network for Quality Assurance in Higher Education, 2004, 19–25.

Schwarz, S. and D.F. Westerheijden. *Accreditation and Evaluation in the European Higher Education Area.* Dordrecht, The Netherlands: Kluwer, 2004.

Shogren, J.F. "Introduction and Overview." In Shogren, J.F. (ed.). *The Political Economy of Government Regulation.* Boston: Kluwer, 1989, 1–12.

Smith, A. *The Wealth of Nations.* Bantam Classic Edition. New York: Bantam Dell, 1776.

Spulber, D. *Regulation and Markets.* Cambridge, MA: MIT Press, 1989.

State Services Commissioner, New Zealand. "Report on the Performance of the New Zealand Qualifications Authority in the Delivery of Secondary School Qualifications." 2005, http://www.ssc.govt.nz.

Stigler, G.J. "The Theory of Economic Regulation." *Bell Journal of Economics* 2.1 (1971): 3–21.

Times Higher Education Supplement. News Round-up. 20 August, 2003.

Tullock, G. "Rents and Rent-seeking." In Rowley, C.K., R.D. Tollison, and G. Tullock (eds). *The Political Economy of Rent-seeking.* Boston: Kluwer, 1988, 51–62.

Viscusi, W.K. "The Political Economy of Risk Communication Policies for Food and Alcoholic Beverages." In Shogren, J.F. (ed.). *The Political Economy of Government Regulation.* Boston: Kluwer, 1989, 83–129.

Westerheijden, D.F. "Where are the Quantum Jumps in Quality Assurance?" *Higher Education* 38.2 (1999): 233–254.

Wheen, F. *How Mumbo-Jumbo Conquered the World.* London: Harper Perennial, 2004.

Williamson, O.E. *The Economic Institutions of Capitalism.* New York: The Free Press, 1985.

Williamson, O.E. "The New Institutional Economics: Taking Stock, Looking Ahead." *Journal of Economic Literature* 38.3 (2000): 595–613.

DAVID D. DILL

WILL MARKET COMPETITION ASSURE ACADEMIC QUALITY? AN ANALYSIS OF THE UK AND US EXPERIENCE

1. INTRODUCTION

A major change that has accompanied the worldwide 'massification' of higher education is the new-found openness of policy makers to the use of competitive markets to steer the university sector. In many countries efforts to improve the quality of publicly provided higher education, both in teaching and in research, are leading to experiments with market-based policy instruments (Teixeira et al. 2004). The perceived quality of universities in the competitive US system – which Trow (2000) has termed the 'American advantage' – has inspired much of this interest in market forces. While a number of these market experiments may also be motivated by a desire to restrict public expenditures in rapidly expanding systems of higher education, many policy makers and academics believe that there is a relationship between the degree of market competition and academic quality (Dill 2005).

This presumed relationship between academic quality and market competition clearly influenced US federal policy decisions on the financing of higher education in the years following World War II (see Chapter 6 by Ewell). In 1972 the US Congress explicitly rejected proposals for federal grants to institutions in favour of federal student assistance on the grounds that student loans and grants would promote competition for academic quality within the US system. In debates during 2003–2005 about the renewal of the Higher Education Act, members of the US Congress expressed growing concern about declining academic standards amid rapidly rising public and private college tuition costs.[1] Consistent with the traditional US commitment to competitive markets for coordinating higher education, Congress proposed legislation in 2005 designed to empower consumers with better information on university academic performance.[2] Similar arguments for a link between market competition and academic quality have been proposed in the United Kingdom (DfES 2003) as policy makers and university leaders debate the most appropriate means of regulating its rapidly expanding system of higher education. Frustration with new state quality assurance regulations has also motivated academics in various parts of the world to look to market competition as a preferred alternative. A former vice chancellor of Cambridge University asserted that "it was time for action to eliminate the [Quality Assurance Agency] external assessment process and allow 'the market' to rule" in the United Kingdom (Maslen 2000).

D.F. Westerheijden et al. (eds.), Quality Assurance in Higher Education: Trends in Regulation, Translation and Transformation, 47–72.
© 2007 *Springer.*

Clark's (1983) classic 'triangle of coordination' suggested three principal modes for coordinating or controlling behaviour in academic institutions: state regulation; professional self-regulation, which Clark termed 'the academic oligarchy'; and market forces. Many economists argue that in mass systems of higher education coordination by 'competitive markets' is more allocatively efficient, all things being equal, than coordination by government regulation or by voluntary or self-regulation (Teixeira et al. 2004). Barr (2004), for example, notes that young adults are better informed about their needs and better able to make choices than school-age students. Furthermore, unlike school-age students, university students' tastes are diverse, university degrees are becoming increasingly varied, and academic innovation is becoming more rapid. For these reasons, Barr (2004) argues that while it is reasonable to question competitive markets for the provision of school education, market provision of higher education is in public interest.

But what has been the experience with market regulation of academic quality? How effective have the existing market for academic programmes in the United States and the emerging market in the United Kingdom been in assuring academic standards? These questions will be explored in the sections to follow. Section 2 provides a brief definition of the concept of academic quality as applied in this analysis. Section 3 examines the experience among universities in the United Kingdom, where market competition has been recently introduced. The analysis continues in Section 4 with a more extensive discussion of the US system, which is generally acknowledged to be the most market-oriented system of higher education in the world. Section 5 reviews the influential role played by commercial university league tables in the UK and US higher education markets. The chapter concludes with an overall assessment of market regulation of academic standards and the possible implications for public policy in Section 6.

2. ACADEMIC QUALITY AND ACADEMIC STANDARDS

In the growing literature on academic quality there is often extensive debate about the meaning of the term (Green 1994). Many have suggested that 'academic quality' is amorphous, non-measurable, or so ambiguous in meaning as to be not appropriate for public intervention. From a public policy perspective I would suggest that academic quality is equivalent to academic standards – to the level of academic achievement attained by higher education graduates. Public subsidies of higher education in all countries are argued to be in the public interest because of the human capital that graduates provide to society (Becker 1964). Human capital is used here in its broadest meaning to include not only the contributions that educated graduates make to the economy, but also the non-monetary benefits they contribute to society through improved parenting, healthier lifestyles, greater civic partici-pation, and increased social cohesion (Haveman, Bershadker, and Schwabish 2003). From this perspective the public interest is best served by an institutional framework of policies, norms, and rules (North 1990) that maximises in as efficient and equitable a manner as possible the academic standards attained by graduates. This definition of academic quality as equivalent to academic standards is also consistent with the emerging focus in higher education quality assurance policies on student learning outcomes – the specific levels of knowledge, skills, and abilities that students achieve as a consequence of their engagement in a particular college or university programme (Brennan and Shah 2000).[3]

Academic quality in this sense is a necessary component of any discussion of cost and access in higher education (Berdahl and Spitzberg 1991). For example, policy makers must consider whether the rapidly increasing public investment in higher education is purchasing more, less or comparable levels of academic achievement among students. Without some knowledge of the relationship between the level of public investment in higher education and the level of academic achievement produced, the public debates about higher education cost can be seriously misleading. Even if a government adopts a market orientation to higher education, which produces as in the United States varying levels of academic quality among institutions, there is an important public interest in academic standards. If the market is to function efficiently, individual consumers need to be able to fairly evaluate the relative educational value-added by colleges and universities of widely varying cost. Similarly, policy makers in most countries who are concerned with access to higher education must confront the often-unasked question "access to what?" (Massy 2003). Investments in access without a commensurate concern with the level of learning outcomes of institutions of higher education may not yield the social and economic benefits expected.

3. MARKET COMPETITION AND ACADEMIC STANDARDS IN THE UNITED KINGDOM

UK universities are to be distinguished from 'public' universities in other parts of the world in that they are autonomous, property-owning institutions whose independence is guaranteed by Royal Charter or by Parliamentary Statute.[4] In this sense, their governance is more similar to not-for-profit, private universities in the United States than to state-sponsored universities of many other countries including the United States. As with US private universities, UK universities are fully responsible for the management of their own financial affairs, appoint and employ their own staff, recruit their own students both nationally and internationally, design their own curricula, and award their own degrees. Into the 1980s there was some competition among English universities for students with the highest 'A' level scores (secondary school-leaving certificates) and for research recognition. The rewards in this competition were greater institutional prestige and more interesting teaching responsibilities, because faculty members can better link their teaching and research when students are more able (Williams 2004).

However, despite the institutional autonomy granted by the state to UK universities, it would be difficult to characterise the higher education market or markets in the United Kingdom prior to 1980 as highly competitive. The expansion of the British welfare state following World War II effectively suppressed rivalry in the market for higher education and provided few incentives for universities to actively compete in the provision of education, research, and public service.

National funding of universities rose from a pre-war average of 30% to more than 70% following the war, and in a number of supposedly independent universities national funding approximated 100% of the operating budget (Williams 2004). Both the scale and the nature of this national funding limited competition. Because government support to universities was provided in the form of 5-year block grants with few strings attached that were more or less incremental over time, the universities had few incentives to seek alternative sources of funding. The block grants also included support for research; therefore, national financing did little to encourage a competitive research market or provide incentives for universities to actively pursue research contracts with business and industry.[5] Student fees were also paid by the state, except for the wealthiest families,[6] and state-funded student maintenance grants lessened cost as a consideration in university choice. By making university education essentially a free good for those who could pursue it, state support may also have lessened student criticism and pressure for academic quality improvements within universities (Johnstone 2004). In addition, pay scales for teaching staff were determined nationally. As a consequence, although universities were supposedly independent institutions competing for the best faculty members, rivalry in the academic labour market was suppressed and there was limited mobility of academic staff among universities. Finally, entry of new universities into the higher education sector was carefully controlled by the government. Only one small university, the University of Buckingham, was recognised by the government as a truly 'private' university in that it was not eligible for government funding. When a need for non-traditional higher education was perceived, the government established the nationally subsidised Open University as a primary provider and thereby suppressed competition in the distance learning market as well.

As a consequence of these national policies, the supposedly independent universities in the United Kingdom through the 1980s operated more similarly to the state monopoly systems of higher education in Western Europe than to the socially responsive competitive higher education market in the United States (Ben-David 1972). Williams (2004) concludes that since the UK higher education market was not truly rivalrous, the noted autonomy of universities failed to produce the levels of social benefits including innovation that economists would normally expect from a market composed of private providers.

3.1. Introduction of Market Forces in the United Kingdom

The Conservative government elected in 1979 was determined to reform the British welfare state in part by introducing market competition into the public sector. In areas such as housing, transportation, and utilities this involved deregulating and/or privatising the public sector to create independent and autonomous entities that would compete in the provision of goods and services. In the case of the old universities, this type of deregulation was unnecessary, because the universities already possessed the legal autonomy necessary to compete as independent organisations.[7] However, the institutions in the former polytechnic sector were not independent. Unlike the university sector they did not have degree-awarding powers.

The academic oversight activities of the Council for National Academic Awards (CNAA) and the influence of Local Education Authorities (LEAs) restricted the academic and managerial autonomy of these institutions. In this sense, the polytechnic sector was more similar to state-regulated university systems in western Europe or in the United States. The 1988 Education Reform Act and the 1992 Further and Higher Education Act made the polytechnics independent of the LEAs and CNAA, eliminating the technical distinction – the so-called binary system – between polytechnics and universities (Barr 2004). These policies essentially privatised the polytechnic sector, more than doubling the number of competitors as well as increasing the potential for rivalry in the newly expanded university sector.

To further increase the efficiency of UK higher education, the Conservative government pursued two general policies: reductions in public support and the introduction of quasi-markets. The first and most obvious policy was massive cuts in public expenditures for higher education. The first two Conservative government budgets combined reduced state support for higher education by an overall 16%, but between 1980 and 2000 public expenditure per student in UK higher education declined by almost 35% in real terms (Williams 2004). While there is some debate as to whether these reductions in university support were motivated by a policy commitment to market forces by the Conservative government (Bird 1994), there is no question that the financial cuts altered the behaviour of the university sector.

With the re-election of the Conservative government in 1984 the universities assumed that financial stringency in the public sector would be a permanent part of the landscape and they began aggressively to pursue cost-saving efficiencies as well as alternative sources of revenue. In their internal affairs universities adopted more proactive forms of management, including the widespread use of resource allocation models for financial decision making, as well as the restructuring of academic units to encourage greater responsibility and accountability for teaching, research, and service activities (Dill 1999; Williams 2004). In their external affairs from the 1980s on they vigorously pursued new strategies for generating income including the recruitment of fee-paying foreign students, the selling of teaching and research services, and the renting of academic facilities at times they were not required for instruction (Williams 1992).

The second policy pursued by the Conservative government, which was more clearly intended to promote market competition in the publicly funded higher education sector, was the introduction of 'quasi-markets' (Johnes and Cave 1994). The concept of quasi-markets has policy utility, but is used with a variety of meanings in the literature on higher education (Niklasson 1996). Therefore, the concept needs to be carefully defined if it is to contribute to our understanding of higher education markets. The discussion that follows therefore adopts the definition of quasi-markets as internal markets used by Le Grand and his colleagues at the London School of Economics (Le Grand and Bartlett 1993; Barr 2004).

Internal or quasi-markets differ from private markets in that they are introduced into existing publicly funded systems. Quasi-markets do not evolve naturally from existing factors of supply and demand, but are created by government to overcome the perceived imperfections of state monopoly or bureaucracy, particularly the problems of efficiency, choice, and responsiveness. Quasi-markets encourage

competition among monopoly state providers by decentralising demand and supply
(Le Grand and Bartlett 1993):

- On the supply side, they introduce competition for state funding, but the
  suppliers need not be private or necessarily profit maximising; nor do they
  face the threat of bankruptcy.[8]
- On the demand side, consumer purchasing power is expressed as a
  earmarked government budget (e.g. performance-based funding). 'Prices'
  are therefore negotiated or administered and are not formed directly from
  the interplay of supply and demand.
- In the market for academic programmes students may make their own
  choice of university or choice may be made for them by a government
  agency.

In the United Kingdom, quasi-markets were implemented both for first-degree level
programmes and for university research.[9] In the case of research, the amount of the
relevant university block grant was influenced by institutional scores on the
Research Assessment Exercise, thereby introducing a more competitive market for
institutional research funding based upon peer evaluations of research performance
in various fields. In the case of first-degree level education, the University Funding
Council (UFC) experimented in the early 1990s with an 'auction' process for
allocating state-funded student places (Johnes and Cave 1994). The UFC clearly
expected that competitive bidding for student places would increase the incentives
for university efficiency in the provision of education. However, amid claims from
the universities that the process of competitive bidding eroded academic standards
and charges from observers that the universities colluded to ensure few differences
in the submitted bids, the UFC eventually abandoned the auction experiment and
returned to more conventional means for allocating resources for teaching among
the universities.[10]

3.2. The Impact of Market Competition on Academic Standards in the United
Kingdom

The crucial and overarching question about the emerging market rivalry in the
United Kingdom is whether universities were influenced to take actions that assure
and improve academic standards. Using a representative sample of old and new UK
universities, Rolfe (2003) explored the effect of the market forces discussed above,
as well as the recent introduction of tuition fees, on UK university strategy and
behaviour. One new emphasis observed in all the universities, which reflected the
emerging environment of competition, was marketing for student recruitment with
substantial expenditures for marketing staff, consultants, and professional agencies
(see also Lindsay and Rodgers 1998). University managers expressed the need to
develop a 'brand image' using professional advice. They also reported that the new
tuition fees had heightened parents' and students' desire to get 'value for money' in
accommodation, sports, and leisure activities. Rolfe noted that university managers

in each of the universities believed that student applicants relied heavily upon the commercial league tables to assess university quality and therefore they focused on enhancing the position of the university in these rankings, particularly by improving the university's RAE scores and by attracting more high-achieving applicants as measured by A level scores. Even though the Higher Education Funding Council for England (HEFCE) provided financial premiums for the enrolment of part-time students, mature students, and students from disadvantaged groups, the principal concern at each of the studied universities, especially the newer universities, was to attract more high-quality full-time students.

Rolfe (2003) discovered that each of the universities, even the newer universities with a regional focus, was intent on improving their research position. In the top-ranked university, all other ingredients for success, such as quality of teaching and quality of student applicants, were ultimately believed to be dependent upon research performance. As a consequence, there was a great emphasis to recruit 'research stars' on research-only contracts in order to enhance research ratings and increase research income. This focus on research was also motivated by the growing transfer market among faculty members as experienced and well-qualified staff became harder to recruit and retain because they were seeking positions at universities with high RAE rankings.

Course provision was reported (Rolfe 2003) to be more important to university strategy, because university managers (correctly) believed that prospective students made application principally because of their interest in a particular course for which they were qualified rather than because of interest in the university itself. However, the focus on courses, particularly in the new universities, was on making them more appealing to applicants in the light of the visible shift in student interests from academic to career concerns. The universities were therefore adding new vocational subjects, increasing the vocational content of modules – even in the humanities – and 're-packaging' modules into courses with clearer relevance to student careers.

Consistent with Rolfe's (2003) analysis, there is increasing evidence that the new competitive market for research funds produced by the tight link between RAE scores and university research funding created stronger incentives for all faculty members to be more research-active, particularly in the newer universities (Dolton, Greenaway, and Vignoles 1997; McNay 1999; Hare 2003).[11] Research performance is now heavily emphasised in all universities with regard to decisions on appointments and promotion. Studies at the academic unit level suggest that the increased incentives for research have altered the traditional roles of academic staff, affected the balance between teaching and research, encouraged more individualistic behaviour on the part of academic staff, and contributed to a more fragmented educational experience for students (Jenkins 1995; McNay 1999; Henkel 2000; Harley 2002).[12] These themes are reflected in the following representative comments from studies of academic staff in the social sciences:

> Appointments are people 'on their way' to higher things and have no commitment to students, to teaching or to colleagues. (Sociologist, new university) (Harley 2002: 199)

The isolation – more individualistic – more ego-centered and more competitive ... I feel 'weakened' by concentrating on students and teaching. (Psychologist, old university) (Harley 2002: 202)

As we go modular there is an unwillingness to give adequate time and debate to crucial teaching issues ... in an atmosphere that promotes research (only papers published in refereed journals) above all other scholarly activities. (Jenkins 1995: 6)

When full-timers are released by part-timers, the quality of teaching may not be worse (some of our part-timers are very good) – but the student experiences a less integrated approach and also finds it more difficult to deal with queries/problems of course organization. (Jenkins 1995: 6)

These observations reflect a growing concern that the strong incentives for research created by market competition may be leading to a cross-subsidisation of research by teaching.[13] McNay (1999: 20), for example, reported in his review of the 1992 RAE for the HEFCE "evidence of teaching funds being raided to support research". Moreover, as more faculty members strive to invest additional time in research and less time in teaching, as teaching loads for productive researchers are cut, and as recognised scholars are replaced in the classroom by junior or part-time teaching staff, the maintenance and improvement of academic standards are likely to suffer. Although the 2001 RAE was particularly designed to discourage the reported practice of 'poaching' high-performing researchers in order to increase RAE scores, there is nonetheless evidence of a growing transfer market in 'research stars'. As noted (Hare 2003; Rolfe 2003), this transfer market further weakens the synergies between teaching and research as recruiting incentives for able researchers de-emphasise involvement in teaching. But increased faculty mobility also affects in more subtle ways the informal processes whereby academic standards were traditionally assured in UK universities. Given the historically low mobility of academic staff, at least in comparison to US institutions (HEFCE 2000), academic departments in the United Kingdom likely possessed a high degree of social cohesion brought about by the 'strong ties' (Granovetter 1985) of long-term close contact, communication and shared norms. This cohesion would have contributed in the past to the capacity of the academic staff to informally coordinate their teaching and assure academic quality. With the increasing mobility of academic staff and the growing reliance on part-time faculty members, the level of social cohesion will inevitably decline and the assurance of academic standards will necessarily require greater reliance on more formal and more visible university processes.

Taken as a whole, the UK experience with quasi-markets offers some valuable insights into the academic responses of universities to the new forces of market competition. The research suggests that perceptions of university prestige based primarily upon research reputation and quality of entering students distort the assumed constructive link between information on academic quality and university efforts to improve human capital. As a consequence, universities have responded to market competition primarily by emphasising admissions marketing, 'cream skimming' of high-achieving student applicants, increased investment in research reputation, with limited attention to improving academic standards. It is important to emphasise that because of the active government efforts to regulate academic quality (Brown 2004) there are many variables at work in the UK equation. Isolating the specific impacts of market forces on academic standards in the UK context is therefore especially difficult. Furthermore, although the recent policy changes on tuition fees may intensify market competition, or at the least increase student sensitivity to the relationship between university price and academic quality, as Barr (2004) notes, the UK reliance on quasi-markets with continued central government controls on price and student numbers has the effect of dampening market competition. For this reason it is particularly helpful to extend this discussion of the effects of market competition on academic standards with an analysis of the US system, where market forces have been less restrained historically by government policy and where government intervention to assure academic standards has been less aggressive than in the United Kingdom.

4. MARKET COMPETITION AND ACADEMIC STANDARDS IN THE UNITED STATES

The conventional view is that market forces have traditionally played a greater role in US higher education than in any other national system (Ben-David 1972; Clark 1983). The restricted role in education assigned to the national government in the US constitution, the Supreme Court decision according the status of private corporations to independently founded colleges and universities, the ease of entry for privately funded colleges and universities into the higher education industry permitted by many of the states, the existence of public universities supported by each of the 50 states, and finally the resource allocation policies adopted by the federal government with regard to federally funded research and student aid all conspired to create a more competitive market for higher education than existed in any other country.

Nonetheless, as noted in the previous discussion of UK higher education, the apparent existence of a market does not necessarily lead to welfare maximising market competition and this was true also for the US system for much of its history.

In a sophisticated analysis of the US baccalaureate degree industry, Hoxby (1997, 2002) has provided valuable insight into the changing nature of competition in higher education since World War II and the effects of this competition on academic and institutional behaviour.[14] Hoxby notes that competition in the US market-oriented system of higher education was suppressed historically by the structure of the market. First, despite the apparent competition among large numbers of public and private institutions for baccalaureate (first-level degree) enrolment, most students as in the United Kingdom and Europe chose a geographically proximate institution of higher education. Second, because there were no federal and few state standards for admission to higher education, US colleges produced educational services at a number of different quality levels. Therefore, many colleges traditionally had few competitors at their particular point in the quality spectrum. As a consequence, prior to World War II both public and private institutions in the United States had a degree of monopoly power that retarded the full effects of a truly competitive student market.[15]

Hoxby (1997) reports that in 1949, for example, 93% of US students pursued a first-level degree at a college or university in their home state, while only 16% of US colleges drew students from 20 or more states and only 2% of colleges drew students from 40 or more states. By 1994 these data had changed significantly, with 74% of all students attending a college in their home state, while 35% of colleges drew students from 20 or more states, and 7% drew students from 40 or more states. Over the same period the proportion of in-state students among 'public' institutions fell from 95% to 84% and among 'private' institutions fell from 80% to 54%.[16] Hoxby notes that studies of students' college decision-making behaviour over time reveal a similar pattern, with an increasing percentage of students applying to more geographically distant colleges and universities.

Hoxby concludes that the growing geographical integration of students observable in college and university enrolment is an indicator of a substantial change in the structure of the market for baccalaureate education in the United States. The baccalaureate degree market has become significantly more competitive as it has transformed from a series of local monopolies to a nationally and regionally integrated market in which each colleges face many potential competitors for inputs and consumers.[17]

Given the emergence of this national student market, Hoxby then explores the effects of increased market competition on the US system of higher education using panel data on baccalaureate colleges from 1940 to the present. In framing her analysis, Hoxby notes that a distinctive characteristic of a university education is that it is a 'complimentary good', in which students serve as both consumers and inputs (Rothschild and White 1995). The quality of education a student receives is supposedly influenced both by the traditional college inputs of faculty time and university resources as well as by the aptitude of peer students. In short, Hoxby assumes that college inputs and peer effects are complements in the production of human capital.[18] Given this distinctive characteristic, Hoxby discovers that increased market competition in the United States has some unexpected impacts. That is, increased competition:

- *Increases stratification between colleges and universities in student admissions test scores.* The loss of monopoly power due to geographic integration encourages the former monopolists to compete with each other more vigorously for able students. As a consequence greater market competition has increased the between-college variance and decreased the within-college variance in student admissions test scores over time. These effects are greater for private than public colleges.

- *Increases average college tuition.* Increased competition is positively related to the rapid growth of college tuition in both the private and public sector.[19]

- *Increases the amount of per-student subsidy that colleges provide to their students.* In an effort to attract the most able students, colleges increase their per-student subsidy (i.e. the difference between college expenditures per student and tuition revenue per student). The increase in these subsidies is greatest in those institutions that also have the greatest increases in tuition and student admissions scores. Hoxby considers these subsidies 'implicit wages' for the most able students.

- *Increases between-college variance in college quality as well as average college quality.* College quality as measured by peer effects (average student admissions test scores) and educational inputs has become more varied between institutions and on average has risen over time as colleges have competed with each other for high-quality students.

Hoxby concludes her analysis by arguing that despite evidence of tuition increases in both the public and private sectors that continually exceed growth in average family income and the cost of living, market competition in the United States has created an efficient system of baccalaureate education. Hoxby asserts that the observed tuition rises under conditions of increased competition are in fact consistent with economic theory because colleges and universities overall have increased their educational quality as measured by their expenditures on educational inputs. Furthermore, those colleges that have increased tuition the most have also provided commensurate educational quality from increased educational inputs and from increased peer effects. In support of this view Hoxby provides evidence in a related paper that the lifetime income benefits to graduates of the more expensive, selective colleges and universities continue to increase over time and far outweigh the students' expenditures for tuition (Hoxby 2001).

Students with low admissions test scores do receive less value for money, primarily because they attend colleges with fewer students with high admissions test scores (i.e. fewer 'peer effects'). However, Hoxby argues that the *average* student is better off because educational inputs have risen more in the sector of the market serving high admissions test score students than they have fallen in the sector serving low admissions test score students. Hoxby concludes that the baccalaureate market is now in equilibrium and that the net benefit to society of the new competitive market in US higher education is positive. She therefore argues that letting the market work is the most effective public policy.

In sum, this intriguing and challenging set of studies suggests that the US market for higher education is now efficiently providing human capital for society. If true, this would suggest that academic standards can be maintained more effectively by market competition than by government regulation or professional self-regulation. However, the accumulating evidence on the current behaviour of US colleges and universities suggests just the opposite, that the increasingly costly market competition among US colleges and universities is negatively affecting the quality of the institutions' teaching and student learning.

4.1. The Impact of Market Competition on Academic Standards in the United States

In a recent national study of US colleges and universities researchers from the Rand Corporation (Brewer, Gates, and Goldman 2002) detected evidence of an increasingly costly 'arms race' for prestige among large numbers of colleges and universities. Many institutions are making extensive investments designed to attract high-ability students. The Rand researchers argue that this attempt to build prestige by 'cream skimming' the student market does not seem to lead to an improvement in the quality of educational delivery and may lessen the overall educational benefits of higher education for students and ultimately for society. The Rand researchers suggest that this pursuit of prestige through increasingly costly investments in admissions selectivity is reinforced by commercial college ranking systems in the United States that use financial and student 'inputs' as a primary measure in national league tables.[20]

The Rand researchers classified the US institutions in their national sample into three strategic orientations: prestige-based (P); prestige-seeking (PS); and reputation-based (R). P institutions already possessed a high level of prestige and operated in markets with few objective criteria of performance. These institutions included those public and private US universities that are readily recognised throughout the world. PS institutions obviously sought to become 'prestige' institutions and R institutions sought to succeed by satisfying customer needs.[21] Since academic institutions operate in one or more markets with different products and customers, the study investigated institutional competition in four markets – student enrolments, research funding, public fiscal support, and private giving – that correspond to the primary sources of revenue for a US academic institution.

Because US colleges and universities can earn discretionary revenues (i.e. 'profit') through their various revenue markets, they can allocate these funds internally to achieve their chosen strategy. The study argues that academic institutions invest in either reputation or prestige as a means of buffering themselves from competitive forces. However, colleges and universities can also invest in consumption that benefits internal constituencies, for example, by providing above-market wages for professors and staff members, lower teaching loads for faculty members, and/or higher quality research facilities that benefit faculty members. Alternatively, these discretionary revenues could be invested in savings, i.e. in endowment.

In the undergraduate baccalaureate market studied by Hoxby, R institutions attempted to build reputation by investing in research on the local business community, on student demand and on labour market demand. These institutions also invest in programme improvement, convenient course scheduling options, and student services.

In contrast and consistent with Hoxby's research, P and PS institutions focused their efforts and strategic investments in the student market on strengthening their perceived prestige. This involved increasing the selectivity of the admissions process by linking tuition discounts with academic merit/student ability,[22] attempting to lower student acceptance/yield rates, and investing in student consumption benefits such as dormitories, eating facilities, or fibre-optic computer networks that will help attract high-quality students (note that these expenditures are reflected in increased operating costs for the institutions). The Rand researchers suggest that this overwhelming focus on admissions selectivity among certain types of US institutions is reinforced in part by commercial college ranking systems in the United States that use student 'inputs' as a primary measure in national league tables.

However, serious questions need to be raised about the assumed positive relationship between university selectivity, as measured by average entering student test scores, and human capital formation. Empirical research in support of this relationship is based largely on econometric studies of the relationship between average entering student test scores and graduate lifetime earnings as well as a small number of studies of the effects of the quality of student peers (again as measured by entering test scores of freshman roommates) on grade point averages in US colleges.[23] In contrast, the extensive research on student learning indicates an inconsistent and trivial relationship between admissions selectivity based upon average entering student test scores and measures of the knowledge, skills, and abilities learned by students during their education (Pascarella and Terenzini 1991).

As previously noted, Hoxby (1997, 2001) assumes that the positive relationship discovered between graduates' lifetime earnings and average entering student test scores provides the major evidence that the admission of higher-achieving students increases the educational benefits of selective universities. However, there are a number of problems with this assumption. The most recent review of educational research casts significant doubt on the supposed relationship between institutional selectivity, as measured by average aptitude scores of entering students, and students' earnings capabilities (Pascarella and Terenzini 2005). First, the research confirms that the impact of institutional selectivity on earnings is nonlinear. Only the most selective institutions may have an impact on earnings. Second, the relationship depends on the students' major field of study, which is often not controlled in relevant studies. Less selective, public institutions in the United States often offer academic majors with less potential earnings capacity than selective schools and this may explain the discovered differences. Finally, and most importantly, when studies control for the types of students who apply to more selective institutions – utilising measures of individual ambition – the earnings advantage of more selective schools disappears. As Dale and Kreuger (1998: 30) conclude in their carefully controlled study of the relationship between college selectivity and earnings:

> After we adjust for selection, our findings cast some doubt on the view that peer group quality, as measured by the average SAT score of the student who attends a college, is an important determinant of students' subsequent life outcomes. The average SAT score of students who attend college – though commonly used as a proxy for peer groups and school quality in previous studies – may be too coarse a measure to accurately reflect a student's actual peer group or college quality once school selection is taken into account. ... It is also possible that peer group effects are trivial for college students.[24]

Research that more directly assesses the educational processes of selective US universities in fact challenges the assumption that these institutions provide the most effective environment for student learning. Kuh and Pascarella (2004) discovered that institutional selectivity and the presence of educational practices known to be associated with student learning were largely independent. A college's selectivity offers no guarantee that it provides a more effective learning environment than a less selective school.

The Rand researchers also note that PS institutions attempt to build prestige in the student market in the United States not by being innovative or by meeting new types of student demands, but essentially by mimicking institutions that already have prestige as will be outlined below. Therefore, prestige-seeking behaviour tends to limit pedagogical improvements in the overall higher education system.

In the United States, research is a revenue market because of the competitive allocation of federal research funds and the growing funding of university research by business and industry. But the amount of external research funding received by a university has also become an important indicator of prestige. PS institutions therefore seek to increase their potential for research funding by investing in PhD programmes, in laboratories, libraries, computer facilities, and research management, as well as by attracting research-oriented faculty. There is also increasing evidence of P and PS institutions subsidising their federal research activity through increased investment in grant matching funds and/or by attempting to lower their indirect cost rate (Feller 2000). Since the funds to support these latter activities are derived from other revenue markets (e.g. public financing, student tuition, and private giving) that are designed to cover the costs of education, this is an example of the means by which US colleges and universities increasingly use teaching to cross-subsidise research as a means of generating or maintaining college and university prestige.[25] In contrast, the R institutions have concluded that competing in the research revenue market has little to do with meeting student needs, and they therefore avoid cross-subsidising research.

In the market for public fiscal support, obviously the vast majority of funds are awarded to public institutions. However, P and PS public institutions are competing with publicly supported R institutions in the market for public funding. As the American states become more interested in improving student learning and economic development and as they increase their accountability mechanisms for higher education funding, P and PS institutions find their preferred strategy increasingly constrained. P and PS institutions may therefore use their political influence to negotiate with critical public stakeholders for greater flexibility from education accountability mechanisms.

Finally, the market for private giving, historically dominated by private institutions in the United States, is becoming increasingly competitive as growing numbers of public institutions seek private funds to supplement or replace declining public support. The Rand researchers note the interaction between student selectivity and private support; prestige in the student market tends to be associated with success in raising private funds. The need for private fund-raising therefore provides a further incentive for universities to adopt a strategy of expenditures that attract the most able and wealthiest students.

The Rand researchers conclude their study with several observations on the overall social benefit of the higher education industry in the United States that provide some perspective on the results of Hoxby's studies. They note that while the market for reputation defined as meeting customers' needs is infinitely expandable, the market for prestige is necessarily a zero-sum game. An increase in student selectivity can only lead to an increase in overall institutional prestige if there are commensurate increases in the academic quality of the national pool of student inputs, which may not in fact be occurring in the United States. Similarly, an increase in research can only lead to an increase in overall prestige if there is real growth in overall federal funding for research. Furthermore, the Rand researchers suggest that competition for prestige in the student market does not seem to improve the quality of educational delivery, while prestige-seeking behaviour in the research revenue market induces many institutions to subsidise research through the building and maintenance of costly research facilities and investment in matching funds. Both of these behaviours may lessen the overall educational benefits of higher education for students and ultimately for society.

5. COMMERCIAL LEAGUE TABLES AND INFORMATION ON ACADEMIC QUALITY

A necessary assumption for efficient markets is that both consumers and producers have 'perfect' information – rational choice requires that economic agents are well informed about both price *and* quality (Teixeira et al. 2004). If government as a consumer of education and student consumers lack sufficient information on the quality of university goods and services, they are unlikely to make choices that positively influence academic standards. However, valid information on academic quality is important not only for consumer protection purposes, but also for producer effectiveness. Accurate information on the educational quality of an academic programme provides an incentive for academic staff to make genuine investments in quality improvement as a means of competing in the market (Dill and Soo 2004).

In theory inadequate consumer information on academic quality may provide incentives for commercial organisations to produce organisational report cards or rankings (Gormley and Weimer 1999). The emergence of commercial university league tables in the United Kingdom and United States is an indicator of the growing role market competition is playing in higher education. Consumer expenditures on these university league tables can be interpreted as an indirect measure of the inadequacy of existing information on academic quality. Unfortunately, as noted in both the UK and US cases, the academic quality information provided by the existing commercial university league tables appears to undermine the assurance of academic standards and the productive efficiency of the market in academic programmes (see Chapter 6 by Ewell).

If university league tables are to correct the information imperfections of the academic degree market, several linked behaviours need to occur (Gormley and Weimer 1999). First, league tables and related consumer information on academic quality need to utilise measures that closely approximate, or are clearly linked to, the development of human capital, i.e. to the knowledge, skills, and abilities achieved by graduates. Second, league tables must inform and influence student choice of university or encourage universities to act in anticipation of the potential effects of published rankings. Third, universities must respond to student choices and/or to the potential effects of rankings by genuinely improving student learning.

An analysis of the primary commercial league tables published in the United Kingdom and United States suggests that they fail to meet these conditions (Dill and Soo 2005). University league tables published by *US News & World Report* (*USNWR*) in the United States and by the *Times* in the United Kingdom place greatest weight not on valid measures of student learning, but on inputs similar to those emphasised in Hoxby's research: quality of entering students, quality and number of faculty, financial resources and facilities. These indicators are known predictors of research reputation and university prestige (Astin 1985; Yorke 1997), but are not valid indicators of the educational value added by attending a particular university or enrolling in a specific academic programme. As a leading US researcher on student learning in higher education (Pascarella 2001: 20) concluded:

> A more serious problem with the national magazine rankings is that from a research point of view, they are largely invalid. That is, they are based on institutional resources and reputation dimensions, which have only minimal relevance to what we know about the impact of college on students.

Ideally, league tables of academic quality should focus on measures of the outputs or outcomes of universities that are valued by society, rather than on input indicators (Gormley and Weimer 1999). The two mentioned league tables include some output measures, such as graduation rates, the number of first- and second-level degrees, job prospects, student satisfaction, and university reputation. However, each of these measures is of questionable validity as a measure of academic quality. The number of graduates and types of degrees produced by a university are certainly socially valued outcomes, but graduation rates can be increased both by more effective teaching and student learning and by lowering academic standards. The issue of university grade inflation and inflation in honours degree awards has in fact been a point of contention in both the United Kingdom and United States (Rosovsky and Hartley 2002; Yorke et al. 2002). Job prospect information utilised in the UK league tables reports the proportion of students who have found a job 6 months after graduation without controlling for the individual's social class background, class of degree, the degree subject studied, or local labour market conditions, all of which have been discovered to influence scores (Smith, McKnight, and Naylor 2000). Neither does this indicator identify whether students are employed on graduate-level jobs or are underemployed. A final limitation of the existing output measures (i.e. job prospects, graduation rate, degree levels awarded) is that they are highly correlated with the quality of entering students. Unless league tables control output measures by the quality of entering students, the rankings provide more information on the universities' recruitment policies than on the actual quality of education.[26]

Reputation is an important component in the *USNWR*'s rankings. *USNWR* claims that their assessment of college and university reputation using the views of institutional administrators is aimed at measuring 'intangibles' such as faculty dedication to 'teaching'. The *USNWR*'s reputation score, however, correlates much more closely with high per-faculty federal research and development expenditures than with good graduation-rate performance (Graham and Thompson 2001). Another problem with *USNWR*'s reputation survey is that while it may be relevant for ranking the best-known schools, even a sample of prominent people are unable to assess accurately the quality of all programmes in all schools. Therefore, their opinion is likely to be influenced more by the existing reputation of the university (i.e. the 'halo effect') than by actual knowledge of programme quality (Clarke 2002).

The *USNWR* output measures include student satisfaction with their educational experience as measured by the proportion of alumni who make contributions to the institution, freshman or first-year student retention, and graduation rate. However, alumni contributions as an indicator of graduate satisfaction is of questionable validity as this measure may be more a function of the vigour of the development office and the tradition of fund-raising at that institution than a measure of student satisfaction (Ehrenberg 2003).

A potential valid alternative to input indicators would be measures of the teaching and educational process known to be related to student learning (Kuh 2003). The *USNWR* does not include such indicators in its overall ranking while in the United Kingdom the *Times* does give some weight to Teaching Quality Assessments (TQA) formally conducted by the UK Quality Assurance Agency (QAA). In response to some of the noted weaknesses in the *Times'* rankings, the *Guardian* published a league table specifically designed to inform student consumers about teaching quality in academic subjects. While the *Guardian*'s league table makes a serious attempt to lessen the influence of university prestige on academic quality rankings by placing greatest weight on QAA teaching assessments, it is questionable whether they actually succeeded. Studies of the relationship between TQA and Research Assessment scores suggest that TQA assessors have a positive research bias and university research ratings are a strong predictor of favourable TQAs (Drennan and Beck 2001).[27]

Finally, not only are the measures used in the *USNWR*'s rankings of questionable validity with regard to the quality of student learning, but they are also unreliable measures. While the UK university league tables are based upon data collected and verified by government agencies, most of the data utilised in the *USNWR*'s league table were supplied by the institutions themselves. Hossler and Litten (1993) reviewed the overall provision of information on academic institutions in the United States. They noted that virtually all of the published data on colleges and universities, whether collected by government or the publishers of guidebooks and commercial rankings, are supplied by the institutions themselves and that no independent source of verification exists. Their concerns were warranted. Since they wrote, there have been numerous reported incidents of US colleges and universities manipulating the data submitted to commercial league tables in an attempt to enhance their rankings (Ehrenberg 2002).

The second necessary condition for commercial league tables to contribute to the improvement of academic standards is that the rankings effectively inform student choice. One indirect measure of the consumer relevance of university report cards is the nature of the readership or purchasers of these league tables. Research in the United Kingdom and United States suggests that commercial league tables are most often designed for, and used by, a narrow segment of the potential student market – students of high achievement and social class (Sarrico et al. 1997; McDonough, Antonio, and Perez 1998). Many of these students appear interested primarily in the 'prestige' rating of a university as reflected in the future opportunities and incomes of an institution's graduates. But research in the United Kingdom and United States on the preferences of student applicants also suggests that league tables that provide university rankings based upon a single weighting scheme do not meet the needs of the majority of students who desire a much more varied list of factors for deciding where to apply (Sarrico et al. 1997; McDonough, Antonio, and Perez 1998; Connor et al. 1999; Moogan, Baron, and Harris 1999).

For example, a recent survey on student choice in the United Kingdom (Connor et al. 1999) indicates that the most important factors influencing the choices of applicants to full-time university education are the course or subject, academic quality (particularly teaching reputation), entry requirements, employment prospects for graduates, location, available academic and support facilities, social life, and costs of study. Despite the differing structure of US higher education, the extensive US research on college choice suggests that similar factors are important for US students and parents in choosing among colleges. The most significant factors include the academic programme (major area of study), tuition costs, financial aid availability, general academic reputation/general quality of institution, location (distance from home), college size, and social atmosphere (Manski and Wise 1983; Zemsky and Oedel 1983; Hossler, Braxton, and Coopersmith 1989; Paulsen 1990).

Information on the academic subject has consistently proven the most influential on student choice in the United Kingdom (Moogan, Baron, and Harris 1999) and raises fundamental questions about the utility of league tables such as the *Times'* that provide rankings and information only for the overall university. First, highly ranked universities may not have the specific subjects sought by a student. Second, entry qualifications may vary across subject fields even within the same university. Finally, and most importantly, the quality of the student learning experience, graduation rates, student satisfaction, employment prospects, and even lifetime earnings are apt to vary significantly by subject field within the same university. Therefore, rankings based upon average data for the university as a whole not only misrepresent the experience for particular subject fields, but fail to provide the type of academic quality information most desired by student consumers.

US league tables also underinform student consumers because they rank whole institutions rather than providing information on academic programmes within institutions. Because most US university students begin their education with a 'general education' programme prior to selecting a 'major', a case can be made that institutional rankings are appropriate for student consumers in the US context. However, there is also reason to believe that in the United States the relative influence of general education on student learning may be declining relative to the influence of the major field or subject (Trow 2000). Consequently, it is likely that similar to their peers in other countries, US university students derive their primary educational benefits from their chosen academic subject or major field. If true, even in the United States, student choices based upon institutional rather than subject field rankings will be less educationally beneficial to themselves and ultimately to society.

In sum, the indicators used for academic quality in the commercial league tables in both the United Kingdom and United States are of questionable validity and appear to be biased towards research reputation and academic prestige rather than student learning. The available research on student choice in the United Kingdom and United States suggests that commercial league tables have not been very influential on applicants' selection of a university or degree programme except in the case of students of high achievement and social class. Furthermore, the lack of high-quality information on the educational value added by specific subjects and the fact that the available output data do not adjust for differences in unit costs and entering student ability between universities mean that potential students do not have the information necessary to promote market efficiency (Coates and Adnett 2003). Not surprisingly, as noted in the previous discussion of UK and US universities' responses to market competition, the information from commercial league tables has not influenced universities to take actions that improve academic standards.

6. MARKET REGULATION OF ACADEMIC QUALITY: AN ASSESSMENT

Many economists and policy makers in the United Kingdom, United States (Hoxby 2001; Barr 2004; Teixeira et al. 2004), and elsewhere assume that market competition can provide an institutional framework for universities that is welfare-maximising for society. The behaviour of producers and consumers in competitive markets, however, often departs from theoretical expectations. The distinctive characteristics of universities and their consumers in mass systems of higher education create imperfect competition that fails to efficiently produce the expected human capital for society. The experience with the emerging market for universities in the United Kingdom as well as the more mature market in the United States suggests a number of reasons for this.

First, and most importantly, academic prestige based primarily upon research performance, faculty reputation, as well as financial and student inputs becomes the dominant goal and signal for all colleges and universities in a competitive market. As noted in both the United Kingdom and United States, the indicators of academic prestige drown out the weaker signals of the quality of teaching and student learning, and the aggressive pursuit of prestige crowds out activities associated with the improvement of academic standards. While prestige based upon scholarly reputation has long been recognised as the primary goal of universities (Garvin 1980), the dominance of the prestige goal in systems of mass higher education encourages all institutions to invest in cream skimming the student market, in building their research capacity, and in incentives designed to recruit and retain the most prominent scholars/researchers. The pernicious effect of this competitive pursuit of academic prestige is that it diverts resources as well as administrative and faculty attention away from the collective actions within universities necessary to actually improve academic standards (Kuh and Pascarella 2004).

Second, the rational choices of student consumers in mass systems are unlikely to create sufficient pressure for universities to improve academic standards. Although it is believed, because of the increased maturity and motivation of university applicants, that student choice will be more influential on quality in higher education than in lower education (Barr 2004), there is little empirical evidence at the first-degree level to support this view (Dill and Soo 2004). Students understandably choose universities primarily for the private benefits they will receive, not because of the social benefits that an effective education may eventually provide to society. High-achieving students in the United Kingdom and United States therefore select universities based primarily upon indicators of academic prestige rather than measures of the quality of teaching and learning in academic programmes, because they believe – correctly – that graduation from these institutions will provide a signal to society that assures their future status (Dill and Soo 2004). Many students, particularly in a mass system, are also attracted to universities for consumption benefits that they value personally, but which may ultimately produce little benefit to society. These include the pleasures of living in attractive university surroundings, the appeal of university social life and, in the United States, the distractions of university athletics. For these reasons, if enrolled students receive satisfactory marks and eventually graduate, only the few in a mass system of higher education may complain if they believe they have actually learned little in the process. This point is not meant to denigrate university students, or the importance of valid information on academic quality to socially beneficial student choice, but does suggest that informed student choice alone is not apt to assure the efficient provision of human capital in a competitive market for higher education.

Third, the void in valid information on academic quality is not likely to be filled by the market (Dill and Soo 2005). With many goods and services, a market failure due to insufficient information may motivate commercial publishers to provide the necessary information to consumers (Gormley and Weimer 1999). The evidence in both the United Kingdom and United States suggests that commercial guides and league tables will not effectively address the information deficiencies in the higher education market (Dill and Soo 2005). The cost and complexity of developing valid indicators of academic quality with relevance to student choice are significant, and for-profit publications already enjoy substantial sales and influence among opinion leaders, higher-achieving students, and even university personnel by focusing on readily available and/or highly subjective indicators of academic prestige. As noted by the different types of quality indicators available in UK league tables as compared to those in the United States, the provision of more valid and reliable academic quality information for student consumers is consequently dependent upon government intervention (Dill and Soo 2005). Therefore, addressing this market failure would entail state regulations obliging institutions to provide reliable academic performance information and additionally may require state subsidies or incentives for valid league tables or guides to inform student consumers. An interesting example of a more socially beneficial commercial league table is the *Good Universities Guide* in Australia (Dill and Soo 2005). This guide provides information not currently available in either the United Kingdom or United States on graduates' perceptions of teaching quality, skills learned, and satisfaction, as well as graduates' employment/further study prospects for all academic subjects in Australian universities (Dill and Soo 2005). This commercial publication is made feasible by the provision of relevant data through Australian education agencies as well as by government-mandated Graduate Destination Surveys and Course Experience Questionnaires.

Finally, the effects of market competition on academic behaviour compromise the capacity of universities to maintain and improve academic standards. The incentives of unregulated academic markets encourage faculty members to 'satisfice' academic quality in first-level academic programmes (Massy 2003), to limit their time investment in undergraduate teaching and the collective activities of academic quality assurance, while maximising their time investment in their preferred activities of graduate instruction and research. In addition to the decline in discretionary time devoted to instructional activities, many universities have also lowered teaching loads as a means of attracting or retaining more visible researchers and scholars, thereby requiring a marked growth in part-time staff to cover the necessary courses. This emerging academic structure, characterised by more atomistic, less coherent, academic programmes, increases both the challenges and the costs of maintaining and improving academic standards. Furthermore, market competition creates incentives for opportunistic behaviour among faculty members that compromises academic standards. Many universities have responded to the more competitive market by linking academic promotion to student evaluations of teachers and tying departmental budget allocations to student enrolments. The absence of meaningful outcome measures and effective collegial oversight therefore provides the opportunity for instructors to increase the demand for their individual courses and programmes by inflating grades and/or lowering academic standards rather than by actually improving student learning.

As already noted, the particular nature of consumer markets in higher education suggests that valid consumer information on academic quality alone, while a worthy and necessary policy intervention, will not strengthen the capacity of universities to assure academic quality. Therefore, if competitive higher education markets are to efficiently maximise the production of human capital for society, state monitoring or incentives for institutional self-regulation may also be needed to maintain the integrity of each university's collective process for assuring and improving academic standards (Dill 2005; see also Chapter 10 by Harvey and Newton; for appropriate words of caution about the efficiency and effectiveness of government intervention in academic quality assurance, see Chapter 2 by Blackmur).[28]

In sum, because the new competitive market context is characterised by inadequate and inappropriate information, an ambiguous conception – 'academic prestige' – comes to represent educational quality in the public mind, which can lead to a price-quality association that undermines productive efficiency. The distorting influence of prestige in both the US and UK markets means that the educational costs of elite universities provide a 'price umbrella' for the rest of the system and present spending targets for less elite institutions that wish to compete by raising their prices (Massy 2004).[29] Competitive markets thereby encourage an academic 'arms race' for prestige among all institutions, which rapidly increases the costs of higher education and devalues the improvement of student learning. As noted in both the United Kingdom and United States, an unregulated academic market can lead to a situation in which no university constituency – students, faculty members, or administrators – has a compelling incentive to assure academic standards. This is a recipe for a classic and significant market failure in which the rising social costs of higher education are not matched by equivalent social benefits (Teixeira et al. 2004).

NOTES

1   For a discussion of regulations affecting accreditation in the amendments proposed in the 2003–2005 reauthorisation of the Higher Education Act, see 'Government Relations' on the website of the Council for Higher Education Accreditation at: http://www.chea.org.

2   Legislation before Congress in 2005 would require institutions to provide the Department of Education with a consumer profile that the Department would disseminate to the public. Recognised accreditation agencies would in turn be required to assess the validity of each institution's profile, which would include descriptions of every academic programme, its learning outcomes, as well as related student completion and graduation rates.

3   Astin (1985) uses a similar definition of academic quality in his 'talent development model'. Astin argues that the major purpose of a university is to develop the talents of its students to their maximum potential. This development is achieved by facilitating changes in students' intellectual capacities, skills, values, attitudes, interests, habits, and mental health. Therefore, in Astin's view, institutions that provide the largest amount of developmental benefits to students possess the highest academic quality.

4   This introductory discussion follows Williams (2004).

5   UK Research Councils did award research funds on a competitive basis. Historically their grants represented a small proportion of UK funding for university research, although the proportion has been increasing over time.

6   In 1976 the Labour government removed the means test on student fees, effectively making university education free for all (Williams 2004).

7   For example, UK universities possessed the autonomy to set and retain their own fees, but had not utilised this authority since World War II (Williams 2004).

8   Note, however, that in the case of UK universities, they are legally autonomous (i.e. private) institutions.

9   Williams (2004) also notes the development of 'third-sector' funding in which competitive grants were made available by the state to encourage university programmes in the market for public service. Arguably this is an additional example of a government-introduced 'quasi-market'.

10 For an informative discussion of the design flaws in the UFC bidding process, see Johnes and Cave (1994) and Witzel (1991).

11 Reflecting on the effects of a similar research assessment exercise introduced into the Hong Kong University system by the University Grants Committee (UGC), Massey noted that it produced a 'land rush' into research by university faculty members and motivated the UGC to implement an academic audit process designed to re-emphasise attention to teaching and student learning (Massy 2003).

12 There is evidence that the internal market created for research has had some clear positive as well as possible negative consequences for society (McNay 1999; Hare 2003), but the focus of this discussion is on the (unintended) consequences of this new competitive market for academic standards.

13 A review by the HEFCE of the interactions between teaching and research as a result of the RAE (HEFCE 1999) reported the widespread view among academic staff that university teaching was not adversely affected, but the 2003 government White Paper on Higher Education (DfES) nonetheless explicitly noted that teaching in universities may be cross-subsidising research and called for increased efforts to strengthen the quality of teaching and student learning.

14 The discussion that follows draws upon analyses in Dill (2003) and Dill and Soo (2004, 2005).

15 As Hoxby (1997) notes, this generalisation was less true in the northeast and middle Atlantic areas of the United States than in other parts of the country.

16 The substantial difference between public and private institutions in the proportion of in-state students is explained by the need for state-supported institutions to give preference to in-state students, an irrelevant consideration for most private institutions. The state of North Carolina, for example, places a limit on the number of out-of-state students that can be admitted as undergraduates to its public universities.

17 Hoxby (1997) identifies a number of significant predictors of this geographic integration of the market for US baccalaureate education including deregulation in the airline and telecommunications industries that resulted in substantially lower prices for long-distance travel and communication; the advent of modern, standardised admissions testing; the information exchange system among students, colleges, and scholarship donors that was initially generated by the National Merit Scholarship

programme; and tuition reciprocity agreements among states' public college systems (for a more extended discussion, see Dill 2003).

18 Hoxby's assumption about students as complimentary goods leads her to advocate 'matching' high-ability students in universities in order to maximise the efficiency of the industry. An obvious competing view is 'mixing' students of different ability levels to maximise benefits to the society. For a discussion of these contrasting perspectives, see Canton and Vossensteyn (2001).

19 Hoxby's assertion that increased competition leads to increased prices (tuition) appears to violate basic economic thinking, a point that will be further explored below.

20 Ehrenberg (2002, 2003) also notes that the heavy weighting on institutional expenditures and faculty salaries in the *US News & World Report* formula provides an incentive to increase costs in higher education, since efforts to cut costs or increase productivity would lower an institution's ranking.

21 Combining the classifications from the Brewer, Gates, and Goldman (2002) study with related data on colleges and universities, Massy (2003) estimates that the categories of P and PS institutions together account for more than half of the 1200 4-year institutions in the United States and almost three-quarters of the financial resources invested in US higher education.

22 The study also reported an increasing tendency in PS and some P institutions of relaxing admissions standards for those students who would pay the full price of admission.

23 For a comprehensive review of this economic research, see Winston and Zimmerman (2003).

24 It is worth noting that the crucial assumptions among educational economists about the existence of peer effects were developed in an economic modelling exercise motivated by observed differences in graduate income (Rothschild and White 1995), not by empirical research on factors influencing student learning. Rothschild and White (1995) do note that the differences in the incomes of graduates of more and less selective colleges and universities may in fact be attributable to factors other than peer effects.

25 For a systematic analysis of such cross-subsidies in US higher education, see Massy (2003).

26 The *Guardian* table commendably controls student degree performance by student entry standards and weights this indicator at 9% of the overall score. The *US News & World Report* (*USNWR*) also controls graduation rates by university spending and entering student test scores. In the case of the *USNWR*, however, the value-added measure contributes only 5% to the overall ranking. Furthermore, faculty salaries and per-student spending independently contribute 17% and relevant characteristics of the entering student body including test scores and class rank contribute another 11%. Thus, the amount of 'correction' provided by the *USNWR* value-added measure, as well as the influence of the measure itself, are effectively compromised in the overall ranking.

27 While there are arguably some educational benefits to the increased emphasis on research and scholarship encouraged by market competition in the United Kingdom and United States noted above (Clark 1997), it is unlikely that the increasing transfer by many institutions of resources and time from teaching to research can be justified by commensurate increases in human capital. Research on student learning suggests that the correlation between research productivity and first-level instruction, the demand for which is the primary rational for the development of mass higher education in all countries, is very small and that teaching and research appear to be more or less independent activities (Fox 1992; Terenzini and Pascarella 1994; Coate, Barnett, and Williams 2001; Marsh and Hattie 2002).

28 There is an obvious parallel here between the recent government regulations designed to strengthen corporate processes for assuring financial integrity in competitive markets and the need for regulations to strengthen university processes for assuring educational integrity in competitive markets.

29 Note that when the UK government adopted the highly controversial policy of permitting universities to raise tuition to £3000, almost all of the less prestigious universities followed the elite institutions in charging the maximum amount.

REFERENCES

Astin, A.W. *Achieving Educational Excellence: A Critical Assessment of Priorities and Practices in Higher Education*. San Francisco, London: Jossey-Bass, 1985.

Barr, N. *The Economics of the Welfare State*, 4th edn. Oxford: Oxford University Press, 2004.

Becker, G.S. *Human Capital*. New York: Columbia University Press, 1964.

Ben-David, J. *American Higher Education: Directions Old and New*. New York: McGraw-Hill, 1972.
Berdahl, R.O. and I.J. Spitzberg Jr. "Quality and Access as Interrelated Policy Issues." In Berdahl, R.O., G.C. Moodie, and I.J. Spitzberg Jr. (eds). *Quality and Access in Higher Education: Comparing Britain and the United States*. Buckingham, UK: SRHE and Open University Press, 1991, 164–171.
Bird, R. "Reflections on the British Government and Higher Education in the 1980s." *Higher Education Quarterly* 48.2 (1994): 75–91.
Brennan, J. and T. Shah. *Managing Quality in Higher Education: An International Perspective on Institutional Assessment and Change*. Buckingham, UK: OECD, SRHE and Open University Press, 2000.
Brewer, D., S.M. Gates, and C.A. Goldman. *In Pursuit of Prestige: Strategy and Competition in US Higher Education*. New Brunswick, NJ: Transaction Press, 2002.
Brown, R. *Quality Assurance in Higher Education: The UK Experience Since 1992*. London: Routledge Farmer, 2004.
Canton, E. and H. Vossensteyn. "Deregulation of Higher Education: Tuition Fee Differentiation and Selectivity in the US." In CPB and CHEPS. *Higher Education Reform, Getting the Incentives Right*. Den Haag, The Netherlands: Sdu Uitgevers, 2001, 67–84.
Clark, B.R. *The Higher Education System: Academic Organization in Cross-national Perspective*. Berkeley: University of California Press, 1983.
Clark, B.R. "The Modern Integration of Research Activities with Teaching and Learning." *Journal of Higher Education* 68.3 (1997): 241–255.
Clarke, M. "Some Guidelines for Academic Quality Rankings." *Higher Education in Europe* 27.4 (2002): 443–459.
Coate, K., R. Barnett, and G. Williams. "Relationships Between Teaching and Research in Higher Education in England." *Higher Education Quarterly* 55.2 (2001): 158–174.
Coates, G. and N. Adnett. "Encouraging Cream-skimming and Dreg-siphoning? Increasing Competition Between English HEIs." *British Journal of Educational Studies* 51.3 (2003): 202–218.
Connor, H., R. Burton, R. Pearson, E. Pollard, and J. Regan. *Making the Right Choice: How Students Choose Universities and Colleges*. London: Universities UK, 1999.
Dale, S.T. and A.B. Kreuger. "Estimating the Payoff to Attending a More Selective College: An Application of Selection on Observables and Unobservables." Working Paper 409, Industrial Relations Center, Princeton University, 1998.
DfES (Department for Education and Skills). *The Future of Higher Education* (White Paper). London: HMSO, Cm 5735, 2003.
Dill, D.D. "Academic Accountability and University Adaptation: The Architecture of an Academic Learning Organization." *Higher Education* 38.2 (1999): 127–154.
Dill, D.D. "Allowing the Market to Rule: The Case of the United States." *Higher Education Quarterly*, 57.2 (2003): 136–157.
Dill, D.D. "Are Public Research Universities Effective Communities of Learning? The Collective Action Dilemma of Assuring Academic Standards." Paper presented at the Symposium: Future of the American Public Research University, Penn State University, 25 February 2005.
Dill, D.D. and M. Soo. "Transparency and Quality in Higher Education Markets." In Teixeira, P., B. Jongbloed, D. Dill, and A. Amaral (eds). *Markets in Higher Education: Rhetoric or Reality?* Dordrecht, The Netherlands: Kluwer, 2004, 61–86.
Dill, D.D. and M. Soo. "Academic Quality, League Tables, and Public Policy: A Cross-national Analysis of University Ranking Systems." *Higher Education* 49.4 (2005): 495–533.
Dolton, P.J., D. Greenaway, and A. Vignoles. "'Whither Higher Education?' An Economic Perspective for the Dearing Committee of Inquiry." *Economic Journal* 107.442 (1997): 710–726.
Drennan, L.T. and M. Beck. "Teaching Quality Performance Indicators: Key Influences on the UK Universities' Scores." *Quality Assurance in Education* 9.2 (2001): 92–102.
Ehrenberg, R.G. *Tuition Rising: Why College Costs so Much*. Cambridge, MA: Harvard University Press, 2002.
Ehrenberg, R.G. "Reaching for the Brass Ring: The *US News & World Report* Rankings and Competition." *Review of Higher Education* 26.2 (2003): 145–162.
Feller, I. "Social Contracts and the Impact of Matching Fund Requirements on American Research Universities." *Educational Evaluation and Policy Analysis* 22.1 (2000): 91–98.
Fox, M.F. "Research, Teaching, and Publication Productivity: Mutuality versus Competition in Academia." *Sociology of Education* 65.4 (1992): 293–305.

Garvin, D.A. *The Economics of University Behavior*. New York: Academic Press, 1980.

Gormley, Jr. W.T. and D.L. Weimer. *Organizational Report Cards*. Cambridge, MA: Harvard University Press, 1999.

Graham, A. and N. Thompson. "Broken Ranks: *US News'* College Rankings Measure Everything but what Matters, and Most Universities Don't Seem to Mind." *Washington Monthly* 33.9 (2001): 9–14.

Granovetter, M. "Economic Action and Social Structure: The Problem of Embeddedness." *American Journal of Sociology* 91.3 (1985): 481–510.

Green, D. *What is Quality in Higher Education?* Buckingham, UK: SRHE and Open University Press, 1994.

Hare, P. "The UK's Research Assessment Exercise: Its Impact on Institutions, Departments, Individuals." *Higher Education Management and Policy* 15.2 (2003): 45–67.

Harley, S. "The Impact of Research Selectivity on Academic Work and Identity in UK Universities." *Studies in Higher Education* 27.2 (2002): 187–205.

Haveman, R.H., A. Bershadker, and J.A. Schwabish. *Human Capital in the United States from 1975 to 2000: Patterns of Growth and Utilization*. Kalamazoo, Michigan: W.E. Upjohn Institute for Employment Research, 2003.

Henkel, M. *Academic Identities and Policy Change in Higher Education*. London: Jessica Kingsley, 2000.

HEFCE (Higher Education Funding Council for England). "Interactions Between Research, Teaching and Other Academic Activities: Report to the HEFCE as Part of the Fundamental Review of Research Policy and Funding." Bristol: HEFCE, 1999, http://www.hefce.ac.uk/research/review/sub/teach.pdf.

HEFCE (Higher Education Funding Council for England). *Fundamental Review of Research Policy and Funding, Report 00/37*. Bristol: HEFCE, 2000, http://www.hefce.ac.uk/Pubs/hefce/2000/00_37.htm.

Hossler, D., J. Braxton, and G. Coopersmith. "Understanding Student College Choice." In Smart, J.C. (ed.). *Higher Education: Handbook of Theory and Research*, vol. V. New York: Agathon Press, 1989, 231–288.

Hossler, D. and L.H. Litten. *Mapping the Higher Education Landscape*. New York: College Entrance Examination Board, 1993.

Hoxby, C.M. "How the Changing Market Structure of US Higher Education Explains College Tuition." NBER Working Paper 6323, Cambridge, MA: National Bureau of Economic Research, 1997, http://www.nber.org/papers/w6323.

Hoxby, C.M. "The Return to Attending a More Selective College: 1960 to the Present." Harvard University, 2001, http://post.economics.harvard.edu/faculty/hoxby/papers/whole.pdf.

Hoxby, C.M. "The Effects of Geographic Integration and Increasing Competition on the Market for College Education." Harvard University, 2002, http://post.economics.harvard.edu/faculty/hoxby/papers/exp_tuit.pdf.

Jenkins, A. "The Research Assessment Exercise, Funding and Teaching Quality." *Quality Assurance in Education* 3.2 (1995): 4–12.

Johnes, G. and M. Cave. "The Development of Competition among Higher Education Institutions." In Bartlett, W., C. Propper, D. Wilson, and J. Le Grand (eds). *Quasi-markets in the Welfare State: The Emerging Findings*. Bristol: SAUS Publications, 1994, 95–120.

Johnstone, R.B. "Cost-sharing and Equity in Higher Education: Implications of Income-Contingency Loans." In Teixeira, P., B. Jongbloed, D. Dill, and A. Amaral (eds). *Markets in Higher Education: Rhetoric or Reality?* Dordrecht, The Netherlands: Kluwer, 2004, 37–59.

Kuh, G. "What We're Learning About Student Engagement from NSSE." *Change* 35.2 (2003): 24–32.

Kuh, G.D. and E.T. Pascarella. "What Does Institutional Selectivity Tell Us About Educational Quality?" *Change* 36.5 (2004): 52–58.

Le Grand, J. and W. Bartlett. *Quasi-markets and Social Policy*. London: Macmillan, 1993.

Lindsay, G. and T. Rodgers. "Market Orientation in the UK Higher Education Sector: The Influence of the Education Reform Process 1979–1993." *Quality in Higher Education* 4.2 (1998): 159–171.

Manski, C.F. and D.A. Wise. *College Choice in America*. Cambridge, MA: Harvard University Press, 1983.

Marsh, H.W. and J. Hattie. "The Relation Between Research Productivity and Teaching Effectiveness." *Journal of Higher Education* 73.5 (2002): 603–641.

Maslen, G. "V-C Says Scrap State Red Tape." *Times Higher Education Supplement*, 15 September, 2000.

Massy, W.F. *Honoring the Trust: Quality and Cost Containment in Higher Education*. Bolton, MA: Anker Publishing, 2003.

Massy, W.F. "Markets in Higher Education: Do They Promote Internal Efficiency?" In Teixeira, P., B. Jongbloed, D. Dill, and A. Amaral (eds). *Markets in Higher Education: Rhetoric or Reality?* Dordrecht, The Netherlands: Kluwer, 2004, 13–35.

McDonough, P.M., A.L. Antonio and L.X. Perez. "College Rankings: Democratized College Knowledge for Whom?" *Research in Higher Education* 39.5 (1998): 513–537.

McNay, I. "The Paradoxes of Research Assessment and Funding." In Henkel, M. and B. Little (eds). *Changing Relationships between Higher Education and the State*. London: Jessica Kingsley, 1999, 191–203.

Moogan, Y.J., S. Baron, and K. Harris. "Decision-making Behaviour of Potential Higher Education Students." *Higher Education Quarterly* 53.3 (1999): 211–228.

Niklasson, L. "Quasi-markets in Higher Education: A Comparative Analysis." *Journal of Higher Education Policy and Management* 18.1 (1996): 7–22.

North, D. *Institutions, Institutional Change, and Economic Performance*. Cambridge: Cambridge University Press, 1990.

Pascarella, E.T. "Identifying Excellence in Undergraduate Education: Are We Even Close?" *Change* 33.3 (2001): 19–23.

Pascarella, E.T. and P.T. Terenzini. *How College Affects Students: Findings and Insights From Twenty Years of Research*. San Francisco: Jossey-Bass, 1991.

Pascarella, E.T. and P.T. Terenzeni. *How College Affects Students: A Third Generation of Research*, 2nd edn. San Francisco: Jossey-Bass, 2005.

Paulsen, M.B. "College Choice: Understanding Student Enrollment Behavior." ASHE-ERIC Higher Education Report No. 6, Washington, DC: The George Washington University, School of Education and Human Development, 1990.

Rolfe, H. "University Strategy in an Age of Uncertainty: The Effect of Higher Education Funding on Old and New Universities." *Higher Education Quarterly* 57.1 (2003): 24–47.

Rosovsky, H. and M. Hartley. *Evaluation and the Academy: Are We Doing the Right Thing?* Cambridge, MA: American Academy of Arts and Sciences, 2002.

Rothschild, M. and L.J. White. "The Analytics of the Pricing of Higher Education and Other Services in Which the Customers are Inputs." *Journal of Political Economy* 103.3 (1995): 573–586.

Sarrico, C.S., S.M. Hogan, R.G. Dyson, and A.D. Athanassopoulos. "Data Envelope Analysis and University Selection." *Journal of the Operational Research Society* 48.12 (1997): 1163–1177.

Smith, J., A. McKnight, and R. Naylor. "Graduate Employability: Policy and Performance in Higher Education in the UK." *Economic Journal* 110.464 (2000): 382–411.

Teixeira, P., B. Jongbloed, D. Dill, and A. Amaral (eds). *Markets in Higher Education: Rhetoric or Reality?* Dordrecht, The Netherlands: Kluwer, 2004.

Terenzini, P.T. and E.T. Pascarella. "Living with Myths: Undergraduate Education in America." *Change* 26.1 (1994): 28–32.

Trow, M. "From Mass Higher Education to Universal Access: The American Advantage." *Minerva* 37.4 (2000): 303–328.

Williams, G.L. *Changing Patterns of Finance in Higher Education*. Buckingham, UK: Open University Press, 1992.

Williams, G.L. "The Higher Education Market in the United Kingdom." In Teixeira, P., B. Jongbloed, D. Dill, and A. Amaral (eds). *Markets in Higher Education: Rhetoric or Reality?* Dordrecht, The Netherlands: Kluwer, 2004, 241–269.

Winston, G.C. and D.J. Zimmerman. "Peer Effects in Higher Education." NBER Working Paper 9501, Cambridge, MA: National Bureau of Economic Research, 2003, http://www.nber.org/papers/w9501.

Witzel, M.L. "The Failure of an Internal Market: The Universities Funding Council Bid System." *Public Money and Management* 11.2 (1991): 41–49.

Yorke, M. "A Good League Table Guide?" *Quality Assurance in Education* 5.2 (1997): 61–72.

Yorke, M., G. Barnett, P. Bridges, P. Evanson, C. Haines, D. Jenkins, P. Knight, D. Scurry, M. Stowell, and H. Woolf. "Does Grading Method Influence Honours Degree Classification?" *Assessment and Evaluation in Higher Education* 27.3 (2002): 269–279.

Zemsky, R and P. Oedel. *The Structure of College Choice*. New York: College Entrance Examination Board, 1983.

DON F. WESTERHEIJDEN

STATES AND EUROPE AND QUALITY OF HIGHER EDUCATION

1. INTRODUCTION: WHAT ARE THE QUESTIONS?

This chapter investigates how quality assurance affected the performance of higher education at the macro, meso, and micro levels. The emphasis will be at the macro and to some extent the meso levels of (collections of) countries and higher education institutions. I shall approach my question first with some theoretical considerations, mainly informed by neoclassical economic theory, broadened to a general theory of (political) behaviour (based on De Vree 1982; Lieshout 1984; Westerheijden 1988) and to some extent by neo-institutional economics (as summarised in Eggertsson 1990). Blackmur gave a more extensive economic perspective on the regulation issue in Chapter 2. The theoretical issue in this partial theory of quality in higher education is what are the interests of actors in quality? The neoclassical theory forcefully underpins the proposition that "what gets measured, gets done", that is, higher education institutions adapt to their steering environment, leading to different emphases in institutions' performance depending on the conception-in-use of 'quality' held by external actors (quality assurance agencies, ministries, supra-national bodies, etc.).

From the higher education institutions' interest not to lose governmental support, derives my second question. Neo-institutional considerations centring on the agency problem (the difficulty for principals to fully control agents' behaviour, while agents have different utility functions from principals) will be used to look at the 'inner life thesis'. This thesis states that there is a disparity between the policy world of '(intermediary) agents' and the 'chalk face' world in higher education institutions with a very limited 'trickle down' of policy concepts into the still highly autonomous 'inner life' of academe with regard to teaching and research. Empirical studies of quality assessment schemes and their impact will be used for informal testing of these two propositions.

A third area, with special relevance at the time, namely the interconnections between countries in what is seen as an increasingly globalising world (almost obligatory quote: Castells 1998), will be looked at in one of the cases of most (and complex) interdependence, namely the European countries, which are involved in the European Union and/or in the Bologna process. Economically oriented behavioural theory will almost completely give way here to institutional considerations; empirical, explanatory research into our interest area of impacts of quality assurance on performance is largely lacking at this level.

73

D.F. Westerheijden et al. (eds.), Quality Assurance in Higher Education: Trends in Regulation, Translation and Transformation, 73–95.
© 2007 Springer.

With these three interconnected questions in a single chapter, the argumentation may be presented densely in parts, as I aim to keep the chapter within reasonable limits of space. Yet I will try to remain clear. To make a clear start, let me begin by going back to some of the basics of higher education economics.

2. BACK TO BASICS: WHY ARE STUDENTS, INSTITUTIONS, AND STATES INTERESTED IN QUALITY ASSURANCE?

In a theory of demand and supply of higher education, two parties play the primary roles: the 'consumers', i.e. the students,[1] and the 'suppliers', i.e. the higher education institutions. However, higher education is the antithesis of a good traded in the idealised market of textbook classical economics. First, it is far from homogeneous – differences in qualities will be the topic of this chapter. Second, its benefits for the consumers will not appear before buying or even immediately upon 'consumption' of the 'service', on the contrary they will only appear after many years; education is the *nec plus ultra* of 'experience goods', which are defined as those whose quality "can be measured only by using the product" (Eggertsson 1990: 195). Use of education in this context means the ex-student enjoys its benefits in achieving better (paid) jobs, partaking more in society's culture, and other elements of the 'common weal', better health, etc. Third, there are no stable preferences, because the utility function according to which the consumers judge a good's value is deliberately changed by the 'consumption' of higher education itself.[2] This is where a third party enters the theory, namely, the states in their role to create and maintain order in markets among their citizens and, more particularly, to counter-balance market failure.

An axiom of classical economic theory, as well as of an axiomatic theory of individual behaviour (De Vree 1982), is that the subjects themselves best know their utility function, which is a given. All individuals have a right to their own false class consciousness, so to say. The upshot of which is that researchers of higher education, for instance, cannot pose a single utility function for all students, for all higher education institutions,[3] or for all states. It is at the expense of empirical predictive power that such assumptions are made (variety among individual objects in a class of actors is not accommodated). I shall have to find a balance in this trade-off, for without such assumptions, it becomes impossible to make predictions or give explanations about classes of actors.

Besides the micro-economic argument of market failure, states may have macro-economic arguments, such as the desire to stimulate the development of a 'knowledge economy' or to obtain a better place in the globalisation process.[4]

How do states take up their role in the higher education system? Here too it is tempting yet dangerous to assume homogeneity: the utility function of states may differ as much as that of individuals – maybe even more so, as the assumption of the state as a single, unitary actor with a single, utility function may already be debatable (Allison and Zelikow 1999). For the moment, I shall assume that states can be unitary actors; internal politics will have to wait till a later occasion. I shall not assume that all states have the same preferences, but will sketch some broad trends below that do seem to affect many states, at least in the part of the world I happen to know best, that is, Europe.

In recent decades, often connected to the idea of 'new public management', the state ideology changed from the welfare state idea, that the state had to intervene whenever it might be beneficial to part of the population, to an ideology influenced by neo-liberalism and neo-conservatism with a much less pronounced role for the state.[5] That discussion affected all areas of state involvement in society, including higher education. The change became visible both in the 'steering philosophy' and in the instrumentation of policies. With regard to the steering philosophy, there was a marked difference between the national debates. National political agendas were turned into scientific terms, debates, and 'truths', as Enders maintained (2002). Dominating in Europe was perhaps the new public management literature from the United Kingdom, but there – at least in higher education – the situation at the outset differed markedly from the one in continental European countries. In broad brush strokes, in the latter the issue was one of moving from strict, and in the Weberian sense, bureaucratic, control to one of more autonomy in order to become more flexible and in that way responsive to contextual (societal) demands. The British perspective, on the other hand and in equally broad brush strokes, was one of bringing autonomous institutions under sufficient state control to make them more responsive to contextual (state) demands. From both sides of the North Sea, though, higher education was seen more than before in terms of its returns to society – and especially to the economy. For the economic discourse at the same time became dominant, at the expense of other, social and socio-critical discourses that had been prominent since at least the eventful year of 1968.[6]

Traditionally, the instruments of state intervention have been primarily its power or authority (regulation and enforcement) and budget (taxes and grants); later, but already before the rise of new public management, information and communication were added (Jenniskens 1997: 48–56). With new public management the array of instruments was extended further. A conspicuous new instrument was connected with the quality of higher education.

To some extent, the new public management movement was a repackaging of old instruments in new terms:

- Regulation was replaced by deregulation, but the remaining regulation should target critical levers, in cybernetic fashion.

- Accountability post factum about money spent was to replace detailed rules and line-item budget ex ante (but required its own (re-)regulation).

- More autonomy for 'lower-level' governmental agencies (among them public higher education institutions) was an instrumentation of deregulation and a condition for those agencies to become innovative (in the sense of trying to find new ways to do their job, which the state intended to be more efficient) that at the same time made accountability more necessary.

- Control over such 'lower-level' governmental agencies was often taken to be a non-political task which was therefore not part of the state's 'core business', and outsourced to intermediary bodies (anti-trust and other market control agencies, in higher education quality assessment or accreditation agencies).[7]

- Funding was more performance-based instead of the traditional input-based formulae or negotiated budgets.

New elements in steering rather than repackaging were associated mostly with privatisation and marketisation. Thus, in higher education, access opportunities increased in many states for private service providers (note here the almost unavoidable 'service' and 'market' metaphors). And those who directly[8] benefited from higher education, the students themselves, were to engage more in market-like behaviour in that they were to pay higher fees for their tuition. By increasing their financial stakes, more rational choice behaviour was intended by the states as well.

With regard to higher education, the drive for economy ('value for money' as a politically dominating view on quality, cf. Harvey and Green 1993), the performance-based funding methods, the deregulation of, for instance, curricula, and the arrival of new non-public providers, in combination undermined old certainties (even if those certainties perhaps were legal fictions) about threshold quality of education being guaranteed by higher education institutions. To counteract these and similar corrupting tendencies, the threshold level of quality of education had to be controlled. Both demands of efficiency and of maintaining a threshold of quality were subsumed under the popular call of quality assurance for *accountability*.

In addition, the rate of change of economies and societies seemed to increase to such a level that the traditional methods of adaptation of higher education institutions to their environments – basically, incremental changes focused on content of teaching and research, instigated by developments in the disciplines[9] (Clark 1983: 234–237) – were no longer trusted to result in curricula that 'produced' graduates fit for the labour market. Formalised and continuous quality *improvement* became a new demand.

These two, or in fact three, demands were combined in a single policy instrument, called quality assessment.[10] This instrument was given additional functions when it had to *inform* (prospective) students (and in the case of young students also their parents) in choosing study programmes and locations to apply for (Weusthof and Frederiks 1997).[11]

In terms of information theory the most efficient form of information about quality is given in a single-bit (yes/no) *accreditation* or in a more refined, graded (rated or ranked) list of higher education programmes or institutions. This consequence was drawn by many state governments, especially in the form of accreditation.[12] Some made the next step to *ranking*, for example, the Russian Federation,[13] and more widely magazine publishers did so, as they perceived a commercial market for ranking lists.[14]

Mentioning accreditation and ranking takes me somewhat ahead of where I am in my argument. Let me return to the instrument of quality assessment and its connection to state utility functions. Some years ago, my colleagues and I argued that there was a logical connection between the preferences – or rather, the perceived priorities – of states and the type of quality assessment instrument they would pursue (Jeliazkova and Westerheijden 2002; see also table 1 below). Moreover, we argued that there was an inherent dynamic, in that (temporarily) bringing a more basic problem to closure would lead to another problem becoming dominant, so that a certain development path presented itself for external quality assessment in any state, with predictable changes in the methodology: from accreditation through different stages of external visits to internally propelled quality management. Even before that scheme was published, events proved it wrong, since with the Bologna Declaration of 1999 a whole new dynamic overtook developments. We added that to our scheme as a trend reversal ('new challenge'), but it showed that the external dynamics dominated inherent developments, and that the utility functions of a large coalition of states could converge in an unpredictable way.

The Bologna Declaration was not, initially, a sign of uniformisation of the states' utility functions, for they had very different reasons, driven by national politics, to join the Bologna process. Some, like Germany or Italy, may have seen in the Bologna Declaration an international lever to enforce national reform (reducing time to degree and drop-out). For others (such as the Netherlands), gaining international recognition for their higher education may have been high on their agenda. A third preference may have been to improve a state's position in the international student competition (also in the Netherlands). Briefly put: there were as many Bologna Declarations as there were countries signing. Afterwards, the process obtained its own dynamic, leading to, perhaps, more convergence of states' priorities and policies for higher education than initially envisaged.

Again I am tempted to run ahead of my line of argument. I shall return to the Bologna process later as the main form of international policy making in higher education in Europe. But before going to the international level, first I need to look at the question of how the introduction of quality assessment instruments affected the performance of higher education systems within the single states.

In economic views on behaviour, it is axiomatic that actors prefer behavioural options more, the higher the net benefits (or the lower the net costs) they expect to be associated with those options. 'Benefits' and 'costs' are taken here in their broadest sense, not necessarily in monetary terms.[15] If a government attaches higher benefits to certain options, these become more attractive to actors; higher costs make them less attractive. Accordingly, if a government puts a premium on graduating as many students as possible, as has happened in some performance-based funding models associated with new public management-like movements, higher education institutions that depend on this premium are (more) tempted to let students graduate, even if that puts quality thresholds in jeopardy. What prevents the system from corrupting, under such circumstances? First, this is not prevented completely, as is shown by the continued existence of 'degree mills'. But that is just a marginal category, showing that, in the majority of cases, *something* prevents total corruption from happening. It must be admitted, though, that no education or bad education is a cheaper option than providing good education, so that corrupting tendencies are rational behaviour for providers of higher education. That it can be rational for 'students' too, may be treated in more detail elsewhere,[16] but is proven empirically again by the continued demand for degree mill services. Gresham's Law of 1558 would apply: bad education drives out the good (more formally, Eggertsson 1990: 196–198).

Table 1. Phases in quality assurance systems. (Adapted from Jeliazkova and Westerheijden 2002: 435; with a few corrections added)

1. Problems	2. Role of quality assurance	3. Information base	4. Nature of external review and reporting
Phase 1: Serious doubts about educational standards.	Identifying sub-standard educational programmes.	Descriptive reports. Performance indicators.	Summative; accreditation, checking standards. Report to state.
Phase 2: Doubts about the efficiency of the higher education system and/or institutions.	a) Public accountability. b) Creating quality awareness in institutions.	Descriptive/strategic reports ('self-selling') covering: a) performance; b) procedures.	Ranking of institutions. One report to state and institutions. Identifying good practices.
Phase 3: Doubt about innovation capacity and quality assurance capacity of institutions.	Stimulate self-regulation capacity of institutions.	Public accountability.	Self-evaluation reports about: a) procedures; b) performance. Audit report to: – the institution; – the state.
Phase 4: Need to stimulate sustainable quality culture in institutions.	Split between: – improvement based on self-regulation; – public accountability.	Split between: – self-evaluative reports about processes and strategies based on SWOT, benchmarking; – self-reporting about performance indicators.	Split between: – audit report to the institution; – verifying data to be incorporated in public databases.
New challenge: Decreasing transparency across higher education systems.	Market regulation, i.e. informing clients (students, employers).	Performance indicators about 'products' (knowledge and skills of graduates).	Publication of comparative performance indicators. Standardised testing of graduates?

Beyond Gresham's law, even neo-institutional economic theory still has a hard time coping with the effects of differential quality of a good on a market. Possibilities multiply very fast. To mention but a few options: to what extent can study programmes in different disciplines be seen as substitutes for one another in the eyes of students considering to enter higher education (to what extent are we talking about a single market for a single good)? To what extent are study programmes in a single discipline only differentiated by their quality (on a one-dimensional scale of utility)?

The counterbalance must come from benefits associated with providing good education, which can be internal or external. *Internal* to the higher education system as a community of scholars (with or without a state) one sees in the first place reputation and esteem in the eyes of peers as the main incentive for behaviour. It is commonly assumed, however, that in the reputation cycles among academic peers (Latour and Woolgar 1979; applied to higher education policy in Välimaa and Westerheijden 1995) research performance is much more important than education performance (borne out by the different reactions of higher education institutions to rankings of research and of teaching, in Dill and Soo 2005).[17] *Externally*, the institutional elements of the market for higher education *may* act as counterbalancing forces: a higher education institution's reputation, to the extent that it can be damaged by signs of bad education (such as bad employment records, loan payback deficits or students suing their university to refund their fee because of bad teaching), does have some relation to education and may affect its turnover (an indicator of utility). But most of the external motivation is often expected from the monitoring of higher education, especially in the form of quality assessment, accreditation, or ranking. The actors willing to spend the effort for such mechanisms in most cases nowadays are state governments. The free market forces play a role mostly in the (less investment-intensive) ranking business, which in many countries thrives on information elicited in the course of (more investment-intensive) state quality assessment and accreditation schemes.

In the middle ground between market actors in the business of selling information and governments stand the professional organisations that initiated what in the United States is called 'specialised accreditation' (usually at the programme level). In some states, these are self-organising actors, in other cases they are related with the state – in fact, in a number of professions the states themselves are the controllers (e.g. medical doctors in many countries, or lawyers in Germany). The incentives for professions to control quality come from protection of the market of their profession (limiting access to keep suppliers' numbers low, or controlling quality of service provision to maintain the profession's reputation hence each member's capacity to charge higher fees). States have more paternalistic motives: they control certain professions to protect the citizens against malicious provision especially of vital professional services (medicine and engineering are the standard examples).

3. ECONOMIC VIEWS ON BEHAVIOUR AND HIGHER EDUCATION PERFORMANCE IN THE FRAMEWORK OF QUALITY ASSURANCE

In this section, the focus is on the question of how quality assessment in all its forms has affected the performance of higher education at the macro, meso, and micro levels. First, though, it has to be admitted that the statement "what gets measured, gets done" is almost like a theorem in economic theories of behaviour, hence supposed to be true theoretically, even before any empirical tests have been taken into consideration. It needs to be specified, however. For the theoretical statement – in fact, a restatement of the basic axiom of expected utility – would be that what gets rewarded gets done. But for behaviour to be rewarded, in an institutional environment of the rule of law, means that it first must be measured. In sum: what gets measured gets rewarded, and what gets rewarded gets done.[18] In the previous section, this statement was the underlying principle in the question: what would have the strongest impact on higher education institutions' behaviour? Would the corrupting tendencies of the performance-based funding (associated with new public management) be more rewarded, or the counterbalancing force of quality assessment?

Now I look at the question in more detail: what does quality assessment measure, what gets rewarded? Basically, there are two way of 'measuring' quality of education: through fixed procedures, often quantitative, associated with performance indicators, or through the intrinsically subjective process of peer review. Of course, things are not as clear-cut as that. On the one hand, some of the most relevant performance indicators are based on subjective (peer) review, for example, feedback from students or fellow-teachers, publication, and citation data (Westerheijden 1991). On the other hand, in current external quality assessment schemes peers are asked to base their judgments on 'objective' data. Still, to the extent that quality assessment schemes are based on performance indicators, they tend to over-emphasise the measurable over the relevant (examples are given in the box below). Many quality assessment schemes use a mixture of input, process, throughput, and output indicators. The choice is based on characteristics of the higher education system (e.g. in some systems, students cannot be selected by the higher education institution so that selectivity data are meaningless), on the quality model popular with the quality assessment agency or ministry, and on the availability of data – which in the end is linked to measurability of information.

Common Performance Indicators

Input factors: staff numbers and their qualifications (available for education), student selectivity, staff-student ratios, funding (per student), facilities (per student), curriculum plans, planned student qualifications (linked with Dublin Descriptors).[19]

Process factors: number of hours for different course units/disciplines or for different work forms (lectures, seminars, etc.), ECTS per course unit or for whole degree programme, student feedback on course delivery, alumni feedback on strong and weak points of the study programme from the point of view of their early career.

Throughput factors (intermediate results): examination results, resits, progress through different phases of study, grade point averages.

Output factors (final results): graduation rates/drop-outs, time to degree, employment rates (in relevant job sectors).

A basic distinction in quality assessment approaches is between mission-based and standards-based evaluation. In mission-based evaluation, which is at the heart of the archetypal US institutional accreditation, the higher education institution's own statement is taken as the standard to be reached: 'fitness for self-defined purpose', so to speak. In standards-based evaluation, external evaluation will first of all establish the 'fitness *of* purpose' judged against an externally given standard. The most popular example of the latter at the moment in Europe is given by the Dublin Descriptors.

A trend in a number of higher education systems in Europe, associated with the Joint Quality Initiative from which the Dublin Descriptors emerged, is to try to focus on output factors, judged in the light of the Dublin Descriptors. Yet, in the Dutch programme accreditation scheme, much more information is asked than just on the competencies of higher education's output (the examples in the box are to a large extent based on the indicators asked of applicants by one of the agencies active in Dutch accreditation (QANU 2004)).[20]

The litmus test of quality assurance is of course if it contributed to an increase in the quality of higher education. This is certainly not a foregone conclusion, because although in theory there ought not be good quality assurance without good quality of the 'product' – the Demings and Jurans of this world were not interested in quality assurance per se, but in pulling US industry 'out of the crisis' (title of Deming's 1986 book) – practice is more stubborn. Good quality assurance procedures may exist without good feedback of their results into the actual management and 'production' in higher education institutions,[21] and what guarantees that good external quality assessment leads to good internal quality assurance in the first place? Or rather in the second place, because in the first place one might wonder if the external quality assessment, which almost always drives internal quality assurance, is good in itself.

To the extent that external assessment indeed drives internal quality assurance, and to the extent that what gets measured gets done, external assessment determines what type of information is available in the higher education institutions. So, if a government demands information about graduation rates, higher education institutions have an incentive to increase graduation rates, *ceteris paribus*.[22] A perverse effect of this (real, Dutch) example is that quality assessment was introduced in an effort to counterbalance the undesired effects on quality of a funding mechanism that rewarded increasing graduation rates but now is seen to reinforce that corrupting tendency. To make matters even more complicated, increased internal efficiency was a major aim of the government's higher education policy as well – so the perverse effect was a desired effect too.

Quality assessment schemes often targeted publicly debated and easily visible information, to show higher education's responsiveness to society's demands. In that way, the use of manifest information and performance indicators engendered a separation between the public, political process of external quality assurance and the 'inner life' of the higher education institution in its academic sense. The attention for a more holistic, education-oriented view on quality of education was left to the less scrutinisable process of peer review. Designers of quality assessment schemes have, however, always been worried that the discretion inherent in peer review might degenerate into arbitrariness: either mutual back scratching among close-knit colleagues or wanton exercise of power by academic barons in the disciplines (Westerheijden 1991). The more external quality assessment itself had to operate in a bureaucratic or legal context (the apex of which was accreditation with its fundamental legal consequences of 'the right to exist', but which could never be absent in an institutional arrangement based on the rule of law), the more the peers had to base their decisions on indisputable, easily visible information. And the less holistic and education-oriented they could be – as D'Andrea argues in more detail later in this volume. The combination of accountability and quality improvement in a single process, however necessary it may have been for other reasons, could therefore never be easy; it always was a matter of navigating between Scylla and Charybdis (not for nothing was this in the title of Vroeijenstijn 1995).

In our research into the use of quality assessment in the Netherlands, our first, global finding was that no matter how exactly the quality assessment scheme was 'measuring' quality, the simple fact that education was targeted already had the effect that this function was given more attention by actors in the higher education institutions than before (Frederiks, Westerheijden, and Weusthof 1994). In many cases, the first self-evaluation process was the first time in many years that teaching staff met to discuss the study programme. Programme coherence and educational innovation increased since then. The government's focus on programme feasibility (in a Dutch neologism 'studeerbaarheid') reinforced these tendencies – another instance of "what gets measured and rewarded, gets done". At the same time, this shows that the 'inner life' thesis was falsified in this case: the primary process of education, which was if not the first then at least the second priority in the minds of academics,[23] was deeply affected by the introduction of quality assessment.

Another effect was the increase in secondary processes around education, such as (computerised) systems to monitor student progress much more closely than before. Until the 1980s, the Dutch tradition regarding students was akin to the German one in which students were expected to find their own way through academia, and they had the right to rot (as one German professor once graphically put it). This changed in the Netherlands after 1988, which in a what-gets-measured-gets-done manner may be linked directly to the fact that from the very beginning of external quality assessment, tables on student progress and drop-out were demanded by the government in each self-evaluation report.[24] Growth in administrative processes might be predicted as a consequence of the rise of quality assurance as a profession, first in the 1970s and 1980s in the business world and since the late 1980s also in higher education, because such 'bean counting' is part of what quality officers are expected to do (partly coming out of education science traditions, the discipline from which many quality officers were recruited in higher education institutions), and because it creates budgets, staff, a specialised jargon, and similar ephemera that give them status, hence utility. However, an alternative explanation is the one I gave before, basing the *priorities* in measurement (which are left unexplained by the Niskanian budget-maximising behaviour of actors in a bureaucratic organisation) on external, in this case, governmental demands.[25]

More impacts at the meso and micro levels were noted in, amongst others, McNay (1997, 1999) and Westerheijden (1997). They emphasised for instance the increased opportunities for higher education institutions' 'managers' (as academic governors increasingly began to call themselves since the new public management revolution) to make differential decisions inside their institutions, using externally proven quality and performance as their main arguments. At the micro level, they noted increased interdependence and cooperation among academics (both in education and in research)[26] as well as increased stress.

4. ADDING THE TRANSNATIONAL LEVEL

Higher education systems function primarily within a country. In mentioning functions of higher education, states tellingly use rhetoric like transmission of the *national* culture to the next generation of *its* population. Or, in macro-economical perspective, states emphasise the need to educate the *country's* workforce. At least until recently, governmental strategic plans for higher education looked at the *nation's* need for higher education institutions, etc.

In colonial states in the first half of the 20th century, the concept of country may have been a bit more ambiguous, and some students in the universities in the 'mother' country came from the colonies, in movements that nowadays would be part of internationalisation – or international trade. Both internationalisation and international trade (for instance, but certainly not only, discussed in relation to GATS) have become important catchwords in higher education since the turn of the century. However, between the decolonisation of Asia and Africa (largely around 1945–1960)[27] and the last decade of the 20th century, the movement of students across continents received little attention from states, perhaps with the exception of the United States, where study abroad and immigration continued to be intertwined.

In international relations, states are sovereign, if not completely autonomous (the difference is explained in e.g. Van Kersbergen, Lieshout, and Verbeek 2000: 37) actors. What, broadly, are states' interests internationally regarding higher education and its quality? International relations, also when it comes to higher education, are simultaneously characterised by interdependence (in partial division of labour, based on comparative advantages) and by competition (among partially similar actors, offering substitutable goods and services to, potentially,[28] a world market).

In classical economic theory, comparative advantages include lower production costs. In all probability, the developed nations had comparative advantages over countries in the third world in producing higher education, perhaps not so much in terms of the monetary running costs (which would be lower in developing countries with their lower salary levels) but in terms of the considerable investments needed to establish higher education systems. Again, the investments must not only be seen in monetary terms but also in terms of cultural and social capital. The monetary advantages for the developed nations were considerable, because they already had large numbers of higher education institutions, so they did not need to invest heavily in setting up higher education systems when globalisation hit higher education. But probably more important was the cultural capital in that the developed nations already had generations of academics ready to engage in teaching, while the numbers of academics in less developed nations were small at best. This advantage would take at least one, and probably more, generations to overcome given the time needed for academic education (perhaps expressed best as *Bildung*, which is more than 'academic training'!).[29]

With regard to higher education, neo-institutional economics points to lower transaction costs on the side of students and/or providers in the sense of not having to learn a new language of instruction. The comparative advantage of English-speaking higher education providers has been tremendous on a worldwide scale ever since at least the middle of the 20th century. Moreover, since what is ostensibly traded in higher education are degrees, the advantage of the English language spilled over into an advantage for the names of higher education degrees used in English-speaking countries. As these were the same in the major countries (i.e. the United Kingdom and the United States), the advantages for these English-speaking countries on the world market for higher education were increased.[30]

A factor in international relations and international trade has been the protection of home markets – or protection of the country as such, which is arguably the 'core business' of states, as philosophers have emphasised ever since the early days of statehood (see e.g. Nozick 1974; or for the classics, Plato 1974). Higher education often has been given a minor role in this, usually expressed in terms of safeguarding, transmitting, or promoting the national culture.[31] Yet, also, the economic argument of higher education's role in preparing the country's workforce may have protectionist connotations.[32]

The attitude in a state towards internationalisation of higher education may probably be explained by these two factors: the comparative advantages or disadvantages it sees for its higher education system on the world market and its tendency for protectionism.[33] The argument in the following will be that both the European Union and the Bologna process have influenced these two factors.

Before I go into that, however, I would like to make two additional remarks. First, I would like to draw attention to the fact that states are not the only actors in international higher education relations. Higher education institutions act as partly autonomous actors on the international student market in their own right. How autonomously they can do so depends on the national institutional framework; public institutions as a rule are at a competitive disadvantage in this respect to private ones.[34] Higher education institutions increasingly are driven to the (world) student market by decreasing state support in many countries; examples are the United Kingdom and Australia, but also the Netherlands. In doing so, they may be supported by their home state (e.g. by support for the 'national brand' of higher education, through funding national foundations such as the British Council or the Goethe Institutes, or practically by support for higher education institutions in recruiting foreign students as the Dutch government does by establishing a network of Netherlands Education Support Offices (NESOs)). On the other hand, higher education institutions in their market behaviour may go against governmental policies; elements of that were visible in the Netherlands where institutional funding arguments made public higher education institutions keener on attracting foreign students than the state thought desirable (for reasons of quality or of its funding). Pursuing the Dutch example a little further, the fact that the Dutch government has funding arrangements giving it an interest in limiting the number of foreign students, while it is also government policy to support the higher education institutions to attract foreign students through NESOs points to the well-known fact that government policies need not be consistent with one another, nor consistent over time. Another inconsistency can be seen in the increased fear of terror since 2001, which made Dutch visa policies much more restrictive, time-consuming, and expensive, while the government also acknowledges that attracting talented people (students and knowledge workers) is essential for the Dutch economy in the long run.[35]

The second remark concerns the fact that internationalisation brought to light a problem that was slowly emerging due to the new public management-related withdrawal of state control from the higher education system. What I mean is that in a market with deceasing homogeneity of the good (which in publicly dominated higher education systems used to be assured through institutional arrangements emphasising homogeneity of higher education institutions (see also Neave 1995) and their funding) the need for information on the side of consumers increases. When internationalisation, both in the form of an ideology forced by the government upon itself (for reasons of EU integration or of international trade – which reason dominated is not the point here) and in the form of actually increasing international mobility of students and higher education institutions, increased the higher education market to cross-border size, the information need became paramount. Even stronger than that, the government's withdrawal from its former type of market control and internationalisation led to such an information lack that the debate turned into terms of 'consumer protection'. Since quality assessment schemes already had an information function, as mentioned above, it was not a surprise that with the changing context the information function of quality assessment schemes was further emphasised – and changed – as well. The rise of accreditation schemes in the Bologna process can be explained in this way.[36]

4.1. The European Union and the Bologna Process

The European Union and its predecessors, as partly international, partly supranational, and therefore more handily called transnational governmental actors[37] focusing on economic cooperation among European countries, at the outset did not have higher education in their area of competence. In a not uncommon development in the EU, (unexpected) consequences of some of the European Court of Justice's judgments,[38] ditto of general agreements among the member states,[39] and smart manoeuvring of the European Commission in the absence of close governmental supervision,[40] higher education increasingly became an issue on the EU agenda. In the route towards accession for the ten countries that joined the EU in 2004, much higher education regulation was even seen to be part of the *acquis communautaire*.

For a long time, in the European higher education policy arena the leading axiom had been that Europe's richness and strength lay in the very diversity of the higher education systems of the member states (Van Vught, Van der Wende, and Westerheijden 2002: section 2). This argument was part of a complex of arguments, mainly emphasising higher education's cultural role, designed to keep higher education as much as possible out of the European, economic community. With the growing dominance of the economic discourse both in domestic politics and in international politics ('globalisation!'), the cultural argument lost attractiveness. Moreover, with the growing European integration, disadvantages of higher education's diversity for the smooth operation of the European (labour) market became more apparent. Diversity of degrees and of the underlying competencies of graduates from an increasing number of countries (the EU had grown from 6 to 15 members by that time) led, as stated above, to a significant increase in transaction costs. Intergovernmental cooperation at first took the form of information exchange through the ENIC/NARIC (European Network of Information Centres/National Academic Recognition Information Centres) network. Although the practice of degree recognition had changed from the principle of 'equivalence' to 'recognition' (Van der Wende and Westerheijden 2003), substantial transaction costs remained the rule. The next step was set in the Council of Europe/UNESCO Recognition Convention of Lisbon (1997), which introduced the principle of 'acceptance' (Van der Wende and Westerheijden 2003).

Apparently and understandably given the international situation (beyond Europe) of increasing competition on the higher education market (Van der Wende and Westerheijden 2003) and the increasing importance of such additional income for the higher education institutions and countries, diminishing transaction costs within the EU was not enough. More harmonisation could aid each of the European countries' higher education institutions in the international competition with, especially, the higher education institutions from Anglo-Saxon countries.[41] In other words, they had a common interest, enough to get together for a temporary coalition. Implicit assumptions are that these countries did see opportunities for making gains on the international higher education market (for the higher education institutions in their country), and that they were not afraid of negative consequences for their economy (no protectionism) and higher education system (no fear of lowering of quality). Although the EU might have been an obvious platform to form such a coalition, this route was not chosen. Instead, ad hoc coalitions first signed the Sorbonne Declaration in 1998 (France, Germany, Italy and the United Kingdom) and then in 1999 the Bologna Declaration.[42]

Why not the EU route? It certainly was not impossible, as shown by the fact that only a year later, the highly ambitious Lisbon Agenda for radical reforms of the national economies, with large financial consequences for especially the research and innovation budgets, was agreed inside the EU framework. From a (neo-institutional) economic-theoretical perspective, the formal reply that in Bologna there were 29 countries – practically double the number of the EU members at the time – is not a sufficient answer. Perhaps the higher education ministers did not want to 'surrender' the culturally sensitive field of higher education to the European actors, the less so as "the Commission has succeeded in weakening the position of the member states in some policy arenas by co-opting previously excluded actors ... into its web of advisory committees" (Van Kersbergen, Lieshout, and Verbeek 2000: 50).[43] And in higher education such actors might be found in the higher education institutions themselves, which were increasingly denationalising, not only because the declining state government funding drove them to the market, but also because the benefits from the EU were increasing (monetary as well as in reputation, through participation in networks for both education and research; think of Socrates, the Framework Programmes and the European Science Foundation, ESF).

Another reason could be that staying outside of the formalised, judicial institutions of the EU by signing an international 'Declaration' of unspecified nature, may not necessarily have been a binding statement – and it is received knowledge that for politicians it is in general wise to keep options open, not to get bound, until really necessary.[44] Such a declaration could act as an exhortation to other actors in national higher education systems to comply with a minister's preferences, without binding the minister in any definitive way. Which might have been a difficult way to go even had they wished to do it, as higher education reform would require legal reform in many countries, something that ministers could not do on their own but would need to get the agreement of their national parliament for.

If (some) ministers responsible for higher education might have had opportunistic reasons for preferring a declaration, without need for follow-up on the nice words, they would have been disappointed by what happened afterwards. The Bologna Declaration turned into a Bologna process of momentous size, speed and impact. And the EU Commission gained perhaps the most central place in it. Major players in the new policy arena formed by the flying circus of Bologna seminars and conferences are the '4Es': ENQA, EUA, ESIB, and the ENIC/NARIC, that is to say, the platform of (until now)[45] mainly national quality assurance agencies (European Network of Quality Assurance Agencies), the association of universities (European University Association) (and, to some extent, the other higher education institutions), the national student unions (National Unions of Students in Europe), and the national degree recognition agencies. ENQA and ENIC/NARIC can be seen to some extent as government-controlled (although the institutional arrangements are of course different in the countries concerned), the EUA represents semi-autonomous albeit public higher education institutions, and the students are of course unguided missiles from the point of view of governments. But the most powerful actor is the presidency of the BFUG, the Bologna Follow-up Group, made up from the *temporary* representatives of the EU-troika (the past, current and immediate future presidents of the EU Council of Ministers, so membership in this group is limited to 18 months) and the *continuous* representative of the EU Commission.

Again in line with the conclusions of Van Kersbergen, Lieshout, and Verbeek (2000) about EU policies in several fields, the impact of the Bologna process on different countries has been different, partially in relation to their national institutional arrangements (in particular its higher education degree structures), but partially also in what seems to be a random manner: some large countries are reacting vehemently, some small ones too, but also some large ones as well as some small ones do not (Reichert and Tauch 2003, 2005). As mentioned twice already, I venture the proposition that the explanation may be in the national (reform) agenda for higher education: the more reform already on the agenda, the more impact 'Bologna' seems to have had. An additional explanatory factor was also indicated earlier: the expected position of a country in the globalisation game for higher education.[46]

5. CONCLUSION: CONSEQUENCES FOR QUALITY ASSURANCE

While it may be early days to make an assessment of the impact of the Bologna process on quality assurance in higher education systems, and especially through that element of the institutional arrangement on the performance of the higher education institutions, let me attempt to indicate some early results.

In parallel to and at least partly influenced by the Bologna process, the number of countries that turned to accreditation as the major quality assurance instrument has increased. The estimate in Schwarz and Westerheijden (2004b) that out of the 20 countries they included in their study, 18 had an accreditation scheme, overstates the issue. Their finding, more exactly, was that in 18 countries there was *at least a minor* accreditation scheme (taken in a theoretical sense, as it might be *called* differently for political or path-dependent reasons) for some *part* of the higher education system. Germany and Flanders/the Netherlands provided clear examples of countries where the impact was to introduce a *major* accreditation scheme – and there are others. In the same countries, major reforms of degree structures took place. In combination, these two reforms may have major impacts on the performance of the higher education systems. In that combination, the impact of the degree structure reform may be recognisable separately. Obviously, programmes according to the new structure were introduced. One of their effects might be to lead to fewer drop-outs as there now is an intermediate 'honourable' exit from the higher education system where in many cases that did not exist before.[47]

The mentioning of the ECTS (European Credit Transfer and Accumulation System) in the Bologna Declaration led to at least an administrative change of course unit sizes. In many cases further modularisation of study programmes was undertaken than a pure administrative recalculation of workload in ECTS. This may have made study programmes more 'school-like', packaging the knowledge in readily consumable packets. On the one hand, this too may show in the quality statistics in higher success rates for students. On the other hand, looking at the content of new modules and especially the higher-order competencies that higher education is expected to transmit, several commentators have voiced the fear that the new bachelor-master structure programmes may be less effective. That would perhaps show in alumni and employer satisfaction results. It is remarkable, however, how fast people adjust their expectation levels to what is on offer in the market of graduates, and relegate their dissatisfaction to coffee-table discussions on how things were better when they were young.[48]

Another consequence of modularisation may have been that students obtained larger autonomy in designing their own learning route, in that way contributing to the 'deconstruction' of the study programme as an easily recognisable unit. At the same time, at least some higher education institutions in that process of modularisation have taken further steps towards 'mass individualisation' of study programmes by addressing the issue of recognition of students' previously acquired competencies. Both developments call the current focus on the degree as a meaningful signal for graduates' knowledge and competencies into question. With it, quality assessment schemes' focus on degree programmes becomes equally doubtful.[49] Luckily, from that perspective, both in Germany and in Flanders/the

Netherlands it seems doubtful if the current programme accreditation scheme will be continued (after completing the first round). In both countries, with actors mainly arguing from a transaction cost perspective, discussions go in the direction of accrediting larger units, probably higher education institutions or faculties, like the Swiss OAQ (Center of Accreditation and Quality Assurance of the Swiss Universities) has done from the beginning.

At the European level, ENQA published its standards and guidelines in the framework of the Bologna process (European Association for Quality Assurance in Higher Education 2005). This document contained "standards for internal and external quality assurance, and for external quality assurance agencies". Do they provide the powerful harmonising force that would make it possible to predict that the Bologna process eventually will be the ostensibly intended unifying influence for higher education from the European perspective at the national level and below, desired by some, feared by others? No. The 'standards' are not at all concerned with the content of education; they are not standards in the sense that the Dublin Descriptors are, or the Tuning outcomes. They do no more than prescribe that all higher education institutions, to be externally evaluated positively, must have a quality assurance system with a policy and instruments, covering (academic) review of programmes and awards, student assessment, staff quality, and adequate learning facilities and resources (European Association for Quality Assurance in Higher Education 2005: 6). That is no more than a minimum definition of areas to be covered by internal quality assurance, and can be fulfilled in many ways, and at many levels (in the sense that 'level' is used in quality audits for e.g. the European Foundation for Quality Management model). Finally, the ENQA standards prescribe that public information about institutions' programmes and awards should be honest. This is a measure of common market regulation – even in commercial marketing outright lying is prohibited.

With regard to standards in external quality assessment, the ENQA standards say only that *formal* decisions (I understand that as accreditation or funding decisions) "should be based on explicit published criteria that are applied consistently" (European Association for Quality Assurance in Higher Education 2005: 7). This does not imply a European level or standard of anything, but the rule of law. The external quality assessment agencies themselves are not subjected to standards regarding academic levels either. Again ENQA states that "processes, criteria and procedures used by agencies should be pre-defined and publicly available", but as for the process, nothing more is set than an expectation that 'normally' the four-step process is followed outlined already over a decade ago (Van Vught and Westerheijden 1993), and which was so general that it hid as much as it revealed about external quality assessment, as Stensaker in Chapter 5 also argues. The most incising requirement on external quality assessment agencies is formal: they "should be formally recognised by competent public authorities in the European Higher Education Area as agencies with responsibilities for external quality assurance and should have an established legal basis" (European Association for Quality Assurance in Higher Education 2005: 7). Recognition power is in the hands of (public) authorities within the states, leaving the intergovernmental game intact and squarely dominated by the states (each of which may apply different, not harmonised, criteria), not by a supranational body. The most far-reaching requirement is that external quality assessment agencies "should have in place procedures for their own accountability", later operationalised as the *expectation* of "[a] mandatory cyclical external review of the agency's activities at least once every five years" (European Association for Quality Assurance in Higher Education 2005: 26).

Meeting the standards, including the just mentioned one of regular review of the quality assessment agency itself, is a condition for quality assessment agencies being listed in the European "Register of external quality assurance agencies operating in Europe" that is to be established (European Association for Quality Assurance in Higher Education 2005: 30–31). Yet even if these standards were fully implemented as access criteria to the European Register and even if that would lead to blackballing a state-related quality assessment agency (which seems only a theoretical possibility)[50] it still does not constitute a force towards harmonisation of higher education in Europe, as nothing is said about the competencies of higher education graduates.

In conclusion, then, it does not seem likely that current European developments will significantly alter the chances of the Bologna process leading to a very harmonised European Higher Education Area. The shape of the European higher education landscape from the point of view of internationally comparable outcomes of higher education study programmes (i.e. graduates' competencies) might be more affected by less official forces. For instance, the shared sets of competencies as defined in the Tuning projects might slowly develop to get the status of de facto standards. After all, ECTS, which now has the status of the way to calculate 'worth' of course units, also began as an 'innocent' pilot project. Admittedly, one does not hear the Tuning outcomes mentioned very often anymore – it is therefore also possible that this project has gone the way of many other innovations: interesting but not adopted.

Whatever will happen to the landscape of the European Higher Education Area, it won't be what we expect now! Prediction of the future will remain difficult – that is the only safe prediction.

NOTES

1   The term 'student' is used in a broad sense here, not implying only the full-time, on-campus student directly out of secondary education, but equally the more mature, part-time and/or distance-education learner.

2   A consequence of the 'transformation' argument put forward in Harvey and Knight (1996).

3   *If* the higher education institution is the correct level of posing a unitary actor, that is. Maybe the level better explaining suppliers' behaviour is the faculty/school within the higher education institution, or even the individual professor – and maybe this level is different in different higher education systems at different points in time. (Think of the different powers of American deans and German professors.)

4   Moreover, states may have reasons of social justice to intervene in higher education, for example, if they state that participation in higher education should be open to all without regard to their purchasing power (income). For our purpose of looking at states' behaviour in relation to quality of higher education in their international environment, these social arguments are irrelevant (i.e. we can take participation as given).

5   From a different theoretical perspective, namely a detailed discourse analysis, a similar shift in utility arguments was found in Dutch higher education policy since ca 1960 (Griffioen 2005).

6   The growing occupation with economics may be explainable from, for instance, the budget crisis many states faced in the 1970s and 1980s partly as a result of their ever-increasing intervention in all spheres of society since World War II. But the reasons need not detain us here; what counts is the fact that the economic discourse gained the upper hand.

7   This control function demanded its own, lower-level regulation, and – especially after some conspicuous failures in, for example, the transport and energy sectors – re-regulation by the state as well.

8   The word 'directly' often seemed to have been forgotten in the political debate, as if the economy and society as a whole did not benefit indirectly (the externalities of higher education).

9   The term 'discipline' will be used here in a broad sense, identifying any area of knowledge, whether it is a traditional discipline or an interdisciplinary field.

10   The discussion on definitions is in principle tedious since we can define terms as we like, and it reached its apogee in Ball's question: "What the Hell is Quality?" (1985) and Pirsig's reply: "It all goes *poof*!" (1984). That discussion need not be repeated here. I simply state that I take 'assessment' and 'control' to refer mainly to the static measurement of quality; assessment usually denoting the external evaluation, while control often is internal. 'Assurance' points to convincing external stakeholders of quality. 'Quality management' denotes the activities in higher education institutions to measure, maintain, and improve quality. I use 'quality audit' for the external evaluation of quality management or of 'educational quality work'. 'Accreditation' is an external assessment resulting in a summary judgment that a (previously defined) threshold of quality is reached or surpassed.

11   Which supposes that students choose studies on the basis of quality of study programmes, rather than, for example, attractiveness of location, social reasons, or the perceived prestige of higher education institutions. This is one example of policy-makers assuming individuals' utility functions to be uniform and of a certain form, or at least, paternalistically, that they *ought* to be uniform and of a certain form.

12   Usually binary, but sometimes graded, as in Hungary (Campbell and Rozsnyai 2002; Schwarz and Westerheijden 2004a).

13   But countries in the EU now also take an interest in more refined yet efficient information in the form of rankings, although officially these are left to newspapers and magazine publishers in the free market.

14   That (commercial) rankings were often criticised for their shaky methodology is not our point of interest here. A thorough example is provided in Dill and Soo (2005).

15   Yet "the scientific relevance of an economic theory of political behaviour is the higher, the more the delimitation of costs and benefits is restricted" (thesis appertaining to Elsinga 1985, my translation – DFW).

16   My argument would be based on the chance of not being found out, so that the chances of student degree fraud would seem to be higher in softer disciplines – however, in many cases in those disciplines the potential gains may be less. Taking these lines of argument in combination, the most fraud-prone type of degree might well be the MBA.

17   This also may have to do with the long term at which effects of good education become visible, confounded further by the fact that for good education to be successful, good students are also needed, which is a factor beyond the control of the individual academic whose reputation is at stake. See also the Chapter 8 by Rosa and Amaral.

18   For that reason, I once stated: "Without the expectation of real consequences, the incentives to organise quality assessment are lacking; with the expectation of real consequences, quality assessment will turn into a power game" (Westerheijden 1990: 206).

19   A term I introduced in Westerheijden and Leegwater (2003) and which became a standard name.

20   Going deeper, namely to the disciplinary level, the Socrates-funded Tuning projects also aimed to provide (West) Europe-wide agreed competencies for graduates in selected disciplines (González and Wagenaar 2003).

21   Of course it could be argued that feedback (in quality jargon: the 'act' phase of the Deming cycle) ought to be an integral part of quality assurance. Again, practice does not always conform to (normative) theory.

22   The, usually implicit, *ceteris paribus* clause is especially relevant here, as the influence of funding mechanisms is so visible that it will probably override the impact of quality assessment information

demands. The design of external quality assessment schemes is, therefore, important for the *type* (if not necessarily the *size*) of their impact.

23 Literally, academics are members of the Academy. It is used here, as often in higher education studies, to denote all who work in higher education institutions to teach and/or research, in contrast to administrative and support staff.

24 Other quantitative data mostly appeared only later in the checklists for the quality assessment scheme.

25 The same *external dynamics* were explored in connection with function and form of quality assurance schemes in Jeliazkova and Westerheijden (2002).

26 Moed (2005) makes the point that increased (international) cooperation among researchers did *not* lead to increased research output.

27 Latin-America had become independent already in the early 19th century, in days when higher education was still a very elite undertaking (in Trow's quantitative sense as much as in sociological sense). Some colonial powers held out longer, such as Portugal.

28 'Potentially', because costs associated with geographical and social or cultural distance (e.g. language) may make part-world markets more attractive, such as geographical world regions (e.g. Europe) or (former) colonial empires connected through use of the same official language (e.g. the British Commonwealth, the *Francophonie*, or the former Russian sphere of influence in Central and Eastern Europe and Central Asia).

29 In the formation of cultural capital, the positive externalities of a sizable proportion of a population's academic education need to be taken into account as well – adding to the number of generations needed for a country to acquire it.

30 Which leads to the counter-factual hypothesis that if the United Kingdom and the United States had used different names for their (in fact different) higher education degrees, countries like Germany and the Netherlands would now not have used the names 'bachelor' and 'master'.

31 Obviously, this cultural argument works best in *nation* states.

32 Non-protectionism does not correlate with national institutional structures of a certain type, for example, corporatism (Van Kersbergen, Lieshout, and Verbeek 2000: 52–53). In other words: there is no direct connection with the structure of the country's higher education system either.

33 This is not the place to delve deeper into why countries may be protectionist, but let me state as a proposition that *ceteris paribus* the more a country's economy is dependent on income from abroad, the less it will be protectionist.

34 Public higher education institutions may have other advantages, such as – in a number of cases and in the eyes of certain potential students – high reputation.

35 We touch here on a factor that I will further ignore, namely the demographic context: the Dutch population – like that in most European countries – is 'greying' and 'degreening', meaning that the birth rate is too low to maintain a stable population size in the long run, with all the negative economic effects that will have on the sustainability of the welfare state (or what is left of it).

36 In Jeliazkova and Westerheijden (2002) we had prophesied the rise of other forms of quality assurance after the Bologna 'challenge', but apparently we did not take the information gap into account sufficiently. See also Section 5 of this chapter.

37 "The EU is a supranational organisation. The establishment of its institutions ... nevertheless rests on intergovernmental bargains" (Van Kersbergen, Lieshout, and Verbeek 2000: 38).

38 The main one being the *Gravier* case (Pertek and Soverovski 1992).

39 In this case the principle of mutual recognition underlying the 1985 white chapter "Completing the Internal Market" (Van Kersbergen, Lieshout, and Verbeek 2000: 41–42).

40 In their conclusion about institutional change at the level of EU policy arenas, Van Kersbergen, Lieshout, and Lock (1999: 51) stated regarding these mechanisms: "Member states maintain policy autonomy in the sense that they can change the game, at any time, into an intergovernmentalist game. Nevertheless, policy autonomy is temporarily lost in two ways. First, many *dossiers* are left to the fight between other actors than the member states. Second, 'European' actors, such as the European Commission and the European Court, make use of the freedom given to them by the member states, and sometimes manage to change the day-to-day rules and policies". Higher education was not among their illustrations.

41 As noted before: the United Kingdom takes a hybrid position, as it is an Anglo-Saxon country and the second-largest in the international higher education trade, yet at the same time it signed the Sorbonne and Bologna Declarations (Van Vught, Van der Wende, and Westerheijden 2002: note 4).

42 Besides, and in line with the finding of international relations studies (Allison and Zelikow 1999; Waltz 1979), there may have been internal political reasons for signing international declarations: I argued above that national reform of higher education was an important driver for the Bologna Declaration (taking my examples from countries involved in the Sorbonne Declaration).

43 This should not be taken as a general tendency for the EU to weaken member states' autonomy or steering capacity. Citing nine studies in very different policy arenas, Van Kersbergen, Lieshout, and Verbeek (2000: 56) conclude that "State autonomy has been increased, decreased, and left unaffected. The EU has nullified the effect of other pressures, has reinforced them, or has failed to have any effect on them".

44 Jocularly known as Lord Falkland's Rule: When it is not necessary to make a decision, it is necessary not to make a decision (Bloch 1977).

45 In 2004, ENQA was transformed into a membership organisation, with a vetting process further detailed in the guidelines for external quality assurance agencies (European Association for Quality Assurance in Higher Education 2005), which are still biased towards (quasi) governmental agencies in the requirement of a legal base. Still, this is not an automatic link with governmental agencies anymore.

46 Note that 'the agenda' and 'the game' are not purely controlled by the government, but are also influenced by other actors, the higher education institutions in particular.

47 Categorising those who step out in the middle as bachelor degree holders rather than drop-outs certainly impacts the official indicators on the higher education systems involved. But does it also improve the quality of the higher education system? Have bachelors learned more, and will they earn more, than drop-outs after the same number of years of study? Does society benefit more from bachelors than from drop-outs?

48 On the other hand, this may be no more than what I call the 'golden age myth' that one can already find in Plato's philosophy, for such stories about ever worse graduates have been around for generation upon generation of academics, so that if there were some truth to it, it would be like the Marxian *Verelendungstheorie* and higher education graduates by now should be completely illiterate (Van het Reve 1978: 57–59) – some elder professors, not necessarily Marxists, might retort that they are, making lecturing "the throwing of false pearls to real swine" (anonymous, cited in Van het Reve 1970: 15).

49 This was our reason for emphasising other, more individualised, means of assessing quality than accreditation of degree programmes in table 1 in Jeliazkova and Westerheijden (2002).

50 This was one of the main reasons for an expert group of the CRE (Association of European Universities) (now EUA) not to propose developing such a selective register, but to remain on the level of a clearinghouse, only publishing information about external quality assessment agencies (Sursock 2000). Remarkably, the information grid proposed in European Association for Quality Assurance in Higher Education (2005) also includes non-complying quality assessment agencies – so that in fact it is the same as the clearinghouse proposed five years before. By the way, the consultative committee on quality in higher education, also proposed in the ENQA document of 2005, was equally proposed by the CRE expert group. Policy development takes time.

REFERENCES

Allison, G. and P. Zelikow. *Essence of Decision*. 2nd edn. New York: Longman, 1999.

Ball, C. *Fitness for Purpose*. Guildford: SRHE and NFER-Nelson, 1985.

Bloch, A. *Murphy's Law and Other Reasons Why Things go Wrong*. Los Angeles: Price/Stern/Sloan, 1977.

Campbell, C. and K. Rozsnyai. *Quality Assurance and the Development of Course Programmes*. Bucharest: CEPES-UNESCO, 2002.

Castells, M. *End of the Millennium, The Information Age: Economy, Society and Culture, Vol. III*. Malden/Oxford: Blackwell Publishers, 1998.

Clark, B.R. *The Higher Education System: Academic Organization in Cross-national Perspective*. Berkeley: University of California Press, 1983.

De Vree, J.K. *Foundations of Social and Political Processes: The Dynamics of Human Behaviour, Politics, and Society*. Bilthoven, NL: Prime Press, 1982.

Deming, W.E. *Out of the Crisis: Quality, Productivity and Competitive Position.* Cambridge: Cambridge University Press, 1986.

Dill, D.D. and M. Soo. "Academic Quality, League Tables, and Public Policy: A Cross-national Analysis of University Ranking Systems." *Higher Education* 49.4 (2005): 495–533.

Eggertsson, T. *Economic Behavior and Institutions.* Cambridge: Cambridge University Press, 1990.

Elsinga, E. *Politieke participatie in Nederland.* Amsterdam: CT Press, 1985.

Enders, J. "Governing the Academic Commons: About Blurring Boundaries, Blistering Organisations, and Growing Demands." Trans. J. File. Enschede: University of Twente, 2002.

European Association for Quality Assurance in Higher Education. *Standards and Guidelines for Quality Assurance in the European Higher Education Area.* Helsinki: European Association for Quality Assurance in Higher Education, 2005.

Frederiks, M.M.H., D.F. Westerheijden, and P.J.M. Weusthof. "Effects of Quality Assessment in Dutch Higher Education." *European Journal of Education* 29.2 (1994): 181–199.

González, J. and R. Wagenaar (eds). *Tuning Educational Structures in Europe. Final Report Phase One.* Bilbao, Groningen: University of Deusto, University of Groningen, 2003.

Griffioen, D. *Kwaliteit vormt opleidingen: Een discursieve analyse van vormende normen binnen het Nederlandse universitaire kwaliteitssysteem tussen 1987 en 1999.* Amsterdam: Universiteit van Amsterdam, 2005.

Harvey, L. and D. Green. "Defining Quality." *Assessment & Evaluation in Higher Education* 18.1 (1993): 9–34.

Harvey, L. and P.T. Knight. *Transforming Higher Education.* Buckingham: SRHE and Open University Press, 1996.

Jeliazkova, M. and D.F. Westerheijden. "Systemic Adaptation to a Changing Environment: Towards a Next Generation of Quality Assurance Models." *Higher Education,* 44.3/4 (2002): 433–448.

Jenniskens, I.G.M. *Governmental Steering and Curriculum Innovation: A Comparative Study of the Relationship Between Governmental Steering Instruments and Innovations in Higher Education Curricula.* Maarssen: Elsevier/De Tijdstroom, 1997.

Latour, B. and S. Woolgar. *Laboratory Life.* Beverly Hills: Sage, 1979.

Lieshout, R.H. "Without Making Elaborate Calculations for the Future." PhD Thesis, Enschede: Technische Hogeschool Twente, 1984.

McNay, I. "The Impact of the 1992 Research Assessment Exercise in English Universities." *Higher Education Review* 29.2 (1997): 34–43.

McNay, I. "The Paradoxes of Research Assessment and Funding." In Henkel, M. and B. Little (eds). *Changing Relationships Between Higher Education and the State.* London: Jessica Kingsley, 1999, 191–203.

Moed, H.F. *Citation Analysis in Research Evaluation.* Dordrecht: Springer, 2005.

Neave, G. "Homogenization, Integration and Convergence: The Cheshire Cats of Higher Education Analysis." In Meek, V.L., L. Goedegebuure, O. Kivinen, and R. Rinne (eds). *The Mockers and Mocked: Comparative Perspectives on Differentiation, Convergence and Diversity in Higher Education.* Oxford: Pergamon, 1995, 26–41.

Nozick, R. *Anarchy, State, and Utopia.* New York: Basic Books, 1974.

Pertek, J. and M. Soverovski (eds). *EC Competences and Programmes Within the Field of Education/Compétences et programmes communautaires en matière d'éducation.* Maastricht: European Institute of Public Administration, 1992.

Pirsig, R.M. *Zen and the Art of Motorcycle Maintenance.* New York: Bantam Books, 1984.

Plato. *The Republic.* Harmondsworth: Penguin, 1974.

QANU. *QANU-kader: Gids voor de externe kwaliteitsbeoordeling van wetenschappelijke bachelor – en masteropleidingen ten behoeve van accreditatie, Versie 3.1, Januari 2004 – Augustus 2005.* Utrecht: Quality Assurance Netherlands Universities (QANU), 2004.

Reichert, S. and C. Tauch. "Trends in Learning Structures in European Higher Education III – Bologna Four Years After: Steps Towards Sustainable Reform of Higher Education in Europe." First draft. Graz: European University Association, European Commission, 2003.

Reichert, S. and C. Tauch. *Trends IV: European Universities Implementing Bologna.* s.l. Brussels: European University Association, 2005.

Schwarz, S. and D.F. Westerheijden (eds). *Accreditation and Evaluation in the European Higher Education Area.* Dordrecht: Kluwer Academic Publishers, 2004a.

Schwarz, S. and D.F. Westerheijden. "Accreditation in the Framework of Evaluation Activities: A Comparative Study in the European Higher Education Area." In Schwarz, S. and D.F. Westerheijden (eds). *Accreditation and Evaluation in the European Higher Education Area*. Dordrecht: Kluwer Academic Publishers, 2004b, 1–41.

Sursock, A. *Towards Accreditation Schemes for Higher Education in Europe?* London: Centre for Higher Education Research and Information, Open University, 2000.

Välimaa, J. and D.F. Westerheijden. "Two Discourses: Researchers and Policy-making in Higher Education." *Higher Education* 29.4 (1995): 385–403.

Van der Wende, M. and D.F. Westerheijden. "Degrees of Trust or Trust of Degrees? Quality Assurance and Recognition." In File, J. and L.C.J. Goedegebuure (eds). *Real-Time Systems: Reflections on Higher Education in the Czech Republic, Hungary, Poland and Slovenia*. Enschede, Brno: CHEPS, Brno University of Technology, 2003, 177–206.

Van het Reve, K. *Marius wil niet in Joegoslavië wonen (Marius Does Not Want To Live in Yugoslavia)*. Amsterdam: Van Oorschot, 1970.

Van het Reve, K. *Uren met Henk Broekhuis (Hours with Henk Broekhuis)*. Amsterdam: Van Oorschot, 1978.

Van Kersbergen, K., R.H. Lieshout, and G. Lock (eds). *Expansion and Fragmentation: Internationalization, Political Change and the Transformation of the Nation State*. Amsterdam: Amsterdam University Press, 1999.

Van Kersbergen, K., R.H. Lieshout, and B. Verbeek. "Institutional Change in the Emerging European Polity." In Van Heffen, O., W.J.M. Kickert, and J.J.A. Thomassen (eds). *Governance in Modern Society: Effects, Change and Formation of Government Institutions*. Dordrecht, Boston, London: Kluwer Academic Publishers, 2000, 35–60.

Van Vught, F.A., M.C. van der Wende, and D.F. Westerheijden. "Globalization and Internationalization: Policy Agendas Compared." In Fulton, O. and J. Enders (eds). *Higher Education in a Globalizing World. International Trends and Mutual Observations*. Dordrecht: Kluwer, 2002, 103–120.

Van Vught, F.A. and D.F. Westerheijden. *Quality Management and Quality Assurance in European Higher Education: Methods and Mechanisms*. Luxembourg: Office for Official Publications of the Commission of the European Communities, 1993.

Vroeijenstijn, A.I. *Improvement and Accountability: Navigating Between Scylla and Charybdis: Guide for External Quality Assessment in Higher Education*. London: Jessica Kingsley, 1995.

Waltz, K.N. *Theory of International Politics*. Reading, MA: Addison-Wesley, 1979.

Westerheijden, D.F. *Schuiven in de Oosterschelde: Besluitvorming rond de Oosterschelde 1973–1976*. Enschede: Universiteit Twente, Faculteit Bestuurskunde, 1988.

Westerheijden, D.F. "Peers, Performance, and Power: Quality Assessment in the Netherlands." In Goedegebuure, L.C.J., P.A.M. Maassen, and D.F. Westerheijden (eds). *Peer Review and Performance Indicators: Quality Assessment in British and Dutch Higher Education*. Utrecht: Lemma, 1990, 183–207.

Westerheijden, D.F. "Promises, Problems and Pitfalls of Peer Review: The Use of Peer Review in External Quality Assessment in Higher Education." In Banta, T.W. (ed.). *Proceedings of the Third International Conference on Assessing Quality in Higher Education*. Knoxville, TN: University of Tennessee, 1991, 130–142.

Westerheijden, D.F. "A Solid Base for Decisions: Use of the VSNU Research Evaluations in Dutch Universities." *Higher Education* 33.4 (1997): 397–413.

Westerheijden, D.F. and M. Leegwater (eds). *Working on the European Dimension of Quality: Report of the Conference on Quality Assurance in Higher Education as Part of the Bologna Process*. Amsterdam, 12–13 March, 2002. Zoetermeer: Ministerie van Onderwijs, Cultuur en Wetenschappen, 2003.

Weusthof, P.J.M. and M.M.H. Frederiks. "De functies van het stelsel van kwaliteitszorg heroverwogen." *Tijdschrift voor Hoger Onderwijs* 15 (1997): 318–338.

PART II: TRANSLATION

BJØRN STENSAKER

QUALITY AS FASHION: EXPLORING THE TRANSLATION OF A MANAGEMENT IDEA INTO HIGHER EDUCATION

1. INTRODUCTION

Stimulated through supranational and international organisations such as the EU and the OECD, picked up and implemented by national governments in various parts of the world, and with an array of new organisations supporting quality both internationally (e.g. the European Foundation for Management Development) and nationally (e.g. intermediate evaluation agencies), the concept of quality has been one of the most dominating and influential 'meta-ideas' globally over the last 20 years, invading both the private and the public sector (Micklethwait and Wooldridge 1996; see also Czarniawska and Sevón 1996). In the mid-1990s, US observers Cameron and Whetten (1996: 265) even argued that the concept of quality had actually replaced effectiveness as the central organisation-level variable in higher education:

> A fundamental shift has occurred recently in the literature of higher education. This shift has been more gradual and less dramatic than it has been in the broader organisational studies literature, but it has been significant nevertheless. It is a shift away from considerations of the construct of effectiveness to describe organisational performance in institutions of higher education and toward considerations of the construct of quality. Quality has begun to replace effectiveness as a central organisation-level variable in higher education. With a few noticeable exceptions, effectiveness has largely been abandoned and quality has become the pre-eminent construct.

This apparent success of the quality concept makes it a very interesting study object for researchers of higher education, not least due to the fact that quality seems to have so many facets. Reeves and Bednar (1994: 419) have, for example, listed numerous ways quality has been perceived. According to them, quality has been defined as value, conformance to specifications, conformance to requirements, fitness for use, loss avoidance, or meeting and/or exceeding customer expectations. An empirical study revealed the same discrepancy when it comes to how the concept of quality was perceived by different stakeholders in higher education (Harvey and Green 1993: 11). Harvey and Green found that stakeholders' views on quality could be categorised according to five broad definitions: quality as exceptional, quality as perfection, quality as fitness for purpose, quality as value for money, and quality as transformation.

99

D.F. Westerheijden et al. (eds.), Quality Assurance in Higher Education: Trends in Regulation,
Translation and Transformation, 99–118.
© 2007 *Springer.*

The diversity concerning definitions of quality has also been echoed by a vast number of organisational manifestations of quality. In higher education, organisational practices related to quality can be found in various types of national quality assurance schemes (accreditations, evaluations, audits and assessments) (see e.g. Frazer 1997), but also within higher education institutions in the form of institutional quality assurance systems where evaluation systems, information systems, and management systems are combined in various ways.

In one of the earliest classifications of the different approaches to quality assurance, Dill (1992) distinguished between three forms: the reputational approach, the student outcome approach, and the total quality (management) approach. The first approach uses the peer review mechanism to assess (and sometimes rate) the quality of programmes and institutions. The second approach is based on measurement of outcome indicators of student achievements both when attending higher education, and also afterwards (career, earnings, etc.). The third approach stresses broad participation, client orientation, organisational learning, and coordination.

However, even if these practices are implemented at different levels and in different forms, they have, over time, increasingly been linked to each other. For example, in several countries such as Australia, Sweden, and Norway, national evaluations in the form of an audit are used as a means to control or improve institutional quality assurance systems, and where the reputational approach is more or less combined with student outcome indicators. And there are also examples that show how institutions design their own (TQM-based) quality assurance system to fit external evaluations (see e.g. Schaik 1996). Hence, to argue for the existence of a clearly distinguished approach or a particular 'quality assurance concept' is rather difficult given the magnitude of existing systems, routines, and templates borrowing the quality label (cf. Birnbaum 2000: 193; see also Harvey and Askling 2003: 76–79). This lack of agreement, both concerning definitions and organisational practices, draws attention to the symbolic dimension of quality, and the fact that, although it is a rather poorly defined and loose concept, it has still been a very fashionable one, attracting a lot of interest.

This chapter is an exploration of why quality has been such a success as an idea in higher education during the last decades, with a special focus on how the concept has been translated into higher education. Using recent research on organisational fashion and the spread of management ideas as a starting point, the objective of this chapter is to improve our understanding of the process related to the diffusion of management ideas in higher education.[1] This is an interesting area to study for several reasons. First, it can shed some light on the vulnerability of the sector, or, put more positively, the potential higher education has for adapting to environmental and societal expectations. Second, since management ideas these days are often diffused as part of governmental reforms in higher education, the chapter may subsequently shed some light on the processes related to policy implementation in higher education.

That being said, one should, of course, acknowledge the difficulties associated with studying the diffusion of quality in higher education. Several points are worth mentioning here. First, if quality is a loosely defined concept with various organisational approaches associated with it, it is hard to set the limits on what should be included or excluded from the study – what exactly is being spread? The pragmatic solution has been to be quite open and include approaches in the chapter, usually labelled as various forms of quality assurance, at both the national and institutional level, and both mandatory and voluntary initiated schemes. Second, since quality is presumed to have been spread globally one also faces the need for some geographical limitation. In this study, the OECD area is the one selected and explored in more detail. Third, since this is a study of the diffusion process, and the translation of the idea of quality in higher education, the study says little about the actual effects of any implemented measures. Fourth, the evidence collected and analysed is based on available *written* material extracted from articles, reports, and books. Although one can imagine that management fads and fashions can be spread in ways other than through the written word there is a lack of alternative and reliable data sources.

2. FASHION AND MANAGEMENT IDEAS IN HIGHER EDUCATION

Fads and fashions have in general not been considered as forces with particularly powerful influence on higher education. Numerous students of higher education rather have shown that higher education organisations are reluctant, or experience difficulties, when trying to adapt to externally initiated reforms and management fashions (March and Olsen 1976; Cerych and Sabatier 1986). Strong values, norms, and cultures within higher education institutions are often highlighted as significant factors for this inertia (Clark 1970, 1983).

However, there also exists a considerable and rather convincing literature pointing to the importance of external forces and government and management fads and fashions in spreading and implementing innovations (Brunsson 1989; Abrahamson 1991, 1996; Czarniawska and Joerges 1996). Recently, there has also been renewed interest in fads and fashions within higher education (Stensaker 1998; Ewell 1999; Birnbaum and Deshotels 1999), not least when it comes to how to live and cope with such management ideas (Birnbaum 2000; Vazzana, Elfrink, and Bachmann 2000).

One can argue that it is important to study fads and fashions, especially since they carry a potential to harm organisations by forcing them to adopt technically inefficient or useless innovations, or because one might overlook local ideas that had the potential to improve the performance of the adapting organisation (Abrahamson 1991: 588–589). On the other hand, management fads and fashions can also have a positive side, changing organisations to be more innovative, quality-minded, and efficient, or at least creating an image of this to the society at large (Abrahamson 1991: 608). Fads and fashions can, in addition, be of relevance for organisations internally by providing prisms through which universities and colleges can examine their own practices and routines from new perspectives (Ewell 1999).

2.1. Quality – Change or Continuation in Management Ideas?

So, what is 'new' or 'different' with the quality concept? What are the distinctive characteristics and the core ideas of quality as a management idea? At first sight, quality is an idea that can be distinguished from other management ideas quite easily. If we, for example, compare the idea of management by objectives with the quality concept, the obvious difference is that while quality, according to the classic definitions, is about optimising the processes of production, management by objectives is focused on setting the right goals. While the basic idea associated with quality is to establish the right regulations and routines, the basic idea of the latter concept is to not interfere in how goals are achieved (Brunsson 2001: 3).

If we compare quality with other current management ideas, equally substantial differences also seem to appear:

> The three most popular public-sector fads – downsizing, re-engineering and total quality management – are, on many points of substance, mutually incompatible. Downsizing argues that workers are expendable; TQM sees them as an invaluable resource. Re-engineering depends on ripping up the organisation and starting again; TQM is a doctrine of continuous, incremental improvement. (Micklethwait and Wooldridge 1996: 330)

Given the different nature of these management ideas, not least related to the quality concept (see e.g. Grant, Shani, and Krishnan 1994), could one still question whether 'quality' or, rather, the assumptions behind this and the other concepts are really as new as often claimed (Dill 1992: 42; Harvey 1995: 133)? Critical observers on the history of management theory have, for example, claimed that, in general, there only exist a small number of management ideas that are constantly reproduced over time (Barley and Kunda 1992; Huczynski 1993).

Following Barley and Kunda (1992) in that the evolutionary character of management ideas may be questioned, one could argue that the whole quality panacea is really a mix between the classic scientific management ideas (cf. Taylor 1911) and the human relation school of thought (cf. Mayo 1933). Pollitt and Bouckaert (1995: 16) argue in a similar way that in principle there are only two major theoretical perspectives on quality: an output-oriented view including definitions such as value for money, consumer satisfaction, zero errors, and vice versa (i.e. 'scientific management'), and a process-oriented view where quality is seen as transformative (i.e. the 'human relations school').[2]

For Pollitt (1993: 189), it is the use of statistical methods and quantitative measuring together with a control-oriented intention that makes the quality concept into some sort of 'Neo-Taylorism'. Tuckman (1994: 731) also claims that an output-oriented definition of quality can be linked to the political 'New Right' movement in Western societies in the late 1980s and early 1990s, with its emphasis on deregulation of public services, greater managerial discretion, the introduction of market and quasi-market mechanisms, and its focus on consumer needs.[3] In this situation:

> Quality itself becomes an icon, a selling point for an increasing number of goods and services. The customer becomes deified, surveyed to find their demand and wishes. Meeting customers' requirement is the definition of quality offered and employed. (Tuckman 1994: 742)

Those who see quality as transformative can be said to have initiated a quite different perspective, arguing that emphasis should be taken away from a mere customer, product, or managerial role, towards an improvement-oriented approach, focusing more on those who can actually make a difference – teachers and students of higher education (see e.g. Barnett 1992; Dill 1995; Harvey 1995; Gosling and D'Andrea 2001). Even if both perspectives acknowledge the need for change in higher education, the difference between the perspectives becomes clear in the views of the latter who favour a process that:

> require[s] re-weaving the collegial fabric of academic communities, the collective mechanism by which faculty members control and improve the quality of academic programmes and research. (Dill 1995: 107)

This way of understanding the quality concept can rather easily be linked to the human relations school, underlining a softer approach for changing higher education organisations (Holmes and McElwee 1995). Quality is, in other words, an idea that can be related to very different meanings. This conclusion also matches a suggestion from Brunsson (2001: 3) who states that the sustainability and diffusion of a fad or a fashion depend on the openness for including other ideas in the original concept, hence its symbolic ability to embrace and incorporate ideas that might even be contradicting and competing with the original one. Based on this insight, one could easily agree with Van Vught (1996: 187) that "from an epistemological point of view, words and definitions (relating to quality) are not very important: words can be given whatever meaning is thought to be appropriate". Hence, the idea of quality seems to be covered by the philosopher Wittgenstein's argument that a term sometimes is used extensively to preclude formulating a definition capable of conveying the full range of the term's meaning. This use, according to Wittgenstein, comprises a family of meanings in the sense that they are united "by a complicated network of similarities overlapping and criss-crossing; sometimes similarities of a general nature; in some cases, similarities in detail" (cited in Wagner 1989: 7). However, the question still remains whether every meaning and every translation of quality are possible and acceptable. This leads us to how quality has been translated into higher education, and the question of whether it is possible to identify some general characteristics attached to the successful diffusion of fads and fashions in higher education.

2.2. Management Fashion – Some Theoretical Reflections

The classic explanation for adapting management fads and fashions is that they are means of legitimation (Meyer and Rowan 1977).[4] By adapting to management fashion, organisations legitimise themselves externally by showing how well they reflect major phenomena in society (Brunsson 1989; Czarniawska and Joerges 1996), although such adaptation may just be a symbolic process signalling good intentions (Meyer 1979) and the willingness to acknowledge important social values and ideas (Feldman and March 1981). Thus, such management ideas could be seen as a 'sign of the times', concepts and templates transmitted from the larger national and international society, and as such could be considered part of the 'fad and fashion' market which, sometimes, is a mandatory requirement as part of governmental reforms, in other instances, ideas voluntary adapted by higher education institutions (cf. Abrahamson 1991, 1996).[5]

One can distinguish between two perspectives as to how this transmission of ideas occurs. The first perspective sees the idea as something original that is diffused throughout a given sector without the original idea being changed (cf. Meyer and Rowan 1977). Adapting organisations then imitate those organisations that have already implemented the idea in question. The second perspective sees the idea as a more abstract entity more difficult to 'imitate', alternatively as a result of powerful and imaginative adapting organisations (or organisational sectors) changing the idea to fit their characteristics and needs. Hence, the spread of the idea happens as a result of translation where the adapting organisations provide their own meaning to what they perceive is the core in the idea (Czarniawska and Joerges 1996; Czarniawska and Sevón 1996). The latter perspective also points to the fact that a given management idea may look very different, or be interpreted very differently depending on the level of analyses, and the context surrounding the adaptation (Newton 1999). For our purpose, separating diffusion and translation is nevertheless most important in the sense that it signals the resistance or, alternatively, the responsiveness of the higher education sector to the concept of quality.

However, even if the distinction between diffusion and translation is important, it focuses attention away from the management idea and the fact that certain characteristics related to a given idea may condition the spread of the idea. Brunsson (2001: 2) has, for example, argued that fashions are particularly strong when people do not perceive them as fashion, but as the natural, obvious thing to do, as taken-for-granted assumptions. Echoing reflections by the political scientist, Christopher Hood, one might say that "shifts in what counts as received ideas in public management works through a process of fashion and persuasion, not through proofs couched in a strict deductive logic, controlled experiments, or even systematic analysis of available cases" (Hood 1998: 172). This is not to say that policy, structures, hierarchies, and institutions are unimportant. Rather, it is an acknowledgment of the fact that symbols (fads and fashion) may sometimes win out over substance.

To be regarded as 'modern' and 'fashionable', the ideas that are transmitted to organisations must have certain attributes (Meyer 1996). In trying to develop a theory of how management ideas are spread and implemented, Abrahamson (1996: 255) has proposed that such a theory should pay attention to the symbolic character of these ideas. Following this assumption, Meyer (1996: 247) has further proposed that the "modern system gives great cultural credence to abstract and universalistic ideas of a rationalistic sort". Credence both individuals and organisations seek to obtain. Hence, because organisations are viewed as entities that should produce services rationally, efficiently, and effectively, the ideas that guide organisational action must therefore also be *rationalistic* (Meyer 1996: 250). In summing up some of these ideas, Røvik (1998: 109–110) has proposed that there are seven central characteristics related to a successful diffusion of management ideas. They need to be:

- *socially authorised*, that is, that the idea is supported and backed by powerful and influential stakeholders within a sector or within the adopting organisation;
- *theorised*, that is, that the idea is launched as a universal means to a universal problem. This means that the concept must have the image of functioning independently of institutional or organisational characteristics such as size, culture, technology, sector etc. (cf. also Meyer 1996: 250). The notion of an idea being theorised does not mean, however, that the idea must be very advanced, only that it can be generalised, and abstracted from practice;
- *productivised*, that is, that the idea is sold as a commodity to be purchased in a market. It follows from this assumption that the idea must be 'objectified' – transformed from an idea into an object in the form of routines, actions, handbooks, etc. (cf. Czarniawska and Joerges 1996: 32). Due to the societal belief that there must be established organisational structures if certain ends are to be met, a basic way of objectifying an idea is to propose more organisations and more organisational activities (Meyer 1996: 251);
- *progressive*, that is, that the idea is distinguished from other management ideas as something better or improved (cf. also Abrahamson 1996: 117);
- *harmonised*, that is, that the idea is not causing disapproval from certain stakeholders, or favouring some people over others;
- *dramatised*, that is, that the idea is supported by dramatic narratives concerning how successful some organisations have been when implementing the idea (cf. also Czarniawska 1997);
- *individualised*, that is, that the idea is edited in a way that visualises it as an attractive opportunity for the individual (and for the organisation) (cf. Sahlin-Andersson 1996: 82).

Do these characteristics match how quality has been diffused and spread in higher education? In Section 3, some empirical evidence is analysed concerning the applicability of these characteristics for higher education.

3. THE DIFFUSION OF QUALITY IN HIGHER EDUCATION – SOME EMPIRICAL EVIDENCE ON THE PROCESS OF TRANSLATION

3.1. The Social Authorisation of Quality

Due to the nature of higher education, it is often expected that social authorisation of new ideas needs to take place from within: where the academics themselves have the key role (Clark 1983). When looking into the arena for communication between academics – academic journals – it is, however, difficult to find much enthusiastic embracing, from academics, of the idea of quality assurance during the last 15 to 20 years. In most cases, one finds contributions commenting upon or analysing governmental initiatives in the quality assurance area, but scepticism and critical analysis seem more dominating than the pure positive voices. In particular, many contributions emphasised that the context of the governmental quality assurance initiatives – often accompanied by budget decline, increased reporting, and accountability claims – did not match the government rhetoric in the quality area (see e.g. Välimaa 1994; Newton 2000).

A somewhat different picture appears if one studies articles considering the possibility for higher education institutions to voluntarily adapt various quality assurance procedures. In the early 1990s, reports from the United States indicated that the concept of TQM was spreading rapidly in higher education, and that some institutions saw TQM as an important tool for improvement (Marchese 1991; Coate 1993). Also in Europe one could find positive judgments concerning the potential of TQM. For example, one commentator argued that TQM was "not panacea, nor placebo, but certainly [had] potential" (Williams 1993: 236) to improve administrative and academic structures and the functioning of higher education. Perhaps Middlehurst (1992) went furthest on the positive side when she stated that 'quality' actually could be 'the' organising principle in higher education. But Middlehurst also stressed that quality should be an intrinsic and not an extrinsic value of higher education thus emphasising the traditional values and characteristics of higher education.

Hence, within the OECD area, it is rather from governmental documents and reports on future challenges for higher education that attempts to socially authorise quality can be seen to have been strongest. This interest can be witnessed by just looking into the titles of governmental reports and white and green papers on higher education from the last 20 years where the keyword 'quality' often accompanied by the equally symbolic word 'freedom' frequently appeared.[6] However, in higher education systems where the state has a significant role, such attempts at social authorisation should not be underestimated. Kogan (2005: 62) has shown, for example, with the United Kingdom as a case, how heroic ministers can be more influential than academic elites in important policy issues. From Norway one can also find examples of how government and academic elites found 'common ground' in how to interpret and define quality (Stensaker 1998: 136). Governmental initiatives to establish intermediate bodies aiming at controlling or promoting quality through evaluation and accountability-related measures are also an important element in this picture. The rise of the numerous evaluation and quality assurance agencies around the world is perhaps more than anything a development that has contributed to 'institutionalise' quality assurance issues on the higher education agenda. The existence of special organisations with the sole purpose of assuring, controlling or improving quality signals that this is an important issue (cf. Brunsson 2001).

3.2. Theorising Quality

The background of the quality concept, with its origins stemming from business and industry, has in the past triggered much discussion within academe as to whether the concept was universal enough to be applicable also in higher education (Bensimon 1995; Owlia and Aspinwall 1996). This debate focused especially on the issue as to whether higher education institutions could be run in a similar way as for-profit private companies, addressing the TQM approach in particular (cf. Dill 1992). Considering the TQM concept, a study from the United Kingdom in the early 1990s suggested, for example, that this was not the case. Chaston (1994) argued that due to important characteristics of higher education institutions, that is, loose coupling and weak coordination, attempts to implement TQM in these organisations would probably fail (see also similar reviews from Dill 1992; Harvey 1995). More positive claims came from both the US and European scenes. In the United States, Seymour (1993) stated that introducing TQM in higher education could be relevant for several purposes including stimulating competition, increasing cost awareness, answering accountability claims, and providing better service. Another positive review of the TQM concept was done by Fry (1995: 62–63, 73) who compared the concepts of ISO 9000, TQM, and procedures related to quality audits and quality assessments in the United Kingdom. Fry argued that only the TQM concept placed strong emphasis on staff development, personal responsibility, and organisational improvement, and that the rest of the concepts were more oriented towards external accountability claims.

However, attempts to theorise quality assurance have not been dominated by the adaptation of more specific quality models from other sectors into higher education even if one can identify a number of such attempts. Within higher education one can witness rather an interest in trying to theorise quality assurance according to the specific characteristics of the sector (cf. Barnett 1992; Harvey and Green 1993; Van Vught and Westerheijden 1994; Harvey 1995). Although some attempts have been made to argue for the existence of 'academic standards' (Ashworth and Harvey 1994), the dominating definition of the concept has been that quality is fitness for purpose (Ball 1985) emphasising the multi-dimensionality and subjective dimensions of the concept. In other words, quality equates with flexibility. As such, this definition fits well with the idea that a well-spread management idea should be launched as a universal instrument, however, without actually identifying the universal problem quality is meant to solve.

The consequence of this definition is that the universal instrument (quality) can then be related not only to one problem, but to numerous problems. Empirical research by Frazer (1997) and Brennan and Shah (2000: 31–32) has accordingly shown how national quality assurance systems have covered a very broad range of purposes, from informing funding decisions to assigning institutional status, supporting mobility of students, or supporting the transfer of authority between the state and higher education institutions, to mention a few. A Nordic study has also illustrated how institutional quality assurance initiatives have been applied in equally numerous ways, for example, to instigate cultural changes, to smooth downsizing operations, or to create new or improved links between higher education and industry (Fahlén et al. 2000). Along the same line, Brennan and Shah (2000: 131–132) state that institutional quality assurance initiatives often deal with problems related to efficiency and effectiveness, or to change or develop institutional strategy and mission. The general nature and general applicability of quality assurance in higher education have in addition been advocated in several of the most influential 'handbooks' on this topic during the last decades (Kells 1992; Vroeijenstijn 1995). However, due to the dominating 'fitness for purpose' definition and the pragmatic organisational practices related to this definition, the need for more advanced theoretical attempts to develop the quality concept seems to have been precluded.

3.3. The Making of Quality into a Product

The latter contributions from Kells (1992) and Vroeijenstijn (1995) have to a great extent also been central to the process of making quality assurance into a product in higher education. Even if it is difficult to evaluate the impact of these and related contributions addressing the quality assurance issue either from the academic side (see e.g. Kells 1988; Dill 1992; Kells and Nilsson 1995; Dill 2000) or from government or various forms of intermediate bodies (see e.g. Kells and Stenquist 1995; HEQC 1996), they should not be underestimated as sources of inspiration in establishing routines, actions, and systems at the institutional level.

At the national level and within (Western) Europe, EU initiatives in the early 1990s to stimulate the establishment of national systems for quality assurance, and to test the methodological foundations related to external quality assurance, are probably the most significant events in transforming the idea of quality assurance into a product in higher education (Thune and Staropoli 1997). Partly based on the outcome of this project, Van Vught and Westerheijden (1994) argued that a 'general model' of external quality assurance was emerging in Europe in the early 1990s with four elements usually considered as typical elements in the evaluation procedures set up on the national level: a national coordinating body that administered the evaluations conducted, an institutional self-evaluation phase, an external evaluation, and the production of a report. Of course, as Brennan (1999: 221) has noticed, this so-called general model of quality assurance may obscure as much as it reveals about what really goes on in these processes. The political context, the power distribution in different higher education systems, methodological differences, and intended outcomes of the evaluation processes are important sources of differentiation. Still, as a conceptual model – objectifying how external quality assurance should be conducted – this general model has been extremely influential in various European countries (Frazer 1997). And even with new purposes added to external quality assurance, i.e. accreditation, these general routines involving self-evaluation and peer review in various forms are still very visible parts of most existing external quality assurance schemes in Europe (Schwarz and Westerheijden 2004).

3.4. The Progressive Aspects of Quality

If quality, as suggested earlier, could be considered to be just a variant of classic management ideas, the question then arises as to how quality has been able to acquire status as something 'new' and 'progressive' compared to other, and often competing, management ideas. An immediate answer when looking into key contributions on this issue during the last decades is that quality by many observers has not been seen as something 'new' but rather as a traditional and intrinsic dimension in higher education at least as old as the modern university itself (Neave 1994: 116). Considering the methods by which quality has been scrutinised also in the newer organisational procedures related to quality, i.e. by using peer review, it is also hard to immediately spot any major differences.[7]

If one takes the new organisational practices related to quality assurance in higher education, both on the national and institutional level, as a starting point, the picture is again not very affirmative. A substantial number of contributions have over the years pointed to the dangers and side effects of quality assurance, highlighting the risk of increased bureaucratisation, centralisation, and 'marketisation' of higher education as not very desirable but likely outcomes of such procedures (Neave 1988; Westerheijden 1999; Stensaker 2003).

Still, a study comparing how academics received a new management-by-objectives based planning system and an external quality assurance system in Norway in the early 1990s illustrated that the quality assurance system was perceived differently from the 'competing' management idea, that is, a new planning system (Stensaker 1998). A likely explanation for this may be related to the perceived progressive character of the quality assurance system. Both the planning system and the quality assurance system were mandatory requirements initiated by the Ministry of Education. Furthermore, both reforms stemmed from management ideas in industry and business, both reforms had the intention of improving the performance of public organisations, and both reforms can also be classified as rationally based reform fashions. Regardless of these similarities, the planning system was still perceived as old-fashioned, adapted to administrative needs compared to the quality assurance system which was seen as more 'academic', hence more relevant to the academic staff. Nevertheless, the academic staff within the higher education institutions admitted in retrospect that there were more administrative and organisational similarities in the effects of the two systems than those given by the image of them (Stensaker 1998: 135). In other words, the difference between the two reforms can mostly be noted during their translation into the sector.

Hence, it is possible to argue that management 'fashions' and strong pressure from external agencies alone are not enough for the successful diffusion of new ideas in higher education. The findings rather support studies showing how important the interplay between fashion and (institutional) culture is for the diffusion of ideas (cf. Brunsson 2001). Stensaker's (1998) study showed that it is not enough for new ideas to have a general image of rationality and progressiveness, but that these two factors must match the specific interpretations of 'rationality' and 'progress' that exist in the adapting organisations. Other contributions have assessed various quality assurance approaches in similar ways. Dill (1992: 142) argued, for example, that TQM approaches can be seen as being compatible but also contesting the culture of higher education, advocating a more nuanced view on the pure progressive dimensions of this approach.

3.5. Harmonising Quality

The question of whether quality assurance could change the existing power balance, thus creating tensions and increased conflict in higher education, has been one of the key issues in the debates surrounding quality during the latter decades (Harvey and Knight 1996; Brennan and Shah 2000). More than anything this tension has appeared through the debates concerning how to balance improvement and accountability in quality assurance. The well-known background for this debate was the policy initiatives concerning quality assurance in the United Kingdom in the late 1980s and early 1990s, and the fear related to how governmental initiatives could dramatically change UK higher education (Harvey and Knight 1996; Henkel 2000).

In commenting upon this dilemma, Van Vught (1994) and others (e.g. Thune 1996) suggested that national quality assessment systems should balance the internal and external needs of the higher education system, both to create an improvement-oriented climate within universities and colleges, and to gain legitimacy from actors outside higher education. The argument was that quality assurance initiatives targeted exclusively at accountability would give external stakeholders too much power and influence. A procedure solely directed at internal improvement would, on the contrary, lack the impetus towards stimulating such processes. Hence, a tilt to either side could, according to Van Vught (1994), result in a risky overestimation of the specific functions and practices of higher education institutions.

However, this suggestion could also be interpreted – regardless of the original intention behind it – as a way to harmonise quality and dampen discontent and potential conflict within the sector (see e.g. Maassen 1998), and can be seen as one of the most important reasons for why the idea of balancing improvement and accountability in quality assurance gained so much ground during the 1990s, and is still the dominating paradigm as to how quality assurance systems should be designed. Saarinen (2005) has recently argued that this mode of harmony is changing – at least in Finland – as a result of the Bologna process, and the renewed interest in accreditation, i.e. the accountability side of external quality assurance. Still, even if various accreditation schemes can be seen as being tilted towards the accountability side, a recent study has indicated that many current accreditation schemes in practice try to combine accountability with improvement-oriented activities and organisational learning (Stensaker and Harvey 2006). In other words, even current quality assurance practices seem adjusted to this balance.

3.6. Dramatising Quality

Management fads and fashions are usually accompanied by a number of narratives – anecdotal but widely known – about how successful some organisations have been when implementing a particular management idea (Micklethwait and Wooldridge 1996; Birnbaum 2000). These dramas are usually also advocating quite radical change: where one has to break with the past to start a bright new future (Micklethwait and Wooldridge 1996). In higher education, such stories are not so common when focusing on quality assurance. On the contrary, governmental rhetoric concerning the quality in higher education has rather emphasised a perceived 'crisis' in higher education, and as such has pointed to the general lack of quality in the sector (Birnbaum and Shushok 2001). Hence, what we have seen is in most cases a negative dramatisation of quality.[8]

Some, quite positive, 'advertisements' can be identified from the United States (see e.g. Seymour 1992; 1993), and the United Kingdom (see e.g. Ellis 1993), but the overall picture is that the wider spread of 'dramas and sagas' related to quality are almost absent.

Even in the various 'handbooks' within the area the promises are few, and measures are adjusted to the sector. For example, in the guide *Evaluation for Quality Assurance and Improvement*, Kells and Nilsson (1995: 11) suggest that the basic characteristics of an institutional scheme for quality development are, amongst others, that "the scheme should be rooted in the nature of the institution in question" and that "the scheme must produce an honest and reality-based view and be responsibly transparent to the public and potential clients without damaging the institution in the process". In other words, what is proposed is not very dramatic and different from everyday practice; the argument is that institutional characteristics and culture should be emphasised and protected – advice often echoed in similar handbooks and guides in the area (see e.g. Kells 1992; Vroeijenstijn 1995; Stensaker 1998).

Even the intermediate bodies, with their main task of stimulating and administrating external quality assurance, seem to be quite balanced when reporting about the (possible) outcomes of this work at the institutional level. For example, in a Nordic report from 2000 aiming at stimulating 'best practice' concerning quality assurance in universities and colleges, Fahlén et al. (2000: 15) underlined that

> The case studies highlighted in this report should not be viewed as completed success stories. Hopefully, they show that there have been, and still are, problems related to the projects, illustrating that quality improvement work is a process that must be continually nurtured for quality to prosper.

Again, it is incremental adjustments and long-term engagement that seem favoured over dramatic and revolutionary change. A similar picture can also be recognised in a larger OECD-financed study on the impact of external quality assessment upon institutional management and decision-making processes where national intermediate bodies reported both on their current and future plans, but also on the effects of external quality assurance (Brennan and Shah 2000).

3.7. Individualising Quality

When looking into the recent history of quality assurance in higher education, there have been many attempts to transform external quality concepts into more beneficial processes for the individual institution, and in particular for those who work in higher education (see e.g. Barnett 1992; Dill 1992; Harvey 1995; Holmes and McElwee 1995; Winn and Cameron 1998; Gosling and D'Andrea 2001; Srikanthan and Dalrymple 2002, 2005). The recurring issue in these and other contributions is often the argument that external quality assurance concepts and models do not acknowledge and emphasise the central place human capital has in higher education (Harvey 1995: 135). What is especially underlined is the collegial organisation of higher education, and how this form of organisation should be a central element in any attempt to develop well-functioning quality assurance schemes. In the words of Srikanthan and Dalrymple (2005: 77), "development of a collective consciousness or a shared awareness is necessary as a fundamental prerequisite across the campus for steadfast progress in implementation of the holistic model" (see also Barnett 1992: 95; Dill 1992: 76; Harvey 1995: 137). Quality has in this way not only been adapted to the central characteristics of higher education, but has also been interpreted as a potential opportunity for academics to strengthen power and influence in general (Holmes and McElwee 1995: 5), not least since some advocates of the 'new collegiality' approach stated that quality could not be managed, but only cared for (Barnett 1992).

However, this approach can also be seen as benefiting other groups within higher education, especially those having the responsibility for human resource management – academic leaders and administrators. In an analysis of the relevance of the Malcolm Baldrige National Quality Framework for institutions of higher education, this point was underlined by Winn and Cameron (1998: 508) who concluded that managers do not have any direct impact on organisational (quality) outcomes, but that their influence is felt more through the (well-functioning) systems and processes they establish. As such, a win-win situation can be seen to appear downplaying the potential conflicts of interest that exist among different actors within higher education, and instead visualising the opportunities involvement in quality assurance could provide to the individual.

4. FROM FASHION TO FITNESS

Considering Røvik's (1998) seven theoretical assumptions on how management ideas are spread in a given sector, Section 3 shows that the diffusion of the idea of quality in higher education does not match the assumptions completely. The idea of quality has to a limited extent been socially authorised and, hence, accepted by those working in the sector. It is also hard to find many examples showing that quality has been dramatised in the translation process, with advocates only highlighting advantages. The progressive dimension of quality compared to other management ideas is partly supported, but with evidence indicating how important it is for external ideas to match cultural characteristics in the organisational adaptive process. It is also hard to find evidence that quality has been instigated as a response to one particular universal problem in higher education – rather it has been launched as a pragmatic tool for addressing a number of issues (Harvey and Askling 2003: 72). Concerning the other characteristics on how management ideas are diffused –

the transformation of the idea into a product, and the harmonisation and indivi-dualisation of the idea – the evidence is more supportive of the theory.

However, looking at all seven characteristics together, and how higher education can be 'positioned' accordingly, one is more than anything struck by the critical and rather sceptical atmosphere through which the translation process has taken place so far. Quality as a management idea has been embraced with little enthusiasm, hence the lack of social authorisation of the idea from within the sector. This did not hinder quality as an idea being transformed into new organisational practices in higher education (see e.g. Frazer 1997; Brennan and Shah 2000). Mandatory requirements from governments and national authorities played, of course, a crucial role in this process, and are still important as driving forces behind existing and new forms of quality assurance schemes. But even such mandatory requirements have not hindered the transformation of quality to fit the intrinsic characteristics of the sector. For example, while quality in other sectors was often associated with the idea of customer satisfaction and market adaptation (see e.g. Birnbaum 2000), one can rather find translations of quality within higher education emphasising staff empowerment and developments of central organisational features such as colle-giality. The place self-evaluation and the peer review mechanism have achieved within various quality assurance schemes in higher education can seldom be found in other sectors where clients, customers, and service-orientation seem to play a more prominent role (see e.g. Peters 2001). Even in the UK system of quality assurance, which was often argued to be the one with procedures and routines less adjusted to the sector (cf. Barnett 1992), these mechanisms are central to the existing system (Henkel 2000). As such, this study confirms classic research on policy implementation in higher education emphasising the ability that the sector has for reinterpreting, translating, and transforming policy to internal needs (cf. March and Olsen 1976; Cerych and Sabatier 1986). Hence, it seems that management ideas – even backed by governmental reform initiatives – do not change much of how adaptation takes place in higher education.

One could interpret this finding as an example of a sector with little vulnerability to external ideas and new societal expectations, or, put more negatively, as a sector not very open to change. A cynical interpretation could, for example, be that quality has been complied with, but then ignored by the sector with only symbolic adjustments and actions taken. But the available data can be interpreted otherwise. The (open-ended) theorisation, harmonisation, individualisation, and the making of quality into a concrete 'product' with certain routines and organisational activities associated with it, can also be seen as signs of a rather adaptive and dynamic sector with great ability to spot the potential in new ideas, and with creative ways of utilising or adapting to them. Birnbaum's (2000: 215) many suggestions on how to 'manage fads' can consequently already be seen as part of the standard operating procedures in the sector. It is, therefore, more the translation of quality that has been socially authorised than the idea of quality as such. Hence, potential resistance appears not to be directed against change as such, but against change that could affect the fundamental characteristics of higher education. The translation of quality into higher education can as a consequence be seen more as a process that has cherished what higher education 'is' rather than what it 'should be'. One can, therefore, agree with Ewell (1999) that management ideas indeed are prisms through which higher education examines existing routines and practice. However, when translating the idea of quality, it seems that more attempts have been directed at reaffirming the identity of the sector rather than changing it.[9] One can also speculate whether the idea of quality has been used by the sector as a way of fighting back other reform and change initiatives in higher education related to funding, management, or governance. The many voices heard relating to the link between maintaining academic quality in an era of budget decline could, at least, be interpreted this way (see Henkel 2000). Ball (1985) in this way was right – quality is 'fitness for purpose', not only for those proposing it, but also for those on the receiving end.

5. CONCLUSION

There are a number of perspectives one can use to analyse how quality has affected higher education. A similarity shared by most of these perspectives is that they have difficulties identifying the effects of quality on higher education. The problems associated with defining what exactly to study, the problems of establishing causal links, and the uncertainties related to how findings should be interpreted are the usual explanations. While not arguing that attempts to study the effects of quality are of little value, this chapter has attempted to launch a different perspective on how to analyse quality. The core of this perspective has been to use common characteristics related to how management ideas are spread, and analyse how the spread of quality within higher education can be deconstructed accordingly.

The advantage of this perspective is that it manages to capture the dynamics related to how new ideas and concepts infuse higher education. By acknowledging the fact that management ideas are not static entities, and that the sector to which they are introduced is not characterised by inertia and stability, one is able to present a more nuanced and interactive picture of how change occurs in higher education. Decades of research on implementation in higher education and elsewhere have shown us that implementation is not a simple linear process, but a highly complex, and sometimes even a paradoxical and contradictory, process. Using perspectives that can capture some of this complexity should therefore be prioritised in future studies in the sector.

The findings of the current study are an illustration of this complexity. Indications that quality was not socially authorised and dramatised within higher education, while still made into a product, harmonised and individualised, are only one example to be mentioned.

NOTES

1   The author would like to thank Jethro Newton, Lee Harvey, and the other participants at the Douro Seminar for comments on an earlier version of this chapter. A special thanks to Johan P. Olsen for providing some clarifying points in the theoretical part.
2   These two perspectives may still be blurred when it comes to how they are manifested in practice. For example, one can imagine that programme assessments can be designed both according to a scientific management and a human relations perspective.

3 However, several reforms having a market-based approach have also been launched by political parties on the left (Olsen 1991), or labour parties, as in New Zealand (Peters 2001).

4 Although one can differentiate between fads and fashion (see e.g. Abrahamson 1991: 591), this is not done in this chapter. While management fashions may (or may not) be beneficial to the adapting organisation, labelling a management idea a 'fad' suggests that an idea is harmful, or at least has no effect upon the adapting organisation. However, in practice, it is empirically hard to differentiate between fads and fashions due to measurement problems.

5 Of course, adapting to management ideas can also be seen as an attempt to increase the legitimation internally in a given organisation for particular groups. Adapting to management ideas can, for example, be seen as a way of legitimising management action and increasing their influence (Harvey 2005, pers comm).

6 Typical examples here are Sweden and Norway.

7 However, one difference is the way peer review committees are put together. While such committees traditionally only consisted of disciplinary experts, modern peer review committees also contain representatives from professions, industry, students or other stakeholders.

8 The author is indebted to Alberto Amaral for guiding my attention to this point.

9 This does not imply that higher education is not changing. Stensaker (2004) has shown how institutions of higher education can go through substantial change processes while trying to maintain and strengthen their institutional identity.

REFERENCES

Abrahamson, E. "Managerial Fads and Fashions: The Diffusion and Rejection of Innovation." *Academy of Management Review* 16.3 (1991): 586–612.

Abrahamson, E. "Management Fashion." *Academy of Management Review* 21.1 (1996): 254–285.

Ashworth, A. and R. Harvey. *Assessing Quality in Further and Higher Education*. Buckingham: Society for Research into Higher Education and Open University Press, 1994.

Ball, C. *Fitness for Purpose*. Guildford: Society for Research into Higher Education and NFER-Nelson, 1985.

Barley, S.R. and G. Kunda. "Design and Devotion: Surges of Rational and Normative Ideologies of Control in Management Discourse." *Administrative Science Quarterly* 37.3 (1992): 363–399.

Barnett, R. *Improving Higher Education. Total Quality Care*. Buckingham: Society for Research into Higher Education and Open University Press, 1992.

Bensimon, E.M. "Total Quality Management in the Academy: A Rebellious Reading." *Harvard Educational Review* 65.4 (1995): 593–611.

Birnbaum, R. *Management Fads in Higher Education. Where They Come From, What They Do, Why They Fail*. San Francisco: Jossey-Bass, 2000.

Birnbaum, R. and J. Deshotels. "Has the Academy Adopted TQM?" *Planning for Higher Education* 28.1 (1999): 29–37.

Birnbaum, R. and F. Shushok Jr. "The 'Crisis' Crisis in Higher Education." In Altbach, P., P. Gumport and D.B. Johnstone (eds). *In Defense of American Higher Education*. Baltimore: Johns Hopkins University Press, 2001, 59–84.

Brennan, J. "Evaluation of Higher Education in Europe." In Henkel, M. and B. Little (eds). *Changing Relationships between Higher Education and the State*. London: Jessica Kingsley Publishers, 1999, 219–235.

Brennan, J. and T. Shah. *Managing Quality in Higher Education. An International Perspective on Institutional Assessment and Change*. Buckingham: Society for Research into Higher Education and Open University Press, 2000.

Brunsson, N. *The Organisation of Hypocrisy*. Chichester: Wiley, 1989.

Brunsson, N. "Quality as a Rule." Keynote speech presented at the Conference on The Meaning of Quality in Education, Karlstad, Sweden, 2001.

Cameron, K.S. and D.A. Whetten. "Organizational Effectiveness and Quality: The Second Generation." In Smart, J.C. (ed.). *Higher Education: Handbook of Theory and Research*, vol. XI. New York: Agathon Press, 1996, 265–306.

Cerych, L. and P. Sabatier. *Great Expectations and Mixed Performance. The Implementation of Higher Education Reforms in Europe*. Stoke-on-Trent: Trentham Books, 1986.

Chaston, I. "Are British Universities in a Position to Consider Implementing Total Quality Management?" *Higher Education Quarterly* 48.2 (1994): 118–134.

Clark, B.R. *The Distinctive College*. Chicago: Aldine, 1970.

Clark, B.R. *The Higher Education System*. Berkeley: University of California Press, 1983.

Coate, E. "The Introduction of Total Quality Management at Oregon State University." *Higher Education* 25.3 (1993): 303–320.

Czarniawska, B. *Narrating the Organisation. Dramas of Institutional Identity*. Chicago: University of Chicago Press, 1997.

Czarniawska, B. and B. Joerges. "Travel of Ideas." In Czarniawska, B. and G. Sevón (eds). *Translating Organizational Change*. Berlin: Walter de Gruyter, 1996, 13–48.

Czarniawska, B. and G. Sevón (eds). *Translating Organizational Change*. Berlin: Walter de Gruyter, 1996.

Dill, D.D. "Quality by Design: Towards a Framework for Academic Quality Management." In Smart, J.C. (ed.). *Higher Education: Handbook of Theory and Research*, vol. VIII. New York: Agathon Press, 1992: 37–83.

Dill, D.D. "Through Deming's Eyes: A Cross-national Analysis of Quality Assurance Policies in Higher Education." *Quality in Higher Education* 1.1 (1995): 95–110.

Dill, D.D. "Designing Academic Audit: Lessons Learned in Europe and Asia." *Quality in Higher Education* 6.3 (2000): 187–207.

Ellis, R. (ed.). *Quality Assurance for University Teaching*. Bristol: Society for Research into Higher Education and Open University Press, 1993.

Ewell, P. "Imitation as Art: Borrowed Management Techniques in Higher Education." *Change* 31.6 (1999): 11–15.

Fahlén, V., A-M. Luihanen, L. Petersson, and B. Stensaker (eds). *Towards Best Practice. Quality Improvement Initiatives in Nordic Higher Education Institutions*. Copenhagen: Nordic Council of Ministers, 2000.

Feldman, M.S. and J.G. March. "Information in Organizations as Signal and Symbol." *Administrative Science Quarterly* 26.2 (1981): 171–186.

Frazer, M. "Report on the Modalities of External Evaluation of Higher Education in Europe: 1995–1997." *Higher Education in Europe* 22.3 (1997): 349–401.

Fry, H. "Quality Judgements and Quality Improvements." *Higher Education Quarterly* 49.1 (1995): 59–77.

Gosling, D. and V.M. D'Andrea. "Quality Development: A New Concept for Higher Education." *Quality in Higher Education* 7.1 (2001): 7–17.

Grant, R.M., R. Shani, and R. Krishnan. "TQM's Challenge to Management Theory and Practice." *Sloan Management Review* 35.2 (1994): 25–35.

Harvey, L. "Beyond TQM." *Quality in Higher Education* 1.2 (1995): 123–146.

Harvey, L. and B. Askling. "Quality in Higher Education." In Begg. R. (ed.). *The Dialogue Between Higher Education Research and Practice*. Dordrecht: Kluwer Academic Publishers, 2003, 69–83.

Harvey, L. and D. Green. "Defining Quality." *Assessment and Evaluation in Higher Education* 18.1 (1993): 9–34.

Harvey, L. and P. Knight. *Transforming Higher Education*. Ballmoor: Society for Research into Higher Education and Open University Press, 1996.

Henkel, M. *Academic Identities and Policy Change in Higher Education*. London: Jessica Kingsley Publishers, 2000.

HEQC (Higher Education Quality Council). *Guidelines on Quality Assurance*. London: Higher Education Quality Council, 1996.

Holmes, G. and G. McElwee. "Total Quality Management in Higher Education: How to Approach Human Resource Management." *TQM Magazine* 7.6 (1995): 5–10.

Hood, C. *The Art of the State. Culture, Rhetoric, and Public Management*. Oxford: Clarendon Press, 1998.

Huczynski, A.A. "Explaining the Succession of Management Fads." *International Journal of Human Resource Management* 4.2 (1993): 443–463.

Kells, H. *Self-study Processes*. New York: Macmillan/ACE, 1988.

Kells, H. *Self-regulation in Higher Education. A Multi-national Perspective on Collaborative Systems of Quality Assurance and Control*. London: Jessica Kinsley Publishers, 1992.

Kells, H. and K-A. Nilsson. *Evaluation for Quality Assurance and Improvement.* Stockholm: Office of the University Chancellor, 1995.

Kells, H. and P. Stenquist. *A Guide to Evaluation Processes in Finnish Higher Education.* Helsinki: Ministry of Education, 1995.

Kogan, M. "The Implementation Game." In Gornitzka, Å, M. Kogan and A. Amaral (eds). *Reform and Change in Higher Education. Analysing Policy Implementation.* Dordrecht: Springer, 2005, 57–65.

Maassen, P.A.M. "Quality Assurance in the Netherlands." In Gaither, G. (ed.). *Quality Assurance in Higher Education: An International Perspective.* San Francisco: Jossey-Bass Publishers, 1998, 19–27.

March, J.G. and J.P. Olsen. *Ambiguity and Choice in Organizations.* Bergen: Universitetsforlaget, 1976.

Marchese, T. "TQM Reaches the Academy." *AAHE Bulletin* 44.3 (1991): 3–9.

Mayo, E. *The Human Problems of an Industrial Civilisation.* New York: Macmillan, 1933.

Meyer, J.W. "Otherhood: The Promulgation and Transmission of Ideas in the Modern Organizational Environment." In Czarniawska, B. and G. Sevón (eds). *Translating Organizational Change.* Berlin: Walter de Gruyter, 1996, 241–272.

Meyer, J.W. and B. Rowan. "Institutionalized Organizations: Formal Structure as Myth and Ceremony." *American Journal of Sociology* 83.2 (1977): 340–363.

Meyer, M.W. "Organizational Structure as Signaling". *Pacific Sociological Review* 22.4 (1979): 481–500.

Micklethwait, J. and A. Wooldridge. *The Witch Doctors. What Management Gurus Are Saying, Why it Matters and How to Make Sense of it.* London: Heinemann, 1996.

Middlehurst, R. "Quality: An Organising Principle for Higher Education?" *Higher Education Quarterly* 46.1 (1992): 20–38.

Neave, G. "On the Cultivation of Quality, Efficiency and Enterprise: An Overview of Recent Trends in Higher Education in Western Europe." *European Journal of Education* 23.1/2 (1988): 7–23.

Neave, G. "The Politics of Quality: Developments in Higher Education in Western Europe 1992–1994." *European Journal of Education* 29.2 (1994): 115–134.

Newton, J. "An Evaluation of the Impact of External Quality Monitoring on a Higher Education College (1993–98)." *Assessment & Evaluation in Higher Education* 24.2 (1999): 215–235.

Newton, J. "Feeding the Beast or Improving Quality? Academics' Perceptions of Quality Assurance and Quality Monitoring." *Quality in Higher Education* 6.2 (2000): 153–163.

Olsen, J.P. "Modernization Programs in Perspective: An Institutional Perspective on Organizational Change." *Governance* 4 (1991): 125–149.

Owlia, M.S. and E.M. Aspinwall. "Quality in Higher Education – A Survey." *Total Quality Management* 7.2 (1996): 161–172.

Peters, B.G. *The Future of Governing.* 2nd edn. Lawrence: University Press of Kansas, 2001.

Pollitt, C. *Managerialism and the Public Services.* 2nd edn. Oxford: Basil Blackwell, 1993.

Pollitt, C. and G. Bouckaert (eds). *Quality Improvement in European Public Services.* London: Sage Publications, 1995.

Reeves, C.A. and D.A. Bednar. "Defining Quality: Alternatives and Implications." *Academy of Management Review* 19.3 (1994): 419–445.

Røvik, K-A. *Moderne organisasjoner.* Bergen: Fagbokforlaget, 1998.

Saarinen, T. "From Sickness to Cure and Further: Construction of 'Quality' in Finnish Higher Education Policy From the 1960s to the Era of the Bologna Process." *Quality in Higher Education* 11.1 (2005): 3–15.

Sahlin-Andersson, K. "Imitating by Editing Success: The Construction of Organizational Fields." In Czarniawska, B. and G. Sevón (eds). *Translating Organizational Change.* Berlin: Walter de Gruyter, 1996, 69–92.

Schaik, M. "Quality Management at the Hogeschool Holland. Internal Auditing and Experience with an EFQM-based Method Adapted for Institutions of Higher Education." Paper presented at the AIR-Forum, Albuquerque, NM, 1996.

Schwarz, S. and D.F. Westerheijden (eds). *Accreditation and Evaluation in the European Higher Education Area.* Dordrecht: Springer, 2004.

Seymour, D. *On Q: Causing Quality in Higher Education.* Washington, DC: ACE/Oryx, 1992.

Seymour, D. "TQM: Focus on Performance, Not Resources." *Educational Record* 74.2 (1993): 6–14.

Srikanthan, G. and J. Dalrymple. "Developing a Holistic Model for Quality in Higher Education." *Quality in Higher Education* 8.3 (2002): 215–224.

Srikanthan, G. and J. Dalrymple. "Implementation of a Holistic Model for Quality in Higher Education." *Quality in Higher Education* 11.1 (2005): 69–81.

Stensaker, B. "Culture and Fashion in Reform Implementation: Perceptions and Adaptations of Management Reforms in Higher Education." *Journal of Higher Education Policy and Management* 20.2 (1998): 129–138.

Stensaker, B. "Trance, Transparency and Transformation: The Impact of External Quality Monitoring in Higher Education." *Quality in Higher Education* 9.2 (2003): 151–159.

Stensaker, B. "The Transformation of Organisational Identities. Interpretations of Policies Concerning the Quality of Teaching and Learning in Norwegian Higher Education." PhD Thesis. Enschede: CHEPS/University of Twente, 2004.

Stensaker, B. and L. Harvey. "Old Wine in New Bottles? A Comparison of Public and Private Accreditation Schemes in Higher Education." *Higher Education Policy* 19.1 (2006): 65–85.

Taylor, F.W. *The Principles of Scientific Management*. New York: Harper and Brothers, 1911.

Thune, C. "The Alliance of Accountability and Improvement: The Danish Experience." *Quality in Higher Education* 2 (1996): 21–32.

Thune, C. and A. Staropoli. "The European Pilot Project for Evaluating Quality in Higher Education." In Brennan, J., P. de Vries, and R. Williams (eds). *Standards and Quality in Higher Education*. London: Jessica Kingsley Publishers, 1997, 198–204.

Tuckman, A. "The Yellow Brick Road: Total Quality Management and the Restructuring of Organizational Culture." *Organization Studies* 15.5 (1994): 727–751.

Välimaa, J. "Academics on Assessment and the Peer Review – Finnish Experience." *Higher Education Management* 6.3 (1994): 391–408.

Van Vught, F.A. "Intrinsic and Extrinsic Aspects of Quality Assessments in Higher Education." In Westerheijden, D.F., J. Brennan, and P.A.M. Maassen (eds). *Changing Contexts of Quality Assessment: Recent Trends in West European Higher Education*. Utrecht: Lemma, 1994, 31–50.

Van Vught, F.A. "The Humboldtian University under Pressure: New Forms of Quality Review in Western European Education." In Maassen, P.A.M. and F.A. van Vught (eds). *Inside Academia. New Challenges for the Academic Profession*. Utrecht: De Tijdstroom, 1996, 185–226.

Van Vught, F.A. and D.F. Westerheijden. "Towards a General Model of Quality Assessment in Higher Education." *Higher Education* 28.3 (1994): 355–371.

Vazzana, G., J. Elfrink, and D.P. Bachmann. "A Longitudinal Study of Total Quality Management Processes in Business Colleges." *Journal of Education for Business* 76.2 (2000): 69–74.

Vroeijenstijn, A.I. *Improvement and Accountability, Navigating Between Scylla and Charybdis, Guide for Quality Assessment in Higher Education*. London: Jessica Kingsley Publishers, 1995.

Wagner, R.B. *Accountability in Education: A Philosophical Inquiry*. New York: Routledge, 1989.

Westerheijden, D.F. "Where Are the Quantum Jumps in Quality Assurance?" *Higher Education* 38.2 (1999): 233–254.

Williams, G. "Total Quality Management in Higher Education: Panacea or Placebo?" *Higher Education* 25.3 (1993): 229–237.

Winn, B.A. and K.S. Cameron. "Organizational Quality: An Examination of the Malcolm Baldrige National Quality Framework." *Research in Higher Education* 39.5 (1998): 492–512.

PETER EWELL

THE 'QUALITY GAME': EXTERNAL REVIEW AND INSTITUTIONAL REACTION OVER THREE DECADES IN THE UNITED STATES

1. INTRODUCTION

Quality assurance is not an easy topic to review from a policy perspective in the United States because of its bewildering variety. The absence of a national system of public higher education (and its associated ministry), coupled with the presence of myriad independent colleges and universities, mean that the function of quality assurance is both decentralised and dispersed. Individual states hold responsibility for funding and governing public institutions with concomitant variations in how they define 'quality' as well as their commitment and approach to determining if it is present. In parallel, responsibility for directly assuring quality for all institutions is delegated to a range of non-governmen·tal accrediting organisations, which operate under the regulatory aegis of the federal government, but which are otherwise diverse and independent. The resulting complexity – which is shared to a lesser degree by other federal systems like Germany[1] – renders any attempt to determine the dynamics and impacts of quality assurance in US higher education a challenge indeed.

Nevertheless, there are some very good reasons for trying to undertake such an analysis. To begin with, the United States has been at this job for a very long time. Explicit attention to reviewing institutional 'quality' as a matter of public policy dates back to the early 1980s, with 'voluntary' institutional accreditation based on peer review just celebrating its centenary. In contrast, the much more focused national processes of quality review undertaken in Europe and Australasia for the most part evolved in the 1990s (Frederiks, Westerheijden, and Weusthof 1994; Dill 1995). Secondly, the decentralisation and dispersion that characterise US higher education provides a lot of cases to examine in search of themes and lessons. Fifty states and eight regional accrediting organisations allow a good deal of variation in approach and potential impact to be observed. Finally, there are reasons to believe that higher education systems in most places in the world are becoming more like that of the United States. The number of independent (and even proprietary) institutions is on the rise in many countries, massification is taking place to match the scale of US postsecondary provision, and market forces generated by a gradual shift in financial support from governments to consumers are becoming significant factors worldwide (OECD 2003). All these reasons suggest that learning from US experience might be valuable.

D.F. Westerheijden et al. (eds.), Quality Assurance in Higher Education: Trends in Regulation, Translation and Transformation, 119–153.
© 2007 *Springer*.

Accordingly, the topic of this chapter is the interplay between external initiatives in the realm of quality assurance in the United States (including the 'public' roles of accreditation organisations) and institutions of higher education over the past three decades. Broad topics of interest under this heading include:

- The effectiveness of various approaches to assuring quality from the point of view of state interest – that is, did these approaches achieve what policy makers said they wanted to achieve with respect to such matters as assuring accountability, 'steering' institutions toward behaviours consistent with public goals and interests, or providing consumer information and consumer protection?

- The impact of these approaches on institutions – that is, did quality approaches act principally as a 'tax' on institutional operations, stimulate institutions to move in new or different directions, or create planning and management assets that institutions could harness for their own purposes?

- The net benefit to the national 'system' of higher education – that is, did engagement with quality assurance influence overall investments in higher education, public perceptions of its merit or effectiveness, the overall 'trust' accorded the higher education sector by policy makers and the public, or the relative engagement of key postsecondary stakeholders like the employment community?

After a brief review of the players, the topic will be addressed in two stages, the first historical and the second analytical. The first section will attempt to characterise the dynamics of quality assurance across four distinct periods of evolution. The second will attempt to analyse the 'historical data' presented to identify a number of policy variables affecting state and institutional interaction in the realm of quality assurance, propose a simple model of this interaction ('The Quality Game') that may be useful in examining other national contexts, and suggest some propositions about how the policy variables identified affect such matters as achieving state goals or promoting positive institutional engagement.

2. THE PLAYERS

The United States currently has some 4100 accredited higher education institutions offering degree programmes. Almost 1100 of these are public community colleges that terminate study at the two-year or associate degree level, together with a smaller number of independent two-year institutions. Among the more than 2300 institutions that offer baccalaureate study and above, independent institutions outnumber public institutions by a substantial margin (77% of these institutions are private while only 23% are public). But most students (77%) attend public institutions.[2]

Quality assurance for this diverse array of institutions is traditionally described as a shared responsibility of the 'Triad', which is made up of states, accreditation organisations, and the federal government. Each entity's role in the 'Triad' is somewhat different and it has frequently been observed that they have particular, and sometimes complementary, sets of strengths and weaknesses in assuring quality (Ewell, Wellman, and Paulson 1997). In addition – and increasingly acknowledged formally as part of the overall system of quality assurance – are the media and the market. As a prelude to understanding the historical review that follows, the specific roles of each of these entities requires a bit of analysis.

2.1. States

States in the Unites States have three distinct roles that connect them to questions of quality assurance. Like most nations, state governments act as 'owner-operators' of public colleges and universities by providing them with substantial direct operating subsidies and by broadly supervising and regulating their operations. For this body of institutions at least, this means that states are as concerned about efficiencies and returns on investment as they are with academic quality per se. And indeed, when state budgets are tight, this becomes their chief concern. Second, many states provide substantial scholarship support that allows students to attend private as well as public institutions. Acting in this role, a state's primary quality assurance concern is that students obtain a credential of value – one that graduates are satisfied with, that (hopefully) has academic integrity, and that has a payoff in the marketplace of employment. Finally, in their role of keepers of the public interest, states are concerned about such matters as economic development, civic participation, and overall quality of life for their citizens. Dimensions of 'quality' in higher education that interest them in this regard include institutional contributions to economic development in the form of well-prepared graduates, contributions to knowledge consistent with identified state needs, and institutional responsiveness to the needs of the communities in which they are located (however these are defined). These elements of quality, of course, can be manifest in both public and private institutions.

2.2. The Federal Government

Because individual states fund and govern public higher education, the federal government plays an indirect role in quality assurance in the United States. But it is an increasingly important role. Beginning with the Higher Education Act (HEA) of 1965, the federal government has provided substantial need-based support to individual students in the form of grants and guaranteed low-interest loans with which they can pay the cost of tuition. These funds can be used at both public and private institutions.[3] Given this role, the primary 'quality' interests of the federal government are to ensure that the institutions administering financial aid are adequate 'stewards' of these funds and, more importantly, that students are provided with a credential of integrity. A more narrowly focused version of the latter concern is that loan-bearing students earn a credential of sufficient value in the marketplace that they can pay back their loans.[4] To discharge this interest, the HEA designates accrediting organisations to serve as 'gatekeepers' governing access to federal funds. Accordingly, the US Department of Education (USDOE) periodically reviews and approves institutional accrediting organisations to ensure that they are acting in the federal interest as they review institutional quality. Since 1990, moreover, federal interest in quality has focused increasingly on the quality of student outcomes – more particularly graduation rates and evidence of student learning (From the States 1993a, 2003). These performance areas are seen not only as elements of institutional 'stewardship' but also as elements of consumer protection.

2.3. Accrediting Organisations

Institutional accreditation in the United States began as a voluntary review process about a century ago, when individual colleges and universities needed a mechanism to accept one another's degrees and credits. It is currently governed through eight separate and independent regional commissions that are membership organisations comprising the institutions they accredit.[5] The typical review process undertaken through accreditation – which changed little until the last decade – involves a periodic comprehensive institutional self-study followed by a multi-day visit by an accreditation team comprised of peer reviewers drawn from faculty and administrators in the region. Following the visit, the team prepares a report to the Commission, which acts to continue the institution's accreditation and/or to impose sanctions and offer recommendations. Except for the accreditation decision itself, the process is typically confidential and most accrediting organisations consciously construct their engagement with institutions as consultative, not as an agent of accountability. This is consistent with their constitution as institutional membership organisations, a factor that also tends to mitigate the severity of any actions they will undertake toward institutions and therefore the legitimacy they are accorded by more 'hard-edged' government actors.

Regional accreditation's traditional interest in 'quality' has been comprehensive – embracing matters ranging from the adequacy of resources, the appropriateness of institutional governance arrangements, the qualifications of administrative and teaching staff, and the adequate provision of instruction. Since their assumption of the 'gatekeeping' role, however, regional accreditors have increasingly been asked to review matters of concern to the federal government including, most prominently in recent years, the quality of student learning outcomes (Ewell 1997).

2.4. Media and the Market

US higher education is also distinctive because of the proportion of institutional operating cost paid by students.[6] Public institutions, on average, derive a third of their support from tuition and fees, and this proportion has been rising in recent years. The vast majority of private institutions, meanwhile, derive almost all their support from tuition charges. This condition renders US institutions unusually sensitive to market forces as they compete for students. At the high end of the institutional selectivity range, this natural competition is intensified by the quest for the most qualified students to enhance the institution's reputation. Not surprisingly, this has meant the emergence of a vast amount of 'market information' issued by institutions themselves and by the media. Perhaps the most notorious among the latter are the rankings of 'America's Best Colleges' issued each fall since 1983 by *US News & World Report*, which pioneered the notion of college and university 'league tables' that has now emerged all over the world. 'Quality' in this view is almost entirely about institutional reputation, which is in turn fuelled by visible institutional assets and, above all, admissions selectivity. The evidence is slim that potential students pay much attention to these rankings (McDonough et al. 1997), but the evidence is overwhelming that the rankings influence administrative choices and behaviours as institutions seek to maximise their prestige (Machung 1998).

Operating alongside the formal 'Triad' of state, federal, and accreditation oversight, the media thus act as a kind of 'fourth estate' of quality review that can occasionally exercise considerable influence. Meanwhile, the market itself exerts its own 'quality' discipline by enacting a wide range of student consumer preferences about the kinds of postsecondary education individual students want to purchase. This view of 'quality' is largely about 'fitness for purpose' and, in contrast to institutional prestige which governs the high end of selectivity, is generally about cost, convenience and to some extent the perceived advantage of a particular credential in the employment market (Zemsky and Oedel 1983). Singularly lacking in this picture, however, is the quality of instruction or of ultimate student learning (Zemsky 2005).

Because of their distinctive roles, these principal accountability actors thus have different perspectives on quality and influence institutional behaviour in different ways. States and accrediting organisations have exerted the most direct influence in the four historical periods to be described, with the exception of an uncharacteristic episode of federal activism in the early 1990s. But all four have been significant in shaping the national conversation.

3. HISTORICAL REVIEW

For purposes of exposition, the evolution of external quality review in United States higher education can be roughly divided into four periods, each of which features a distinctive mix of lead actors and institutional reactions. Borders between periods are admittedly arbitrary and could certainly be drawn differently. More importantly, each successive period preserved some of the approaches and behaviours characteristic of previous periods, yielding a 'layered look' of policy tools. This is especially true for the earliest 'Pre-Quality' period reviewed, as the access and efficiency measures used to describe principal elements of 'quality' in this period continue to be used today.

3.1. Pre-Quality [1965–1982]

The context for this period was significant expansion of higher education capacity, beginning with the passage of the HEA in 1965 which established accreditation's 'gatekeeping' function as it is today. Enrolments doubled from some 6 million to over 12 million students (USDOE 2004), partly through the creation of new public institutions (most notably among two-year community colleges) and partly through the significant expansion of existing public four-year institutions. Higher education policy questions under these conditions were almost entirely about growth and how to manage it, and most states evolved some form of per capita funding approach to support (and provide incentives for) rapid expansion (Jones 1984). This was also the period in which most of today's higher education governance arrangements were put into place – structures that would later be harnessed for quality review. In addition to accreditation's new role as federal agent, these included the establishment of many state-level higher education coordinating boards (the so-called SHEEO agencies) intended to rationalise growth, coordinate institutional missions, and in many cases to recommend funding policies and levels. These new agencies joined established multi-institutional governing boards for public university systems in states that had already had such bodies as the primary public authority for higher education in each state (Berdahl 1971).

The primary policy actors in this period were states, with the federal government acting to finance expansion through heavy investments in student financial aid. The states' overall approach to policy during this period can be described as higher education as a 'public utility' (Ewell 1997). Postsecondary credentials were seen as separable benefits for the individuals who possessed them, with their value apparent in higher incomes and an enhanced quality of life. The principal task of the state was to ensure that a) the public funds invested in providing these individually worthwhile services were spent appropriately and efficiently; and b) the chance to benefit through postsecondary education was available to all citizens regardless of circumstances. The notion of 'quality', where present at all, was simply an expression of established institutional reputation and prestige or, later on in the period when admissions selectivity tiers among institutions became firmly established, an expression of the tested abilities of entering freshmen (Lemann 1999). Both of these phenomena affected only a small percentage of institutions and both were enacted through the marketplace, not public policy.[7]

Consistent with the 'public utility' analogy, institutional accountability in this period was largely based on annual reporting to state SHEEO agencies about access and efficiency. For access, measures emphasised the proportions of students served by race/ethnicity, reflecting the dominant civil rights concerns of the 60s and 70s – especially in southeastern states. For efficiency, measures concentrated on output in the form of student credit hours per units of input as expressed in faculty time or dollar expenditures.[8] In some states, these measures were supplemented by statewide programme review – a process that looked at particular academic programmes to determine their priority for investment in relation to institutional mission and perceived state need (Barak 1982). Here, however, the overwhelming concern was resource based, with little attention given to teaching–learning processes or student learning outcomes.

Under these circumstances, institutions bore relatively little accountability burden. Public colleges and universities were easily able to absorb the additional marginal costs of compliance reporting – especially in the context of funding growth that characterised much of this period. Indeed, the enrolment-based, average-cost resource allocation mechanisms adopted by most states were of particular benefit to institutions in the context of enrolment growth characterised by this period because they allowed more and more 'profit' to be taken as fixed-to-variable expenditure ratios decreased (Jones 1984).[9] Meanwhile, the need for statistical reporting to states and the federal government stimulated the profession of institutional research, which could straightforwardly harness new computerised student records systems to generate the needed numbers. Independent institutions, except for federal reporting for statistical purposes, remained largely unaffected by any of these developments.

All of these developments, moreover, took place within a relatively benign policy environment in which the higher education sector enjoyed significant professional deference and was accorded a high level of trust by public officials. Academics were presumed to know their subjects and to deliver high quality instruction and, for the most part, the subjects delivered corresponded to political perceptions of what was needed. At the same time, heavy federal investments in basic science research capacity increased institutional prestige and resulting public perceptions of professional competence. Higher education was simply assumed to be part of the 'public good' and questions about specific performance were not explicitly raised.

3.2. Quality I [1983–1991]

The emergence of 'quality' as a distinct arena of higher education performance in the United States was the result of several convergent forces (Ewell 2002a). First, the 1980s saw the end of the significant period of enrolment expansion that had taken place over the previous 15 years. With flat enrolments and a largely enrolment-driven funding approach, public higher education had to come up with new reasons to argue for increased resources. Beginning in the state of Tennessee – which explicitly raised the 'quality question' in 1979 as the justification for its pioneering performance funding programme (Banta 1986) – more and more advocates began suggesting such a shift of emphasis in budget requests in the new decade. Second, calls for investments in quality were significantly reinforced by the impact of a prominent federal report on declining quality in elementary and secondary education. Entitled *A Nation at Risk* (USDOE 1983), this report fuelled significant investments in school reform that have continued to this day. Finally, led by a bipartisan group of 'education governors' that included the future President Bill Clinton,[10] the dominant 'public utility' policy model of higher education began to be displaced by one that emphasised strategic investment: higher education was increasingly seen by states as a 'public good' that could serve as an engine of economic development (Boyer 1985; ECS 1986). All three of these developments converged on a particular view of 'quality' as manifest in student learning.

Nourished by these developments, formal calls for the assessment of collegiate learning came simultaneously from two directions. First, in the wake of *A Nation at Risk*, two reports came out that called for learning assessment as an integral component of curricular reform. *Involvement in Learning*, the report of the Study Group on the Conditions of Excellence in American Higher Education convened with federal support, argued that institution-initiated assessments of learning were essential to transforming the teaching–learning process toward active and engaging pedagogies (NIE 1984). *Integrity in the College Curriculum*, issued by the prominent Association of American Colleges, argued in parallel that coherent undergraduate courses of study were essential to improving quality and that more systematic assessments of learning were needed to help develop them (AAC 1985). Both were advanced from within the academy as self-directed reform initiatives. But a second development was embodied in yet a third report, issued by the National Governors Association revealingly titled *Time for Results* (NGA 1986). This report was in many ways an action response to *A Nation at Risk* and primarily addressed K–12 education. But echoing the new conviction that higher education was a strategic investment for states, it called for equivalent attention to assessing the outcomes of higher education to help determine the return on this investment. Both these developments were thus multifaceted rather than being narrowly responsive: as Stensaker's chapter in this volume observes about the diffusion of quality concepts in the European context a decade or so later, they were not stimulated by a single problem but were instead seen as "a pragmatic tool for addressing a number of issues".

Through their SHEEO agencies, many states responded immediately to the call for assessment. Understandably, their first proposals to colleges called for the development of standardised achievement tests to determine collegiate outcomes – a mechanism with which they were already familiar in elementary and secondary education. Because of the influence of *Involvement in Learning*, however, college and university leaders had a reasonable alternative to offer. If public institutions could agree to undertake serious local assessment programmes, use the results to make visible improvements, and report publicly on what they found, the states' call for learning-based accountability could be met while simultaneously advancing the internal reform agenda and continuing to accord the higher education sector a significant level of deference. In the relatively benign accountability climate of the mid-1980s, with lead governors championing higher education as a public investment, it seemed like a good idea to many public officials. Sometimes such proposals were initiated by state leaders themselves. In Virginia and Missouri, for example, they came from the SHEEO agency, while in states like Colorado and South Carolina, they were written directly into law (Ewell and Boyer 1988; Boyer et al 1987). Sometimes, they were the result of a protracted set of negotiations, as in Washington where an original testing proposal was converted to a full-scale pilot, then dropped when it became clear that the resulting programme was neither useful nor cheap (Thorndike 1990).

Whatever their origins, such 'institution-centred' state assessment mandates had been adopted by some two-thirds of the states by 1990 (Ewell, Finney, and Lenth 1990). Virtually all first required public institutions to prepare 'assessment plans' for approval by the governing or coordinating board. Within these plans, institutions were to a) develop statements of student learning outcomes for general education and for each major programme; b) propose concrete evidence-gathering mechanisms on student performance against these goals; c) create organisational pathways to use the resulting information to improve curriculum and pedagogy; and d) prepare a public report summarising both assessment results and what was done with them. In return, about half the states established additional funding to pay for the process.

The rapidity with which this basic pattern emerged – and the relative uniformity of its features across states – were in retrospect astonishing. The diffusion process was in many ways similar to the one Stensaker describes in his chapter in this volume (using a scheme derived from Røvik) with respect to the spread of more general quality concepts in Europe. 'Social authorisation' came entirely from government, which certainly saw such developments as something new and 'progressive'. As a result, much of the practice of rapid adoption was through direct imitation, with guidelines and frameworks literally adopted verbatim from one state to another. But until institutions found ways to shield faculty from the direct effects of these mandates there was, at best, indifference on the part of the academy and, at worst, resistance. Institutional assessment was heavily 'theorised' by the scholarly work behind *Involvement in Learning* and it quickly became 'productivised' in the form of an infrastructure of 'how to' products and publications for widespread institutional use (e.g. Nichols 1989). Implemented quickly, however, it was neither 'harmonised' nor 'individualised' at this point. In only a few cases, moreover, was it 'dramatised' in the form of transformative institutional narratives and these were mostly at low prestige institutions.

Compared to access and efficiency reporting, the resulting burdens on institutions of these requirements were substantial. Not only were colleges and universities required to create new processes to collect new kinds of information, but they were asked to do so in the sensitive arena of student learning that had previously been off limits to state scrutiny and adjudicated by individual faculty members. The first condition created new organisational costs, while the second generated significant (though often passive) political resistance (e.g. Peters 1994). These, in turn, led to at least two important patterns of institutional behaviour in response. The first of these was administrative. Because compliance was required, and because the best way for states to determine if it was occurring was to examine institutional reports to see if the requisite structures and processes to gather and use the needed information were in place, most institutions began to develop formal (and therefore visible) institution-level assessment operations. But the result was in many cases an increasingly isolated 'assessment superstructure' that did little to further the internal agenda of improving teaching and learning (Ewell 2002a, 2002b).[11]

The second behavioural pattern was one of uneven development. The majority of institutions followed this dominant strategy of trying to administratively accommodate assessment while isolating it from the academic core. But some responded with outright resistance. The latter, especially since it most often occurred among high prestige institutions unused to public scrutiny, began to significantly erode political trust in the sector and its responsiveness. Eroding levels of mutual trust, together with worsening fiscal conditions, helped set a tone for the next historical period. But some institutions actually *did* seize the opportunity to harness this mandated process for their own purposes. While academic improvement was certainly one of those purposes, it is interesting how some of these institutions also used their wholehearted adoption of 'quality assessment' (and its implied message for student return on investment) to leverage their market and prestige positions. Prominent examples here included Northeast Missouri State University (later Truman State University) and James Madison University (Banta and Associates 1993).[12]

3.3. Performance Measures [1992–1999]

Although some signs were apparent before this point, the early 1990s saw a progressive loss of momentum for the 'institution-centred' approach to assessment (Ewell 1996). For one thing, this decentralised approach meant that there was no 'bottom line' about effectiveness that could be succinctly communicated to the public. Institutions adopted their own goals and metrics to assess learning, and their public reports were frequently both inaccessible and voluminous. While capable of assuring the fact that institutions had processes of their own to look at quality, they were collectively incapable of providing the public with assurances that the actual enterprise of higher education in a given state was any worse or better (Ewell 2005). At the same time, an altered context meant that the underlying quality question was changing. A new recession meant immediate funding pressure on higher education and although the nation recovered from it relatively quickly, state budgets did not. Partly this was because of substantial tax cuts, which were increasingly popular throughout the 1990s in many states. And higher education funding was hit especially hard because funding for other state functions (chiefly health care insurance and elementary/secondary education) was mandatory and states had to balance their budgets with the leftovers. Finally, as noted, isolated instances of institutional resistance to assessment – especially by high-visibility institutions – helped erode the basic conditions of trust and 'residual deference' to the academy that characterised the 'Pre-Quality' and early 'Quality I' periods. Under these conditions, 'quality' was much more likely to be seen in a hard-edged way as 'performance' – especially in the realm of the cost-effectiveness of outputs (Ewell 1997).

Layered on to the original 'public utility' conception of higher education and the newer 'public good' conception of higher education as a strategic investment in economic development, was therefore an updated synthesis of the two. In this view, higher education was seen as a 'public enterprise', which must be disciplined and 'steered' by state authorities consistent with public purposes. This view, of course, was beginning to emerge simultaneously in policy studies of European higher education at about the time these national systems also began wrestling with 'quality' as part of the 'new public management' approaches described by Westerheijden in Chapter 4. In the United States, the policy tool of choice for state governments quickly became performance indicators (Ruppert 1994). By the mid-1990s the majority of states had adopted such measures addressing a variety of domains ranging from degree completion (by far the most common measure), cost per unit of output, employment rates for students in vocational programmes, equity of access with respect to race/ethnicity, and degree production in relation to designated employment needs (Burke and Serban 1998). In contrast to the previous period's policy approach based on institution-centred assessment, public perform-ance reporting was deliberately quantitative and comparative – intended to con-sciously steer institutions to act in particular ways. [13]

The obvious way to try to make this kind of 'steering' effective was to attach money to these indicators (Folger and Jones 1993). As a result, toward the middle of this period, many states began experimenting with 'performance funding' or 'performance budgeting' schemes that linked indicator-based performance with various kinds of incentives (Burke and Associates 2002). Like the institution-centred assessment approaches of the 'Quality I' period, many of these schemes spread rapidly from state to state without much examination or reflection, again echoing the dynamic of 'quality as fashion' described by Stensaker (in this volume). Most of these approaches only involved a limited amount of money – usually from 2% to 5% of overall operating funds[14] – and were driven by established formulae linking allocation levels to achieved indicator levels. The most extensive such performance funding scheme, only partially implemented, was enacted by South Carolina and sought to link all state support to a set of legislated performance measures (From the States 1997).

In the middle of all this, the federal government made one of its few direct forays into the realm of 'quality'. Its first instalment, enacted in 1990 under the 'Student Right to Know and Campus Security Act', was to require all institutions (public and private) to calculate degree-completion rates according to a prescribed methodology and provide them to prospective students and parents. Its second instalment, enacted with the 1992 reauthorisation of the HEA, was to require states to develop new measures and review processes directed at institutions 'triggered' by high default rates on federal student loans (From the States 1994a; NCHEMS 1999).[15] Its third instalment, following up on a goal first proposed by a national summit of the President and the fifty governors in 1989, began an initiative on whether and how to develop a national assessment of baccalaureate-level communications and problem-solving skills (USDOE 1992). Only the first of these survived more than a few years.[16] But all three were consistent with the culture of statistical performance reporting already evolving in the states.

Despite the apparent complexity of the reporting requirements typical of this period (and the myriad and inevitable complaints that are always associated with new requests of this kind), actual institutional burden was actually quite low. This was true for a number of reasons. First, many state performance measures could be calculated directly by SHEEO agencies themselves, using the rapidly expanding capabilities of their centralised student unit record databases. To be sure, prudent institutions would want to match these records with calculations of their own to ensure that they were treated fairly and not surprised, but the majority already had the necessary analytical capacity. Second, statistical performance measures could to some extent be 'gamed' by institutions to yield maximum apparent performances without really changing behaviour very much. As the experience of performance funding in Tennessee over three decades illustrates, this can lead to a constant revision of guidelines for calculating performance measures that puts as much burden on state agencies as it does on institutions (Ewell 1994). Third, because the stakes associated with marginal performance funds were relatively small in the face of overall enrolment driven resource allocation mechanisms, not much 'steering' actually occurred – especially if one looks for impacts at the all-important teaching unit or departmental level within institutions (Burke 2005). Institutions were once again able to protect their academic cores from external 'interference', but this time without a lot of burden to themselves. But doing so still required a 'tax' on these operations that provided few local benefits.

3.4. Quality II [2000–date]

Significant changes in the context for higher education again marked the beginning of the final period to be considered historically. On the economic front, the recession of 2001 badly shocked public support for higher education, causing the first absolute declines in real dollar allocations in two decades.[17] This had two important and immediate effects. First, states had few discretionary dollars available to 'steer' anything, and performance funding schemes for the most part disappeared.[18] At the same time, budget cuts in SHEEO agencies themselves meant that it was more and more difficult to fund the staff needed to enforce existing quality review processes or to construct performance indicators. Second, public institutions rapidly increased tuition and fees to cover their operating expenses. The resulting rapid return to the marketplace increased competitive pressures and enhanced the influence of market forces on institutional behaviours. At the same time, it began seriously eroding remaining distinctions between public and private institutions with respect to quality because both were now marketing heavily to students and because accreditation – the principal remaining quality assurance mechanism in higher education – treated both kinds of institutions the same.

The other significant development affecting quality in this period was a substantial change in institutional accreditation itself. Despite accreditation's assumption of the federal gatekeeping role, its actual organisation and conduct had remained until now little altered since the process began. This started changing in the late 1990s, with the result that by about 2001 regional accreditation organisations not only were the major quality assurance players in place in the United States, but were also reviewing institutions in new and distinctive ways (Eaton 2001; From the States 2002). Part of this change was because of renewed federal pressure, exercised through the USDOE's recognition process, that directed accreditors to pay much more attention to student learning outcomes. Such a requirement had been in place for federal recognition since at least 1989, but it was made increasingly prominent each successive year. By 2003, some accrediting organisations were being asked explicitly by federal recognition panels what 'standards' of learning they held their constituents to. The other stimulus for change arose from institutions that had become increasingly weary of what appeared to them to be costly but excessively ritualistic reviews that added little value to an institution's own planning and management processes.[19] Stimulated by these countervailing pressures, and supported by substantial infusions of grant money from private foundations, six of the eight regional accrediting organisations had made major changes in their institutional review processes by 2003 (Ewell 2005).

The first such change was to visibly separate accreditation's 'compliance' role from its traditional emphasis on institutional consultation and improvement. In some cases, this distinction was formal,[20] while in others it was a matter of emphasis negotiated for particular institutions.[21] But the net result was to give institutions an unprecedented opportunity to harness the accreditation process to deeply engage a set of quality issues of their own choosing.

A second change, less fully enacted to date, was to adopt a wider array of quality review techniques than the traditional multi-day comprehensive site visit conducted by largely untrained peer reviewers. Among the alternatives being enacted are the academic audit process imported from Europe and Australasia[22] and more narrowly focused protocol-based reviews borrowed from such areas as health care or industry quality assurance (Dill 2000; Dill et al. 1996). These approaches potentially allow quality reviews to delve much more deeply and effectively into institutional practices, but they also demand a level of training and discipline among reviewers that has been up to now atypical of US accreditation practice. As Blackmur points out in Chapter 2, moreover, the effectiveness of these approaches (at least in the Australasian context) depended a great deal on the willingness and ability of quality assurance agents to really press institutions about performance. And as already noted, US accreditors are significantly limited in this respect by their status as membership organisations.

A third change, stimulated substantially by USDOE, was to place far greater emphasis on examining the teaching–learning process and its outcomes (Ewell 2001a). While most accreditors had referenced this topic in some way in their review standards before this point, all are now more aggressive in actually pursuing it – to the point of citing as out of compliance high prestige institutions that had up to that point not done much in this arena. Fortunately, most accreditors are also encouraging institutions to address the complexities of determining quality in teaching and learning as part of the more flexible 'deep engagement' component of their reviews instead of adopting overly simplistic approaches. At the same time, prominent reports from both inside and outside the academic community have emphasised the importance of getting on with this work, lest the federal government impose uniform outcomes standards through the HEA.[23]

A final change, again far from fully enacted, was a growing trend toward public disclosure of the results of institutional accreditation. Traditionally, the only information disclosed to the public after an accreditation review was the institution's accredited status – essentially a 'yes/no' ratification of minimum quality. While this provides some assurance to the public and to potential students that the institution meets minimum standards, it is far from the kind of detailed information needed to make an informed consumer choice based on observed strengths and weaknesses (Jones 2002). There has been a spirited debate in the accreditation community over the past year about how far to go with respect to public disclosure (e.g. Ewell 2004), and some movement on the part of institutional accreditors to provide more information about accreditation decisions to the public has in fact taken place.[24] While this matter is far from settled, the momentum seems clearly in the direction of greater public disclosure. This is leading to concerns expressed by both the institutional and accrediting communities about the extent to which loss of confidentiality will lead to information distortion in reporting.

'Quality II', of course, is still very much in play so it is impossible to diagnose its impacts with precision. Nevertheless, a couple of trends appear to be developing. One is that the states at this point appear ready to let accreditation take the lead on quality, so long as they reserve the right to intervene if their own interests are not served (Ewell 2005). This latter point unavoidably raises the 'principal-agent' problems that are associated with any attempt by government to 'delegate' quality assurance functions to third parties. As Blackmur notes in his discussion of this topic in Chapter 2, delegating pursuit of state objectives to a third party is frequently subject to 'capture' if the party to whom responsibility is delegated is associated closely with the stakeholders whose actions it is supposed to be monitoring – and the constitution of US accreditors as institutional membership organisations makes this risk real indeed. But given current budget conditions, SHEEO agencies are in no position to undertake extensive quality reviews themselves, and there are early signs that states see their interests as increasingly aligned with accreditation's 'new look'.[25] At the same time, given a recent shift in state rhetoric toward a 'public agenda' for higher education based on civic priorities and inclusive of all institutions, accreditation's indifference to the public/private distinction has the potential of being equally welcome. So there is a chance that the new approach will succeed and a measure of trust between regulators and regulatees be re-established.

The impacts on institutions of these new accreditation practices are also just beginning to emerge. Certainly one major impact is a notable increase in burden, particularly with respect to assessing the quality of student learning.[26] While most public institutions had created the necessary administrative infrastructure to govern assessment during the 'Quality I' period, few were in a position to undertake the kind of serious, sustained and thematic investigations of effectiveness now being asked for in the name of 'building a culture of evidence'.[27] Increased direct costs of engaging these new review processes are also reported by some institutions, while others – especially larger and more complex institutions that can more straightforwardly meet the required compliance components of accreditation reviews – report lower total costs. But in many cases, increased burden is made up for by the increased institutional benefit realised by more flexible review approaches and the ability to incorporate some in-depth investigation of an issue of the institution's own choosing.[28] Taking advantage of this opportunity, though, is entirely at the discretion of institutional leadership. Proactive leaders at large well-resourced institutions have so far shown a tendency to embrace these new processes, and therefore see increased burdens offset by greater institutional benefits. Less proactive leaders – especially if they feel their institutions are at some risk from the accreditation process – are more likely to adopt a compliance posture and, if they can, opt for a more traditional 'follow the standards' review.[29]

4. SOME ANALYSIS

Over-determination is a classic problem confronting those who try to analyse any complex historical phenomenon (Althusser 1969), and the evolution of quality assurance policies in the United States just described is no exception. Multiple contexts and conditions not only exert their individual influences on institutional impacts and behaviours, but also interact in complicated ways that vary from state to state. Despite these challenges, applying a simple model of action and reaction to begin to interpret this mass of historical 'data', using a limited set of policy variables that can to some extent be varied by government authorities, may be fruitful in uncovering generalisations about what constitutes effective quality assurance policy.

4.1. Policy Variables

Quality assurance policies may vary along six important dimensions that are likely to affect institutional impact and reaction. All are meant to be continuous, and the conceptual domains they address may to some extent overlap. But each encompasses a relatively distinct set of policy choices.

4.1.1. Directness

This dimension addresses the extent to which government acts directly on institutions with respect to assuring quality, or acts through other organisations (or mechanisms like the market) to which it may delegate such action. Allowing all determinations of 'quality' to be decided by the marketplace represents one extreme on this continuum, while an aggressive state-run quality review process represents the other. Third party quality review that serves government purposes, like the role institutional accreditors play in the United States, represents a middle position.

4.1.2. Institutional Discretion

This dimension addresses the latitude the institution has to determine or shape the process of determining 'quality'. Using a set of uniform, precisely defined statistical indicators over which institutions have no control, applied without adjusting for differences in institutional contexts, represents one extreme on this continuum. 'Self-accreditation', a condition not enjoyed by any US institution but common in Europe before the advent of quality review, in which the only quality assurance mechanisms present are internal, probably best represents the other. In between but tending toward less discretion are mechanisms like the market, which institutions can attempt to influence, and performance indicator approaches where institutions are allowed a choice of indicators. Also in between, but tending toward greater discretion, are review approaches that allow institutions to make important choices about what is to be reviewed and how the review should be conducted.

4.1.3. Quality Domain

This dimension addresses the specific ingredients of 'quality' that are the object of review. As Blackmur points out (in Chapter 2), 'quality' is an inappropriately uni-dimensional concept and discussion may be better served by noting a limited set of 'qualities' as the focus of concern. As such, 'quality' is less a continuum than a list, whose most prominent topics include efficiency/productivity, equity of access, and effectiveness with respect to outcomes (especially including the quality of student learning). Also included and cutting across these specific topics, may be particular conceptions of 'quality' such as absolute performance or 'fitness for purpose'.

4.1.4. Basis for Judgment

This dimension addresses the principal method by which judgments of 'quality', however defined, are arrived at. One end of this continuum is anchored by purportedly 'objective' approaches, which rely on empirical indictors and defined standards of performance. The other extreme comprises peer review, in which the professional judgment of colleagues or experts is relied upon (Ewell 2002b). The marketplace may represent an interesting intermediate position here, where the aggregate choices of consumers collectively determine 'quality'.

4.1.5. Consequentiality

This dimension addresses what is at stake for institutions in the quality assurance process. Performance funding represents the highest form of consequentiality as performance directly influences institutional resource payoffs. Performance report-ing schemes, on the other hand, are relatively inconsequential for institutions – especially if reports are only provided to the state (Burke and Minnassians 2003). Market forces will likely vary in consequentiality depending on the institution's current reputation and resource base. Adverse accreditation decisions in the United States, for instance, are among the most consequential quality mechanisms in place for small private institutions that are heavily dependent upon tuition and fees, while remaining less consequential for larger institutions. And as the accreditation example points out, consequentiality in some cases may not involve a smooth continuum of high to low: as traditionally practiced, institutions are generally either in the majority position of no consequences or, more rarely, in the uncommon but highly disadvantageous position of losing accreditation and access to federal funds.

4.1.6. Burden

This dimension addresses the direct and indirect costs to the institution of engaging in the quality assurance process. Costs are most commonly incurred in the form of personnel time, but may also include the direct costs of assembling data or producing performance measures, of constructing internal review mechanisms such as those involved in assessing student learning, or of underwriting the expenses of a visiting team.[30] An important additional component of cost in this context are opportunity costs – more particularly, the diversion of institutional attention and planning/evaluation resources from the institution's own purposes.

The actions of these policy variables also take place within a larger policy context that is characterised by at least two factors. The first, government intentionality, centres on the extent to which the state actually *has* a conscious policy agenda of some kind, and acts deliberately and consistently to further this agenda through various mechanisms for 'institutional steering'. The second, climate of trust, centres on the extent to which policy makers and members of the academic community operate in a context of mutual respect and can implicitly count on one another to discharge what are seen as shared responsibilities. Though intentionality and trust might seem antithetical in relationships between government and the academy, this need not be the case if the objectives of both are broadly coincident. In the 'Pre-Quality' period in the United States, for instance, both government and the academy agreed on the need to fund and expand the system, and that time-honoured 'professorial' ways to maintain quality could be counted upon.

Although classifications are admittedly arbitrary, Table 1 attempts to portray each of the four historical periods reviewed in the previous section in terms of these policy variables. The 'Pre-Quality' period reflects concerns only with access and efficiency, and employs relatively indirect policy approaches that involve minimal consequences and burden, and that allow a significant degree of institutional discretion. As noted, this was also a period in which the objectives of government and the academy were roughly coincident and mutual trust was high. 'Quality I' based on the 'institution-centred' approach to the assessment of student learning, in contrast, shifted the domain of quality to the adequacy of the institution's internal processes for examining student learning outcomes, but remained a relatively indirect approach to policy that maintained a good deal of institutional discretion in an environment of relatively low consequentiality. This clearly represented a new and more proactive government approach, yet policy makers were persuaded that institutions could be trusted to carry out this more pointed approach to quality assurance. But institutions experienced a significant increase in burden as they struggled to establish whole new assessment processes against the grain of established academic culture.

The 'Performance Measures' period signalled a very different policy direction, characterised by a shift of central topic to effectiveness and public return on investment, a directly regulatory approach with very low institutional discretion about how policy tools were to be applied and (at least in the case of performance funding) relatively high levels of consequentiality for institutions. Government intentionality had not diminished, but trust was decidedly eroded. Uneven institutional response to the institution-centred approach of 'Quality I' convinced states that institutions could not be counted upon to discharge these responsibilities themselves and the academy, in turn, saw increasing government requirements for specific performance as indicative of a broader loss of professional respect and integrity. Yet, ironically, actual institutional burden receded as states were able to calculate many of these measures themselves using centralised data resources.

Table 1. Policy variables by historical period

	'Pre-Quality'	Quality I	Performance Measures	Quality II
Regulatory approach	Indirect	Indirect	Direct	Indirect
Institution discretion	High	High	Low	Negotiated
Quality domain	Efficiency access	Quality of institutional Q/A process	Productivity Return on investment	Quality of institutional Q/A process Quality of teaching and learning
Quality assessment approach	Quantitative	Professional judgment [state reviewers]	Quantitative	Professional judgment [3rd party reviewers]
Consequentiality for institutions	Low	Low	High	Moderate
Institutional burden	Low	High	Moderate/Low	High [but with potential for recovery]

Finally, the emerging 'Quality II' period involves a shift of domain back toward the quality of student learning and teaching–learning process, but largely through the indirect, third party venue of institutional accreditation. State interests were coincident with this thrust and had little ability to exercise much 'steering' on their own in any case. At the same time, the venue of accreditation was in some sense 'owned' by the academy so some measure of trust was re-introduced into the relationship.[31] New review processes separating compliance from 'deep engagement' allowed institutional discretion to be negotiated so that institutions have a substantial influence on the course and topics of a review. The institutional burden of engaging in such a review, if it chooses to take the process seriously, is high but with a concomitant potential for decreasing opportunity costs if the process allows the institution to engage a topic that it wants to improve.

4.2. The 'Quality Game'

This historical review also suggests a simple general interpretation of the cycle of impact and reaction that occurs between state authorities and institutions in the implementation of any quality assurance process. In what can be called the 'Quality Game', these sequential moves tend to play out differently under different configurations of institutional consequentiality and discretion.

Under conditions of low consequentiality (shown in Figure 1), the state leads with a requirement (Step 1) that the institution can meet in a relatively straightforward fashion through reporting (Step 2). If the level of government intentionality is relatively low, or if the objectives of the state and the academy are roughly coincident, this requirement is not very onerous in the first place. As the dynamic of state action and institutional response is repeated across multiple exchanges, the institution 'accommodates' quality reporting by insulating it from the academic core. The insulated zone (shown here as the 'assessment superstructure') is able to fully discharge the responsibilities of quality reporting because it has become a specialised functional area specifically attuned to an externally imposed operating requirement – much like the institution's need for an extramural fund-raising function or for legal counsel. As long as the state gets what it wants (or isn't aware of what it wants) levels of mutual trust can remain high.

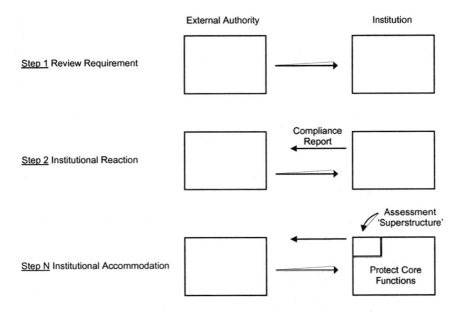

Figure 1. Some potential moves in the 'Quality Game': Low stakes

Where the burden on the institution is low, as in the 'Pre-Quality' period in the United States, this insulated zone is almost inconsequential and the implied 'tax' on the enterprise is relatively low. But as the experience of most institutions in the 'Quality I' period illustrates, institutions are able to 'accommodate' quite burdensome internal quality processes so long as they can be Where the burden on the institution is low, as in the 'Pre-Quality' period in the effectively insulated from the academic core.[32] Ironically, this was not at all what external authorities wanted in this period. Instead, the policy objective was to induce institutions to develop and use assessment processes that were locally meaningful and would lead to academic improvement. But the fact that assessment arose as an external mandate – perceived by academics as being done for somebody else and not for themselves – tended in most cases to confine the activity to the realm of 'administration' and to diminish academic respect for these processes (Ewell 2002b, 2005).

Under conditions of high consequentiality (shown in Figure 2), accompanied by a good deal of government intentionality, the situation can unfold in several ways. As Step 2a illustrates, the institution may act directly to combat the mandate if it has little choice about how to go about meeting it. As cycles of action and reaction under these conditions are repeated, mutual trust can diminish rapidly. A classic case is provided by performance funding in South Carolina occurring in the 'Performance Measures' period, where a declining funding base and legislation to allocate all resources on the basis of 37 institutional performance measures was ultimately met by sufficient institutional resistance that the programme all but ceased operating last year.[33] At the same time, the three major research universities in South Carolina essentially threatened secession in the form of a demand to the governor and legislature that their governance be reconstituted under a new board unrelated to the South Carolina Commission on Higher Education. An additional example drawn from the 'Quality I' period can be found in New Jersey, which was a striking exception to the period's general pattern of 'institution-centred' assessment. While the Department of Higher Education in New Jersey indeed called for 'institution-centred' assessment, this was only one component of an unusually complex and proactive effort to examine the quality of student learning statewide whose centrepiece was a new examination (From the States 1992). Institutional 'push-back' to this effort was one of a number of areas of resistance which ultimately led to the demise of the department itself and its replacement by a less powerful SHEEO authority in 2004 (McGuinness 1995). State experiences in Washington and Colorado, where state initiated testing proposals emerged early in this period but were diverted to create the original 'institution-centred' assessment model, were less dramatic, but essentially similar (Ewell 2005).[34] In all of these situations, a proactive government requirement, implemented with high consequentiality and no institutional discretion, led to sufficient 'push-back' that the policy (and sometimes the agency) was eliminated.

Under conditions of substantial institutional discretion, however, a quite different dynamic can unfold as illustrated by Step 2b. As in the last step of the low-consequentiality case, the institution principally meets the mandate by deploying its information and analysis capacity to demonstrate quality. But instead of insulating planning and management assets from the academic core, it is able to 'incorporate' the external opportunity provided by quality review to engage in analyses that are internally beneficial. A classic case here is drawn from the most recent 'Quality II' period, where the University of California Berkeley completed the deep engagement portion of a WASC accreditation review in 2003 by conducting several quality-related studies directed at problems of its own choosing – including one on the quality of the undergraduate learning experience and one on the consequences and opportunities associated with growing racial and ethnic diversity. WASC reviewers were satisfied with this 'in motion' demonstration of the institution's internal analytical and review capacity, while the institution was able to generate information that could lead to actual improvements in the way it operated.[35] If continuing cycles of this nature are maintained, mutual trust is reinforced and states can achieve their objectives indirectly through the proxy of institutional accreditation – so long as the all-important principal-agent problem can be overcome.

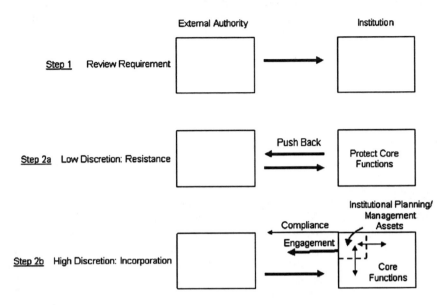

Figure 2. Some potential moves in the 'Quality Game': High stakes

The same outcome can occur even under conditions of low consequentiality if institutional leadership chooses to seize the opportunity to harness an external review process. As noted, this occurred for those few institutions like James Madison and Truman State universities in the 'Quality I' period that chose to seriously invest in assessment because their presidents saw assessment as a chance to simultaneously gather useful information and enhance institutional reputation. Heightening institutional discretion can generate this dynamic even under the apparently inhospitable conditions of quantitatively driven performance funding. One of the most powerful (and widely imitated) features of Missouri's Funding for Results (FFR) programme in the 'Performance Measures' period was its incorporation of several performance indicators chosen by individual institutions (From the States 1994b). If appropriately chosen, presidents could use the mechanism of a public performance measure aligned with the institution's strategic plans to focus and mobilise institutional resources and attention. Truman State and Northwest Missouri State universities, for example, both chose indicators for this state programme that were aligned with measures in their own internal quality programmes.

4.3. Some Propositions

The dynamic of action-reaction framed by the 'Quality Game' provides an opportunity to generate hypotheses that can be tested in the light of further US experience and that of other nations. These propositions should be interpreted in the light of the three questions that opened this discussion: what combinations of characteristics of an approach to quality assurance a) further state interest; b) result in positive institutional engagement; and c) provide a net benefit to the 'system' of higher education with respect to stakeholder interest and investment? Based on the historical exposition and analysis presented above, the following broad propositions can be advanced.

4.3.1. The likelihood that state interests will be served increases as quality approaches convey a clear and carefully delimited message about what the state values, and when consequentiality visibly reinforces this message

One of the biggest challenges faced by US approaches to quality throughout all four periods was the states' difficulty in signalling to institutions exactly what was wanted or expected.[36] The majority of state approaches were multifaceted, sending mixed (or at best extremely complicated) messages to institutions about what constituted 'effective' performance. This was especially true of the 'Performance Measures' period where the majority of performance indicator and performance funding schemes put in place included too many dimensions of performance for institutions to perceive the central policy message (Massy 2003).

Some notable exceptions to this trend are worth pointing out, though, because they appear to have been particularly effective. One such narrowly tailored message occurred in the southeastern states in the 'Pre-Quality' period, where an overriding equity agenda held public institutions accountable for increasing the proportion of African American students enrolled and graduated – a process monitored by performance indicators for each institution that proved quite effective in garnering institutional attention. In a similar vein, Missouri's FFR programme in the 'Performance Measures' period had only a single consequential state-level performance measure for allocating funds – the number of African American students earning a baccalaureate degree. Oklahoma's new performance funding scheme is similarly focused solely on graduation, but with an emphasis on maximising degree granting for underserved students from low income groups.

The importance of focusing the states' message also implies that states that are pursuing more than one quality objective may be better served by implementing separate programmes in pursuit of each, instead of launching a single complex approach that attempts to subsume all of them. Ohio's longstanding 'Selective Excellence' programme in the 'Quality I' period, for example, consisted of five separate incentive programmes addressing goals as diverse as workforce education and increased research productivity, each of which was narrowly tailored to accomplish a particular objective (From the States 1993c). This approach provides a substantial contrast to South Carolina's performance funding scheme in which almost 40 quantitative indicators were used to drive allocation indiscriminately and homogenously. The recent separation of 'compliance' from 'deep engagement' components in institutional accreditation provides another example of physically distinguishing processes with different objectives in order to clarify the 'quality message' being sent to institutions.

Finally, despite multiple ventures into the realm of performance funding by states in the 'Performance Measures' period, the vast majority of these schemes allocated only marginal resources to them.[37] Both at the time and in retrospect, some commentators argued that these amounts were simply too small to exert any meaningful leverage in the face of the dominant incentive pattern provided by enrolment-driven fund allocation in most states (NCHEMS 1992; Jones, Ewell, and McGuinness 1998). But others argued that the problem was not so much the amount of these allocations (above a minimum threshold, of course), but the fact that they were not narrowly targeted and were driven by too many indicators (Massy 2003). Superb performance on any one indicator did not yield much return, and putting an institutional focus on all of them was simply not worth the effort.

4.3.2. *The likelihood of institutional engagement with quality initiatives increases with consequentiality (but this reaction may not always be consistent with state interests)*

Significant consequentiality appears to be a necessary condition for the effectiveness of any quality initiative because of the demonstrated ability of institutions to insulate the impact of such initiatives from the academic core under conditions of low consequentiality. This was most markedly played out in the United States in the 'Quality I' period, where institutions successfully constructed 'assessment super-structures' that successfully met mandates without changing behaviours. As noted, there were exceptions in this period when institutional leaders deliberately chose to engage assessment and derived benefits as a result, but this was not because state action 'steered' this response.

When consequentiality is high, however, institutions have little choice but to engage the requirement in some way. But high consequentiality in itself does not determine the *direction* of this response. Institutions may 'push-back' politically in an attempt to defeat the requirement. Or, if they are allowed to, they can act to 'incorporate' it by investing the resources needed to engage quality in a manner that adds value to their own institution. What they cannot do under these conditions is simply isolate the requirement as a regrettable, but necessary, tax of doing business because the stakes have become too high.

4.3.3. *The likelihood that state interests will be served increases when quality approaches allow significant institutional discretion, and are implemented flexibly to empower local leadership and recognise significant differences in institutional circumstances*

Because of the power of the logic of incorporation demonstrated by the innovative approaches to institutional accreditation that are emerging in the 'Quality II' period, this proposition suggests that the most effective state actions are indirect. Inducing meaningful institutional engagement is thus a prerequisite to furthering *state* interests as well as institutional interests (Jones and Ewell 1993). As a result, state authorities need to be mindful of local practices and attempt to enlist them to serve identified public purposes if they hope to succeed (Harvey and Knight 1996).[38]

The examples already cited of institutions in the 'Quality I' period that forcefully engaged assessment while most others adopted a compliance mode suggest the importance of institutional leadership in the quality equation. Similarly, the high levels of institutional discretion to explore institution-chosen problems and issues in the course of carrying out a required quality review now being demonstrated by accreditation's 'new look' in the emerging 'Quality II' period appear to be increasing both institutional engagement *and* accountability. If state and local leadership interests can be rendered complementary, each can 'exploit' the other to get what it wants accomplished.

Two state programmes emerging in different periods can serve to illustrate this dynamic.[39] Ohio's Selective Excellence programme, already mentioned, contained a simple provision intended to focus institutional priorities: an institution could earn an additional 1% of discretionary resources provided it could demonstrate that this increment was used to increase investments in any one academic unit by at least 5%. This feature proved immensely popular among academic vice-presidents because it offered them a ready tool to focus and prioritise programmatic effort which was consistent with their own strategic plans. Confidential interviews conducted as part of an external evaluation of the project (NCHEMS 1992) also revealed the familiar pattern that academic vice-presidents could partially cover their own agendas with the argument that state rules allowed them no choice in the matter.[40] A second example is provided by the Priorities Quality and Productivity (PQP) programme in Illinois in the mid-1990s, which was similarly aimed at focusing institutional effort by eliminating duplicative or unproductive programmes. Rather than making the needed decisions about programme discontinuance themselves, the SHEEO agency provided institutions with common data about individual programme performance. But it then left the decision about which programmes to eliminate up to the institutions themselves so long as they moved their aggregate performances within established guidelines. The result was to provide institutional leadership with a lever to focus programmatic effort that they had previously lacked but badly wanted (Walhaus 1996).

Even in cases where institutional discretion cannot be increased or leadership empowered, institutional engagement can be harnessed by quality approaches that acknowledge legitimate differences among institutional capacities to respond. Put simply, it makes little sense to hold institutions accountable for matters that are outside their control. Attending to this is especially important in policies such as those implemented frequently in the 'Performance Measures' period where the dominant approach to enacting quality was empirical, leaving little room for professional judgment. During this period, most state approaches to establishing performance indicators or implementing performance funding recognised important contextual differences between four-year colleges and universities and two-year community colleges (Ruppert 1994). But there were few other instances of approaches that took into account the fact that contexts often differed substantially across institutions within each of these sectors.

A striking exception to this dominant pattern was the approach to performance funding crafted by the State Board of Community and Technical Colleges (SBCTC) in the state of Washington (From the States 1998a). This agency knew that its constituent colleges varied a great deal in their relative abilities, for example, to place vocational programme completers in related employment because regional employment markets within the state also differed substantially. In a process in some ways similar to the 'negotiated discretion' governing self-study topics established by accrediting organisations, the system analysed these contexts carefully to define individualised performance goals – challenging, but attainable – for each institution in the system. A second example of 'contextualised' accountability for performance is currently emerging in the form of individualised state-institutional 'compacts', which spell out what the state expects from each public institution depending upon its mission and circumstances. Arrangements of this kind are now in place in Kentucky, West Virginia, Colorado, and Kansas and are currently being developed in several other states.

4.3.4. The likelihood that institutions will be meaningfully engaged increases when quality approaches are implemented by 'quasi-governmental' third party organisations (but state interests are served only if such organisations pursue an agenda that is consistent with state objectives)

Institutional accreditation is a process dating back almost a hundred years in some regions in the United States and, as noted, the review processes and standards used by accrediting organisations remained essentially unaltered until only a few years ago. The explicit topic of 'quality' was instead first raised by states with the mandates that emerged early in the 'Quality I' period. As noted, most institutions were able to accommodate these requirements without substantial changes in internal behaviour. States acting directly were also the lead actors in the 'Performance Measures' period that followed, where the level of institutional consequentiality for institutions increased markedly with programmes like performance funding. Again, the pattern here was one of relatively little institutional impact. In many cases, institutions were able to 'game' allocation formulae to their advantage without affecting behaviour and in most institutions, the effects of performance funding reached few below the top administrative levels (Burke 2005).

During this latter period, however, the federal government gradually increased pressure on accreditation organisations to require institutions to assess student learning outcomes and this was reflected increasingly in their reviews. While there was certainly a substantial amount of institutional foot-dragging in this process, the vast majority of institutions had by the end of the 1990s developed the kind of assessment infrastructure originally envisioned – but not accomplished – by the state mandates of the 'Quality I' period.[41] And in the 'Quality II' period that is still unfolding, early evidence suggests positive institutional engagement in response to new accreditation approaches that allow institutions substantial discretion.

While far from definitive, this pattern of reaction suggests the efficacy of non-governmental third party organisations over direct state action in influencing institutional engagement with quality. Indeed, such organisations have several advantages over states in the current US policy climate. First, states are now severely challenged by resource shortfalls. Most could not undertake today the kinds of quality programmes they embarked upon in the late 1980s nor could they set aside sufficient funds to ground the performance funding schemes of the 1990s. Second, in a political climate of legislative term limits and severe partisanship, most states find it difficult to sustain a long-term policy agenda in higher education with any degree of consistency. The relatively rapid rise and fall of performance funding and statewide testing schemes in many states is a case in point: these are intricate and complex policy approaches that take a long time to put into place and require constant bureaucratic attention to make them work (From the States 1998b; Ewell 2001b). Together, these conditions render states relatively poor stewards of quality initiatives in the United States compared to accreditation organisations, at least at the moment.

But this dynamic poses a compelling associated problem for the states: how to effectively manage discretion to ensure that institutions address matters of *public*, not narrowly institutional, interest. This 'principal-agent' problem is the main issue with which US accrediting organisations are currently wrestling as the 'Quality II' period unfolds. High levels of institutional discretion are seen as key to building the kind of trust that a meaningful and effective quality assurance system demands. But allowing institutions to act too much on their own will not discharge the public purposes of accountability that governments are looking for.

Most accreditors are trying to manage this dilemma by requiring institutions to engage in a carefully negotiated process to determine the specific topics that institutions will address in the 'deep engagement' component of their quality reviews. For WASC, these negotiations are addressed up front, as institutions are asked to submit a proposal for formal approval by the Commission well in advance. For SACS, it is crafted in the form of a 'Quality Enhancement Plan' (QEP) that institutions develop as a formal part of their self-study process. Under AQIP, these negotiations are part of the continuous quality improvement programme that each participating institution commits to undertake and document. Many of these processes were developed explicitly in response to instances of excessive institutional discretion that moved the focus of review away from matters of public interest.[42]

4.3.5. The likelihood that public interests will be served increases when quality approaches are open, transparent and provide meaningful public information

Because virtually all institutions are public in most countries, public disclosure of review results is frequently a matter of course. But opinions differ about whether institutions will be less candid under these conditions than if results were kept confidential. In the US context, where large numbers of institutions are private, public disclosure of information about quality – in the form of detailed accreditation results – is more controversial. As noted earlier, a small proportion of accrediting organisations are beginning to provide the public with more information about the results of their reviews, but this process is only just beginning. More revealing, though, is the fact that the primary reason cited by those accreditation leaders who chose to disclose such information was their obligation to the 'public interest' (CHEA 2005). At the same time, public officials in the United States are increasingly raising questions about higher education's transparency, so responding to such questions proactively helps build credibility (SHEEO 2005). Finally, recent corporate accounting scandals like Enron have built a public expectation[43] of openness and disclosure that is increasingly hard to resist. Despite legitimate worries about information distortion, a consensus seems to be emerging that the public interest will be better served by quality processes that err on the side of openness.

In addition to the role of openness and transparency in promoting the credibility of information about quality, the information itself needs to be readily accessible to important stakeholders and the public. The 'institution-centred' assessment processes established in response to state mandates during the 'Quality I' period in states like Virginia and Colorado were certainly publicly available, but this by no means meant that they were publicly meaningful. Reports were issued annually or biennially and frequently ran to the hundreds of pages, with little guidance about which measures were most important. Institutional accreditation reports, where these are made public at all, have similar drawbacks for public communication. Under such circumstances, even though communication is open, it is difficult to claim that the public interest is served.

Similarly, performance indicators have the virtue of being succinct but do not always focus on topics that key stakeholders want to know. Virtually all of those produced by states in the 'Performance Measures' period, for instance, focused on matters associated with individual institutions, rather than addressing benefits to the states' economy and social well being (McGuinness 1994). Beginning in 2000, this began to change somewhat with the publication of *Measuring Up 2000*, the first edition of a biennial 'report card' on state-level benefits and performance. *Measuring Up* looked at joint products of *all* the institutions in a given state (public and private) in societal benefit terms (NCPPHE 2000). Because its message about return on investment is clearly focused, *Measuring Up* has proven immensely popular with governors and state legislators who can use it to help shape a higher education policy agenda for their states. Kentucky has been particularly aggressive in this regard, packaging all public communication – including data about performance and quality – around five 'key questions' posed from a 'state benefits' perspective.[44] While such examples are few, early evidence suggests that they are particularly effective in furthering public communication about performance.

4.3.6. The likelihood that all interests will be served depends on the level of trust accorded to higher education institutions by states (and their agents undertaking quality reviews), and upon the level of respect accorded to quality reviewers by the academics under review

One of the advantages of taking a long view of the dynamics of quality assurance processes is that it emphasises the impacts that one cycle of experience can have upon the next. An important consequence of a completed cycle that leaves all parties reasonably satisfied is the willingness to engage in a further cycle, perhaps with a few more risks. And the reverse. At the bottom of any ultimately successful regimen of quality review, therefore, is a relationship of mutual trust and respect between the state (or its agents) who undertake quality assurance, and the institutions they review. High levels of institutional discretion, the implementation of a flexible review process and the use of third parties as state surrogates are all claimed by previous propositions to increase the likelihood of an effective quality assurance process. But all three depend fundamentally on the state's willingness to trust the actors involved to do the right thing. Similarly, because the state cannot inspect everything, it must expect myriad institutional actors to implement desired practices without continual supervision. And this will not happen – especially among academics – unless these actors themselves respect the process and see good reasons for it. Examples of this general process in the US context have already been discussed. Among the most prominent are the erosion of previously accorded state trust in higher education institutions at the end of the 'Quality I' period due to uneven institutional response to assessment requirements, and the beginning of a recovery of respect for examining quality on the part of institutions with the implementation of accreditation's 'new look' in the emerging 'Quality II' period.

But this dynamic can also be seen in microcosm. Tennessee's original performance funding programme has survived for almost three decades now, while similar initiatives in many other states have been faddish and fleeting. One reason ascribed for this is that the various actors involved have been in place for a long time and have learned to communicate and accommodate one another. Personnel turnover at the state agency in the early years of the initiative was minimal, as was the case among the presidencies of key institutions (Banta 1986; From the States 1990). Furthermore, the leaders of the state's higher education agency were recognised as academics by their peers at institutions and were therefore less likely to be regarded as 'bureaucrats' unfamiliar with collegiate operations and values. Moreover, they launched the programme as an experiment at first and responded quickly and appropriately to institutional concerns prior to actual implementation. The opportunity to review the entire programme by all stakeholders every five years and suggest changes has been equally important. It has now been through five such reviews, each of which has yielded substantive changes. More importantly, these reviews provide all stakeholders with an opportunity to formally revisit the purposes of the programme and reaffirm them.

Similarly, the Western Association of Schools and Colleges (WASC) Senior Commission developed its new review model over an eight-year period in 1992–2000 through a series of gradually more ambitious experimental reviews.

Institutional participants in these experiments were recruited from those that already had well-established internal quality processes and could therefore be trusted to undertake a less directed course. And this circle of institutional participation was gradually widened as mutual confidence increased with the successful (and public) conclusion of each new review. All of this took place before the formal adoption of the new standards and review process in 2001. This posture of experimentation itself (WASC 1999), regional forums for two-way discussion held regularly throughout this period, and a demonstrated willingness to listen on the part of the Commission staff were cited by many as key to obtaining institutional buy-in and success in a recent systematic evaluation of the implementation process (WASC 2002).

The Tennessee and the WASC examples both emphasise the lesson that mutual trust and respect are reinforced through successive successful rounds of experience. Sufficient experience of this kind may take considerable time to be amassed, and sensitivity on the part of quality agency leaders – as well as willingness to change and experiment – are therefore critical to getting through the first steps successfully.

These six propositions are, of course, cast at a high level of generality and they are not the only ones that could be advanced. And, as noted, the very complexity of the US case means that plenty of apparent counterexamples in all four historical periods can probably be identified. But taken collectively, these propositions do suggest some lines of comparative verification in other national contexts that might usefully be pursued.

NOTES

1   The 16 German Lander have somewhat similar independent responsibilities for funding and governing higher education as the 50 US states, and the recent emergence of regional consortia such as the Nordverbund to conduct quality reviews has interesting parallels with regional accreditation in the United States.
2   All statistics cited are drawn from USDOE 2004.
3   The federal government also provides substantial research grant support to universities through the National Science Foundation, the National Institute of Health and the Defense Department, but 'accountability' for these funds is outside the scope of this discussion. The Department of Education also provides limited grant support to institutions for a range of purposes, and these have their own built-in evaluation mechanisms.
4   Indeed, a major stimulus of one of the few direct federal forays into institutional quality review occurred with the 1992 amendments to the HEA, spurred by escalating student loan default rates (From the States 1993b).
5   The United States also has more than 60 'specialised' accrediting organisations that accredit individual courses of study and function much like subject reviews in other countries. But these organisations do not serve the 'gatekeeping' function performed by regional accrediting organisations and instead operate more to provide market signals of 'quality' influencing student choice.
6   Although again, as noted, student charges are beginning to emerge in many countries whose higher education systems had previously been entirely financed by government (OECD 2003).
7   A possible exception could be argued for the few state systems that formally incorporated admissions selectivity into the missions of particular types of public institutions as, for instance, in the California Master Plan.
8   Perhaps the highest expression of the latter is the enduring Cost Study established by the Illinois Board of Higher Education that calculated dollar costs per credit generated by academic programme by level of instruction (IBHE 2004).

9   The same phenomenon, of course, would increase institutional cost pressures when enrolment flattened in the next period – leading institutional leaders in many cases to begin advocating for 'quality funding' to supplement 'enrolment funding'.

10 Then governor of the state of Arkansas.

11 Contemporary descriptions labelled this development at the state level 'assessment as a train on its own track' (Ewell and Boyer 1988).

12 Both are now ranked highly in the regional rankings of 'institutional quality' published by US News & World Report.

13 It is interesting to note that the US News ranking, based on a somewhat similar set of principles but issued in the name of 'consumer information', also came into its own at about this time.

14 And, in practice, this was frequently limited to 'new money' over and above the previous year's allocation, which under the declining higher education revenue conditions that often characterised this period sometimes meant no money at all.

15 This was popularly titled 'SPRE' after the acronym for the organisations that all states were supposed to create to enforce these provisions – 'State Postsecondary Review Entities'.

16 Graduation rate reporting was incorporated into the regular cycle of institutional reporting to the federal statistical agency and remains in place to this day. But SPRE was killed by extensive institutional lobbying against it. The potential national assessment was meanwhile killed by cost and the formidable technical difficulties involved in developing such a test.

17 Higher education's share of most states' overall public expenditures had steadily declined over this period, but real dollar allocations did manage to outpace inflation (Wellman 2002).

18 Like the institutional assessment reporting typical of the 'Quality I' period, performance funding tended not to be disestablished in state law or policy; instead, these policies simply were not enforced (Ewell 1996; Ewell and Ries 2000).

19 For the most part, these voices arose from prestigious and well-resourced institutions that were unlikely to 'fail' accreditation, but that were nevertheless required to go through it.

20 The Southern Association of Colleges and Schools (SACS), for instance, now requires a 'desk audit' to determine preliminary compliance with the Commission's standards in advance of an improvement oriented team visit centred on the institution's own Quality Enhancement Plan, while the Western Association of Schools and Colleges (WASC) Senior Commission actually requires two successive visits.

21 The Higher Learning Commission's elective AQIP (Academic Quality Improvement Program) process, for instance, is based on the Malcolm Baldrige National Quality Award originally developed for corporations, while all other regional accreditors increasingly allow 'focused' or 'special topics' self studies and reviews for institutions that are deemed not at risk of losing accreditation.

22 The Teacher Education Accreditation Council (TEAC) uses a version of the audit process exclusively, while the Western Association Senior Commission is increasingly experimenting with this approach (From the States 2001).

23 These include a report by the Business Higher Education Forum (2004) calling on all institutions to formally assess student learning in key areas and publicly report results, a comprehensive report by SHEEO's National Commission on Accountability (SHEEO 2005) calling on states to assess the 'educational capital' of their citizens, and a report by a prominent independent association of colleges and universities calling on institutions to spell out common learning outcomes then assess and publish the results (AAC&U 2004).

24 The Higher Learning Commission has just adopted the practice of publishing a summary of strengths and weaknesses after each review and the Council of Regional Accrediting Commissions (CRAC) has developed a template for doing this if member Commissions elect to use it. Nevertheless, a recent survey of accreditors indicates that only about 18% disclose information to the public about the results of individual reviews (including three of the eight regional Commissions), although about a fifth say that they plan to make changes in this area in the near future (CHEA 2005).

25 States like West Virginia and North Dakota, for example, have provided assistance to institutions in preparing assessment approaches that will enable them to meet Higher Learning Commission standards on student learning, and the California State University System has visibly linked several undergraduate improvement initiatives to the learning-centred 2001 Accreditation Standards of the Western Senior Commission.

26 Seventy per cent of institutional respondents to a 2002–2003 survey conducted by the Council on Higher Education Accreditation reported significantly more emphasis on the quality of student

learning in the accreditation reviews they experienced recently than five years before, and more than half reported that they were significantly challenged to meet these requirements (CHEA 2003).

27   The language of 'culture of evidence' to describe sincere institutional adoption of a quality culture began in the Western Association of Schools and Colleges (WASC) Senior Commission, and has quickly spread to other regions.

28   A substantial majority of 30 presidents of prominent institutions interviewed as part of a project undertaken by CHEA indicated major support for new review provisions that allow institutions to investigate local topics in greater depth (CHEA 2006). They also overwhelmingly supported the 'third party' approach to assuring quality represented by accreditation over any increased state or federal role in assuring quality. Partly for this reason, most are also not opposed to greater public disclosure of the results of individual reviews.

29   These admittedly over-generalised conclusions are based on personal observations of dynamics in the Western Senior, Southern, and North Central regions.

30   In contrast to many countries, this is the common practice in US accreditation review.

31   Whether in fact this delicate balance can in fact be maintained, of course, remains to be seen.

32   Arguably, a similar process occurred in the United Kingdom in the late 1990s with the Quality Assurance Agency's first iteration of Academic Audit. Institutions were able to develop internal quality assurance processes that passed muster under outside review, but were often unconnected to local academic decision processes and unknown to the majority of teaching staff.

33   Like so many 'quality' mandates in the United States, the statute is still on the books but no funding is being provided and many of the quality measures were not calculated this year.

34   These examples appear to parallel the Oxbridge and University of London 'push-back' on the QAA in the United Kingdom that led to so-called 'lightness of touch' in 2000–2001.

35   Author's personal observation of and engagement with this process throughout the redesign.

36   Arguably, the accreditation-based quality approaches of the 'Quality II' period have been even worse in this respect as increases in the generality of review standards designed to promote flexibility have frequently provoked confused responses from institutions about what was really expected.

37   Typical allocations ranged from 1% to a high of about 5%, with South Carolina's full performance funding approach a marked exception (Burke and Serban 1998).

38   This case is made particularly effectively for state action generally in Scott 2001.

39   This same dynamic is frequently exercised even in traditional accreditation reviews where it is customary for the visiting team to confidentially ask the institution's leadership to identify any potential review findings that might help leverage a local agenda.

40   Interestingly, despite these strong positive incentives, some vice-presidents confessed that they were unable to overcome deeply held institutional pressures for 'equity' of allocation among academic programmes and could not accept the money (NCHEMS 1992).

41   In fact, as mentioned earlier, states such as Wisconsin, North Dakota and West Virginia essentially 'delegated' the function of reviewing student learning outcomes – as addressed earlier in their assessment mandates – to regional accrediting organisations (Ewell 2005).

42   For example, in the experimental period leading up to WASC's adoption of its *2001 Handbook of Accreditation*, several institutions conducted focused studies on topics like fundraising capacity which were of considerable internal interest, but were not consistent with the quality thrust of the emerging new standards. In response, the region adopted a guideline that at least one such focused study had to visibly engage the topic of undergraduate student learning (WASC 1999).

43   As well as federal legislation such as Sarbanes-Oxley, which apply to colleges and universities as well as corporations.

44   The five questions are 1) are Kentuckians prepared for postsecondary education; 2) is Kentucky postsecondary education affordable to its citizens; 3) do more Kentuckians have certificates and degrees; 4) are college graduates prepared for life and work in Kentucky; and 5) are Kentucky's people, communities and economy benefiting? These questions adopt the perspective of the state and its citizens instead of that of institutions and the students they enrol (see http://cpe.ky.gov/).

REFERENCES

AAC (Association of American Colleges). *Integrity in the College Curriculum: A Report to the Academic Community*. Washington, DC: Association of American Colleges, 1985.

AAC&U (Association of American Colleges & Universities). *Our Students' Best Work: A Framework for Accountability Worthy of Our Mission*. Washington, DC: Association of American Colleges & Universities, 2004.

Althusser, L. *For Marx*. Trans. Ben Brewster. New York: Random House, 1969.

Banta, T.W. *Performance Funding in Higher Education: A Critical Analysis of Tennessee's Experience*. Boulder, CO: National Center for Higher Education Management Systems (NCHEMS), 1986.

Banta, T.W. and Associates. *Making a Difference: Outcomes of a Decade of Assessment in Higher Education*. San Francisco: Jossey-Bass, 1993.

Barak, R.J. *Program Review in Higher Education*. Boulder, CO: National Center for Higher Education Management Systems (NCHEMS), 1982.

Berdahl, R.O. *State Coordination of Higher Education*. Washington, DC: American Council on Education (ACE), 1971.

Boyer, C.M. *Five Reports: Summary of the Recommendations of Recent Commission Reports on Improving Undergraduate Education*. Denver, CO: Education Commission of the States (ECS), 1985.

Boyer, C.M., P.T. Ewell, J.E. Finney, and J.R. Mingle. "Assessment and Outcomes Measurement: A View from the States." *AAHE Bulletin* 39.3 (1987): 8–12.

Burke, J.C. "Reinventing Accountability: From Bureaucratic Rules to Performance Results." In Burke, J.C. and Associates, *Achieving Accountability in Higher Education*. San Francisco: Jossey-Bass, 2005, 216–245.

Burke, J.C. and Associates. *Funding Public Colleges and Universities for Performance: Popularity, Problems, and Prospects*. Albany, NY: Rockefeller Institute of Government, State University of New York, 2002.

Burke, J.C. and H. Minnassians. *Performance Reporting: 'Real' Accountability or Accountability 'Lite'?* Albany, NY: Rockefeller Institute of Government, State University of New York, 2003.

Burke, J.C. and A.M. Serban. *Performance Funding for Higher Education: Fad or Trend? New Directions for Institutional Research*. San Francisco: Jossey-Bass, no. 97, 1998.

Business Higher Education Forum. *Public Accountability for Student Learning in Higher Education: Issues and Options*. Washington, DC: American Council on Education (ACE), 2004.

CHEA (Council for Higher Education Accreditation). "The 2002–2003 CHEA Survey of Degree-granting Institutions, Accrediting Organizations, and Higher Education Associations." *CHEA Chronicle* 6.8 (2003), 6 pages.

CHEA (Council for Higher Education Accreditation). *Results of a Survey of Accrediting Organizations on Practices for Providing Information to the Public*. Washington, DC: Council for Higher Education Accreditation, 2005.

CHEA (Council for Higher Education Accreditation). *The Presidents Project: Conversations with Higher Education Leaders on Accreditation*. Washington, DC: Council for Higher Education Accreditation, 2006.

Dill, D.D. "Through Deming's Eyes: A Cross-national Analysis of Quality Assurance Policies in Higher Education." *Quality in Higher Education* 1.1 (1995): 95–110.

Dill, D.D. "Is There an Academic Audit in Your Future? Reforming Quality Assurance in US Higher Education." *Change Magazine* 32.4 (2000): 34–41.

Dill, D.D., W.F. Massy, P.R. Williams, and C.M. Cook. "Accreditation and Academic Quality Assurance: Can We Get There From Here?" *Change Magazine* 28.5 (1996): 16–25.

Eaton, J.S. "Regional Accreditation Reform: Who is Served?" *Change Magazine* 33.2 (2001): 38–45.

ECS (Education Commission of the States). *Transforming the State Role in Undergraduate Education: Time for a Different View*. The Report of the Working Party on Effective State Action to Improve Undergraduate Education. Denver, CO: Education Commission of the States, 1986.

Ewell, P.T. "Developing Statewide Performance Indicators for Higher Education: Policy Themes and Variations." In Ruppert, S. (ed.). *Charting Higher Education Accountability: A Sourcebook on State-level Performance Indicators.* Denver, CO: Education Commission of the States (ECS), 1994, 147–166.

Ewell, P.T. "The Current Pattern of State-level Assessment: Results of a National Inventory." *Assessment Update* 8.3 (1996): 1–2, 12–13, 15.

Ewell, P.T. "Accountability and Assessment in a Second Decade: New Looks or Same Old Story?" *Assessing Impact, Evidence and Action.* Washington, DC: American Association for Higher Education (AAHE), 1997, 7–21.

Ewell, P.T. *Accreditation and Student Learning Outcomes: A Proposed Point of Departure.* Washington, DC: Council for Higher Education Accreditation (CHEA), 2001a.

Ewell, P.T. "Statewide Testing in Higher Education." *Change Magazine* 33.2 (2001b): 21–27.

Ewell, P.T. "An Emerging Scholarship: A Brief History of Assessment." In Banta, T.W. and Associates (eds). *Building a Scholarship of Assessment.* San Francisco: Jossey-Bass, 2002a, 3–25.

Ewell, P.T. *Perpetual Movement: Assessment After Twenty Years.* Washington, DC: American Association for Higher Education (AAHE), 2002b.

Ewell, P.T. *Accreditation and the Provision of Additional Information to the Public About Institutional and Program Performance.* Washington, DC: Council for Higher Education Accreditation (CHEA), 2004.

Ewell, P.T. "Can Assessment Serve Accountability? It Depends on the Question." In Burke, J.C. and Associates (eds). *Achieving Accountability in Higher Education.* San Francisco: Jossey-Bass, 2005, 104–124.

Ewell, P.T. and C.M. Boyer. "Acting Out State-mandated Assessment: Evidence from Five States." *Change Magazine* 20.4 (1988): 40–47.

Ewell, P.T., J.E. Finney, and C. Lenth. "Filling in the Mosaic: The Emerging Pattern of State-based Assessment." *AAHE Bulletin* 42 (1990): 3–5.

Ewell, P.T. and P. Ries. *Assessing Student Learning Outcomes: A Supplement to Measuring Up 2000.* San Jose, CA: National Center for Public Policy in Higher Education (NCPPHE), 2000.

Ewell, P.T., J. Wellman, and K. Paulson. *Refashioning Accountability: Toward a Distributed System of Quality Assurance.* Denver, CO: Education Commission of the States (ECS), 1997.

Folger, J.K. and D.P. Jones. *The Use of Financing Policy to Achieve State Objectives.* Denver, CO: Education Commission of the States (ECS), 1993.

Frederiks, M., D. Westerheijden, and P. Weusthof. "Stakeholders in Quality." In Goedegebuure, L. and F. van Vught (eds). *Comparative Policy Studies in Higher Education.* Utrecht: Lemma, 1994, 95–126.

From the States. "Assessment in Tennessee: A State Profile." *Assessment Update* 2.3 (1990): 8–9.

From the States. "Assessment in Hard Times: A Tale of Two States." *Assessment Update* 4.1 (1992): 11–14.

From the States. "A New Federal Role in Assessing Outcomes." *Assessment Update* 5.3 (1993a): 12–13.

From the States. "More Federal Follies." *Assessment Update* 5.4 (1993b): 12–15.

From the States. "'Program Excellence' in Ohio: An Indirect Approach to Assessment." *Assessment Update* 5.1 (1993c): 12–13.

From the States. "Part H: The Shape of the Camel's Nose." *Assessment Update* 6.1 (1994a): 12.

From the States. "Performance Funding: New Variations on a Theme." *Assessment Update* 6.4 (1994b): 11.

From the States. "Putting it all on the Line: South Carolina's Performance Funding Initiative." *Assessment Update* 9.1 (1997): 9–11.

From the States. "Implementing Performance Funding in Washington State: Some New Takes on an Old Problem." *Assessment Update* 10.3 (1998a): 7–13.

From the States. "Statewide Testing: The Sequel." *Assessment Update* 10.5 (1998b): 12–13.

From the States. "Auditing Assessment: The Teacher Education Accreditation Council." *Assessment Update* 13.3 (2001): 8–10.

From the States. "Taking Stock of Accreditation Reform." *Assessment Update* 14.1 (2002): 9–11.

From the States. "Reauthorization." *Assessment Update* 15.5 (2003): 8–10.

Harvey, L. and P.T. Knight. *Transforming Higher Education.* London, UK: Open University Press, 1996.

IBHE (Illinois Board of Higher Education). *Guidelines for Submission of Operations and Grants Historical Cost, Staff and Enrollment Data*. Springfield, IL: Illinois Board of Higher Education, 2004.

Jones, D.P. *Higher Education Budgeting at the State Level: Concepts and Principles*. Boulder, CO: National Center for Higher Education Management Systems (NCHEMS), 1984.

Jones, D.P. *Different Perspectives on Information About Educational Quality: Implications for the Role of Accreditation*. Washington, DC: Council on Higher Education Accreditation (CHEA), 2002.

Jones, D.P. and P.T. Ewell. *The Effect of State Policy on Undergraduate Education*. Denver, CO: Education Commission of the States (ECS), 1993.

Jones, D.P., P.T. Ewell, and A.C. McGuinness Jr. *The Challenges and Opportunities Facing Higher Education: An Agenda for Policy Research*. San Jose, CA: National Center for Public Policy in Higher Education (NCPPHE), 1998.

Lemann, N. *The Big Test: The Secret History of the American Meritocracy*. New York: Farrar, Straus and Giroux, 1999.

Machung, A. "Playing the Rankings Game." *Change Magazine* 30.4 (1998): 12–16.

Massy, W.F. *Honoring the Trust: Quality and Cost Containment in Higher Education*. Bolton, MA: Anker Publishing, 2003.

McDonough, P.M., A.L. Antonio, M.B. Walpole, and L. Perez. *College Rankings: Who Uses Them and With What Impact?* Los Angeles, CA: Graduate School of Education and Information Studies, The University of California at Los Angeles (UCLA), 1997.

McGuinness, Jr. A.C. *A Framework for Evaluating State Policy Roles in Improving Undergraduate Education*. Denver, CO: Education Commission of the States (ECS), 1994.

McGuinness, Jr. A.C. *Restructuring State Roles in Higher Education: A Case Study of the 1994 New Jersey Higher Education Restructuring Act*. Denver, CO: Education Commission of the States (ECS), 1995.

NCHEMS (National Center for Higher Education Management Systems). *An Evaluation of the Ohio Selective Excellence Program*. Boulder, CO: National Center for Higher Education Management Systems, 1992.

NCHEMS (National Center for Higher Education Management Systems). *Federal/State Partnerships in Postsecondary Education: SPRE as a Test Case*. Boulder, CO: National Center for Higher Education Management Systems, 1999.

NCPPHE (National Center for Public Policy in Higher Education). *Measuring Up 2000: The State-by-State Report Card for Higher Education*. San Jose, CA: National Center for Public Policy in Higher Education, 2000.

NGA (National Governors Association). *Time for Results*. Washington, DC: National Governors Association, 1986.

Nichols, J.O. *Institutional Effectiveness and Outcomes Assessment Implementation on Campus: A Practitioner's Handbook*. New York: Agathon Press, 1989.

NIE (National Institute of Education). *Involvement in Learning: Realizing the Potential of American Higher Education*. Report of the Study Group on the Conditions of Excellence in American Higher Education. Washington, DC: National Institute of Education, US Government Printing Office, 1984.

OECD. "Changing Patterns of Governance in Higher Education." *Education Policy Analysis*. Paris, France: Organisation for Economic Cooperation and Development, 2003, 59–78.

Peters, R. "Some Snarks are Boojums: Accountability and the End(s) of Higher Education." *Change Magazine* 26.6 (1994): 16–23.

Ruppert, S.S. (ed.). *Charting Higher Education Accountability: A Sourcebook on State-level Performance Indicators*. Denver, CO: Education Commission of the States (ECS), 1994.

Scott, J.L. *Seeing Like a State: How Certain Schemes to Improve the Human Condition Have Failed*. New Haven, CT: Yale University Press, 2001.

SHEEO (State Higher Education Executive Officers). *Accountability for Better Results: A National Imperative for Higher Education*. Denver, CO: State Higher Education Executive Officers, 2005.

Thorndike, R.M. "The Washington State Assessment Experience." *Assessment Update* 2.2 (1990): 7–9.

USDOE (US Department of Education). *A Nation at Risk: The Imperative for Educational Reform.* Report of the National Commission on Excellence in Education. Washington, DC: US Department of Education, US Government Printing Office, 1983.

USDOE (US Department of Education). *National Assessment of College Student Learning: Issues and Concerns.* Washington, DC: US Department of Education, National Center for Education Statistics, US Government Printing Office, 1992.

USDOE (US Department of Education). *The Condition of Education 2003.* Washington, DC: US Department of Education, National Center for Education Statistics, US Government Printing Office, 2004.

Walhaus, R.A. *Priorities, Quality, and Productivity in Higher Education: The Illinois P*Q*P Initiative.* Denver, CO: Education Commission of the States (ECS), 1996.

WASC (Western Association of Schools and Colleges). *Invitation to Dialogue II: Proposed Framework for a New Model of Accreditation.* Oakland, CA: Western Association of Schools and Colleges, Senior Commission, 1999.

WASC (Western Association of Schools and Colleges). *A Learning History of the Intentional Evolution of WASC.* Oakland, CA: Western Association of Schools and Colleges Senior Commission, 2002.

Wellman, J.V. *Weathering the Double Whammy: How Governing Boards can Negotiate a Volatile Economy and Shifting Environments.* Washington, DC: Association of Governing Boards of Colleges and Universities (AGB), 2002.

Zemsky, R.M. "The Dog that Doesn't Bark: Why Markets Neither Limit Prices nor Promote Educational Quality." In Burke, J.C. and Associates (eds). *Achieving Accountability in Higher Education.* San Francisco: Jossey-Bass, 2005, 275–295.

Zemsky, R. and P. Oedel. *The Structure of College Choice.* New York: College Entrance Examination Board (CEEB), 1983.

JUAN F. PERELLON

ANALYSING QUALITY ASSURANCE IN HIGHER EDUCATION: PROPOSALS FOR A CONCEPTUAL FRAMEWORK AND METHODOLOGICAL IMPLICATIONS

1. INTRODUCTION

This chapter sets up the basis of a conceptual framework for the comparative study of quality assurance in higher education. It approaches quality assurance as a policy domain and looks into the policies that are formulated and implemented therein. The objective pursued by the construction of such a framework is to check for cross-national policy convergence and the extent to which national idiosyncrasies still play a role – and, if so, of which nature – in the current context of international harmonisation. More generally, the proposed framework aims at providing a range of tools to understand cross-national convergence in quality assurance policy, the mechanisms through which this convergence takes place, the components of the quality assurance policy that converge and those that, on the contrary, do not.

This questioning is organised in three stages. After this introduction, the prospect of looking into quality assurance policies is developed. It is argued that public policies encompass two different but complementary dimensions: an ideational one, based on normative beliefs about how a policy domain should be organised, and a material one, composed of the instruments to translate these ideas and beliefs into concrete action. The notion of *policy paradigm* is brought forward to account for this double dimension of public policies and is constructed on the basis of the determination of fundamental choices within a policy domain and their temporal and spatial actualisation. Section 3 draws on and expands the theoretical discussion with a discussion of the fundamental choices in the domain of quality assurance policy and some potential answers. Examples drawn from England, the Netherlands, and Switzerland highlight the different situations. Then, in Section 4, the discussion turns to some of the methodological implications stemming from the adopted approach for the analysis of quality assurance in higher education. This is done by addressing the actualisation of the fundamental policy choices as well as by distinguishing between the emergence of quality assurance as a political issue, and its translation into a set of systematised policies. In the conclusions, the arguments presented are summed up.

Before commencing, I would like to stress two important points. First, most of the elements discussed in the coming pages – and indeed the theoretical posture that is developed – have been dealt with, in one way or another, in other different

155

D.F. Westerheijden et al. (eds.), Quality Assurance in Higher Education: Trends in Regulation, Translation and Transformation, 155–178.
© 2007 *Springer.*

publications, especially in my doctoral thesis (Perellon 2001a). To a substantial extent, this chapter constitutes both a summing up of the thoughts and suggestions brought forward in these publications, and a modest attempt to take them a step further. Second, I consider this chapter mainly as a theoretical contribution to the study of comparative higher education. As such, it concentrates principally on the discussion of various conceptual tools, while, as often as possible, also providing concrete examples drawn from the European context. I leave the reader to judge the validity of the approach and the relevance of the method.

2. QUALITY ASSURANCE AS A POLICY DOMAIN

In this chapter, I approach quality assurance as a policy located within the broader domain generally known as higher education. Such an approach places the object of investigation under the general label of policy analysis. As a field of knowledge, policy analysis is composed of a wide range of disciplines, models, and theories (Wildawsky 1979: 15). It therefore requires the adoption of a multidisciplinary approach to social reality, an approach able to account for the conceptual devices of institutionalised academic areas and to acknowledge the importance of the historical, societal, legal, and institutional contexts within which policies are formulated and implemented. Scholars involved in policy analysis pursue a variety of concerns. These can address the links between a 'problem' and the policies formulated to address it or the content of a policy. They can deal with the action (or absence of action) of policy makers or be concerned with the impact of a public policy in terms of outputs and outcomes (Parsons 1995: 29).

In comparative studies, policy analysis can be considered as a "field of study concerned with variations in the products of governmental activity over time and across different jurisdictions" (Hofferbert and Cingranelli 1996: 593). From another perspective, Heidenheimer, Helco, and Adams (1990: 3) consider comparative public policy as "the study of how, why and to what effect different governments pursue a particular course of action or inaction", which sums up the stages of the policy cycle generally addressed in the literature: policy formulation, policy implementation, and policy evaluation.

Higher education studies have not been exempt from the influence of the policy analysis approach. Despite Premfors' remark that researchers in the area of higher education do not take a crucial part in the development of policy analysis as a (sub)discipline (Premfors 1992: 1910), the interest of these researchers for policy analysis has grown considerably in recent years. They have engaged in the theoretical avenues opened by the proponents of policy analysis and taken up most of their concerns. They have done so with a national or cross-national perspective, thus providing a wide range of investigations (see, for instance, Braun 1999; Capano 1996, 1998; Cerych and Sabatier 1986; Goedegebuure and Van Vught 1994; Kogan et al. 2000; Kogan and Hanney 2000).

The questioning developed here takes up this tradition while concentrating on the role of ideas in policy analysis. Its concerns are with the 'problem' of quality assurance, the responses to address it in terms of public policies, and the content of these policies. This stresses the necessity to specify the components of a public policy. This notion has been extensively discussed in the traditional political science literature (see, for instance, Heclo 1972; Lasswell 1970). As Heclo notes, policy is not a self-evident notion and cannot be straightforwardly defined. Two characteristics are salient. Policy is a 'middle-range' concept "bigger than particular decisions but smaller than general social movements" (Heclo 1972: 84). It relates to more or less long sequences of activities undertaken under governmental action and their consequences, than to limited and isolated decisions. This view is interesting because it highlights the importance of duration in the analysis of public policy, which permits looking at the elements of continuity within a given policy domain. The second characteristic of a policy has a more practical sense inasmuch as it encompasses some kind of 'purposiveness' (Heclo 1972: 84). This implies that those legitimated to formulate a policy do so with a certain objective in mind. Whether this objective is achieved is a matter of empirical enquiry. What is certain, however, is that the purposes of the policy will not necessarily be reflected in their outcomes, as unintended consequences may derive from the action undertaken. At the heart of the notion of policy lies, thus, the project of action (or inaction) encompassed in a group's programme to accomplish some end.

For the purpose of the present discussion, the notion of policy is understood as the proposals formulated by governmental authorities as a course of action in a particular domain. It is a construction based on beliefs about the organisation of that domain, which results in the formulation of instruments through which the beliefs are translated into action. From this perspective, it is possible to argue that a policy is formed by two different, though interconnected, dimensions. The first is the ideational dimension and relates to the normative elements that support public action. The second dimension, the material one, consists of the instruments developed as a means for public action. Their combination in a common analytical framework permits the assessment of cross-national policy convergence. In effect, national policies may (or may not) use similar procedures to assess quality but these are just one aspect of the policy and many others are still to be investigated, among which are the beliefs supporting the implementation of particular procedures. Let us see how this can be done.

2.1. Ideas and Public Policy Analysis

Despite increasing interest, there is still a lack of theory about the role of ideas in public policy. Ideas themselves are not an easy concept to understand. Among the different approaches that can be found in the literature (Colander and Coats 1989; Hall 1989; Corbett 2003; Musselin 2000), Goldstein and Keohane (1993) offer a valuable and encompassing contribution which can prove helpful, at least partially, for our own discussion. For them, ideas are simply 'beliefs held by individuals' that can be grouped into three main categories: worldviews, principled beliefs, and causal beliefs (1993: 3–11). Beliefs as worldviews refer to wide perceptions of how things should be. Principled beliefs help to distinguish between what is morally 'right' and what is 'wrong'. These principles are deeply rooted in people's minds and are derived from socialisation in a particular society or social group. Finally, causal beliefs establish a cause-effect relationship between two, or more, dimensions of social life. This type of belief provides general guidelines about how a given objective can be reached.

The authors emphasise the differences between the three notions in order to obtain clear categories. By so doing, however, they underestimate the interdependency of the notions they address. Two points are particularly problematic and examples from higher education can highlight them. First, worldviews on the role of the state in the organisation of higher education systems cannot be translated into practice if 'principles' about what is 'right' or 'wrong' about it are not already formed. Considering that the state should step back from higher education is a view that implies the pre-existence of principles about it, so that it is accepted by its proponents, who act accordingly. Policy formulation combines the three types of beliefs within a single, general worldview. In addition, and despite the usefulness of this approach, it is important to account for the plurality of concurrent worldviews and the process by which some become more powerful than others with regard to the organisation of policy domains: analysing the emergence of particular views on quality assurance policy implies relating them to developments in other domains and, indeed, in society at large.

A way to expand this approach is to refer to the notion of policy paradigm as developed by Thomas Kuhn. For him, a paradigm encompasses two dimensions:

> On the one hand, it stands for the entire constellation of beliefs, values, techniques, and so on shared by the members of a given community. On the other, it denotes one sort of elements in that constellation, the concrete puzzle-solutions which, employed as models or examples, can replace explicit rules as a basis for the solution of the remaining puzzles of normal science. (Kuhn 1970: 175)

Transposed into the field of policy analysis, this approach can be understood as follows. Each policy is composed of two different elements: the ideational and the material. The latter refers to the implementation of the policy, the tools used to make it as efficient as possible and the procedures of evaluation of the policy. The ideational dimension, on the contrary, is the set of cognitive values and norms underpinning the production of new policies in a given domain. As noted, however, the ideational dimension of public policies tends to be similar from one domain to another. In this respect, the emergence of a new sectoral policy has to be understood as the expression, in that particular domain, of a wider worldview.

How, then, does policy change occur within such a framework? Here, Lakatos' conceptual apparatus can prove helpful (Lakatos 1968; Lakatos and Musgrave 1974) since he differentiates between two components of a research programme: the core and the protective belt. The core refers to the fundamental methodological orientations dominating the entire programme. It consists of hard values, beliefs, and norms acting as the ideational basis governing all behaviours and actions. The protective belt is the "set of hypotheses and specific predictions that can be submitted to the test of empirical evidence without compromising the integrity of the core" (Majone 1991: 191). They are the elements that protect the fundamental assumptions of the programme by continuously adapting themselves to the results of empirical tests. They are more flexible and can be modified more easily thus allowing the general structure to continue to exist (Sabatier 1993). From this perspective, scientific change occurs progressively through a movement going from the exterior to the interior, that is, from the protective belt towards the core of research programmes. Following Lakatos, the protective belt can be understood as the material counterpart to the ideational core elements.

The paradigm approach referred to above can gain from being combined with the research programme one. Both Kuhn and Lakatos pay tribute to the ideational dimension in the production of scientific knowledge. The existence of a set of common beliefs shared among a scientific community is at the heart of their analysis, though leading to different views about the process of change itself. Kuhn refers to scientific change as a revolution, stressing a more radical path towards new dominant theories. This view can be misleading when it comes to analysing change in public policy. Contrary to Kuhn, through the research programme approach, Lakatos provides more helpful elements. His distinction between the core and the protective belt allows the re-introduction of the temporal dimension less explicitly referred to by Kuhn. By differentiating the core from the protective elements, Lakatos leaves room for an analysis of the process going from the erosion of the protective belt to the attack on the core values.

2.2. Policy Paradigms and Policy Domains

A policy paradigm is always time and space dependent. It will always reflect the reality of the moment in a particular national setting. Also, it will always bring together elements related to the particular domain under investigation and to broader domains of which the one studied is a part. To highlight the relevance of this approach for the study of quality assurance policy, a detour through the broader domain of higher education policy can be useful.

In his discussion of policy analysis in higher education, Premfors outlines the existence of six fundamental choices: size, structure, location, admission, governance, and curricula (Premfors 1992: 1911). These issues are considered as elements to be addressed by all higher education policies. For him, policy formation in higher education then results from the application of five basic values – excellence, equality, autonomy, accountability, and efficiency – to the six fundamental choices (Premfors 1992: 1912).

We only partially endorse Premfors' views. In effect, arguing that policy formation in higher education results from the combination of the fundamental choices with the basic values can be misleading, since Premfors' basic values in higher education are actually features that have gained major importance in the last two decades or so. Premfors' description of the basic values highlights the transformation that has taken place in the terms used in higher education in recent years. In line with the above discussion, a paradigm shift has occurred from notions such as academic freedom and professional integrity to accountability, efficiency, and social responsibility. This shift corresponds to a redefinition of the place of higher education within society where the previous structure of the policy domain, in terms of beliefs and instruments, is questioned in a context marked by expansion, financial cutbacks and increased influence of the economic value of higher education for national wealth, among other trends.

From this perspective, the responses to the fundamental choices in higher education policy are not to be found according to predetermined values. Rather, the basic values upon which responses to the fundamental choices are provided are not fixed once and for all but are always space- and time-dependent. How these responses are formed is an issue that can only be addressed empirically by assessing the role played by a certain number of factors. As Premfors (1992) notes, the fundamental choices are basic issues all systems of higher education have to address through the formulation and implementation of particular policies. The process of policy formation can therefore be seen as the actualisation of these fundamental choices in different temporal and spatial locations. The fundamental choices are actualised into particular policies consisting, as noted, of an ideational and a material dimension. The combination of these two dimensions, as responses to the fundamental choices, constitutes the paradigm governing, at a given moment and in a given place, the policy domain under investigation.

Following this line of reasoning, the actualisation of the fundamental policy choices of a policy domain can be regarded as the formulation of a particular policy for that domain. Once actualised in a particular place and at a particular moment in time, the policy domain will be governed by a policy paradigm, that is, a combination of the ideational and material dimensions of the policy. The ideational dimension relates to the basic beliefs about the organisation of the domain and the objectives it should aim at. These beliefs encompass values and norms upon which a majority of the actors concerned agree, or at least those actors with sufficient resources to impose their own worldviews. These beliefs are translated into practice through the formulation of different instruments as means to address the fundamental choices of the domain. The actualisation of the fundamental policy choices, that is, the formulation of a public policy, reflects choices deriving from beliefs about the organisation of the policy domain as well as from more formal constraints such as the political organisation of the territory, the structure of the decision-making process or the environment, national as well as international.

3. ANALYSING FUNDAMENTAL POLICY CHOICES IN QUALITY ASSURANCE

I noted at the beginning the comparative concern that accompanies the proposal of the conceptual framework presented in this chapter. This concern implicitly starts from the assumption that national policies for quality assurance are temporal and spatial actualisations of the fundamental policy choices. These have to reflect intrinsic elements of the policy domain, elements that need to be addressed in any case, although the way this is achieved may vary across time and space. Once identified, these fundamental policy choices offer a valuable basis for comparison since they make it possible to look into the decisions that have been made to address them and how they differ from place to place with regard to each dimension of the policy, that is, the beliefs (or ideational dimension) and the instruments (or the material dimension).

With respect to the domain of quality assurance in higher education, the fundamental choices to be made concern the following dimensions: *objectives*, *control*, *areas*, *procedures*, and *uses*. They refer to the following questions:

- *Objectives*: What should be the aims and objectives of quality assurance policy?
- *Control*: Who should control the process of quality assurance?
- *Areas*: What are the domains covered by the quality assurance procedures?
- *Procedures*: How are the quality assurance procedures set up?
- *Uses*: How is the information collected used?

These five questions offer a general overview of quality assurance as a policy domain. They are general issues which actors involved in policy making in quality assurance cannot avoid. The responses would reflect power relationships among stakeholders struggling to impose particular worldviews and beliefs as to how the domain should be organised.

The construction of general categories similar to the fundamental choices to address quality assurance is not uncommon in the literature (see, for instance, Harman 1998). This is generally done by pointing out certain categories from the observation of a number of cases. The studies then go on to inform the reader about how the different countries studied compare in each of the categories. The number of categories and the number of countries differ from case to case. For instance, Van Vught and Westerheijden (1993) addressed five areas and discussed how France, the Netherlands, and England compared. Brennan (1997), drawing on Van Vught and Westerheijden's categories, addressed the variations that can be found among different countries, thus offering fruitful information. However, similar to the Dutch colleagues, Brennan's description says little about either the reasons for the observed variations or the beliefs the observed procedures respond to. Reporting on the results of an international project, Thune (1998) followed a similar approach to describe how different countries showed both similarities and differences in quality assurance. As with the former cases, the author provided fruitful information on how the practice of quality assurance was undertaken but said little about the reasons for it.

Although it shares the concerns for the determination of clear categories through which quality assurance can be analysed, this discussion departs from the above-mentioned works in two regards. First, it considers quality assurance as a policy domain within which policies are formulated. According to the theoretical discussion, these policies are assumed to encompass an ideational and a material dimension or, in other words, policy beliefs and policy instruments. Second, the present conceptual discussion identifies a-temporal and a-spatial choices to be made within the domain of quality assurance and, by assessing the national responses to them, determines whether and to what extent, cross-national convergence is taking place. In addition, by systematically assessing the importance of certain factors in both the emergence of quality assurance as a political issue and the formulation of a particular policy in that domain, the approach defended here can provide fruitful insights into the reasons for cross-national differences and/or similarities, something the above-mentioned studies fail to address.

I now discuss how the above-mentioned choices can be addressed empirically. This is done by constructing a set of categories from each of the five choices. These categories are approached as pairs of oppositions to be addressed by the actors involved in the formulation of quality assurance policy. Which choices are eventually made is a matter of empirical investigation within each national context; the following discussion provides some examples drawn from the European context.

3.1. Objectives: What Should be the Objectives of the Quality Assurance Policy?

The objectives of quality assurance policy reflect the beliefs about the organisation of the domain. Admittedly, trying to wholly uncover the real objectives is a difficult task. Actors are rarely rational and their actions may be motivated by a wide variety of agendas, even if this rationality is sometimes reconstructed a posteriori. The policy objectives for quality assurance in higher education can be expressed in the form of official statements addressing the role quality assurance can play in the national higher education system. They can be presented as being of two different kinds: summative or formative.

Summative objectives stress the importance of linking the results obtained through the procedures to some particular consequences. In the field of higher education this has taken the shape of subordinating the amount of funds delivered to the universities to how they are able to perform in the evaluation of their activities. The proponents of formative objectives argue that no matter what type of procedures are introduced, these should by no means influence the amount of funds institutions receive. Emphasising the learning dimension, they advocate that quality assurance procedures, by means of evaluation or otherwise, have primarily a formative role, that is, they allow for pointing out weak points of the domain under scrutiny and learning how to improve them.

To a substantial extent, shifts in the objectives are likely to modify, at least partially, the type of responses, understood as instruments, that will be developed. In this respect, the current emphasis placed on accreditation highlights a modification of the objectives of quality assurance policy in favour of a more summative-oriented approach. In this new context, which constitutes a very large proportion – if not the totality – of the recent analysis in quality assurance studies, the emphasis is placed on external regulation, mutual recognition, and international comparability of standards (Harvey 2004; Westerheijden 2003). Formative objectives, pursuing a real improvement of pedagogies of teaching and learning and organisational models within higher education institutions are, slowly but surely, losing out to more regulatory concerns aimed at making higher education institutions and study programmes as compatible as possible worldwide. This is not necessarily a bad thing, since the increasing mobility of students and academic staff actually requires the kind of transnational regulation provided by accreditation. However, it should not make us – and political decision makers – forget that what is actually requested by students from all over the world is not only subject to international compatibility but also, and more importantly, to the experience of learning, to which formative objectives for quality assurance certainly contribute.

3.2. Control: Who Should be Responsible for Quality Assurance?

Choices about ownership relate to the bodies that should be responsible for the implementation of the policy and to the extent to which this responsibility should be controlled. In the context of the present study, several scenarios can emerge.

First, the opposition between the political authorities and the higher education institutions reflects two different ways of dealing with quality assurance. In theory, one could find a situation where either the political authorities or the higher education institutions are solely responsible for the development and implementation of the policy. However, this is unlikely to be found in practical cases. It is much more appropriate to investigate the intermediary arrangements between these two extremes, that is, mixed political, and institutional control of the procedures. To a substantial extent, this situation characterised the 'early experiences' with quality assurance in the European context. For instance, the Dutch model, which developed from the early and mid-1980s to well into the 1990s, shared the control of the policy domain between the Minister of Education, through the Higher Education Inspectorate, and the institutions themselves, through the umbrella organisations of both the universities and the higher professional education institutions. In the debates that surrounded the division of competencies, the institutions themselves came up with a clear design of the instruments to be used and under whose responsibility they were going to be placed.

The discussion of the opposition within the two levels mentioned above needs to be carried out in two stages. With regard to the political authorities, a distinction has to be drawn between central and regional governments. With regard to the opposition within the institutions, the focus should be on the way the higher education sectors deal with quality assurance. Are the institutions' umbrella organisations playing a predominant role in the procedures or is this the responsibility of the individual institutions?

Finally, attention will also have to be paid to the autonomy enjoyed by those responsible for the procedures of quality assurance. This point is important. For practical reasons, it will be addressed only through the angle of independence from the political authorities. In effect, the independence of the agencies responsible for quality assurance is generally seen as a supplementary security for the validity of the entire process.

3.3. Areas: What Are the Areas Covered by the Quality Assurance Procedures?

Three categories are generally addressed by quality assurance procedures: research activities, study programmes, and general institutional management. The first two regard the traditional missions of higher education institutions, whereas the third encompasses the broader activities of these institutions such as the proper use of financial subsidies or the type of institutional government. Looking into the study programmes and research performance is generally done through different procedures and, most of the time, by different bodies and agencies.

3.4. Procedures: How Are the Quality Assurance Procedures Set Up?

Addressing the choice of methods means entering the exclusive area of the policy instruments. This is the moment when policy beliefs are translated into practice. This process can be looked into at two different levels. The first refers to methodological questions, which have to be addressed in three pairs of oppositions: outcome-oriented vs. process-oriented procedures; internal vs. external procedures and qualitative vs. quantitative methods. The second concerns the degree of involvement of the higher education institutions.

The first opposition emphasises two different approaches to quality assurance procedures. Depending on the domain where they are implemented, outcome-oriented procedures aim at answering the question, "How good is the product delivered by the institution?" As such, this is a difficult point to make. It directly raises the concomitant question of defining what 'good' is and how it should be measured. Outcome-oriented procedures are based on two assumptions. The first is that there is an objective 'product' that comes out of higher education institutions, such as numbers of graduates or publications. The second assumption is that these outcomes can be assessed against a number of predefined criteria and standards. In contrast to outcome-oriented procedures, process-oriented ones do not have as a prime objective the measurement of a supposed product. In this case, emphasis is on the general process through which education is delivered and/or research carried out in the different institutions.

The second pair of oppositions, that is, internal vs. external procedures, focuses on the different stages of the procedures as well as on the actors involved in these stages. In this case, attention can be paid to the presence or absence of a combination of internal and external reviews as well as to the organisation of these two phases. The principle of the internal procedures relies on the draft of self-assessment reports. These reports are usually prepared on the basis of guidelines defined by the body responsible for the whole process of quality assurance. In contrast, the external procedures rely on the involvement of peer reviewers commenting on the different element of the procedures.

The third pair of oppositions, the quantitative/qualitative distinction, can be re-formulated to highlight two widely used methods to assess quality in higher education: the use of performance indicators and the use of peer reviews. More than opposed methods, they can be seen as complementary ones. As noted by, among others, Van Vught and Westerheijden (1993: Appendix 2), performance indicators provide clear, objective, and measurable information, and can serve as a solid basis for political decisions. This point links together the development of quality assurance procedures with the objectives stated. There are also some problems in the use of performance indicators. The first is the pertinence of such indicators in the field of higher education and, implicitly, in education itself. Another problem concerns the actual comparability of the data collected, which sometimes makes it difficult to undertake valid comparisons.

Alongside the methodological issues, addressing the *how* question also implies making a decision with regard to whether taking part in the quality assurance procedures is compulsory or, on the contrary, if higher education institutions can decide not to participate in such procedures. This dimension of the procedural arrangements may look out of place in the current world of higher education and, in particular, the quality assurance policy. However, when first developed in the European context, teaching or institutional evaluations were made on a totally voluntary basis. This exercise, as was seen by many, helped higher education institutions to learn from others and improve existing procedures. Mutual trust and will to improve were at the heart of participation. Nowadays, opting out is not an option. Evaluations are increasingly part of the day-to-day life of universities with accreditation of study programmes or whole institutions as the prime objective.

3.5. Uses: How Is the Information Collected Used?

What to do with the information gathered during the procedures is the fifth fundamental choice to be made in the domain of quality assurance policy. In this case, the use would reflect previous decisions regarding the objectives and the control of the system. It would also reflect broader policy orientations observable in other domains of public activity.

Different responses can be provided. On the one hand, the information collected can be made available not only to the institutions that have been assessed but also to broader sectors of society. This is, for instance, the choice made by the Quality Assurance Agency in England, whose institutional audit reports can be found free of charge on the Agency's website. On the other hand, the information can also be used to rank the units assessed according to their results, even if the procedures were not elaborated to that end (see, for instance, Dill and Soo 2005). This way of dealing with the information collected has become more and more frequent throughout Europe and impacts on the three areas identified above, that is, study programmes, research and institutional management. League tables and rankings are established in several countries and widely published in books, newspapers, and magazines. They are seen as a means of allowing students, parents, and other interested actors to select the best place to study and, as such, they echo and even promote the process of commercialisation of higher education. Despite their multiplication, we still lack in-depth studies into their actual impact on student and parent behaviour when it comes to choosing a field of study or a university. In this respect, it is worth mentioning that a 1999 report by the private firm Segal Quince Wicksteed (SQW) noted that:

> By far the most important sources of information informing student choice are prospectuses and open days. Parents, friends, advisors and publications such as the UCAS Big Book are collectively important too. But different types of applicants use different sorts of general information and they are influenced by peers in different ways. In particular, mature students rely far more on friends and guidance services and less on publications than school leavers. (SQW 1999: 6)

In the current context – and business – of globalised higher education, this analysis could be challenged.

4. MAKING SENSE OF THE CONCEPTUAL FRAMEWORK: METHODOLOGICAL SUGGESTIONS

The discussion so far has concentrated on the construction of the framework itself. In this section, I propose a number of avenues through which it could be used empirically to compare quality assurance policies across countries and – potentially too – across times. These avenues are methodological suggestions and are organised around the actualisation of the fundamental policy choices identified earlier. To do so, it is important to identify the structure of the policy paradigm at a given moment in time. To that end, two moments should be distinguished: the emergence of quality as a political issue and the translation of this debate into a set of formalised policies through the actualisation of the fundamental policy choices.

4.1. Factors at Play in the Emergence of Quality Assurance as a Political Issue

The emergence of the quality debate as a political issue at the national level can be seen as the result of several factors originating from various sources. On the one hand, the factors can be internal or external to the national higher education system. On the other hand, they can originate either from within or outside the national context.

In the first case, the emergence of the quality debate reflects transformations internal to the national higher education system. These transformations can be qualitative and/or quantitative and are the result of national trends, although similar trends can be observed in other countries. What are the transformations of the systems of higher education that can be at play in the emergence of the quality debate? The first is the quantitative and qualitative expansion of higher education. The reason why the expansion is seen as a key element in the emergence of the quality debate is because the shift from elite to mass higher education is characterised by the entrance of traditionally excluded social categories. This results in new and differentiated demands on the higher education systems but also on a differentiation of standards and subsequent fears that these may fall, especially if the expansion is accompanied by a decline in funding.

The emergence of the quality debate can also be considered to be the result of political concerns regarding the level of student achievement and the time students take to complete their studies. This constitutes a second category of the internal-national dimension of the factors at play and can be analysed through the level of dropouts. The extent to which dropout rates are related to the massification of higher education is difficult to determine precisely. What is less doubtful, however, is the fact that these two factors have often been brought forward as key elements in the emergence of quality assurance in higher education as a political problem. This was particularly true, for instance, in the Netherlands and Switzerland. In the Netherlands, quality assurance in higher education was not an issue until the end of the 1970s. In fact, until then, 'efficiency' in Dutch universities simply consisted of remaining within the norms and legislation fixed by the government (Dockrell 1990: 119). The emergence of the quality debate in Dutch higher education can be traced back to the profound transformations that took place during the late 1970s and early 1980s, aimed at meeting the expansion of the system and the dropout rates, which were considered to be high. As Maassen and colleagues (1993: 140) put it:

> At the end of the 1970s, the circumstances of higher education were not very bright. The main problems concerning the university sector were the student drop-out rate being very high and the average length of study very long compared to the situation in other countries.

These factors would, however, be encapsulated within much broader policy orientations. In the Swiss case, quality assurance became a real issue only in the mid-1990s, precisely when the numbers of new entrants were beginning to increase, though rather modestly compared to the other European countries. Here, however, dropout rates were never considered an issue at that time, although they were portrayed as a potential threat for the future because of the deterioration which cutbacks would cause to student support (CUS 1994: 18).

Finally, a third internal factor worth looking into is the role of institutional bodies and professional associations at the national level. Institutional bodies, such as the associations of higher education institutions, or rectors' associations, can play a role in launching the debate on quality, although their role may be more important in shaping and organising the operationalisation of the procedures as further discussed below. In England, for instance, the Committee of Vice-Chancellors and Principals (CVCP) – 'rebranded' Universities UK in November 2000 – representing the universities reacted promptly to political expectations, best expressed by the then Secretary of State for Education, Keith Joseph, by setting up the Academic Standards Committee in 1983. In the following years, this Committee was to play an important role in the construction of the quality assurance policy domain, especially through the development of external enquiries into university businesses. Renamed Academic Audit Unit in 1990, just two years before the demise of the binary divide, it would ensure that universities had introduced adequate procedures for assuring the quality of their standards and the degrees they were awarding. The establishment of this unit was an important recognition of external pressures by the university sector, although it lacked any powers of sanction, which largely reduced the impact of its work (Perellon 2001a: 105).

The emergence of the quality debate as a political issue can also be influenced by factors originating outside the national higher education system. It can, for instance, be related to general policy orientations advocated by the political authorities. In this case, higher education, as a policy domain, is affected by the transformations that impact upon other sectors of public activity such as the health service or public transport, for instance. Consequently, policies devised for higher education and quality assurance reflect broader societal and political trends, while at the same time mirroring the peculiarities of the national higher education system.

Among the general policies that can most affect the emergence of the quality debate, two seem particularly important. The first is the extent to which there is a reduction of financial support from the political authorities. The financial argument was used as a key lever in the transformations experienced by the higher education systems of, notably, the Netherlands, Switzerland, and England. In these three cases, the emergence of quality assurance as a political problem coincided with substantial cutbacks imposed on higher education and most public domains together with concerns about accountability and efficiency. At the turn of the 1970s and in the early 1980s, Dutch political authorities had formulated a series of policies aimed at reducing the involvement, partly financial, of the state within large parts of society. It is within the context of the corrective and facilitative reforms for higher education that the specific debate on quality assurance was encapsulated. Similarly, from the mid-1990s, the Swiss federal government progressively diminished its financial support of the universities. The cantons did not compensate universities for these financial withdrawals but, rather, imposed further cuts. This was cause for concern because of the potential danger from the combination of financial reductions and numerical expansion, especially in terms of student–staff ratio. In England, the Conservative government elected in 1979 soon imposed a series of cuts in the amounts allocated to higher education. However, in contrast to the Netherlands and Switzerland, these cutbacks took place at a time when expansion was not on the agenda.

An important aspect of the reduction of funds is the influence of what is generally referred to as the marketisation of higher education, in the broadest meaning of the word. When implemented as part of a broader policy, the marketisation of higher education can have direct consequences on the process of quality assurance. The process of marketisation in higher education encompasses an objective and a subjective dimension. The objective dimension is best characterised by the already mentioned diversification of financial resources and the parallel setting up of a market for higher education. This has also influenced the internal structures of management of the institutions, making the entrepreneurial model the dominant organisational type of institutional governance. In parallel, the marketisation of higher education also encompasses a subjective dimension. This refers to the changing perception of the idea of the university and the ways of behaving in it. The introduction of the entrepreneurial model in the institutions of higher education is one of the most important characteristics. In this context, academics are requested more and more to act and behave as if the higher education institutions were private companies providing a particular product, education, and/or research to different types of clients, that is, students, public and private collectivities etc. In such a context, quality assurance procedures can be part of the way through which funds are allocated to the different institutions. In addition, in a context characterised by strong competition for research funds and/or students among the institutions, the development of quality assurance can also be understood as a means of providing the potential users of university services with the information needed to make a rational choice. However, as these two examples tend to demonstrate, it is not the existence of quality assurance procedures that is of interest in the context of the marketisation of higher education but much more the use of the information collected during these procedures. This point is important. It once again stresses the close interconnectedness of quality assurance procedures with the other policies developed in the higher education sector as a whole.

Of special importance, in this respect, is the increasing importance of cross-border and commercial provision of higher education as a result of the internationalisation of the sector. There are concerns that since cross-border and commercial provision are not always taken into account by national policies for quality assurance and accreditation, potential students would be victims of untrustworthy providers offering low quality programmes and unworthy educational experiences. In parallel, the multiplication of providers and modalities of provisions can lead to a multiplication of accreditation bodies of poor quality and reputation, making it necessary to develop mechanisms that would be able to 'accredit the accreditors'. I will come back to this point in the conclusions.

The second factor is more general. It relates to variations in the role or place of the state in the management of public activities and the struggles between the different political levels having prerogatives in the formulation of higher education policy.

This factor was, again, at play in the emergence of quality assurance as a policy in England, the Netherlands and, to a lesser extent, Switzerland. In England and the Netherlands, the emergence of quality assurance as a political issue coincided with the coming to power of right-wing majorities in the respective parliaments. In England, the Conservative project of rolling back the frontiers of the state had been explicit since the publication of the 1979 Manifesto, although what eventually happened was an increase in the control exercised over the system, as the directions adopted since the mid-1980s clearly indicate. The early stages of the project reflected themselves in financial cutbacks, as just noted, and demands for greater financial accountability and efficiency. Higher education institutions on both sides of the binary divide were increasingly under pressure not only through the financial cutbacks but also through the requirements to demonstrate that they were meeting government expectations in terms of mechanisms to ensure quality. The quality debate, in this country, was directed by Sir Keith Joseph for whom the most important success of his years as Secretary of State for Education was to shift the debate from quantity to quality and to put quality on 'top of the agenda' (Joseph cited in Ribbins and Sherratt 1997: 83).

In the Netherlands, a coalition formed by the Liberal Party and the Christian Democrats took power in 1982. This coalition was determined to put the Dutch economy back on track by a set of measures that strongly hit higher education. It was also decided to put an end to the traditional planning policies that had characterised previous governments and that had failed to face up to the aftermath of the first oil crisis. The effects on higher education were substantial. Retrenchment policies were introduced and the type of relationship between higher education and the political authorities was transformed. The shift in the policy style from planning to the steering-at-a-distance type meant that the type of control moved from ex ante to ex post procedures, and, within this context, more room for manoeuvre was granted to the institutions with the subsequent requirement that they develop some instruments to ensure the quality of the provision in a context characterised by system-wide transformations, expansion, and concern about dropouts.

The Swiss situation shows some of the elements present in the English and Dutch experiences. Although less radical than the other two cases, Switzerland has also experienced a period in which views regarding the role of the state have shifted. New-right attacks on the welfare state and the involvement of the state in the management of public affairs were observable in the mid-1990s and late 1990s (Perellon 2003). They culminated in the publication of a White Book proposing a set of measures to reduce the (financial) involvement of public authorities (De Pury, Hauser, and Schmid 1996). However, the peculiar organisation of the political arena and the deeply embedded belief in negotiated policy outcomes prevented any radical move. Changes in the role and place of the state, however, were certainly at play in the emergence of the quality debate, but in a different form from the English and Dutch experiences. In Switzerland, what was observable throughout the 1990s was an increasing trend, from the Confederation, to gain more power in higher education policy, a domain largely under the responsibility of the cantons. This trend had been visible since the early 1990s. It acquired great relevance with the appointment of Charles Kleiber as Secretary of State for Education and Research and through the adoption of a new Act on Federal Assistance to Cantonal Universities in 1999 (Perellon 2001b).

The emergence of the quality debate in a particular country can also be influenced by international factors. Within the domain of higher education, the role of international professional bodies and associations as catalysts of the quality debate in a particular country is important to assess. Like their national counterparts, they can be seen as places where ideas and impressions are shared and from which lessons can be learnt from international partners. Professional bodies and associations are not the only factors potentially influencing the emergence of the quality debate. The process of the internationalisation of higher education policy can also be at play. The latter can influence, among other things, student exchanges, through international schemes, and the conditions to be met if a particular country wishes to comply with regulations passed by non-national bodies.

The last category of factors relates to those originating outside the national context that are external to the domain of higher education itself. Here, the emergence of the quality debate can be analysed in relation to the increasing importance of supra-national institutions and the type of relationships individual countries have with them. In this case, the role of the European Union deserves some attention inasmuch as it can be seen as a place where decisions are taken regarding the organisation of policy domains, among which is higher education. Although these decisions do not bind the different member states, they do have a substantial impact on policy making at the national level. In addition, the European Union is also a producer of international projects on quality assurance in higher education involving several member states.

4.2. Factors at Play in the Construction of the Quality Assurance Policy Domain

The previous section looked at the emergence of quality in higher education as a political issue. The following paragraphs prolong the discussion by turning to the process through which the debates are translated into policies in the domain of quality assurance. In this sense, the discussion points out the factors potentially involved in the actualisation of the fundamental choices.

If we start with the factors at play inside the system of higher education at the national level, three elements can be of relevance: a) the organisational features of national systems of higher education; b) the governance of higher education in general, and quality assurance in particular, as policy domains; and c) the role of the institutional bodies and professional associations.

The organisational features of national systems of higher education are important factors in the actualisation of the fundamental choices in quality assurance inasmuch as the policies that will be formulated will have to address the particularities of the system within which they are implemented (Brennan et al. 1992). Binary systems would dispose of differentiated types of policies for quality assurance. Differences would not only reflect variations in the type of education provided but also in the origins of the binary divide and in the type of relationship each sector has with the political authorities. For instance, in England, the important differences that characterised the two components of the binary sector developed into totally different traditions of quality assurance. The universities had reacted promptly to concerns from the government about standards and quality. These reactions, however, focused primarily on means to retain and improve the traditional system of external examination and, by so doing, to prevent any intervention from outside the sector. It was only by the end of the 1980s that the universities agreed on the establishment of an agency of their own, the Academic Audit Unit, to run institutional audits. But even this decision might be considered a protective move from true external scrutiny of the universities. On the other hand there were the polytechnics. These had been the object of strong scrutiny from various external bodies. To a very large extent, the polytechnics were accustomed to having people from outside their walls evaluating and assessing them. From this perspective, the coming together of the two sectors also meant the coming together of radically different ethoses with regard to the way of approaching quality assurance and, more generally, the accountability requirement. The different policy instruments previously in operation on each side of the binary divide had to be somehow reformulated to fit within the two different traditions.

This latter point has to be related to the role of the bodies made responsible for quality assurance after the passage of the 1992 Further and Higher Education Act. The latter divided responsibilities for quality assurance between the universities – both 'old' and 'new' – and the newly established Higher Education Funding Council for England (HEFCE). How the new university sector dealt with its responsibilities was a crucial element in the construction of the policy domain. The body created to that end, the Higher Education Quality Council (HEQC), soon engaged in animated discussions with the CVCP, its formal mentor. When the debates emerged regarding the possibility of abandoning the binary divide in quality assurance, the difficult relationship did not help the universities much. Rather, it substantially favoured the Funding Council's views on the role of the sector in the domain of quality assurance and the objectives the system would have to pursue. In this regard, the accountability concern and the provision of information were re-confirmed as the central policy beliefs upon which the domain of quality assurance had to be based. Eventually, the division of tasks between the HEQC and the HEFCE was abandoned in 1997, when the Quality Assurance Agency was set up to cover the entire quality assurance policy domain (Perellon 2001a: 116; Brennan and Williams 2004: 483–489).

Alongside the organisational features within which they make sense, the policies for quality assurance have to be located within the broader set of policies formulated for the whole higher education policy domain. This point relates to a second important factor in the actualisation of the fundamental choices: the governance of higher education in general, and quality assurance in particular, as policy domains. This factor can be addressed in three ways. First is the question of who decides higher education policies and, in particular, policies related to quality assurance. Three possibilities can emerge: the central government of the country under investigation, the regional governments, or the higher education institutions themselves. Second is the way a decision is taken regarding higher education and quality assurance. Here, the focus turns to the degree of diffusion or centralisation of power in the two policy domains. Third is the question of what is decided regarding quality assurance between the different actors involved. Altogether, the analysis of the structure of higher education policy offers an insight into the type of relationships between the higher education institutions and the political authorities, on the one side, and between the different levels of government, on the other. This is based on the assumption that the actualisation of the fundamental choices does not only reflect forms of political control of higher education but also forms of power distribution between levels of government in a given territory. For instance, in the Netherlands, the shape of the quality assurance policy domain as known up until the late 1990s, owed much to the governance of the system of higher education and the role played by the bodies responsible for policy formulation therein. Changes in governmental policy style and policy beliefs in the early 1980s led to a modification of the relationships between the political authorities and the higher education institutions. The changing governance patterns meant that universities and the higher professional education institutions were granted increased autonomy. These changes in the policy beliefs affected the domain of quality assurance. The institutions themselves, through their respective umbrella organisations, played a crucial role in the formulation of the responses to the fundamental policy choices, through the policy instruments, and the implementation of the procedures. Within this context, the sector retained large prerogatives, whereas the political authorities maintained the supervision of the procedures via the Higher Education Inspectorate. The structure of the Dutch higher education system certainly played a role in the differences in the policy instruments that could be found in the early stages. However, these would mainly concentrate on the areas to be looked at and the procedures to be used. The difference between the university and non-university sectors, in terms of policy instruments, eventually faded away when the higher professional education institutions adopted, at the end of the 1980s, a structure very similar to that in place in the universities. This situation lasted up until the late 1990s and the substantial changes that were introduced in the domain of quality assurance, through the implementation of the Bologna agenda and the globalised world of higher education it heralded, which made accreditation the key policy objective of national policies for quality assurance.

Together with the organisation of the systems of higher education and their overall governance, a third internal factor can potentially be influential in the formulation of quality assurance policies: the institutional bodies and professional associations. Their influence on the actualisation of the fundamental choices would reflect the general organisation of the domain as well as their respective influence in it.

With regard to national factors at play outside the domain of higher education, political features are important dimensions. This requires a consideration of the formal political framework of a country as a configuration of constraints and opportunities in the formulation of public policies. In this case, the emphasis is on the political organisation of the national territory and how it influences the organisation of policy domains. Attention has to be paid to the degree of political devolution to sub-national entities and the concomitant prerogatives with regard to the formulation of public policies having statutory power over the sub-national territory. This factor is particularly relevant in cases where higher education policy is, as a whole, a shared prerogative of different political levels, as for instance in Switzerland, Spain, or Germany.

Empirically, these two dimensions – that is, national political institutions and political organisation of the national territory – can hardly be separated since the political organisation of the territory largely determines the type of political institutions. For instance, federal systems would tend to have a greater diffusion of power over the national territory, thus granting (some) autonomy to the sub-national level in the formulation and/or implementation of public policies.

International factors are also at play in the formulation of national policies for quality assurance. Here similar factors as those discussed above can be seen as potentially influential.

With regard to the factors from within higher education, two are of particular importance. The first, as noted, refers to the institutional bodies and professional associations and is similar to what has been presented above when discussing the emergence of the quality debate, although their role may be more important here. Professional associations and networks such as the International Network for Quality Assurance in Higher Education (INQAHE), the European Network for Quality Assurance (ENQA), or the European Consortium for Accreditation (ECA) are forums where discussions are held among actors holding key positions at the national level. Experiences are exchanged and ideas debated; new impressions can arise and alternatives emerge. To a very substantial extent, these forums also perform a function of normalisation of national policies. They contribute to the formulation of the general framework for action, within which each individual country, or agency, can elaborate its own responses to the fundamental policy choices. ENQA has played, in this perspective, a fundamental role in spreading the model of institutional evaluation throughout Europe.

The second dimension that can be looked at is the internationalisation of higher education policy. This trend has gained increasing importance and will continue to do so in the coming years. It can influence national policy on quality assurance because it heralds the emergence of the global village and the freedom of movement of individuals. In this respect, the consequences of the Bologna Declaration on the quality assurance agenda deeply impact the signatory countries not only because they would work towards a harmonisation of study programmes but also because this harmoni-sation will foster student mobility, thus requiring harmonisation of the instruments through which standards can be assured. As a matter of fact, the internationalisation of higher education has resulted in the historical models of quality assurance being largely outdated. Formulated to fit the national context of higher education systems, these models now fail to address the current needs.

5. CONCLUSIONS

In this chapter, I have proposed a theoretical and analytical framework for the comparative study of quality assurance in higher education and suggested some guidelines as to how it could be used empirically. For that purpose, quality assurance has been approached as a policy domain, within which particular policies are formulated and implemented. These policies are formed by an ideational and a material dimension. The combination of these two dimensions at a given moment in time and in a given place provides the structure of the policy paradigm governing the quality assurance policy domain. The structure of the policy paradigm results from the actualisation of the fundamental choices of the policy domain. This is done by, first, formulating ideas and beliefs about the general organisation of the domain in a particular spatial and temporal location (the policy beliefs) and, second, by translating these beliefs into policy instruments. The fundamental policy choices constitute a-temporal and a-spatial categories that have to be actualised into policies. It is this process of actualisation that needs to be investigated in order to compare how different national environments make sense of the fundamental features and, consequently, to assess whether, and to what extent, they tend to converge.

The proposed framework contributes to the analysis of cross-national conver-gence in the domain of quality assurance policy in higher education. In this respect, national policies can converge, diverge, or continue on previous patterns. The actual orientation can only emerge from cross-national comparisons of the two dimensions of the policy. Such an approach can prove useful for the study of cross-national policy convergence since it allows going beyond the immediate observation of the structure of the policy paradigm to address its ideational basis. Therefore, it allows for a more accurate determination of the extent of the convergence among national policies.

A definite answer to the question of the extent of policy convergence can only be provided after in-depth empirical investigations. These have not been provided here, although this chapter has pointed out ways of using the conceptual apparatus to, firstly, identify the structure of the quality assurance policy paradigm in different national settings and, secondly, to compare differences and similarities. In a recent publication (Perellon 2005), I have noted that empirical evidence shows a clear shift in the ideational basis underpinning quality assurance policies across countries. Accreditation of study programmes and, in some cases, of institutions has become the norm – or, rather, the dominant policy objective of quality assurance. In the era of globalised higher education, consumer protection is as important as cross-national comparability of degrees. The need for comparable structures and procedures of quality assurance is increasingly voiced in Europe, and national agencies involved in this domain have been eager to respond – or comply. The extent to which the commonality of the policy objective – accreditation of study programmes or institutions – is reflected in the other fundamental choices is, again, an empirical question. Here, national responses tend to vary, mainly with regard to the control of the policy domain, that is, the distribution of power within the quality assurance policy domain (Perellon 2005: 291–294; more generally, see the different national chapters in Schwarz and Westerheijden 2004). In terms of cross-national convergence of the quality assurance policy domain, the conceptual framework proposed here would suggest that an 'ideational convergence' has indeed taken place, at least across countries of the European higher education area. To a substantial extent, this convergence has been imposed upon them by the supranational events that have been experienced since the 1990s. In the dialectic tension that cuts across globalisation, contextual idiosyncrasies affect the extent of policy convergence. While not fully immune to supranational trends, national realities certainly shape global agendas for their own purposes and in their own terms. Whether this traduction work is a mere adaptation of common and accepted trends and agendas – so-called 'travelling policy' (Ozga and Jones 2006) – or a real departure from them, potentially leading to a clash with existing priorities and practices, is a matter that deserves further investigation.

Current developments in the domain of quality assurance policy are somewhat imposed upon it by wider trends, especially the already mentioned globalised context within which the sector now fluctuates. The (re)emergence of accreditation as the 'solution' to new demands is a clear sign of this imposition. But, in parallel, the developments of quality assurance policy also contribute to changes in the higher education sector as a whole. Let me finish with an example of the effect of the close interconnectedness from a situation I know well, the Swiss case. Here, institutional and programmatic differentiation have been on the agenda for a long time. The quality assurance mechanisms introduced in the late 1990s have, so far, mainly addressed the university sector. Quality assurance and accreditation mechanisms can be used to promote the much needed diversity of Swiss higher education. To that end, it is important to set up mechanisms that meet the demands and profiles of the different institutions as well as the strategies they wish to pursue. Currently, such mechanisms are still lacking and, with them, a valuable tool to support further differentiation. The policy for quality assurance that could be developed should directly support a more wider objective for the entire Swiss higher education system. If I generalised from this situation I would suggest that the current liberalisation of the quality assurance 'market', characterised by the multiplication of bodies and agencies being involved in various ways in the process of evaluation and/or accreditation, will foster differentiation of higher education institutions and their educational provision across Europe while, at the same time and because of the close interconnectedness, being stimulated by the emergence of new educational providers, as discussed earlier in this chapter. The challenge here will be the regulation of these new agencies and bodies, taking into consideration the variety of models, procedures, and certainly also standards, they could develop to meet the variety of institutional types and modes of education delivery. In this respect, the 'accreditation of the accreditors' will constitute an important aspect of quality assurance policy, this time at the European level – and maybe beyond. The creation of a European register, as proposed by ENQA (2005) and agreed to at the 2005 Bergen Summit of European Ministers in charge of higher education, will certainly be a crucial part in this new job. But this is certainly another story to be told.

REFERENCES

Braun, D. "New Managerialism and the Governance of Universities in a Comparative Perspective." In Braun, D. and F. Merrien (eds). *Towards a New Model of Governance for Universities? A Comparative View.* London: Jessica Kingsley Publishers, 1999, 239–261.

Brennan, J. "Authority, Legitimacy and Change. The Rise of Quality Assessment in Higher Education." *Higher Education Management* 9.1 (1997): 7–31.

Brennan, J., L. Goedegebuure, T. Shah, D.F. Westerheijden, and P.J.M. Weusthof. *Towards a Methodology for Comparative Quality Assessment in European Higher Education.* London: CNAA, CHEPS, HIS, 1992.

Brennan, J. and R. Williams. "Accreditation and Related Regulatory Matters in the United Kingdom." In Schwarz, S. and D.F. Westerheijden (eds). *Accreditation and Evaluation in the European Higher Education Area.* Dordrecht: Kluwer Academic Publishers, 2004, 465–490.

Capano, G. "Political Science and the Comparative Study of Policy Change in Higher Education: Theoretico-methodological Notes from a Policy Perspective." *Higher Education* 31.3 (1996): 263–282.

Capano, G. "Replacing the Policy Paradigm: Higher Education Reforms in Italy and the United Kingdom, 1979–1997." Contribution to the 26th Joint Sessions of Workshops of the European Consortium for Political Research, 1998.

Cerych, L. and P.A. Sabatier. *Great Expectations and Mixed Performance. The Implementation of Higher Education Reforms in Europe.* Stock-on-Trent: Trentham Books, 1986.

Colander, D. and A. Coats (eds). *The Spread of Economic Ideas.* Cambridge: Cambridge University Press, 1989.

Corbett, A. "Ideas, Institutions and Policy Entrepreneurs: Towards a New History of Higher Education in the European Community." *European Journal of Education* 38.3 (2003): 315–330.

CUS (Conférence universitaire Suisse). "Plan pluriannuel des universités et hautes écoles suisses pour la période 1996–1999." Berne: Conférence universitaire Suisse, 1994.

De Pury, D., H. Hauser, and B. Schmid. *Ayons le courage d'un nouveau départ. Un programme pour la relance de la politique économique de la Suisse.* Zurich: Orel-Füssli, 1996.

Dill, D.D. and M. Soo. "Academic Quality, League Tables, and Public Policy: A Cross-national Analysis of University Ranking Systems." *Higher Education* 49.4 (2005): 495–533.

Dockrell, W.B. "Evaluation Procedures Used to Measure the Efficiency of Higher Education Systems and Institutions: The Netherlands". In Dockrell, W.B. et al. (eds). *Evaluation Procedures Used to Measure the Efficiency of Higher Education Systems and Institutions.* Paris: UNESCO, 1990, 117–154.

ENQA (European Network for Quality Assurance). *Standards and Guidelines for Quality Assurance in the European Higher Education Area.* Helsinki: ENQA, 2005.

Goedegebuure, L. and F. Van Vught (eds). *Comparative Policy Studies in Higher Education.* Utrecht: Lemma, 1994.

Goldstein, J. and R. Keohane. "Ideas and Foreign Policy: An Analytical Framework." In Goldstein, J. and R. Keohane (eds). *Ideas and Foreign Policy. Beliefs, Institutions, and Political Change*, Ithaca: Cornell University Press, 1993, 3–30.

Hall, P. (ed.). *The Political Power of Economic Ideas.* Princeton: Princeton University Press, 1989.

Harman, G. "The Management of Quality Assurance: A Review of International Practice." *Higher Education Quarterly* 52.4 (1998): 345–364.

Harvey, L. "War of the Worlds: Who Wins in the Battle for Quality Supremacy?" *Quality in Higher Education* 10.1 (2004): 65–71.

Heclo, H. "Review Article: Policy Analysis." *British Journal of Political Science* 2.1 (1972): 83–108.

Heidenheimer, A., H. Heclo, and C.T. Adams. *Comparative Public Policies. The Politics of Social Choice in Europe and America*. London: Macmillan Press Ltd, 1993.

Hofferbert, R. and D. Cingranelli. "Public Policy and Administration: Comparative Public Policy." In Goodin, R. and H. Klingemann (eds). *A New Handbook of Political Science*. Oxford: Oxford University Press, 1996, 593–609.

Kogan, M., M. Bauer, I. Bleiklie, and M. Henkel. *Transforming Higher Education. A Comparative Study*. London: Jessica Kingsley Publishers, 2000.

Kogan, M. and S. Hanney. *Reforming Higher Education*. London: Jessica Kingsley Publishers, 2000.

Kuhn, T. *The Structure of Scientific Revolutions*. Chicago: University of Chicago Press, 1970.

Lakatos, I. "Criticism and the Methodology of Scientific Research Programmes." *Proceedings of Aristotelian Society* 69 (1968): 149–186.

Lakatos, I. and A. Musgrave (eds). *Criticism and the Growth of Knowledge*. Cambridge: Cambridge University Press, 1974.

Lasswell, H. "The Emerging Conception of the Policy Sciences." *Policy Sciences* 1.1 (1970): 3–14.

Maassen, P., L. Goedegebuure, and D. Westerheijden. "Social and Political Conditions for the Changing Higher Education Structures in the Netherlands." In Gellert, C. (ed.). *Higher Education in Europe*. London: Jessica Kingsley Publishers, 1993, 135–151.

Majone, G. "Research Programmes and Action Programmes, or Can Policy Research Learn from the Philosophy of Science?" In Wagner, P., C. Weiss, B. Wittrock, and H. Wollmann (eds). *Social Sciences and Modern States. National Experiences and Theoretical Crossroads*. Cambridge: Cambridge University Press, 1991, 290–306.

Musselin, C. "The Role of Ideas in the Emergence of Convergent Higher Education Policies in Europe: The Case of France." Harvard University Center for European Studies, Working Paper 73, March, 2000.

Ozga, J. and R. Jones. "Travelling and Embedded Policy: The Case of Knowledge Transfer." *Journal of Education Policy* 21.1 (2006): 1–17.

Parsons, W. *Public Policy. An Introduction to the Theory and Practice of Policy Analysis*. Cheltenham: Edward Elgar, 1995.

Perellon, J.F. "The Development of Quality Assurance Policy in Higher Education. A Comparative Analysis of England, the Netherlands, Spain and Switzerland." PhD Thesis, London: Institute of Education, 2001a.

Perellon, J.F. "The Governance of Higher Education in a Federal System. The Case of Switzerland." *Tertiary Education and Management* 7.2 (2001b): 211–224.

Perellon, J.F. *La qualité dans l'enseignement supérieur. Reconnaissance des filières d'études en Suisse et en Europe. Analyse d'une révolution*. Lausanne: Presses polytechniques et universitaires romande, 2003.

Perellon, J.F. "Path Dependency and the Politics of Quality Assurance in Higher Education." *Tertiary Education and Management*, 11.4 (2005): 279–298.

Premfors, R. "Policy Analysis." In Clark, B. and G. Neave (eds). *Encyclopedia of Higher Education*. Oxford, UK, and New York: Pergamon Press, 1992, 1907–1915.

Ribbins, P. and B. Sherratt. *Radical Educational Policies and Conservative Secretaries of State*. London: Cassell, 1997.

Sabatier, P. "Policy Change Over a Decade or More." In Sabatier, P. and H. Jenkins-Smith (eds). *Policy Change and Learning*. Boulder: Westview Press, 1993, 13–39.

Schwarz, S. and D.F. Westerheijden (eds). *Accreditation and Evaluation in the European Higher Education Area*. Dordrecht: Kluwer Academic Publishers, 2004.

SQW (Segal Quince Wicksteed). *Providing Public Information on the Quality and Standards of Higher Education Courses*. London: Higher Education Funding Council for England, 1999.

Thune, C. "The European Systems of Quality Assurance. Dimensions of Harmonisation and Differentiation." *Higher Education Management* 10.3 (1998): 9–25.

Van Vught, F. and D.F. Westerheijden. *Quality Management and Quality Assurance in European Higher Education. Methods and Mechanisms*. Luxemburg: Office for Official Publications of the European Communities, 1993.

Westerheijden, D.F. "Accreditation in Western Europe: Adequate Reactions to Bologna Declaration and the General Agreement on Trade in Services?" *Journal of Studies in International Education* 7.3 (2003): 277–302.

Wildawsky, A. *Speaking the Truth to the Power. The Art and Craft of Policy Analysis*. Boston: Little Brown, 1979.

PART III: TRANSFORMATION

MARIA JOÃO ROSA AND ALBERTO AMARAL

A SELF-ASSESSEMENT OF HIGHER EDUCATION INSTITUTIONS FROM THE PERSPECTIVE OF THE EFQM EXCELLENCE MODEL

People who study quality say that *good people working according to good processes accomplish more than good people working with poor ones*. Processes reflect the way people organize their work and the kinds of data they use to inform decisions. Good processes represent a necessary condition for high quality. It's true, of course, that good processes are not sufficient. Sufficiency also requires the right resources.

(Massy 2003: 165)

1. INTRODUCTION

Fifteen years ago Peter Drucker (cited in Massy 2003) predicted that "universities will be relics in 30 years". Although Drucker may have overstated the case, the fact is that nowadays higher education can no longer take its values and privileges for granted (Massy 2003). For Amaral, Magalhães, and Santiago (2003: 131), higher education is being exposed to the influence of significant external pressures that result from the "convergent effects of financial restrictions ... rising expectations and social demand, mandates of the new economy and a weakening of its symbolic capital". Santos (1996) argues that the university today lives a triple crisis: loss of its social legitimacy and of its hegemony relative to knowledge production, as well as an institutional crisis. Massy (2003) has labelled this situation "the Erosion of Trust", stating that "settling for good enough erodes the public's trust in higher education and puts institutions and faculty at risk" (Massy 2003: 3).

For Trow "the claim that higher education is losing the trust of the larger society is a convenient one for those who have an interest in increasing the accountability of higher education to the state ..." (1996: 312). And Harker (1995: 31) finds that:

It is curious that universities, which are ostensibly concerned with excellence and which have enjoyed traditional autonomy on that basis, are currently facing quality assurance demands which, by their nature, call into question the capacity of the university sector to deliver quality outcomes.

According to Massy (2003) higher education institutions need to be "Honoring the Trust"; they need to repair the breach of trust that has been eroded. They can do this by being better than they actually are, through continuous and sustained improvement of their "quality of education without spending more, dismantling their research enterprise, or undermining their essential values" (Massy 2003: 5). However, this may

D.F. Westerheijden et al. (eds.), Quality Assurance in Higher Education: Trends in Regulation, Translation and Transformation, 181–207.

prove a very difficult task as Trow (1996: 318) emphasises: "Trust cannot be demanded but must be freely given".

This chapter analyses the increasing importance given to higher education's quality and to the development of more adequate quality assurance and assessment models. The chapter starts by discussing the reasons behind the increasing public interest in the implementation of quality assessment systems and their results, emphasising the evolution of quality concerns within higher education and the development of models and schemes for its assurance, assessment, and improvement, including those developed in the business world. We will discuss the applicability of the latter inside academe, with special reference to the European Foundation for Quality Management (EFQM) Excellence Model. This will be done using the results of research conducted[1] in Portuguese higher education institutions with the main goal of empirically validating a self-assessment model derived from the EFQM Excellence Model.

2. THE QUALITY MOVEMENT IN HIGHER EDUCATION

For Vroeijenstijn (1995), the present attention given to quality in higher education may give the impression that it is an invention arising from the last few decades and that there was no notion of quality prior to 1985. This is, of course, not true. The quality concept is not new; it is in fact as old as the medieval ages. It has been a permanent concern of universities since their foundation, having always been part of the academic ethos. Van Vught (1995) argues that it was already possible to distinguish two models of quality assessment in the 13th century, the French model of vesting control in an external authority being the archetype of quality assessment in terms of accountability, and the English model of a self-governing community of fellows being an example of quality assessment by means of peer review (Cobban 1988).

At the University of Paris the external authority was represented by the chancellor of Notre Dame Cathedral acting in the name of the bishop of Paris, while at Oxbridge the fellows of the colleges were a community that had power to judge the quality of their colleagues and the right to remove incompetent masters and to co-opt new members. There is also the case of the University of Bologna, the *alma mater studiorum*, an institution controlled by students who had the power to freely hire the professors on an annual basis, fining those who did not discharge their duties to the students' satisfaction or even firing them when their quality was beyond any hope. The University of Bologna was therefore an extreme example of the principles of customer satisfaction (if one considers students as customers, which is obviously a rather controversial matter).

The French and English models address two dimensions of quality: extrinsic and intrinsic, the French model being linked to accountability and the English model representing the traditional academic peer review. The Bologna model is based on the direct link between quality and the demands of the clients.

Over the centuries the intrinsic dimension of quality has been dominant in academe. It was only in the 1980s that the extrinsic dimension emerged as a new form of public policy. Concerns with higher education quality, its assessment, management, and improvement, have only started to be a central policy issue for governments and society during the 1980s (Liaison Committee of Rectors' Conferences 1993):

- In 1984, Sir Keith Joseph declared that the main goals for UK higher education should be quality and value for money.
- In France, also in 1984, the *Comité National d'Évaluation* was created.
- In the Netherlands, in 1985, the government published a policy paper entitled *Higher Education: Quality and Autonomy*.

This change in the approach to quality in higher education can be linked to the emergence of a number of factors, such as the massification of higher education, changes in the relationship between higher education institutions and governments (from a model of state control to a model of state supervision), the increasing role of market regulation, increasing institutional autonomy and the problems of the principal/agent, and the loss of trust in universities associated with new public management.

Until the 1960s, the relationship between governments and higher education institutions was characterised by the *Model of State Control* (Neave and Van Vught 1991). The development of the welfare state was coterminous with the movement of higher education systems towards massification in most European countries. Arguably the traditional model of the modern university did not lose legitimacy until the end of the 1960s. One may add that it survived without external attacks so long as the traditional welfare state survived. Scott (1995: 72) states:

> It is not unreasonable, therefore, to regard the modern university as intimately bound up in the welfare state. They are near-simultaneous formations. So any retreat, or reach beyond, the welfare state is likely to have important consequences for higher education.

Massification has had a very strong effect on higher education systems and their institutions. The explosive growth of higher education systems, their increasing complexity and difficulty with effective implementation of many educational reforms, due to the extremely diffuse character of the universities' power structure, have led to a change in governmental attitude towards higher education institutions, granting them greater autonomy leading to the state supervision model (Neave and Van Vught 1991). However, greater autonomy also meant more responsibility. As a result evaluation has become a common practice in many countries. Systems of accountability (the other face of institutional autonomy) have been progressively enforced and an emphasis on quality assurance and minimum standards has replaced the legal homogeneity principle used to maintain similarity of educational standards and programmes. This corresponds to what Neave (1996) calls the emergence of the evaluative state.

Other factors have also contributed to the emergence of the evaluative state. As the increasing costs of higher education were felt by taxpayers who also had to support a bigger share of the costs of other public systems, such as health and social security, the universities were forced by society to demonstrate that they were making proper and efficient use of the funds made available to them. In the late

1960s and early 1970s, the welfare state model ran into difficulties by accumulating a huge public debt to meet the increasing financial burden of social benefits, leading to the fiscal crisis of the state. Therefore, the rising costs of higher education systems, together with a more difficult economic situation, have led to changes, both at the level of funding and in its mechanisms. Governments have tried to control or even reduce public expenditure on higher education while also attempting to share costs in order to decrease the taxpayers' burden, without creating too much dissatisfaction among students and their families. This included the use of quality assessment to ensure that, despite decreasing per capita funding, higher education institutions still provided education with acceptable quality (Amaral 1997).

These factors have led to the emergence of the 'market' as a possible solution for these problems. However, for a market to be efficient, both producers and consumers need to have perfect information about price, quality, and other relevant characteristics of the goods or services being traded. But, in many cases, the relevant information is not available (imperfect information) or the producer has much more detailed knowledge than the consumer (asymmetric information). The growing emphasis paid to quality assessment and the demand for public disclosure of assessment reports may be seen as an attempt to address the problem of consumer information about the quality of education provided by different institutions.

Another interesting aspect is linked to three concurrent characteristics of higher education (Dill and Soo 2004: 61): it is an experience good (its quality can only be appreciated by consumption, when the student starts attending classes), it is a rare purchase (in general, students complete only an undergraduate study programme during their working life) and it has very high opting-out costs (changing to another programme and/or institution is difficult and expensive). The simultaneous presence of these three characteristics builds a strong case in favour of state intervention to guarantee consumer protection, and it legitimates public disclosure of different forms of information, such as licensing, accreditation and the provision of information on the quality of goods and services (Smith 2000).

Simply providing information may not be enough. There is no guarantee that students and/or their families will use the available information to make rational economic choices, which raises the problem of the immature client (Dill 1997: 180). This has been the rationale for replacing consumer-oriented markets with quasi-markets in higher education. In a quasi-market the state or a state agency acts in the name of the final consumers (the students) to negotiate with competing providers of higher education, assuming that this monopsonistic buyer will be more effective in bargaining with providers. However, the implementation of quasi-markets raises the classical principal/agent dilemma:

> ... how the principal [government] can best motivate the agent [university] to perform as the principal would prefer, taking into account the difficulties in monitoring the agent's activities. (Sappington 1991: 45 cited in Dill and Soo 2004: 68)

Therefore, one may argue that governments have been introducing an increasing number of performance indicators and measures of academic quality to monitor the behaviour of institutions and to ensure that they will self-regulate their behaviour within parameters acceptable to government. The emergence of the market in higher education has gone hand-in-hand with increased institutional autonomy as the rules of the market demand that producers have decision-making freedom to compete and to adapt to the new environment. But increased institutional autonomy poses a new and difficult challenge to the state: how to ensure that autonomous institutions competing in a market will pursue the public good under conditions of financial stringency (Massy 2004: 32)? This means that the principal/agent dilemma may also reinforce the need for quality assurance mechanisms.

The shift of the decision-making responsibility to producers has had "substantial implications for institutional governance and management" (Dill et al. 2004: 340). Starting in the 1980s, and especially at the political level, several voices were raised against the traditional model of governance and management of higher education institutions, considered to be inefficient and unable to face the new challenges confronting these organisations (Rosa, Saraiva, and Diz 2005). In fact, almost everywhere, higher education has been under pressure to become "more accountable and responsive, efficient and effective and, at the same time, more entrepreneurial and self-managing" (Meek 2003: 179). The last two decades have seen the intrusion of the rhetoric and management practices of the private sector into higher education, leading to important changes in the operation of higher education institutions. This pheno-menon that several authors have interpreted using concepts such as 'managerialism' (Miller 1995; Amaral, Magalhães, and Santiago 2003), 'new managerialism' or 'new public management' (Deem 1998, 2001; Meek 2002; Reed 2002) is associated with the emergence of market or quasi-market modes of regulation.

The rise of managerialism in higher education is usually justified by two types of arguments: on the one hand, it is considered that both the higher education system and its institutions are not capable of renewing themselves at a pace commensurate with the changes that occur in their environment; on the other hand, it is claimed that the traditional collegial decision-making bodies of these institutions tend to perpetuate academics' collective corporative interests, "creating irrationalities and inefficiencies, in both the system and its institutions" (Santiago and Carvalho 2003: 1). It is in this context that traditional criteria of social and cultural relevance of higher education are seen as obsolete and inefficient, progressively being replaced by criteria of economic rationality. Higher education institutions are forced to explicitly demonstrate to society that they make effective and efficient use of their resources, and that their activities are relevant to the economy and the labour market.

To Santiago and Carvalho (2003:1) managerialism is usually identified as:

> ... a set of management processes and instruments, technically unquestionable and socially and politically neutral. Its main goals are both the achievement of efficiency and the measurement of the performance of the higher education systems ...

Nevertheless, the authors alert us to the fact that its frame of reference has a broader scope, being theoretically and ideologically well established. In particular it combines:

> ... political, institutional and organisational assumptions with rationality principles that apparently do not seem to be organised but in which it is possible to detect some coherence around the notions of market, competition, individual choice, responsibility and efficiency. (Santiago and Carvalho 2003:1)

The emergence of new managerialism has had two major consequences for higher education. Firstly, it has promoted a "vision of public managers as the entrepreneurs of a new, leaner, and increasingly privatized government, emulating not only the practices but also the values of business" (Denhardt and Denhardt 2000: 549), which has led to the use of private sector management techniques (some of which will be analysed in the next section). And, secondly, it has destroyed trust in public services, including universities, and has attacked the academic profession.

The traditional concept of professions is associated with giving up market benefits in exchange for the monopoly of professional practice (Slaughter and Leslie 1997). Professionals claim to be guided by ideals of service and altruism, not aiming at maximising their profits and giving priority to the interests of clients and the community. No ideal could be more distant from the new ideology based on market values, relevance for the labour market, operational efficiency and entrepreneurship. Academics belong to a profession that has remained specifically isolated from the market. As they work for not-for-profit institutions, in general financed from the state budget, academics have avoided exchanging their services for payment by clients.

The privileges of autonomy and freedom of decision making granted to professionals imply enjoying trust and an ethical underpinning in the services they provide. However, under new public management the public are clients of government, and administrators should seek to deliver services that satisfy clients. In higher education, too, students are referred to as customers or clients. This transformation of students to clients also transforms academics into contractors and as such they lose their previous aura of disinterested dedication to teaching and research, becoming venal contractors. Therefore, academics are seen as having private interests in institutional decisions and need to be replaced in governance bodies by representatives of society or professional managers, and to be periodically inspected, even if under the respectable excuse of transparency and accountability.

The expansion of the European higher education systems, that some authors interpret as the move from an elite to a mass system (Scott 1995), allied to their growing costs, has made it necessary for higher education institutions to legitimate any special benefits they have, and has also contributed to the loss of trust in institutions. Trow (1996: 317–318) reminds us that in the former elite system there was a great amount of trust in academics, grounded in professional behaviour, guided by "the dictates of conscience, or considerations of honor, or professional norms, depending on their social origins". With massification, the higher education systems have become far more heterogeneous, and especially those in the non-elite sector are now seen as full of less able students and teachers (p. 320).

Recent concerns with quality have emerged from the intersection of several factors. At the same time, the balance between the two distinctive objectives of quality assessment: quality improvement (of higher education) and accountability (of higher education institutions)[2] – the first objective being mainly pursued by academics and higher education institutions and the second by governments – has now moved more towards the second objective. Therefore, the means found to address the quality issues point towards the fact that the extrinsic higher education qualities, that is, the qualities found in the services provided to society by higher education institutions (Van Vught 1994), are the ones that have received the attention of Europe over the last two decades. However, one should not forget the quality improvement objective, and higher education institutions must search for quality assessment systems and models that allow them to internally assure and improve their quality, regardless of the external quality assessment system they are subject to.[3] The ideal situation would probably be one of an external quality audit system of the higher education institutions' quality assurance and improvement systems (Dill et al. 1996).

3. TOTAL QUALITY MANAGEMENT (TQM) AND HIGHER EDUCATION

Despite its visible presence in political discourses and academic debates "managerialism as an ideology has not imposed a single, convergent model of behaviour on higher education systems and their institutions" and "governments have espoused managerialism, whether as ideology or as practice, to different degrees or not at all, and institutions have responded in very different ways, largely influenced by their historical, economic, and social backgrounds" (Amaral, Fulton, and Larsen 2003: 291–292).

It is important to distinguish between managerialism as an ideology for the strategic change of public services and the need to give higher education institutions a more flexible and effective administration (Rosa, Saraiva, and Diz 2005). In the latter case, the new management processes and tools should be mere instruments at the service of institutions and their governance and management boards, without assuming determinant roles in defining institutions' goals and strategies (Meek 2003; Amaral, Magalhães, and Santiago 2003). Or, as Trow (1994: 11) claims, when establishing a distinction between 'hard' and 'soft' managerialism:

> ... the 'soft' managerialists still see higher education as an autonomous activity, governed by its own norms and traditions, with a more effective and rationalised management still serving functions defined by the academic community itself.

To Amaral, Fulton, and Larsen (2003: 276), 'soft' managerialism has, in fact, a place in higher education as "no one in his senses will raise his voice against the idea that higher education institutions should be efficiently run". And despite considerable resistance from the academic community, some private sector management practices have to a variable extent intruded into the higher education world. One of the most popular management tools – at least in terms of marketing – has been TQM.

Williams (1993: 229) considers that the rise of TQM in higher education institutions is a "product of the market ideologies of the 80's and of the managerialism that accompanied it". He recognises that, although higher education institutions have specific and particular characteristics connected to the existence of a set of activities based on knowledge creation and dissemination, which must not be forgotten, there is still potential for the application in these organisations of certain TQM principles and concepts.

As is the case with the definition of the concept of quality, it is also very difficult, or even impossible, to find a unique and unequivocal understanding about what TQM is. To Harvey (1995: 124), "although there is no single definition or approach to total quality management a number of issues can be found in most approaches" (see Figure 1).

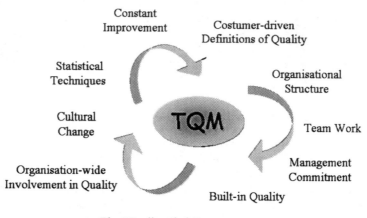

The "Quality Chain"

Figure 1. Ten issues found in most TQM approaches. (Adapted from Harvey 1995)

Williams (1993) considers that continuous quality improvement, quality consistency, participation of academics, students, and non-academic staff, satisfaction of the clients' needs and the existence of management procedures that reinforce quality are a number of TQM principles that nobody would consider irrelevant within the higher education context. In the author's opinion all these principles can significantly contribute to the development of massified higher education systems and their institutions, either explicitly oriented towards the market or not.

However, it is well known that the application of TQM principles, methods, and tools to higher education institutions is not free of criticism, due to their alleged specific nature. In fact, although not much publicised, it is well known that in several institutions the application of this management tool did not contribute to internal quality improvement (Harvey 1995).

TQM is not a management approach easily applied to higher education institutions, especially because the academic culture of these organisations is quite strong and resistant to TQM concepts, principles, and practices. And this resistance begins with TQM terminology. Terms such as product, client, empowerment or even strategy, not to mention TQM or reengineering do not easily resonate in higher education institutions. For Massy (2003: 165):

> The greatest resistance to quality process improvement comes from professors who think it's just another business-oriented fad. The language of some TQM advocates contributes to this view ... Customer, scientific method and removal of all forms of waste are sure to raise the hackles of academics.

Besides this basic difficulty there are others that can become real barriers to the implementation of TQM in academe. Some of these are:

- As occurs in other service-oriented professional bureaucracies, higher education institutions have several purposes and objectives, which usually are not sufficiently clear, and their priority relations may be mixed up (Kells 1995).

- TQM implies the a priori definition of the organisation's mission, as well as the identification of the needs and expectations of its customers. But, according to Birnbaum (2000), most higher education institutions are unable to give clear answers to these issues. In practice, there are several groups inside and outside a higher education institution that may be considered its customers, which most of the time have quite different needs and expectations to be fulfilled (Youssef et al. 1998; Birnbaum 2000).

- And who are the actors in higher education? On the one hand, there is the academic staff, participating in the teaching/learning, research, and services to the society processes. On the other hand, there are the students who must be accountable for their own learning, motivated to learn, and to maximally develop their capacities. And one still has to consider the non-academic staff that also plays a relevant role in a higher education institution.

- Higher education institutions today are still organisations where there is an emphasis on individualism, as well as a significant degree of internal competition; where there are few incentives for teamwork, centred around common and clearly assumed organisational goals (Coate 1993; Kells 1995; Youssef et al. 1998).

- It is well known that the measurement of results is fundamental when implementing a total quality system in an organisation, as it is their analysis that allows for the continuous quality improvement of processes. But how to measure the results of a higher education institution? Most of the time several performance indicators are used, such as students/teacher ratios, financial resources, public/private funds ratios, final exam results, dropout, and scholarly success rates. But these are almost exclusively institutional efficiency measures, and to rely on them only can be dangerous, for there are also important qualitative performance aspects that should not be forgotten (Harvey and Green 1993).

- The absence of effective communication channels, the presence of weak management information systems, and the bureaucracy affecting the decision-making circuits are also relevant barriers to TQM implementation in academe. Kells (1995) argues that it is normal for higher education institutions not to have useful and updated information about themselves and the way they function, or systems that allow for the collection, treatment, and use of data.

- Leadership is a crucial factor when a TQM approach is to be adopted, whatever the organisation. The successful implementation of TQM implies strong leadership, open to dialogue, committed to the ideas and principles it wants to implement, and capable of involving all other organisation members in the project. These conditions are hardly met in a higher education institution. In this type of organisation it is usually difficult to assume true leadership, authority delegation is complicated, and it is dispersed by many, and excessively large, collegial bodies that make change and the adoption of new approaches very difficult.

To Birnbaum (2000) these do not seem to be the greatest difficulties for TQM implementation. Rather, the most relevant barrier has to do with the need for a compromise between TQM and the traditions, values, and purposes of higher education institutions. According to the author, TQM has probably been the first management tool capable of provoking a serious discussion not just about its technical merits and demerits, but also about its educational and social implications. For Kells (1995: 458):

> An extremely important question is the extent to which managerial innovations can be successfully adapted to the environments they seek to serve, rather than, as is feared by many in the higher education world, there being the expectation that the institution must comply with the method.

Harvey (1995: 123) considers that some TQM aspects can be adapted to higher education institutions:

> The debate is repetitive, tedious and sterile and it is time to go beyond TQM. Rather than debate suitability it is time to look at practice and determine the worthwhile aspects of TQM and relocate them in the higher education context, stripped of alienating managerialist jargon and linked firmly to existing quality processes.

To Harvey (1995), when going beyond TQM one is re-evaluating and reorienting the higher education institutions' collegial values, and it is in this context that TQM lessons are most beneficially situated. The new collegialism, that Harvey defends, puts its emphasis on professional accountability and cooperation, reflecting two TQM key elements: delegation of the responsibility for quality and teamwork. The new collegialism emphasises the continuous improvement within the existent academic framework.

Dill (1995) assumes a not very different perspective but replaces the notion of social capital for Harvey's new collegialism. For Dill (1995) there are also some important lessons that higher education institutions can learn from TQM, the most relevant being the central place that social capital should occupy inside organisations. Dill (1995: 107) argues that:

> Through Deming's eyes we can see that assuring quality in academic programmes will require more than encouraging rational university choices by students, or providing positive incentives for faculty members to teach. It will also require re-weaving the collegial fabric of academic communities, the collective mechanisms by which faculty members control and improve the quality of academic programmes and research.

This is especially relevant in massified higher education systems with self-regulated and autonomous higher education institutions, because it is in this context that academic cohesion becomes more problematic. Efforts directed at enhancing quality should then be put into identifying networks and integration mechanisms that promote social capital development, leading to increased academic cohesion, communication, and integration (Dill 1995).

Kells (1995) suggests some strategies to successfully introduce and implement TQM in higher education:

- It may be necessary to present TQM stripped of its more superficial elements, such as "acronyms, industry-based terms and team-related symbolisms" (p. 466).

- The way the TQM scheme is introduced is crucial for its adoption; the organisation leaders' role, both formal and informal, is critical and they should be convinced that adhering to TQM will allow them to better fulfil the higher education institutions' main goals.

- Before trying to introduce a TQM approach it is necessary to "think deeply about the extent to which the organisation(s) in question has an interest in becoming a self-regulating institution" (p. 466), and even if it has the basic technical capacities to become one, including an adequate basic capacity for shared attitudes, and it requires courageous leaders to act in a self-regulating manner.

- Finally, it is important to emphasise that the introduction of a new management approach in a higher education institution must never 'damage it'.

To conclude, it can be said that applying TQM principles, concepts, and tools in higher education is not an easy process or one exempt from critics. Nevertheless it is a possible pathway for higher education institutions to follow if they wish to do so and if they believe that this is the way to continuously improve their quality. It should never, of course, be a path imposed from outside, but rather an internal option of each particular institution. More recently, there have been some empirical studies aimed at probing the possibility of using TQM for evaluating and improving the quality of the management and services of higher education institutions. Rosa (2003) has explored the use of the EFQM Excellence Model as a self-assessment tool for Portuguese higher education institutions, while Calvo-Mora, Leal, and Roldán (2005) have proposed a model for evaluating and improving the quality of Spanish higher education centres. In what follows we explore the Portuguese case to illustrate possible applications of TQM in higher education.

4. THE EFQM EXCELLENCE MODEL

The most well-known quality awards are the European Quality Award, the Deming Prize and the Malcolm Baldrige National Quality Award. All have the ultimate goal of promoting quality in organisations. These prizes are based on measurement and orientation approaches to quality assessment and improvement, and they can have a national, international or regional scope. Basically, they are based on a set of criteria that is used to assess organisations. Each organisation is assessed according to the same criteria and in the end a global score is given to the organisation by a group of external assessors. Initially, these prizes were exclusively awarded to business organisations, but more recently their scope has been extended to service and public sector organisations, including education and health care. An interesting characteristic of these prizes is that in a number of cases the criteria that underlie them have been used by organisations as tools to support their quality self-assessment and improvement efforts, even if the organisations are not candidates for the prizes.

The European Quality Award is a European creation that nowadays involves about 38 countries. It was created by the EFQM[4] in 1991, with the support of the European Organization for Quality (EOQ) and the European Commission. The award is based on the EFQM Excellence Model, whose main purpose is to provide a sound framework for the diagnosis and evaluation of the excellence levels attained by organisations, leading to their continuous improvement. Since 1991 the model has been subject to periodic reviews, the most profound of them being the 1999 one. In 2003 this revision was complemented by some minor adjustments, resulting in its present version.

As was the case with the other quality awards, the European Quality Award was initially available to business organisations only. Nevertheless their criteria rapidly started to be used by public sector organisations, both as a quality diagnosis and a self-assessment tool. Today there is a version of the model tailored for this sector, as well as having its own prize category.

The EFQM Excellence Model is based on eight fundamental concepts (see Figure 2) that are the foundations upon which organisations should build their excellence: "outstanding practice in managing the organisation and achieving results" (EFQM 2003).

When implementing the EFQM Excellence Model, those concepts are operationalised using nine criteria (divided into 32 sub-criteria), belonging to one of two possible categories: *Enablers* and *Results* (see Figure 3). Enablers (or implementation factors) are directly related to what is done and the way it is done, while results have to do with what a given organisation derives from the way the enablers are managed and what they achieve as performance (Saraiva, Rosa, and Orey 2003). For the model to be complete one has to mention *Innovation and Learning* as horizontal vectors essential for the model's architecture. They reflect the need to continuously revise the way enablers are applied and managed using this *learning* process to *innovate,* aiming at improving the organisation's quality. In Figure 3, the arrows emphasise the dynamic nature of the model that is based on the premise that:

> Excellent results with respect to Performance, Customers, People and Society are achieved through Leadership driving Policy and Strategy that is delivered through People, Partnerships and Resources, and Processes. (EFQM 2003)

It is around these building blocks that an organisation's progress towards excellence is assessed. For each sub-criterion, assessment teams identify the organisation's strong points and areas for improvement, giving numerical scores to the results. From these partial scores an overall aggregate excellence level (ranging from zero to a theoretical maximum of 1000 points) can be quantified for each organisation.

Figure 2. The eight EFQM Excellence Model fundamental concepts. (Adapted from EFQM 2003)

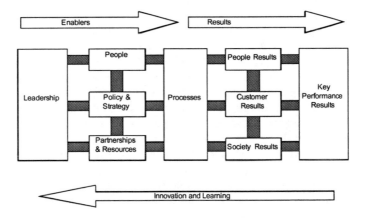

Figure 3. The EFQM Excellence Model. (Adapted from EFQM 2003)

In the framework of EFQM, the Excellence Model is a practical tool that can be used in a number of different ways, namely as a self-assessment tool, a way to benchmark with other organisations and a guide to identify areas for improvement. It is a non-prescriptive framework that recognises that there are different ways to achieve organisational excellence (Saraiva, Rosa, and Orey 2003). It is indeed a tool developed to help organisations in their efforts to make a quality diagnosis and assessment, and to stimulate their continuous improvement efforts. This is why the model has been used much more as a framework for organisations' self-assessment than for competing for the European Quality Award.

EFQM (1999) proposes five different approaches to self-assessment in organisations: questionnaire, matrix, workshop, pro forma and award simulation. EFQM (1999) considers that each of these approaches presents benefits and risks, the best approach for one organisation depends on its maturity in doing self-assessment exercises and in using the model, and on the organisation's resources and commitment to the project. The most widely used approaches are the questionnaire and pro forma.

In the questionnaire approach, the questionnaire is the basic instrument for self-assessment, allowing the organisation to have relevant information on its actors' perceptions about its present quality situation. Questions with lower scores indicate areas where the organisation should concentrate its improvement efforts. The main advantage of this approach is that it allows for the participation of a large number of people in the self-assessment effort. Nevertheless, when using only this approach, the organisation gets no more than quantitative information about its quality status in the model's different criteria. No qualitative information is collected about strong points, areas for improvement, and possible improvement actions. To get this type of information, a pro forma approach is more suitable. It is an approach based on the fulfilment of a set of forms (one for each of the model's sub-criterion) by the organisation's actors involved in the self-assessment exercise (in this approach the number of participating actors is obviously significantly smaller). Analysing the areas within each sub-criterion, and taking into account the present situation of the organisation under analysis, assessment teams establish its strong points, areas for improvement, and possible improvement actions.

Being a model associated with business, it has obviously been resisted by academics and so far it has not received broad-based support inside higher education institutions. Nevertheless, the growing concern with quality, the need to be accountable towards society and the increasing presence of the market in higher education systems have made quality assessment, management, assurance, and improvement an unquestionable reality, covering teaching, research, services, and institutional-level approaches. And, in this context, some higher education institutions have started to consider the application of the EFQM Excellence Model (Cortadellas 2000; Farrar 2000; McAdam and Welsh 2000; Hides and Davies 2002; Saraiva, Rosa, and Orey 2003; Schmidt and García-Legaz 2003; Calvo-Mora, Leal, and Roldán 2005).

5. A SELF-ASSESSMENT MODEL FOR HIGHER EDUCATION INSTITUTIONS – AN EFQM APPROACH

Since the EFQM Excellence Model is internationally recognised and accepted as a framework for quality assessment, management and improvement in European organisations, it can be hypothesised that an adaptation of its underlying structure could work as a self-assessment model for higher education institutions, serving as a tool for their internal quality management, assurance, and improvement. Figure 4 (cf. Figure 3) condenses the four results' criteria of the EFQM Excellence Model, renaming the People criterion, labelling it Actors, placing the organisation's Culture under the Policy and Strategy criterion and adding a new criterion, labelled Structure and Organisation. All these modifications have occurred based on the results of a previous study conducted in Portugal that led to the emergence of a set of criteria to be included in a self-assessment model for Portuguese higher education institutions (Rosa, Saraiva, and Diz 2001).

Figure 4. A self-assessment model for higher education institutions

The self-assessment model suggested here is then an adaptation of the original EFQM model. It assumes that the quality of a higher education institution will depend primarily upon its **processes** (namely teaching/learning, research, and services provided) and its achieved **results. Actors, resources, and partnerships**, are also important factors in a higher education institution that wants to assure and/or improve its organisational quality. But actors, partnerships, resources, processes, and results alone do not define a higher education institution. It also depends on and is characterised by its internal **structure and organisation, leadership, policy, strategy, and culture**.

Although the EFQM model's structure (see Figure 3) is based on the assumption that there are causal relationships between means and results, so far these have not been explicitly established. Nevertheless, as is the case with the Malcolm Baldrige National Quality Award (Flynn and Saladin 2001; Meyer and Collier 2001), some studies have been conducted to probe and verify these relationships (Eskildsen and Dahlgaard 2000; Rosa 2003; Calvo-Mora, Leal, and Roldán 2005), though social research is still at an early stage. Following this research direction, a set of possible causal relationships can be established between the self-assessment model's criteria (see the arrows in Figure 4), based on the premise that higher education institutions' excellent results are achieved through a leadership driving policy, strategy, and culture that is delivered through Actors, Structure and Organisation, Resources and Partnerships, and Processes.

Following what has been established in different excellence models (Kanji 1998; BNQP 2003; EFQM 2003), leadership is the prime factor responsible for an organisation's development, acting upon the definition of its policy, strategy, and culture, making available the resources needed for its processes, establishing necessary partnerships, intervening in the recruitment, and training of its different actors and contributing to its structure and internal organisation.[5] Previous research has also confirmed the positive correlation between leadership and other quality management implementation factors (Flynn and Saladin 2001; Meyer and Collier 2001). Eskildsen and Dahlgaard (2000) and Calvo-Mora, Leal, and Roldán (2005), in their analysis of possible causal relationships between the EFQM Excellence Model's criteria, have also found significant relationships between leadership, people management, policy and strategy, and partnerships and resources. This leads to the following research hypothesis:

H1: Leadership has a positive influence on Policy, Strategy and Culture, Actors, Structure and Organisation, and Resources and Partnerships.

From the EFQM model's internal logic, one can speculate that an appropriate definition and implementation of higher education institutions' policy and strategy, as well as the development of an appropriate organisational culture, may contribute to enhanced performance with respect to their basic processes: teaching, research, and service. Similarly, and following a processes approach, it can be assumed that processes occur because there are available resources, partnerships (or that they can be established when necessary), actors (who intervene where necessary), and a structure and organisation that allow for their occurrence. Other empirical studies (Eskildsen and Dahlgaard 2000; Calvo-Mora, Leal, and Roldán 2005) have proved the existence of significant causal relationships between policy and strategy, people management and partnerships, and resources and processes. From this argument the following research hypothesis can be postulated:

H2: Policy, Strategy and Culture, Actors, Structure and Organisation, and Resources and Partnerships all have a positive influence on Processes.

The logic underlying the EFQM model establishes that it is the occurrence of processes that leads to the achievement of results, relative to people and customer satisfaction, impact over society, and key performance results. In the self-assessment model proposed, one also postulates that it is by developing its activities (teaching, research, and services) that a higher education institution achieves its desired results:

H3: Processes have a positive influence on results.

It can be concluded that the suggested self-assessment model tries to cover a set of criteria and their relationships in an illustrative graphical perspective, allowing each higher education institution to have a clear idea about the areas under analysis, reflection, assessment and improvement. As is the case with the EFQM Excellence Model, each of the model's seven criteria has been properly defined, and the areas to be addressed when an institution assesses itself according to them are identified. The sub-criteria structure of the EFQM Excellence Model has also been followed, each criterion being divided into two or more sub-criteria. The main goal is to provide institutions with a better understanding of the points to be studied (see Appendix).

After having developed the model from a theoretical point of view, the next step is to validate it. To do this one can use structural equation modelling (SEM) multivariate technique. SEM is a powerful statistical technique that combines a measurement model (confirmatory factor analysis) with a structural model (regression or path analysis) (Garver and Mentzer 1999), allowing for the assessment of both the extent of fit between the measurement items and the criteria they are supposed to measure and the set of causal relationships between criteria that are embedded in the model.[6]

A structural equation model can then be hypothesised, containing seven latent variables, or constructs (the model's criteria), leadership being the only exogenous one (see Figure 4). Each one of these latent variables has to be operationalised in terms of a set of directly measurable variables, since criteria are abstract constructs that cannot be directly observed or measured. In order to do so, as in other similar approaches (EFQM 1999; Tambi 2000; Schmidt and García-Legaz 2003), a questionnaire was designed that included seven sets of questions (corresponding to the model's seven criteria) covering practices and factors considered fundamental for quality management and improvement (measurement items or manifest variables). Previous research efforts (Kanji and Wallace 2000; Sá 2002) suggest that closed questions should be put to the respondents, asking them about their perceptions of the organisation's performance on the various critical success factors on a 1 (Very Little) to 10 (Very Much) point scale. This type of answer scale increases the criteria measurement reliability (Kanji and Wallace 2000). The data thus obtained is then subject to structural equation modelling techniques. The structural equation model combines a set of related equations, some of which are related to the causal relationships between criteria hypothesised (structural equations) and others to the relationships between each construct and the manifest variables that operationalise it (Rosa, Saraiva, and Diz 2003).

6. PORTUGUESE HIGHER EDUCATION INSTITUTIONS – A CASE STUDY

The self-assessment model presented in the preceding section has been applied in the context of Portuguese higher education institutions. This exercise has allowed both the model's validation, following the methodology just described, and the establishment of an overview of the present quality management situation of Portuguese higher education institutions.

A written survey was conducted covering all Portuguese higher education institutions (mailed to their rectors/presidents and to the directors and scientific council presidents of their organic units). One hundred and twenty-nine valid answers were received, which corresponds to a response rate of about 30%. The measurement model scales were assessed by carefully analysing their reliability, content and construct validity. To Garver and Mentzer (1999: 34) content validity refers to "the degree that the construct is represented by items that cover the domain of meaning for the construct". Since the model's measurement items were derived from both previous empirical work and a comprehensive analysis of quality assessment models that were and are already applied in the context of higher education institutions, content validity is established (Rosa, Saraiva, and Diz 2003).

For the measurement scales reliability and for construct validity, the same approach has been used as for previous research (see Rosa, Saraiva, and Diz 2003, 2005). Table 1 presents the main results obtained from the correlation analysis performed over the manifest variables, as well as the Cronbach coefficient (α) computed for the seven constructs (criteria) under analysis. Looking at the values presented, it is possible to say that the constructs proposed have an acceptable reliability.[7] The discriminant validity of the scales was positively assessed using the two approaches suggested by Ghiselli et al. (1981 cited in Flynn and Saladin 2001). The comparison of scale internal consistency values (Cronbach's alpha values) with average inter-scale correlations indicates that the reliability for each scale is higher than its correlation with the other scales. The last two columns in Table 1 clearly show that the average correlation between the scale and non-scale items is lower than between the scale and scale items, indicating that the items selected for each scale do indeed operationalise the latent variable they are supposed to address.

Table 1. Measurement model analysis

Criteria	Mean	S.D.	Cronbach Alpha	Average inter-scale correlation	Average item correlations	
					Scale items	Non-scale items
Leadership	7.94	0.24	0.89	0.71	0.65	0.44
Policy, Strategy, and Culture	7.88	0.50	0.72	0.70	0.57	0.45
Resources and Partnerships	6.94	1.01	0.72	0.64	0.33	0.31
Actors	7.18	0.69	0.85	0.62	0.53	0.34
Structure and Organisation	7.14	0.73	0.76	0.65	0.48	0.35
Processes	6.76	0.59	0.91	0.69	0.64	0.42
Results	7.11	0.71	0.87	0.59	0.48	0.33

It is worth mentioning that the measurement model had initially 55 measurement items, linked to the seven latent variables (criteria) under analysis. But, when one estimates the measurement model's structural coefficients using PLS (partial least squares), only the ones higher than 0.1 (in absolute terms) can be considered as statistically significant for samples with 100–500 cases (Tambi 2000; Sá 2002). So, measurement items with coefficients lower than 0.1 should be eliminated from the model; only this will assure that the measurement items included are the ones that really reflect the empirical content of the latent variables. For this reason, the final measurement model had only 34 manifest variables, the criterion *Actors* being the one where more variables have been removed from the analysis. One gets the impression that the application of this quantitative approach to applying and validating the proposed self-assessment model is somehow restrictive, essentially because it eliminates *tout court* from the higher education institution self-assessment, management practices that could be qualitatively relevant.

Figure 5 illustrates the structural equation model obtained. The values presented are the structural parameters of the model, which give a measure of the strength of the relationships between independent and dependent variables of the model. As is possible to see from the figure, all structural parameters have positive values and are statistically significant. The quality of the structural model has been assessed by computing for each structural equation the percentage of variation in the endogenous constructs accounted for by the others with which they are related (R^2) (these results are also presented in Figure 5). As can be seen, all the values obtained but one are greater than 50%, which can be considered quite reasonable especially when compared to other studies reported in the literature, for example, Flynn and Saladin (2001) and Bart, Bontis, and Taggar (2001).

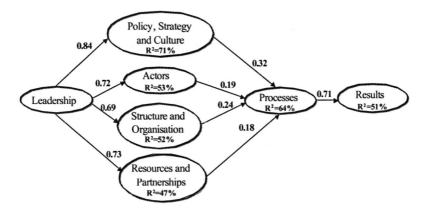

Figure 5. Structural equation model with estimated causal connections between criteria and the percentage of variance in each of the endogenous constructs accounted for by the others with which they are related (R^2)

So, from the statistical analysis performed, one can postulate that the developed structural equation model is a plausible representation of the data collected in Portuguese higher education institutions, and that the formulated hypotheses were validated. This means that in Portuguese higher education institutions *leadership* effectively works as the main driver for their management, significantly contributing to their improvement by directly acting upon their *structure and organisation, policy, strategy and culture, resources and partnerships,* and *actors.* Also, these four criteria help determine the performance of the higher education institutions with respect to their core *processes*, namely, teaching, research, and service. Finally, better quality of the processes will lead to better *results.*

The input data collected through the questionnaire and the structural model obtained, made it possible to compute a score for each of the model's seven criteria (see Figure 6), according to a mathematical expression derived by Fornell (1994 cited in Kanji and Wallace 2000).

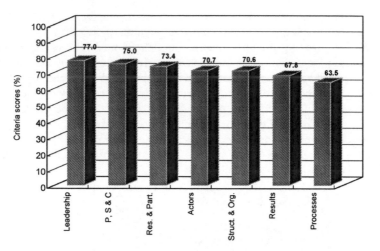

Figure 6. Scores obtained for each of the seven criteria regarding Portuguese higher education institutions

The analysis of these values allows conclusions to be drawn about the degree of internal application of management practices considered to be relevant for quality assurance and improvement of Portuguese higher education institutions. Overall, Portuguese higher education institutions received quite good scores on all criteria, the lowest values corresponding to the *Processes* and *Results* criteria, where it seems they have room to improve their performance. This is quite an optimistic and somewhat unexpected assessment of the implementation of the management practices under analysis.

7. CONCLUSIONS

If one assumes, as Drucker (1999: ix–x) does, that the present is a time of 'profound transition', in which society regularly faces new challenges, it is easy to understand the relevance of education in today's world and its impact on the economic, social, and cultural development of nations. The profound changes and challenges that humankind faces will only be successfully overcome in contexts where the capacity to manage information and knowledge is optimised. Organisational learning and intellectual capital promotion are key factors, and societies that promote the development of education have a clear competitive advantage.

In the last decades, several factors have contributed to raising public concern over higher education institutions' quality, leading to the emergence of quality measurement and improvement devices such as performance indicators, accreditation, programme and institutional assessment, and quality audits, and there have been attempts to import models from the private sector into higher education systems and institutions.

This chapter has examined the use of the EFQM Excellence Model as a self-assessment tool for higher education institutions, using as an example the results of research conducted in Portuguese higher education institutions. Despite the apparent success of the model's implementation it needs to be recognised that the scores obtained for Portuguese higher education institutions (see Figure 6) probably present a too-positive picture for these organisations regarding the internal implementation of the set of quality assurance and improvement practices included in the questionnaire. This scenario was not expected in the light of the interviews conducted with higher education institution managers during a previous exploratory study and the opinions usually expressed by these organisations' rectors and presidents. On the other hand, it appears that the model is sufficiently demanding in terms of quality practices so as to not allow Portuguese higher education institutions to have such a positive global score, unless answers to the questionnaire were overly optimistic and did not reflect reality. Consequently, there are two recommendations:

- First, that the questionnaire should be answered not just by the higher education institutions' top managers, but also by other members of the institution, including teachers, non-academic staff and students (see Rosa, Saraiva, and Diz 2005).

- Second, that besides this quantitative approach, also a qualitative one should be used, as suggested in Rosa, Saraiva, and Diz (2005: 218):

  ... the results obtained from the model's application lead to the conclusion that both approaches (the qualitative and the quantitative one) should be combined and used simultaneously. ... during the institutional self-assessment, while the self-assessment teams must fill a set of forms, the institution's actors (including students) must answer a questionnaire. Through this combination it is possible to quantify the quality level of the institution (obtaining a quantitative score for each one of the criteria under analysis), and to estimate the intensity of the criteria's relationships and, simultaneously, to obtain a set of the institution's strong points and areas for improvement, and to identify which improvement actions need to be implemented.

To conclude, one may ask if there are reasons to believe that this self-assessment model can indeed be used by higher education institutions to assess and continuously improve their quality. Is it a methodology capable of "re-weaving the collegial fabric of academic communities, the collective mechanisms by which faculty members control and improve the quality of academic programmes and research"? (Dill 1995: 107). Is it capable of going "beyond TQM to develop a new collegialism responsive to the twenty-first century"? (Harvey 1995: 141). Will it contribute to "Honoring the trust placed in academe by the larger society"? (Massy 2003: 337).

Two aspects must be considered when trying to answer these questions. One is the self-assessment model on its own and the criteria, sub-criteria, and areas to address embedded in it. The other is the approach suggested for its application to higher education institutions.

Relying on a quantitative approach only may not sufficiently identify higher education institutions' social capital, or promote sustained academic cohesion and connectedness. But, if the self-assessment model incorporates both the quantitative and the qualitative approaches suggested elsewhere (see Rosa, Saraiva, and Diz 2005), it may indeed contribute to enhance "the networks by which academic cohesion and professional control are achieved" (Dill 1995: 106).[8]

The self-assessment model may well contribute positively to enhancing higher education institutions' quality, since it places a strong emphasis on the idea that a higher education institution's quality implies good communication between all actors, teamwork, and sharing information relative to their work. Hopefully the application of the proposed model will empower academic communities and practitioners to make, rather than take, the quality agenda (see Harvey and Newton, Chapter 10).

NOTES

1   The empirical component of this chapter uses the results of the PhD thesis of Maria João Rosa under the supervision of Pedro Saraiva and Henrique Diz.
2   See Harvey and Newton, Chapter 10, this volume.
3   For a discussion on the influence of external quality assessment over the quality improvement of higher education institutions' day-to-day activities associated with teaching and learning see the chapter by D'Andrea, Chapter 9, this volume.
4   Following the success achieved in the United States by the Malcolm Baldrige Award (created in 1987), 14 European companies created the EFQM in 1988, with the mission of promoting excellence in Europe in a sustained way.
5   This last criterion, *Structure and Organisation*, does not appear as such in the EFQM model; instead it is disseminated, as areas to approach, through the other four enablers' criteria (Leadership, Partnerships and Resources, People, Policy and Strategy). Nevertheless it was included as a separate criterion as in the exploratory study conducted for developing the self-assessment model, the internal structure, and organisation were referred to as having considerable influence over institutional dynamism (Rosa, Saraiva, and Diz 2005). Moreover the inclusion of this criterion does not substantially change the configuration proposed by the EFQM model: leadership continues to be the key factor influencing the remaining enablers at the disposal of higher education institutions to conduct their processes in order to achieve the desired results.
6   Partial least squares (PLS) can be used to estimate the structural parameters (or path coefficients) of the entire structural equation model, since it is a rather robust estimation approach that deals in a reasonably robust way with multicollinearity, skew response distributions and various types of model misspecification (Hackl and Westlund 2000).
7   According to Van de Ven and Ferry (1979 cited in Curkovic et al. 2000), Cronbach's coefficient (α) should be 0.7 or higher for narrow constructs, and 0.55 or higher for moderately broad constructs.
8   To give an example, the proposed self-assessment model was applied in a department of the University of Aveiro, the purpose being the self-assessment of its teaching function. The application relied on the simultaneous use of the two approaches suggested. According to those responsible for the exercise, the self-assessment meeting was considered to be its most important phase. In the meeting it was indeed possible to discuss the department's reality and simultaneously to find convergences among the different discourses about what areas have good quality and which ones need further improvement.

REFERENCES

Amaral, A. "Sistemas europeus de avaliação da qualidade." *Revista Portuguesa de Gestão* II/97, 1997, 19–32.

Amaral, A., O. Fulton, and I.M. Larsen. "A Managerial Revolution?" In Amaral, A., V.L. Meek, and I.M. Larsen (eds). *The Higher Education Managerial Revolution?* Dordrecht: Kluwer, 2003, 275–296.

Amaral, A., A. Magalhães, and R. Santiago. "The Rise of Academic Managerialism in Portugal." In Amaral, A., V.L. Meek, and I.M. Larsen (eds). *The Higher Education Managerial Revolution?* Dordrecht: Kluwer, 2003, 131–153.

Bart, C., N. Bontis, and S. Taggar. "A Model of the Impact of Mission Statements on Firm Performance." *Management Decisions* 39.1 (2001): 19–35.

Birnbaum, R. *Management Fads in Higher Education. Where They Come From, What They Do, Why They Fail.* San Francisco: Jossey-Bass, 2000.

BNQP (Baldrige National Quality Program). *Education Criteria for Performance Excellence.* Gaithersburg, MD: Baldrige National Quality Program, 2003, http://www.quality.nist.gov/Education_Criteria.htm.

Calvo-Mora, A., A. Leal, and J.L. Roldán. "Relationships Between the EFQM Model Criteria: A Study in Spanish Universities." *Total Quality Management* 16.6 (2005): 741–760.

Coate, E. "The Introduction of Total Quality Management at Oregon State University." *Higher Education* 25 (1993): 303–320.

Cobban, A.B. *The Medieval English Universities; Oxford and Cambridge to c.1500.* Berkeley: University of California Press, 1988.

Cortadellas, J. Aplicação do modelo EFQM no ensino – Universidade Politécnica da Catalunha. Comunicação apresentada na conferência Sistemas de Avaliação da Qualidade no Ensino Superior, ISEP, Porto, Portugal, December, 2000.

Curkovic, S., S. Melnyk, R. Calantone, and R. Handfield. "Validating the Malcolm Baldrige National Quality Award Framework Through Structural Equation Modelling." *International Journal of Production Research* 38.4 (2000): 765–791.

Deem, R. "New-managerialism and Higher Education: The Management of Performances and Cultures in Universities in the United Kingdom." *International Studies in Sociology of Education* 8.1 (1998): 47–70.

Deem, R. "Globalisation, New Managerialism, Academic Capitalism and Entrepreneurialism in Universities: Is the Local Dimension Still Important?" *Comparative Education* 37.1 (2001): 7–20.

Denhardt, R.B. and Denhardt, J. "The New Public Service: Serving Rather Than Steering." *Public Administration Review* 60.6. (2000): 549–559.

Dill, D.D. "Through Deming's Eyes: A Cross-national Analysis of Quality Assurance Policies in Higher Education." *Quality in Higher Education* 1.1 (1995): 95–110.

Dill, D.D. "Higher Education Markets and Public Policy." *Higher Education Policy* 10.3/4 (1997): 167–185.

Dill, D.D., W.F. Massy, P.R. Williams, and C.M. Cook. "Accreditation and Academic Quality Assurance: Can We Get There From Here?" *Change Magazine* 28.5 (1996): 16–24.

Dill, D.D. and M. Soo. "Transparency and Quality in Higher Education Markets." In Teixeira, P., B. Jongbloed, D. Dill, and A. Amaral (eds). *Markets in Higher Education: Rhetoric or Reality?* Dordrecht: Kluwer, 2004, 61–85.

Dill, D.D., P. Teixeira, B. Jongbloed, and A. Amaral. "Conclusion." In Teixeira, P., B. Jongbloed, D. Dill, and A. Amaral (eds). *Markets in Higher Education: Rhetoric or Reality?* Dordrecht: Kluwer, 2004, 327–352.

Drucker, P. *Management Challenges for the 21st Century.* New York: HarperCollins, 1999.

EFQM (European Foundation for Quality Management). *Assessing for Excellence – A Practical Guide for Self-assessment.* Brussels: EFQM, 1999.

EFQM (European Foundation for Quality Management). *O modelo de excelência da EFQM*. Lisboa: APQ/EFQM, 2003.

Eskildsen, J.K. and J.J. Dahlgaard. "A Causal Model for Employee Satisfaction." *Total Quality Management* 11.8 (2000): 1081–1094.

Farrar, M. "Structuring Success: A Case Study in the Use of the EFQM Excellence Model in School Improvement." *Total Quality Management* 11.4–6 (2000): 691–696.

Flynn, B. and B. Saladin. "Further Evidence on the Validity of the Theoretical Models Underlying the Baldrige Criteria." *Journal of Operations Management* 19.6 (2001): 617–652.

Garver, M.S. and J.T. Mentzer. "Logistics Research Methods: Employing Structural Equation Modelling to Test for Construct Validity." *Journal of Business Logistics* 20.1 (1999): 33–57.

Hackl, P. and A. Westlund. "Customer Satisfaction Measurement: PLS and Alternative Estimation Methods." In *Proceedings of the 44th EOQ Congress*, Budapest 2 (2000): 45–53.

Harker, B. "Postmodernism and Quality." *Quality in Higher Education* 1.1 (1995): 31–39.

Harvey, L. "Beyond TQM." *Quality in Higher Education* 1.2 (1995): 123–146.

Harvey, L. and D. Green. "Defining Quality." *Assessment & Evaluation in Higher Education* 18.1 (1993): 9–34.

Hides, M. and J. Davies. "Implementation of the EFQM Excellence Model in the UK Higher Education Sector. A Comparison with Other Sectors." *Proceedings of the 7th World Congress for Total Quality Management – Business Excellence, Make it Happen!*, Verona, Italy, 1 June 2002.

Kanji, G. "Measurement of Business Excellence." *Total Quality Management* 9.7 (1998): 633–643.

Kanji, G. and W. Wallace. "Business Excellence Through Customer Satisfaction." *Total Quality Management* 11.7 (2000): 979–998.

Kells, H. "Creating a Culture of Evaluation and Self-regulation in Higher Education Organizations." *Total Quality Management* 6.5/6 (1995): 457–467.

Liaison Committee of Rectors' Conferences. *Quality Assessment in European Higher Education. A Report on Methods and Mechanisms, and Policy Recommendations to the European Community*. Brussels: Liaison Committee of Rectors' Conferences, 1993.

Massy, W.F. *Honoring the Trust. Quality and Cost Containment in Higher Education*. Bolton: Anker Publishing, 2003.

Massy, W.F. "Markets in Higher Education: Do They Promote Internal Efficiency?" In Teixeira, P., B. Jongbloed, D. Dill, and A. Amaral (eds). *Markets in Higher Education: Rhetoric or Reality?* Dordrecht: Kluwer, 2004, 13–35.

McAdam, R. and W. Welsh. "A Critical Review of the Business Excellence Quality Model Applied to Further Education Colleges." *Quality Assurance in Education* 8.3 (2000): 120–130.

Meek, V.L. "On the Road to Mediocrity? Governance and Management of Australian Higher Education in the Market Place." In Amaral, Alberto, Glen A. Jones, and Berit Karseth (eds). *Governing Higher Education: National Perspectives on Institutional Governance*. Dordrecht: Kluwer, 2002, 235–260.

Meek, V.L. "Governance and Management of Australian Higher Education: Enemies Within and Without." In Amaral, A., V.L. Meek, and I.M. Larsen (eds). *The Higher Education Managerial Revolution?* Dordrecht: Kluwer, 2003, 179–201.

Meyer, S.M. and D.A. Collier. "An Empirical Test of the Causal Relationships in the Baldrige Health Care Pilot Criteria." *Journal of Operations Management* 19.4 (2001): 403–425.

Miller, H. *The Management of Change in Universities*. London: SRHE and Open University Press, 1995.

Neave, G. "Homogenization, Integration and Convergence: The Cheshire Cats of Higher Education Analysis." In Meek, V.L., L. Goedegebuure, O. Kivinen, and R. Rinne (eds). *The Mockers and the Mocked: Comparative Perspectives on Differentiation, Convergence and Diversity in Higher Education*. Oxford: Pergamon, 1996, 26–41.

Neave, G. and F. Van Vught (eds). *Prometheus Bound: The Changing Relationship Between Government and Higher Education in Western Europe Relationships*. London: Pergamon, 1991.

Reed, M. "New Managerialism, Professional Power and Organisational Governance in UK Universities: A Review and Assessment." In Amaral, Alberto, Glen A. Jones, and Berit Karseth (eds). *Governing Higher Education: National Perspectives on Institutional Governance*. Dordrecht: Kluwer, 2002, 163–186.

Rosa, M.J. "Desenvolvimento de Bases Estratégicas e de Excelência para o Desenvolvimento do Ensino Superior em Portugal." PhD thesis, Aveiro, Portugal: Universidade de Aveiro, 2003.

Rosa, M.J., P. Saraiva, and H. Diz. "The Development of an Excellence Model for Portuguese Higher Education Institutions." *Total Quality Management* 12.7/8 (2001): 1010–1017.

Rosa, M.J., P. Saraiva, and H. Diz. "Excellence in Portuguese Higher Education Institutions." *Total Quality Management* 14.2 (2003): 189–197.

Rosa, M.J., P. Saraiva, and H. Diz. "Defining Strategic and Excellence Bases for the Development of Portuguese Higher Education." *European Journal of Education* 40.2 (2005): 205–221.

Sá, P. "Organizational Excellence in the Public Sector: With Special Reference to the Portuguese Local Government." PhD thesis, Sheffield, UK: Sheffield Hallam University, 2002.

Santiago, R. and T. Carvalho. "Effects of Managerialism on the Perceptions of Higher Education in Portugal." Paper presented at the 16th CHER Annual Conference – Reform and Change in Higher Education: Renewed Expectations and Improved Performance, Porto, Portugal, 4–6 September, 2003.

Santos, B.S. *Pela mão de Alice. O social e o político na pós-modernidade*, 5th edn. Porto: Afrontamento, 1996.

Saraiva, P., M.J. Rosa, and J. Orey. "A Large-scale Application in Portuguese Schools of the EFQM Excellence Model." *Quality Progress* 36.11 (2003): 46–51.

Scott, P. *The Meanings of Mass Higher Education*. Buckingham: Society for Research into Higher Education and Open University Press, 1995.

Schmidt, A. and F. García-Legaz. "Análisis del poder predictivo del modelo EFQM para la gestión y mejora de la calidad en la universidad pública española." *Proceedings of the XIII Jornadas Hispano-Lusas de Gestión Científica – La empresa familiar en un mundo globalizado*, Lugo, Spain, 2003.

Slaughter, S. and L. Leslie. *Academic Capitalism: Politics, Policies and the Entrepreneurial University*. Baltimore: Johns Hopkins University Press, 1997.

Smith, R.L. "When Competition is Not Enough: Consumer Protection." *Australian Economic Papers* 39.4 (2000): 408–425.

Tambi, A. "Total Quality Management in Higher Education: Modeling Critical Success Factors." PhD thesis, Sheffield, UK: Sheffield Hallam University, 2000.

Trow, M. "Managerialism and the Academic Profession: The Case of England." *Higher Education Policy* 7.2 (1994): 11–18.

Trow, M. "Trust, Markets, and Accountability in Higher Education: A Comparative Perspective." *Higher Education Policy* 9.4 (1996): 309–324.

Van Vught, F.A. "Intrinsic and Extrinsic Aspects of Quality Assessment in Higher Education." In Westerheijden, D., J. Brennan, and P. Maassen (eds). *Changing Contexts of Quality Assessment: Recent Trends in West European Higher Education*, vol. 20: *Management and Policy in Higher Education*. Utrecht: Uitgeverij Lemma BV, 1994, 31–50.

Van Vught, F.A. "The New Context for Academic Quality." In Dill, David and Barbara Sporn (eds). *Emerging Patterns of Social Demand and University Reform: Through a Glass Darkly*. Oxford: Pergamon, 1995, 194–211.

Vroeijenstijn, A.I. *Improvement and Accountability: Navigating Between Scylla and Charybdis. Guide for External Quality Assessment in Higher Education*. London: Jessica Kingsley, 1995.

Williams, G. "Total Quality Management in Higher Education: Panacea or Placebo?" *Higher Education*, 25.3 (1993): 229–237.

Youssef, M., P. Libby, A. Al-Khafaji, and G. Sawyer. "TQM Implementation Barriers in Academe: A Framework for Further Investigation." *International Journal of Technology Management* 16.4/6 (1998): 584–593.

APPENDIX
INSTITUTIONAL SELF-ASSESSMENT MODEL FOR PORTUGUESE HIGHER
EDUCATION INSTITUTIONS

(Source: Rosa, Saraiva, and Diz 2005)

C1 – Actors (academics, students and non-academic staff)
      C1.1 Selection and recruitment
      C1.2 Training and development
      C1.3 Work conditions

C2 – Resources
      C2.1 Management of financial resources
      C2.2 Management of facilities, equipment, and materials
      C2.3 Management of information and knowledge

C3 – Partnerships
      C3.1 Partnerships established with external entities
      C3.2 Relationship between the institution and its providers
      C3.3 Internationalisation

C4 – Leadership
      C4.1 Institution's mission, vision, and values
      C4.2 The institution's actors
      C4.3 Relationship with external environment
      C4.4 Institution's continual improvement

C5 – Policy, Strategy, and Culture
      C5.1 Development of the institutional policy and strategy
      C5.2 Quality – policy, strategy, and culture
      C5.3 Teaching/learning – policy, strategy, and culture
      C5.4 Research – policy, strategy, and culture
      C5.5 Services to the community – policy, strategy, and culture
      C5.6 Other institutional policies and strategies

C6 – Structure and Organisation
      C6.1 Structure and organisation
      C6.2 Internal structures created by the institution
      C6.3 Quality – structure and organisation

C7 – External Regulation
      C7.1 Relationship with external entities
      C7.2 Institution's autonomy degree

C8 – Processes

C8.1 Processes' identification and design
C8.2 Processes' development and control
C8.3 Processes' revision and improvement

C9 – Results (Stakeholders)

C9.1 Results – Accomplishment of the defined mission and goals
C9.2 Results – Stakeholders
C9.3 Results – Teaching/learning
C9.4 Results – Research
C9.5 Results – Services to community
C9.6 Results – Financial performance
C9.7 External society impact

VANEETA-MARIE D'ANDREA

IMPROVING TEACHING AND LEARNING IN HIGHER EDUCATION: CAN LEARNING THEORY ADD VALUE TO QUALITY REVIEWS?[1]

> [W]hat differences, if any, are these [quality review] systems, which are claiming time and energy from staff, making to our performance in terms of the quality of the courses. ... Because if they're not working and not making any difference ... let's forget it.
>
> (Respondent quoted in Newton 2000: 156)

1. INTRODUCTION AND BACKGROUND

The ongoing debate surrounding quality reviews in higher education continues to raise a number of issues that would benefit from further exploration and development. One of these concerns is the micro-level outcomes of the increasing use of externally imposed and implemented macro-level regulatory quality assurance systems[2] in higher education (Brown 2004). Micro level in this chapter refers to the teaching/learning processes in tertiary institutions including curriculum planning, the interaction between teachers and students in the learning environment and the development of learning communities, among others. Macro-level refers to national/state higher education policies that affect tertiary institutions. Many questions remain unanswered about how micro-level, day-to-day activities associated with teaching and learning in higher education can be improved through macro-level quality reviews.

Equally, the theoretical basis of quality reviews has rarely been considered. Quality reviews are a form of evaluation research and it could be expected that they are informed by the principles and practices of such research activities.

> Evaluation research tries to discover whether programmes work. Programmes are theories. Therefore it follows that evaluation is theory-testing. A theory tells us where to look for evidence, theories drive learning. (Pawson 2002 cited in Van der Knaap 2004: 21)

At present, it could be said that most quality reviews in higher education are both undertheorised and underutilised as a systematic means of organisational learning. Thus, quality reviews do not derive the benefit of a theory-based approach such as providing a focus for the reviews, a framework of reference, a deliberate choice for improvement and innovation, and relevance to the organisation (Van der Knapp 2004: 25). Yet, all quality reviews operate within an implicit theoretical framework.

This chapter begins by addressing these outstanding issues firstly by exploring the implicit theoretical aims of higher education quality reviews; it then considers

D.F. Westerheijden et al. (eds.), Quality Assurance in Higher education: Trends in Regulation, Translation and Transformation, 209–223.

the explicit application of learning theory to quality review processes. The chapter concludes by suggesting that quality reviews that are underpinned by learning theory have the potential to contribute to improving teaching and learning in higher education (D'Andrea and Gosling 2005). That is, macro-level quality reviews can have an impact on micro-level higher education activity thus adding value to the process.

Before directly exploring these issues and by way of background, it would be useful to briefly consider the broader quality debate in higher education. This will help to frame the more specific discussion on quality reviews and improving teaching and learning which follows. Some of the ongoing discussions of the broader debate include definitions of quality, types of quality reviews, underlying values of quality reviews, and the political drivers for quality schemes, including the rapidly changing higher education environment, among others.

1.1. Definitions of Quality

Anyone familiar with the quality literature in higher education will know that the definition of quality remains highly contested. Rather than review the various definitions available, this chapter takes as read that a definition of quality in the context of higher education continues to lack clarity and, therefore, is a particularly dynamic concept (Boyle and Bowden 1997 cited in Lauvås 2000). Although this circumstance could be viewed as problematic from the standpoint of establishing a basis for comparative analysis, it also means that there are still many opportunities for researchers to contribute to the development of an analytical framework for quality reviews and to further theorise quality and its related conceptual areas. This is one of the starting points for this chapter.

1.2. Types of Quality Reviews

The lack of an agreed definition for quality in higher education has contributed to an ongoing debate in the higher education quality literature surrounding the types of quality reviews best suited to higher education. A prominent theme in this discussion has been the question of whether the use of corporate business models of quality assessment is appropriate to higher education (see Rosa and Amaral, Chapter 8). Debates on the application of total quality management (TQM), for example, and its numerous clones are among those most often considered. Although there are exceptions to the rule, as in Portugal, governmental regulatory accountability, where it is required, has been a major driver for applying these types of quality assessment models in higher education.

In the United Kingdom, after over a decade of intense quality assessment activity of this type, it was found that less than 1% of all subjects and institutions reviewed were designated as being below acceptable standards (see PAQ Consulting Report in HEFCE 2000a, 2000b). Consequently, the debates influencing the regulatory quality review systems have begun to take other models of quality review into consideration. Most are some type of quality enhancement model. These are now gaining support in the higher education sector (see Elton 1996; QAAHE 2003a, 2005; Harvey and Newton, Chapter 10).

To summarise, the two dominant models currently considered in the quality review debate in higher education are quality assessment and quality enhancement:

- *Quality assessment* places an emphasis on measurement, external accountability and regulatory control. It identifies issues and uses negative sanctioning to get institutions to take action to comply with the regulatory framework. It does not, in and of itself, bring about improvements in teaching and learning at the micro level and does not necessarily engender an attitude among staff which is focused on improvement. It is more about compliance (see Newton 2000, 2001; Harvey 2001, 2002).

- *Quality enhancement* places an emphasis on a range of teaching and learning activities across the institution, from curriculum development to communities of practice. It uses a formative feedback process to bring about change. It places institutional learning at the core of its framework and therefore has the potential to engage staff in bringing about improvements in teaching and learning (see Gosling and D'Andrea 2001; D'Andrea and Gosling 2005).

1.3. Underlying Values of Quality Reviews

The quality review processes that have been imported from the business world focus on quality assessment and are based on corporate values, such as production efficiencies and customer satisfaction. Academic values on the other hand focus on the transformative enhancement-based processes of teaching and learning and, because of this, differ from those of the corporate world in important and significant ways (see also Smith 1992). The quality enhancement approach to quality reviews which is more developmentally focused and more closely aligned with the intrinsic value structure of higher education (see Van Vught 1994) would on this basis appear to be a more compatible model for quality reviews in higher education. As noted above, where most quality assessment reviews focus on problems, summative judgements and sanctioning mechanisms to achieve quality improvements, quality enhancement reviews are:

> a process whereby the judgements are formative and assist in improving teaching and learning while avoiding summative sanctions for areas where improvement is needed. Sanctions on their own do not necessarily create the conditions to improve the learning experience of students or bring about needed change. (D'Andrea and Gosling 2005: 178)

There are a number of examples of national quality review systems moving to this type of approach. In the United Kingdom, for example, Scotland emphasises quality enhancement (QE) and has done so for several years. The current position of the Scottish Higher Education Funding Council (SHEFC) is that: "... QE strategies should be developmental and challenging in the goals which they set for institutions" (SHEFC 2000: 7; see also QAAHE 2003a). Similarly, in the United States, the North Central

Association of Colleges and Schools (a regional accreditation agency) has instituted the Academic Quality Improvement Program (AQIP). AQIP is a voluntary alternative to the usual quality assessment processes within the North Central accreditation region of the United States. As in the Scottish approach, the central focus of AQIP (see box below) is on institutional enhancement:

> AQIP's Criteria see the education of students as the central focus of any institution, and will not permit a college to 'do quality' while ignoring the processes that shape students' minds. ... The Criteria are not normative, prescriptive, or proscriptive: they do not tell an institution how it should organise or operate itself, nor do they suggest specific inputs or outputs institutions should have. (Spangehl 2001: 3)

Characteristics of AQIP Process

- focuses on institutional processes and results rather than resources
- focuses on the improvement of teaching and learning
- supports institutions to improve students' educational performance
- customizes its processes to fit institutional needs and priorities
- uses information and communication technology to reduce costs
- provides useful information for public understanding
- is a dynamic process

Source: Spangehl 2001

1.4. Political Drivers of Quality Review

The political context of quality review processes also cannot be ignored. The rationale most often cited for importing the ready-made quality assessment review processes from the world of business and industry is the need for governments and others who fund higher education to seek assurance that the rapidly changing higher education environment, including increasing massification and the concomitant shift in student demographics, technological change, and globalisation among others, is not adversely affecting higher education outcomes. Even when the outcomes of the reviews indicate there is little to worry about, as was noted earlier, the political momentum for external accountability remains a strong driver for maintaining an external quality assessment review system, especially as a means of assuring the appropriate spending of public monies.

Yet by employing systems that for the most part have originated outside of higher education there is an implied statement of lack of trust in academic professional judgement and the peer review processes which have traditionally been in place, for example, the external examiner system in the United Kingdom. Despite the improvements that could be made to these peer review processes (Trow 1994, 1996; Warren Piper 1994; Shore and Wright 1999; Henkel 2000; Newton 2001; Olssen 2001; see also Harvey and Newton, Chapter 10; Rosa and Amaral, Chapter 8), the fact that, as was noted above, nearly all institutions were found to be of an acceptable standard would suggest these processes are doing an adequate job of ensuring quality in the higher education sector. This situation reflects the ideological struggle which is occurring at the macro-level over the purpose of higher education and whether it should primarily serve extrinsic values, that is, the economic needs of the society, or intrinsic values, by maintaining the traditional liberal ideals of pursuit of knowledge and personal intellectual transformation (again, see Van Vught 1994). These value differences have dominated the debates on quality in higher education in the past few decades and have influenced the types of quality reviews carried out, as well as how they are theorised.

2. THEORISING QUALITY REVIEWS IN HIGHER EDUCATION

The two major types of quality reviews carried out in higher education, as discussed earlier, link to two major competing theories of quality in higher education and these reflect the dominant ideologies surrounding quality reviews. One centres on the regulatory assurance function of quality reviews and the other centres on the enhancement improvement function. Although they appear to be theoretically oppositional, they can in fact overlap in practice (see Harvey and Newton, Chapter 10). However, there is a degree of uncertainty about whether either approach, on its own, can adequately address the outstanding questions surrounding the micro-level outcomes of the macro-level policies related to quality reviews.

Both theories have a wide range of methods and methodological approaches at their disposal. The assessment model mostly utilises quantitative approaches while the enhancement model mostly utilises qualitative approaches. An over-reliance on measurable outcomes has dominated higher education quality review processes to date. This has led quality assessment reviews to focus primarily on what is measurable thus sidelining significant, and often important, less measurable data on the higher education system, such as the processes of curriculum development, knowledge of current pedagogical theory among the teaching staff, and scholarly reflections on teaching and learning. A mature quality review process could, if supported by a solid theoretical framework, find ways to achieve robust reviews through the systematic analysis of enhancement data as well.

It is also interesting to note, if somewhat ironic, that the application of learning theory to quality reviews is rarely considered in the development of quality review models. For example, it might be beneficial to the theorising of quality reviews if learning assessment theory and the corollary knowledge of summative and formative assessment were used as the underlying framework for the process. Or, how would quality reviews be affected if problem-based learning theories were applied and knowledge of active learning was used to understand the mechanisms of quality? And, what would be the effect of employing the full range of educational theories to this theorising process?

This chapter will now consider some of these questions by examining several examples of possible applications of learning theory to quality reviews. To para-phrase Biggs (1993), there are a number of useful options for investigating the wide range of learning theories available for this exercise, including those theories specific to learning in higher education (see also Candy 1993; Ramsden 1993; Haggis 1996; Pascarella and Terenzini 2005). However, because this is an exploratory investigation, which is limited in scope, aggregate categories of 'generic' learning theories provide an efficient way into this inquiry. A useful summary of four major categories of learning theory is available from Smith (1999) (see Table 1). For the purpose of illustrating how learning theory might be applied to quality reviews, these broad categories will be used as the framework for discussing some examples.

Table 1. Major categories of learning theory. (Adapted from Merriam and Caffarella 1991 cited in Smith 1999)

Aspect	Behaviourist	Cognitivist	Humanist	Social and situational
Learning theorists	Thorndike, Pavlov, Watson, Guthrie, Hull, Tolman, Skinner	Koffka, Kohler, Lewin, Piaget, Ausubel, Bruner, Gagne	Maslow, Rogers	Bandura, Lave and Wenger, Salomon
View of the learning process	Change in behaviour	Internal mental process (including insight, information processing, memory, perception)	A personal act to fulfil potential	Interaction/observation in social contexts. Movement from the periphery to the centre of a community of practice
Purpose in education	Produce behavioural change in desired direction	Develop capacity and skills to learn better	Become self-actualised, autonomous	Full participation in communities of practice and utilisation of resources
Educator's role	Arranges environment to elicit desired response	Structures content of learning activity	Facilitates development of the whole person	Works to establish communities of practice in which conversation and participation can occur

3. SOME EXAMPLES OF LEARNING THEORY APPLIED TO QUALITY REVIEWS

It would seem that any of the learning theories included in the broad categories summarised by Smith – behaviourist, cognitivist, humanist, and social and situational – have the potential to add value to both assessment- and enhancement-focused quality reviews. In this section, a few illustrative examples have been selected from earlier work on an enhancement-focused quality review process called the quality development model (Gosling and D'Andrea 2001). Examples have been drawn from this work because it has earlier suggested some possible links between quality reviews in higher education and learning theory (D'Andrea and Gosling 2005). Details of the model are not especially relevant to the purposes of this discussion and therefore are not considered here except in the context of the examples.

Furthermore, before beginning this discussion, it needs to be noted that the purpose of this section is to explore the possible application of learning theory to quality review processes and therefore it is meant to be suggestive rather than comprehensive in its consideration of Smith's categories of learning theories. It is also important to recognise that examples could, in fact, draw on a number of categories of learning theory. In the discussion to follow, one example is included in order to demonstrate the possible links to multiple learning theories more generally.

If this initial exploration proves helpful to the discussion of quality review theory, more substantive work in this area can be taken forward in the future.

3.1. Examples of Humanist Learning Theory

The first example chosen illustrates several direct links with humanist learning theory. To start with, the quality development model uses the paradigm shift from teaching to learning (Barr and Tagg 1995) as its underpinning principle and identifies learning as the key organising structure of higher education. Using this approach to teaching and learning is exemplified by student-centred learning. A quality review process using this theoretical framework could focus on identifying student-centredness in a wide range of activities in higher education, such as the processes for designing curricula and choosing content and teaching methods, analysis of various forms of teacher–student interaction, the uses of student assessments, and the broader activities of institutional learning communities.

To further illustrate the point let us take a closer look at the process of designing the curriculum. Increasing student diversity has been a major outcome of widening access to higher education. But has this had any direct impact on curriculum?

> What is at issue here is 'the politics of recognition'. 'Enlarging and changing the curriculum is essential not so much in the name of a broader culture for everyone as in order to give due recognition to the hitherto excluded' (Taylor 1995: 65). Inclusivity requires that we examine the curriculum specifically to ensure that the histories of minorities are not being excluded (D'Andrea and Gosling 2005).

A quality review based on a humanist learning paradigm would place an emphasis on a better understanding of the student and the student's learning experience which in turn has the potential to contribute to micro-level improvements in teaching and learning in the institution.

3.2. Examples of Social and Situational Learning Theory

Two examples from the earlier work on quality development link to social and situational learning theory. The two examples involved include what is called 'appreciative inquiry' and communities of practice.

3.2.1. Appreciative Inquiry

Appreciative inquiry draws on social and situational learning theories including social constructivist models; it is a transformative process that focuses on strengths rather than weaknesses (Cooperrider and Srivastra 1987; Bushe 1998; Cooperrider and Whitney 1999). There are a number of areas where this framework could be employed in quality reviews. The following discussion considers the application of appreciative inquiry to the example of teaching observations.

The view of the quality development model is that for teaching observations to be developmental they must be separated from other university assessment processes and be supported by formative feedback. Appreciative inquiry does both and demonstrates how this can be done in practice. One application that helps to illustrate this process occurred in the 1970s when the author ran a teaching observation video-feedback programme as part of a teaching improvement programme at a major land-grant university in the north-eastern part of the United States. The quality development review procedures developed in this example were aimed at dealing with improving teaching and learning at the micro level with individual faculty/staff.

Over a 5-year period, the author conducted teaching observations via video-feedback. Records of these observations were systematically compiled both in writing and via videotape (but never published). The faculty/staff involved represented a wide range of subjects and were at different points in their academic careers: some were teaching assistants brand new to teaching, some were tenured faculty nearing retirement and others could be described as mid-career professionals.

As others have also discovered, "when you do more of what works, the stuff that doesn't work goes away" (Hall and Hammond 1998). Simply put, during the video-feedback sessions conducted with individual members of the faculty/staff they were asked to focus on themselves in the sociologically defined role of the teacher. By doing so, this helped to objectify the video review process that is usually fraught with significant subjective meaning. During replay feedback sessions, rather than letting the person get stuck on responding to how they physically appeared to the viewer (most often it was concern over personal features such as weight, height, accent, baldness, etc.), the author asked each one to describe what they saw the teacher (themselves) doing to assist the students' learning. This required them to look closely at themselves in the role of a teacher and to describe those aspects of the teaching role that were working well. This process also helped them to understand what their strengths were and, in turn, allowed them to build on these strengths instead of dismantling their weaknesses. In each case, within three years, noticeable improvements in teaching were reflected both in the student ratings received and also in the processes used to plan and execute teaching and learning experiences. These improvements were the outcome of the process of appreciative inquiry applied to teaching observations within a developmental model of quality review, that is, it was a transformative process that focused on strengths. In this case, the social constructivist learning model within social learning theory was successfully applied at the micro level.

3.2.2. Communities of Practice

Another example of the application of social and situational learning theory to quality reviews involves an in-depth look at institutional communities of practice (Wenger 2004). Often, assessment-led quality reviews interrogate the work of university committees in order to confirm that quality assurance practices are being adhered to. University committees usually spend most of their time dealing with the business of the committee. For instance, in a typical university a teaching awards committee spends its time deciding on criteria for selection of awards and reviewing award applications. Rarely are there discussions of the ideas, the research or principles underpinning those decisions. In the case of a teaching awards committee, this could be done through having the committee read and discuss research papers on the meaning of excellence in teaching in higher education. By engaging in this activity, in addition to dealing with the decision-making process, the committee is transformed into a type of community of practice.

In one university in the United Kingdom, the chair of the teaching awards committee sought to do this and reorganised the work of the committee so that it, in effect, became a community of practice on rewarding excellence in teaching. This was done by first changing the agenda of the meetings to include a period of time set aside to debate and discuss selected research findings on rewarding excellence. In this case, half of the time already set aside for the meeting was used as a seminar with a member of the committee acting in the role of 'seminar' facilitator. It included reading published articles on teaching excellence before the seminar, discussing key issues from the articles in the seminar and taking the results of these discussions into the second half of the meeting when the business of the committee was dealt with. The seminar activities provided a more informed consideration of the meaning and purpose of the teaching awards, as well as the selection criteria to be used for the decisions taken on who would receive the awards.

Changing the focus of the committee work from business only to a combination of business and learned discussion redefines both the work and the relations of the committee and its members; through this process, a community of practice on teaching excellence was created. Communities of practice such as these create an environment which allows increased opportunities for faculty/staff to discuss related issues on teaching and learning which in turn increases the opportunity to improve the teaching and learning process for students. It also provides faculty/staff with a personal learning opportunity directly linked to the jobs they perform. Quality reviews which focus on the learning of committees through communities of practice can again be informed by the principles of social and situational learning theory.

3.3. Examples of Overlapping Behaviourist and Humanist Learning Theories

Student evaluations have been used for quality review processes for decades in the United States and more recently in other parts of the world. Depending on how and why they are used, they can be linked to either the behaviourist and/or humanist categories of learning theory. This example illustrates how learning theory can be applied to both quality assessment and quality enhancement review processes.

In the United States, where student evaluations have had a somewhat chequered history, the student movement of the 1960s demanded that they be used so that the student 'voice' could be heard to improve the learning experience, redress the power imbalance between teacher and student and bring about changes to make the curriculum more relevant to the times and student needs. Students believed that student evaluations would allow for their views to be recorded and become the vehicle for bringing about changes that would make their learning more relevant. In this case, the evaluations were, consciously or unconsciously, conceptualised as a quality enhancement review process informed by humanist learning theory.

However, over time, student evaluations in the United States have become used primarily as a means to judge an individual teacher's work with students and to evaluate the performance of faculty/staff. This shift in emphasis on the summary judgement of teachers and not on the relevance of the curriculum they are teaching has decreased the power of the student voice to bring about improvements in the total learning experience. Student evaluations in this context have become linked to assessment models of quality review and more influenced by behaviourist theories of learning.

Interestingly, contrary to the expectations of the behaviourist approach, a number of studies done on student evaluations (Braskamp and Ory 1994; Cashin 1995) have indicated that student feedback on teaching per se has had little or no effect on identifying areas of change for individual faculty/staff. Student views about the personal performance of faculty/staff are therefore of little use for improving teaching and learning at the individual faculty/staff level.

This understanding of the limitations of student responses for bringing about change in individual teachers has led to a refocusing of student feedback surveys on the student experience itself. The Course Experience Questionnaire (CEQ) in Australia and the National Survey of Student Engagement (NSSE) in the United States are examples of a way in which student responses can be used for a wide range of developmental goals such as identifying areas for improvement for teachers as well as strengths and weaknesses of the course in promoting approaches to learning. Instruments like the CEQ and NSSE can provide data to enhance the teaching and learning process overall whereas faculty/staff-focused student evalua-tions are limited to assessment functions.[3] As Taylor (1993: 69) notes: "If quality is to be the watchword in Australian higher education, then we might assess it better by the extent of and commitment to dialogue with students than by the more easily measured outputs of the academic staff."

3.4. Summary of Examples

In summary, through the discussion of some illustrative examples (see Table 2) it has been possible to demonstrate that learning theories can be linked to and inform many elements of higher education quality review processes. The examples considered also suggest that by using learning theories to frame quality reviews there are increased opportunities to better understand how macro-level quality systems can be linked to improving micro-level teaching and learning activities. There are, however, a number of questions that remain unanswered, these are identified in the section to follow.

Table 2. Some examples of learning theory applied to quality review

Learning theory	*Examples considered*
Humanistic Theory	• Learning paradigms • Assessment theory
Behaviourist Theory	• Assessment theory
Social and Situational	• Appreciative inquiry • Communities of practice

4. SUMMARY AND CONCLUSIONS

This chapter has attempted to better understand "how micro-level, day-to-day activities associated with teaching and learning in higher education can be improved through macro-level quality reviews". It has done this, firstly, by analysing the two dominant quality review approaches currently employed in higher education, and discussed in the quality literature, through locating them within the larger quality assurance debates. Similarities and differences between the two approaches identified in these discussions are summarised in Table 3.

Additionally, this chapter has considered ways in which both approaches have been theorised to date and extended this theorising by applying learning theory to quality reviews. Through the analysis of selected examples of quality review mechanisms it has become apparent that there is scope for quality reviews to be underpinned and framed by various types of learning theory. More importantly, when this is done the opportunities for using the macro-level quality review findings to improve micro-level teaching and learning activities is also more evident.

Table 3. Comparison of quality assessment with quality enhancement approaches in higher education. (Based on D'Andrea and Gosling 2005)

	Quality assessment	*Quality enhancement*
Focuses on intrinsic values		√
Focuses on extrinsic values	√	
Linked to external authority	√	
Linked to internal authority		√
Contributes to accountability needs	√	√
Employs summative judgements and sanctioning	√	
Employs formative feedback		√
Emphasis on documentation	√	
Emphasis on educational experience		√
Focuses on learning outcomes		√
Focuses on measurable data and scores	√	
Trusts academic professionalism		√
Process identifies ways to improve teaching and learning at the micro level		√

4.1. Limitations and Further Questions

Nevertheless, this chapter has clear limitations, some of which were acknowledged from the start. It is, and was meant to be, an exploratory investigation of how micro-level improvements can be achieved through macro-level quality reviews when learning theory is used to frame quality reviews. As an exploratory process it did not attempt to address all possible learning theories nor apply these systematically to both types of quality reviews. In addition, the examples used to illustrate the theories considered came primarily from the enhancement approach. Thus, there are a number of unanswered questions remaining prompted by the discussion in this chapter. Some of these are:

- Can learning theory also be applied in similar ways to the quality assessment approach?
- Does learning theory change the quality review process and its outcomes?

- If quality reviews, of either type, can be underpinned by learning theory does this make a link between macro-level quality reviews and micro-level improvements in teaching and learning more likely?
- Is there identifiable added value for using learning theory to frame quality reviews?

Our purpose has been to stimulate new ways of conceptualising quality reviews in higher education in order to increase their value to the institutions and the students they serve. It would seem that from this initial discussion it can be concluded that quality reviews in higher education could contribute more to the micro-level improvement of teaching and learning in higher education if policy makers consciously considered the application of learning theory to the macro-level process. This could be facilitated through working in partnership with higher education researchers. To paraphrase Harvey (2001), one of the primary aims of quality reviews in higher education should be to ensure that the outcome is improvements in the teaching and learning experience of students, not bigger and better regulatory agencies to conduct quality assessment reviews.

NOTES

1   I would like to acknowledge the advice of four colleagues who kindly read earlier versions of this chapter: David Dill, Stephen Jackson, Maria João Rosa and Bjørn Stensaker. Many thanks to each of them; any remaining misunderstandings are solely my responsibility.
2   I use quality assurance to refer to any regulatory process of quality review; quality assessment is used to refer to any summative quality review process and quality enhancement refers to a formative quality review process. 'Quality development' is one type of quality enhancement which has been considered in its own right in previous publications by the author.
3   However, as is well known about any data collection process, the data can be used for a multitude of purposes. For example, the CEQ has been used by the federal government in Australia to publish league tables of university performance, which has coloured faculty/staff perceptions of its value as a developmental tool.

REFERENCES

Barr, R. and J. Tagg. "From Teaching to Learning: A New Paradigm for Undergraduate Education." *Change* 27.6 (1995): 13–25.

Biggs, J.B. " From Theory to Practice: A Cognitive Systems Approach." *Higher Education Research and Development* 12.1 (1993): 73–85.

Braskamp, L.A. and J.C. Ory. *Assessing Faculty Work: Enhancing Individual and Institutional Performance.* San Francisco: Jossey-Bass, 1994.

Brown, R. *Quality Assurance in Higher Education: The UK Experience Since 1992.* London: Rutledge Farmer, 2004.

Bushe, G.R. "Five Theories of Change Embedded in Appreciative Inquiry." Paper presented at the 18th Annual World Congress of Organizational Development, Dublin, Ireland, July 1998, http://www.bus.sfu.ca/homes/gervase/5theories.html.

Candy, P.C. "Learning Theories in Higher Education: Reflections on the Keynote Day, HERDSA 1992." *Higher Education Research and Development* 12.1 (1993): 99–106.

Cashin, W.E. "Student Ratings of Teaching: The Research Revisited." IDEA Paper no. 32. Manhattan, Kansas: Center for Faculty Evaluation and Development in Higher Education, 1995.

Cooperrider, D.L. and S. Srivastra. "Appreciative Inquiry in Organizational Life." In Pasmore, W. and R. Woodman (eds). *Research in Organization Change and Development*, vol. 1. Greenwich, CT: JAI Press, 1987, 129–169.

Cooperrider, D.L. and D. Whitney. "When Stories Have Wings: How 'Relational Responsibility' Opens New Options for Action." In McNamee, S. and K. Gergen (eds). *Relational Responsibility*. Thousand Oaks, CA: Sage, 1999, 56–64.

D'Andrea, V. "Higher Education Quality Assurance Systems in Europe and the United States: Doing the Right Thing and/or Doing it Right." Paper presented at the American Sociological Association Annual Meeting, Los Angeles, CA, August 1994.

D'Andrea, V. and D. Gosling. *Improving Teaching and Learning in Higher Education: A Whole Institution Approach*. Maidenhead, UK: McGraw-Hill, Society for Research into Higher Education and Open University Press, 2005.

Elton, L. "Partnership, Quality and Standards in Higher Education." *Quality in Higher Education* 2.2 (1996): 95–104.

Gosling, D. and V. D'Andrea. "Quality Development: A New Concept for Higher Education." *Quality in Higher Education* 7.1 (2001): 7–17.

Haggis, T. "Models and Experiences: An Investigation into Theories of Learning in Adult and Higher Education." MA in Adult and Continuing Education Dissertation, London: Institute of Education, University of London, 1996.

Hall, J. and S. Hammond. "What is Appreciate Inquiry?" *Inner Edge Newsletter*. 1998, http://www.thinbook.com/thinbook/chap11fromle.html.

Harvey, L. "The End of Quality?" Keynote Address at the 6th QHE Seminar, Birmingham, UK, 26 May 2001.

Harvey, L. "Evaluation for What?" *Teaching in Higher Education* 7.3 (2002): 245–264.

HEFCE (Higher Education Funding Council for England). *Better Accountability for Higher Education*. A review for the HEFCE by PAQ Consulting. Bristol: Higher Education Funding Council for England, 2000a.

HEFCE (Higher Education Funding Council for England). *Council Briefing*. Bristol: Higher Education Funding Council for England, December, 2000b.

HEFCE (Higher Education Funding Council for England). *Performance Indicators in Higher Education in the UK, 1997–1998, 1998–1999, 00–04*. Bristol: Higher Education Funding Council for England, October, 2000c.

Henkel, M. *Academic Identities and Policy Change in Higher Education*. London: Jessica Kingsley, 2000.

Lauvås, P. "Quality Enhancement Systems to Improve Teaching and Learning." Paper presented at the 3rd Conference of the International Consortium for Educational Development, Bielefeld, Germany, July 2000.

Newton, J. "Feeding the Beast or Improving Quality? Academic Staff Perceptions of Quality Assurance and Quality Monitoring." *Quality in Higher Education* 6.2 (2000): 153–163.

Newton, J. "Views from Below: Academics Coping With Quality." Keynote Address at the 6th QHE Seminar, Birmingham, UK, 26 May 2001.

Olssen, M. "The Neo-liberal Appropriation of Tertiary Education Policy: Accountability, Research and Academic Freedom." New Zealand Association for Research in Education, State-of-the-Art Monograph, no. 8, October 2001.

Pascarella, E.T. and P.T. Terenzini. *How College Affects Students: A Third Decade of Research*, vol. 2. San Francisco: Jossey-Bass, 2005.

QAAHE (Quality Assurance Agency for Higher Education). *Handbook for Enhancement-led Institutional Review*. Gloucester: Quality Assurance Agency for Higher Education, 2003a.

QAAHE (Quality Assurance Agency for Higher Education). *Learning from Subject Review 1993–2000: Sharing Good Practice*. Gloucester: Quality Assurance Agency for Higher Education, 2003b.

QAAHE (Quality Assurance Agency for Higher Education). *Learning from Developmental Engagements: Sharing Good Practice*. Gloucester: Quality Assurance Agency for Higher Education, 2005.

Ramsden, P. "A Performance Indicator of Teaching Quality in Higher Education: The Course Experience Questionnaire." *Studies in Higher Education* 16.2 (1991): 129–150.

Ramsden, P. "Theories of Learning and Teaching and the Practice of Excellence in Higher Education." *Higher Education Research and Development* 12.1 (1993): 87–98.

SHEFC (Scottish Higher Education Funding Council). *Consultation HEC07/00 Consultation on Quality Enhancement Strategy*. Edinburgh: Scottish Higher Education Funding Council, 2000.

Shore, C. and S. Wright. "Audit Culture and Anthropology: Neo-liberalism in British Higher Education." *Journal of the Royal Anthropological Institute* 5.4 (1999): 557–575.

Smith, M.K. "Learning Theory." *Encyclopedia of Informal Education*. 1999, http://www.infed.org/biblio/b-learn.htm.

Smith, R.S. "The University – Some Differences from Other Organizations." *Canadian Society for the Study of Higher Education* 12 (1992): 1–11.

Spangehl, S.D. "Quality Improvement Alive and Vital in US Accreditation." Paper presented at the 6th QHE Seminar, Birmingham, UK, 26 May 2001.

Taylor, C. *The Politics of Recognition Multiculturalism*. Princeton, NJ: Princeton University Press, 1995.

Taylor, G. "A Theory of Practice: Hermeneutical Understanding." *Higher Education Research and Development* 12.1 (1993): 59–72.

Trow, M. *Managerialism and the Academic Profession: Quality and Control*. Higher Education Report no. 2. Quality Support Centre, London: The Open University, 1994.

Trow, M. "Trust, Markets and Accountability in Higher Education: A Comparative Perspective." Paper CSHE1–96. Berkeley, CA: Center for Studies in Higher Education, University of California, 1996, http://repositories.cdlib.org/cshe/CSHE1-96.

Van der Knaap, P. "Theory-based Evaluation and Learning: Possibilities and Challenges." *Evaluation* 10.1 (2004): 16–34.

Van Vught, F.A. "Intrinsic and Extrinsic Aspects of Quality Assessment in Higher Education." In Westerheijden, D.F., J. Brennan and P.A.M. Maassen (eds). *Changing Context of Quality Assessment: Recent Trends in West European Higher Education*. Utrecht: CHEPS, 1994.

Warren Piper, D. *Are Professors Professionals? The Organization of University Examinations*. London: Jessica Kingsley, 1994.

Wenger, E. "Communities of Practice: A Brief Introduction." 2004, http://www.ewenger.com/theory/index.htm.

LEE HARVEY AND JETHRO NEWTON

TRANSFORMING QUALITY EVALUATION: MOVING ON

1. INTRODUCTION

Quality assurance of higher education has become ubiquitous. The International Network of Quality Assurance Agencies in Higher Education is worldwide, embracing every continent, with membership from about 80 countries. Stensaker (Chapter 5) argues that quality assurance is not just the latest fad but is a remarkably successful management fashion: a success, this chapter suggests, that is sustained by government endorsement because it provides a means of securing accountability.

Quality assurance of higher education is ubiquitous because it provides a means for governments to check higher education. Harvey and Knight (1996) illustrated how quality assurance underpinned processes of delegated authority in systems as diverse as market arrangements in the United States, autonomous public systems in the United Kingdom, previously ministerial-controlled systems in Scandinavia and tightly constrained systems such as China. The beauty of the approach, from the government's point of view, is that quality assurance ensures not only accountability but can be used to encourage a degree of compliance to policy requirements or to control a burgeoning private sector. Even in tightly controlled systems, there is a degree of autonomy in higher education that ministerial decree and laws on higher education can only constrain to a limited extent. While countries such as the United States, United Kingdom, and the old Commonwealth wanted to rein in the autonomy of the sector, much of the rest of Western Europe, for example, wanted to decrease ministerial control in the 1990s. In both cases, quality assurance was a useful mechanism by which to do this.

There are, though, several fundamental questions to be asked about the ubiquity of quality assurance. These include: What is the relation of quality assurance to quality in higher education? To what extent does quality assurance ensure the accountability of the quality of higher education? To what extent does quality assurance constrain higher education: does the accountability requirement prioritise compliance and control over improvement? Is it time to replace quality assurance with quality improvement (or enhancement)?[1]

This chapter explores these questions through suggesting an alternative approach to quality assurance. The chapter adapts and extends a proposal, made at the 26th EAIR Forum in Barcelona, in 2004, to transform quality evaluation (Harvey and Newton 2004).[2] The approach in this chapter is one that deconstructs the existing dominant approaches to quality assurance and reconstructs an alternative,

D.F. Westerheijden et al. (eds.), Quality Assurance in Higher Education: Trends in Regulation, Translation and Transformation, 225–245.

research-informed approach. Not so much a change from assurance to improvement but a shift from externally imposed procedures to internally generated creativity.

At the core, the contention is that asking an amorphous group of academics to identify their strengths and weaknesses and for an agency or ministerial department to send out a raiding party to pass summary judgment on the quality of provision may ensure compliance to policy or regulation or contribute to some form of control over the sector, and it may satisfy the illusion of accountability, but has nothing to do with the essential nature of quality. It is a bureaucratic process quite removed from either the student learning or the creative research processes, which, it is argued, lies at the heart of quality in higher education. What follows is a far-reaching critique of quality assurance. However, this is not a criticism of the way agencies operate; indeed, within their operational parameters, the vast majority of national agencies do a good, conscientious job. The critique is with the fundamental nature of quality assurance per se.

2. APPROACH, OBJECT, FOCUS, RATIONALE AND METHODS

There are four broad approaches to quality assurance: accreditation, audit, assessment and external examination (or external review of service and outcomes standards of one sort or another).[3] Their object of attention ranges from the institution, through subject and programme to the service provision, the learner or the learning outcomes. Different systems vary the emphasis placed on each of these elements. The focus of quality evaluations can also be diverse, ranging from governance and regulation and financial viability to the student experience of learning, curriculum design, programme content and teacher competence. Although methods vary, the process of self-assessment followed by peer review is also prevalent (see Figure 1).[4]

Furthermore, the rationale for quality assurance is often opaque. Accountability is a dominant rationale but that obscures the compliance and control functions. It also obfuscates the improvement function. In policy discourses (i.e. the approach set out in, or underpinning, policy documents on quality assurance in higher education) accountability is pre-eminent; but what exactly accountability is, or requires of the sector, and how that relates to the quality of higher education, is less clear. The often-cited tension between accountability and improvement and the policy discourse that prioritises accountability, means that the improvement essence of quality is sidelined in assurance processes by a focus on demonstrating compliance.

Before elaborating a framework for a new form of quality assurance, the chapter explores:

- the nature of accountability
- the illusory tension between accountability and improvement
- the disregard for the essence of quality, which results in the attenuation of quality assurance into bureaucratic processes propped up by tenuous, albeit popular, 'definitions' of quality

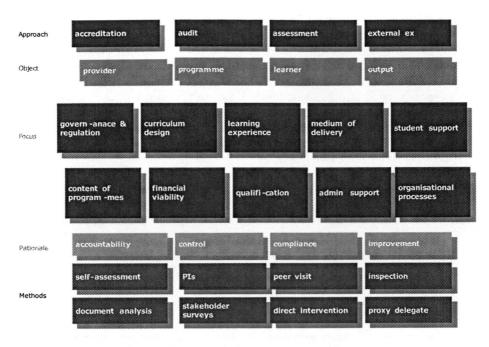

Figure 1. External evaluation (Harvey 2003)

2.1. The Nature of Accountability

Accountability has, since the 1990s, been a widely used term linked to all public service, including higher education. The usually stated reasons for the rise of accountability in higher education include the cost and potential problems of massification, the concomitant need to account for increasing amounts of public money, the need to ensure value for both private and public monies (as students are increasingly faced with paying for higher education), lack of clear lines of accountability within higher education systems, globalisation and the need to keep control of an increasingly unrestricted market (Harvey 2002a; Rosa and Amaral, Chapter 8, this volume).

Accountability is seen as a major purpose of external quality processes. However, although policy discourses give primacy to accountability, it is a rather elusive term when it comes to pinning down exactly what it means. A synthetic view of accountability in higher education is that it is "the requirement, when undertaking an activity, to expressly address the concerns, requirements or perspectives of others" (Harvey 2004–2005).[5]

In the higher education context, Campbell and Rozsnyai (2002) provide the all-encompassing, albeit somewhat circular, definition that "accountability is the assurance of a unit to its stakeholders that it provides education of good quality".

Quality assurance is about ensuring accountability, which is an assurance that it is good quality!

Higher education is usually seen as responsible to a range of stakeholders, although being held to account for expenditure of public money predominates in most elaborations of accountability. For Lewis, Ikeda, and Dundar (2001), accountability is defined as demonstrating the worth and use of public resources. Higher education in most countries has been faced with greater demands to demonstrate its worth and to account for its use of public resources, partly as a result of fierce competition for tightened state funds and partly as a result of other restructuring taking place throughout the public sector.

In a similar vein, the PA Consulting (2000: 6) study for the Higher Education Funding Council for England (HEFCE) of the UK audit methodology noted that higher education institutions in England receive over £6 billion of public money a year for which they are held to account via statutes, regulations, and contracts.

> The independent, self-governing status of higher education institutions does not absolve them from accountability for their use of public funding. ... Accountability in this context refers to the purposes for which public money is voted by Parliament, and the conditions under which institutions receive public funding.

This is, in effect, operationalised by a view that relates accountability directly to performance evaluation:

> Accountability implies the assessment of performance, the public communication of information about performance, and the potential for sanctions or rewards. Combining these words leads quickly to questions about content, power relationships, and legitimacy in educational accountability. At the outset one must ask, who is accountable, for what, and to whom? Then, are the goals and standards appropriate, are the measurements of performance valid and reliable, do those seeking to hold others accountable have legitimate expertise and authority (NCAHE 2004)?

An alternative take on this is that accountability is bound up with governance:

> Accountability: A public or private organisation must be accountable to the organisation and to society in general to ensure good governance. This means that information about set goals that have been achieved and how they have been achieved should be transparent. Universities, as public organisations, also work to establish the appropriate mechanisms to make themselves accountable to their sector and to citizens. (GUNI 2003: 1)

An alternative view relates accountability to collective responsibility:

> *Accountability* [in education] is defined as: the assurance that all education stakeholders accept responsibility and hold themselves and each other responsible for every learner having full access to quality education, qualified teachers, challenging curriculum, full opportunity to learn, and appropriate, sufficient support for learning so they can achieve at excellent levels in academic and other student outcomes.
>
> By implication in this definition, where the system and those who are responsible for it fail the learner, they also share the blame. No one group of stakeholders can point the finger of blame at any other. *All stakeholders* bear the responsibility for student school success and the blame when students are not successful. (IDRA 2002)

A Canadian definition places responsibility on governments to make higher education institutions accountable to the public:

Accountability is defined as the degree to which provincial governments ensure that universities and colleges are in fact accountable to the public, and not to corporations or individual sponsors or clients. In addition, it means that universities and colleges, and their functions of teaching, research and community service remain in the public domain and are not privatized. This is determined largely by the amount of public funding dedicated to post-secondary education budgets, as compared to funding from private donations or student fees, which download the cost of education to individuals. (Doherty-Delorme and Shaker 2001: 9)

2.1.1. Functions of Accountability

For NCAHE (2004):

The ultimate purposes of accountability systems [are] to improve performance, to assure quality, to sustain confidence.

Harvey (2002a) suggested that accountability is somewhat more complex and has five main functions. First, to ensure that the institution or programme is accountable for the money it gets, which is reflected in the definitions above. A second accountability function is to ensure that the core principles and practices of higher education are not being eroded or disregarded. This form of accountability is mainly used to control the development of private providers but can be used to ensure that public providers do not become lax. Third, accountability to students requires that the programme is organised and run properly and that an appropriate educational experience is both promised and delivered: an implicit service agreement. A fourth accountability purpose of quality evaluation procedures is the generation of public information that funders can use to aid funding allocation decisions, and prospective students and graduate recruiters can use to inform choice. A fifth accountability purpose is to use quality evaluation as a vehicle to achieve compliance to policy. The PA Consulting study (2000: 10) also draws out the clear link between accountability and compliance:

But accountability expectations increasingly go beyond this fiduciary compliance to include the achievement of Government policy objectives, even when the service providers, namely the HEIs, are constitutionally independent of Government. The Government has placed increasing emphasis on securing specified outputs and outcomes from publicly funded activities in response to community expectations about improving service quality and policy effectiveness. This is reflected in output-based funding models and increasing attention to outcome-based performance targets.

Governments around the world are looking for higher education to be more responsive. This includes responding to value-for-money imperatives, making higher education more relevant to social and economic needs, widening access to higher education and expanding numbers, usually in the face of decreasing unit cost. In addition, there is pressure to ensure comparability of provision and procedures, within and between institutions, including international comparisons.

It is also worth noting at this point, although it is discussed further below, that accountability is also intrinsically bound up with the fitness-for-purpose definition of quality. Peter Williams (2002: 1), Chief Executive of the UK Quality Assurance Agency, for example, alludes to this interrelationship when he notes:

> In the world at large, 'quality assurance' describes all aspects of the ways in which
> organisations try to make sure that their activities are fully fit for their intended
> purposes, that they are doing 'what it says on the tin'. The reasons for organisations to
> want to do this are numerous: it may be to satisfy themselves that they are meeting the
> needs of their clients, or to account to paymasters for financial assistance received. It
> may be to gain a marketing advantage over their competitors, or simply a wish to be
> sure that they are doing a fully professional job. All these reasons can apply to higher
> education.

All of this suggests that accountability is an inclusive phrase for various compliance, control and value-for-money expectations. Accountability is supposedly a
guiding force but, like a mirage in a desert, it is illusory as a quality destination.
Quality assurance for accountability is, as the quote above suggests, fulfilling a
purpose. This may be admirable but the purpose is not at the essential heart of quality,
as will be explored below. But first, another mirage: the Scylla and Charybdis of
accountability and improvement.

2.2. The Illusory Tension Between Accountability and Improvement

The perpetual debate about accountability and improvement is as old as quality
assurance in higher education. The tension between accountability and continuous
quality improvement was pointed out by Vroeijenstijn and Acherman (1990). The
dichotomy is much discussed in the quality literature (Frederiks, Westerheijden, and
Weusthof 1994; Middlehurst and Woodhouse 1995; Vroeijenstijn 1995). Quality
assurance, so the argument goes, is between a rock and a hard place. It is torn
between improvement and accountability.

However, the discussion of the dichotomy conceals as much as it reveals. First, it
specifies just two of the four purposes of quality processes: concealing compliance
and control. Second, it reinforces a perceived irreconcilable tension: to be accountable, it is claimed, requires different mechanisms than to improve. There are those,
though, who think that the tension can be patched up:

> If accountability and enhancement are key elements of quality assurance, then they
> should be inextricably linked, not placed in opposition to one another. (Williams
> 2002: 1)

Indeed, many systems of quality evaluation attempt to be accountable while
advocating improvement. This is usually based on the idea that improvement
follows accountability. The accountability-led view sees improvement as a
secondary function of the monitoring process. Such an approach argues that a
process of external monitoring of quality, which is ostensibly for purposes of
accountability, is likely to lead to improvement as a side effect. Requiring
accountability, it is assumed, will lead to a review of practices, which in turn will
result in improvement.

However, this has been questioned on three grounds (Harvey 1994). First, it is
likely that, faced with a monitoring system that demands accountability, academics
will comply with requirements in such a way as to minimise disruption to their
existing academic practices. Second, where accountability requires the production of
strategic plans, clear objectives, quality assurance systems, and so on, then there

may be an initial impetus towards quality improvement. However, there is little evidence to suggest a sustained momentum as a result of this initial push. Accountability systems, in short, are unlikely to lead to a process of *continuous* quality improvement. The argument is that improvement comes from a changed culture and local ownership, which compliance processes do not encourage. Third, accountability approaches tend to de-motivate staff who are already involved in innovation and quality initiatives. Not only do they face the added burden of responding to external scrutiny, there is also a feeling of being manipulated, of not being trusted or valued, by managers and outside agencies.

Indeed, as has been argued elsewhere (Newton 2002a), it is important to reflect on the 'career' of quality as a concept and compare the formal meanings of 'quality' that were dominant in the early 1990s with the 'situated' perceptions of quality of front-line academics, which had become embedded within institutions by the mid-1990s. Accordingly, as Newton illustrates, drawing on his ethnographic study of how academics experienced 'quality as accountability' in the 1990s:

- Quality became associated with 'ritualism' and 'tokenism', with academics using procedures primarily to satisfy external requirements and improvement at best merely a residual feature of quality systems.

- Quality became linked with 'discipline' and 'technology', with academics perceiving 'improvements in quality assurance' as distinct from improvements in quality.

- Quality was 'lack of mutual trust', with an emphasis on front-line academics' responsibilities and no real reciprocal accountability on the part of senior managers.

The counter to the view that accountability will lead to and result in improvement is to reverse the accountability-led view: improvement is its own accountability. If an organisation continually improves it is being accountable. This reverses the taken-for-granted view that agencies have to first discharge an accountability function and then encourage improvement. The proposed framework works on placing emphasis on research-based improvement, which itself will discharge accountability, unless, of course, 'accountability' is in reality about control rather than delegated responsibility.

A more recent development, as D'Andrea (Chapter 9) has also noted, has indeed been to shift the focus of agency approaches (for mature agencies) from assurance to enhancement (see note 1). Williams (2002: 1) asked:

Is quality enhancement the new quality assurance? After many years of discussion and argument about whether or not, and if so how, an external agency should review the academic quality and standards of higher education, primarily for the purpose of accountability, the spotlight has now turned away from questions of accountability towards enhancement. A new and influential committee [in the UK], the Teaching Quality Enhancement Committee (TQEC) ... has drawn a distinction between 'quality assurance' and 'quality enhancement'. Although this has been done mainly for convenience – so as to recognise the particular and unique role of the Agency in the quality assurance landscape – it nevertheless raises the question once again of what quality assurance actually is, and whether we in the Agency have any part to play in the enhancement of quality in higher education.

However, all these positions tend to miss the point. If accountability is fundamentally about ensuring compliance to financial and policy requirements and regulations, then the notion of a conflict between that and improvement is illusory. Quality assurance processes may find that in practice they are unable to encourage improvement while demanding compliance but these are not two ends of a single continuum but two distinct and only partly related dimensions. At the very least, we have a two-by-two grid of opportunities: compliance/non-compliance by improvement/non-improvement. Whether it is possible to have a set of quality assurance conditions that simultaneously encourages action in the upper-left quadrant is a moot point: but an irrelevant one. Compliance has nothing to do with improvement. Compliance may or may not lead to improvement in certain features of the higher education landscape, although being a holistic system it may result in deterioration elsewhere. Put another way, accountability is about value for money and demonstrating fitness for purpose, while continuous improvement in teaching and learning is about improvement of the student experience, and empowering students as lifelong learners.

Improvement is not something that is regulated but something that occurs through critical engagement. Accountability and improvement are not two related dimensions of quality, rather they are distinct and there is no intrinsic tension between them. Quality assurance has created an illusory tension by pretending that quality is intrinsically linked to the process of monitoring quality, an illusion that is exemplified in the 'fitness-for-purpose' approach. The illusory relationship between accountability/compliance and improvement evaporates when the focus is on the essential nature of quality itself.

2.3. The Disregard for the Essence of Quality

There is little theorising of quality in higher education. Worldwide, the preponderant approach to external quality evaluation is pragmatic, often working backwards from the political presumption, driven by new public management ideology, that higher education needs to be checked if it is to be accountable. In some cases, the method is determined before the purpose. Self-assessment and performance indicators, peer review and public reporting, although not a universal method, have become the norm and this approach is applied irrespective of the purpose, rationale, object and focus of external evaluation. Phrases such as 'fitness for purpose', 'fitness of purpose', 'value for money', 'achieving excellence' are linked to quality in higher education, all purporting, in some way or another, to be definitions of a concept that, deep down, there appears to be a reluctance to define at all. Such definitions are without any solid theoretical framework. Quality as fitness for purpose, for example, is not a definition and lacks any theoretical or conceptual gravitas. Fitness for purpose, even if linked to a fitness of purpose, thus implying a non-trivial purpose, still fails to evoke the core concept of the concept of quality.

As a noun, quality implies élite status – 'The Quality' was a term used in Britain in the 19th century to refer to the upper class (Harvey and Green 1993). As an adjective, quality implies not just exclusivity, but goodness, desirability, even reliability. In its adverbial form (qualitatively), quality is about change from one thing to another, about transformation; but more on process later.

The most famous 'quality' line in literature is Portia's in Shakespeare's *The Merchant of Venice*: "The quality of mercy is not strain'd".[6] Imagine that as: "The fitness for purpose of mercy is not strain'd"!

A quality is something we possess, something that also emanates from an object or service. We could, of course, deconstruct any object, service or person, for that matter, into a set of *qualities*: we could specify all the attributes that make the object of attention what it is. The more complex the object of attention, the longer and the more multidimensional is the list.

For example, we could describe the text of *The Merchant of Venice* by referring to the leather binding, the embossed gold-leaf title, the number and quality of the pages, the typeface. We could add to that the qualities of the content, the intricacies of the plot, the play with words, the characterisation, the ambiguity about racial discrimination, the effectiveness of the court scene. We could further elaborate its qualities by setting it in a wider context of the social context of the time it was written, or restrict the context to Elizabethan drama, or Shakespeare's own oeuvre; and by dint of so doing compare its qualities. We could endlessly undertake a reductionist analysis but, in the main, we do not. We home in on the core quality that makes the play so gratifying for us as readers, viewers or actors. It is not the reductionist list of qualities but a synthetic essence that conveys the quality of the play as a whole.

We do not explore whether *The Merchant of Venice* fits a purpose let alone specify the fitness of its purpose. Who is to specify the purpose? Us, the reader, Shakespeare, the writer, the director of the theatre that is putting on a production, the publisher of the text, a drama critic, a professor of Elizabethan drama? It makes no sense. Yet the play does have a purpose, or a set of purposes, that are context dependent: they are to entertain, amuse, inform, pose questions, challenge preconceptions or reproduce ideology. Given the complexity of purposes, the nonsense of attempting to specify the correctness of purpose is only outranked in its absurdity by the attempt to specify whether it fits said purposes. Who is to judge? Texts, as Umberto Eco argued (1979), do not exist in isolation with a fixed meaning. They are created as social objects through the role of the reader. Whatever the author intended is just one interpretation of the text.

If, then, it is a nonsense to talk of the fitness for purpose (let alone of purpose) of a single Shakespearean play, what then is the sense of applying this vague, untheorised concept to the complexity of a university? Taking the analogy of the role of the reader, a university is a text with many nuances and each participant is reading it in his or her own way, not least because they *are* the university. The university is not a thing but an ever-changing, multifaceted text that is being read and reread, not by policy makers but by the active participants. If we must adhere to the fitness-for-purpose definition, then every reader/participant has several purposes and everyone reflects on the fitness of each purpose in unique and dynamic ways. But that still misses the fundamental of quality.

Quality is about essence and transformation. It is about the dialectical process of deconstruction and reconstruction. Returning to Portia:

PORTIA: The quality of mercy is not strain'd,

It droppeth as the gentle rain from heaven

Upon the place beneath: it is twice blest;

It blesseth him that gives and him that takes:

'Tis mightiest in the mightiest: it becomes

The throned monarch better than his crown;

His sceptre shows the force of temporal power,

The attribute to awe and majesty,

Wherein doth sit the dread and fear of kings;

But mercy is above this sceptred sway;

It is enthroned in the hearts of kings,

It is an attribute to God himself;

And earthly power doth then show likest God's

When mercy seasons justice.[7]

This is an expression of the essential nature of mercy: not a definition, not an account of the purpose of mercy, not an attempt to measure mercy against some set of procedures. This is the core essential nub of the concept. And just as much as the play pivots around this essential moment, so an understanding of quality assurance revolves around the pivotal notion of quality as essence. This means that quality assurance needs to explore, dig down, to the essential quality of the programme or institution that it is reviewing: a mission-based, fitness-for-purpose checklist will not do.

But essence is not the goal of dialectical analysis. It is the key concept, the fulcrum around which pivots the deconstruction/reconstruction process of dialectical understanding (Marx 1975 (1887); Harvey 1990; Harvey and MacDonald 1993). The essential quality enables deconstruction and subsequent reconstruction of an alternative understanding of the way in which the institution (teaching programme or research project) can fundamentally enable an improvement in the creative/ learning process.

What does this mean in practice? A critical dialectical approach to quality evaluation begins with the idea that both the object of attention of the evaluation (the programme, subject area or institution) and the evaluation process itself are historically specific, situated in a holistic context and imbued with ideology. That is, the process evaluation and the object evaluated are not 'value neutral' nor apolitical, do not exist in isolation and do not transcend their historical setting. To understand the process of evaluation and thus to provide an evaluation of the object of study requires stripping away the surface appearance to reveal the ideology and to identify the essential nature of (in the case of the generalised evaluative process) the nature of quality and (in the case of the specific object under evaluation) its essential core. The essential core is determined through an iterative, dialectical process of shuttling back and forth, conceptually, between the concept/object and the wider context, and between the present and the past.

It is precisely that dialectical process that leads to the conclusion that quality itself has been cloaked in an ideological gloss that transmuted it into quality process and that quality as concept requires reconstitution. In so doing, it was possible to identify an alternative understanding of the evaluative process: that it disregarded the creative process in favour of monitoring checklists.

This view suggests that evaluation against an agenda, whether that of the evaluating agency or of the future plans of the evaluated, fails to engage quality.

Quality as fitness for/of purpose deflects us from this dialectical discourse. The cynical view would be that that is precisely the purpose of fitness-for/of-purpose approaches: to conceal the decline of essential quality and to legitimate that decline. A less cynical approach might suggest that fitness for/of purpose is merely lazy pragmatism that ends up believing itself and cloaks transformation in procedures of accountability. As noted above, fitness for purpose is intrinsically linked as a definition of quality with the accountability approach to quality assurance. Indeed, fitness for purpose, as has been suggested, transmutes quality into quality assurance.

3. A RESEARCH-INFORMED, IMPROVEMENT-LED APPROACH TO QUALITY EVALUATION

Harvey and Newton (2004: 159) made a case for a research-based approach to quality evaluation and one that prioritised self-regulation. It was noted that:

> We do not, though, as yet, have available to us a robust evidence base to illustrate what it is that works in practice for quality evaluation and quality enhancement, and why it works. ... The methods and frameworks adopted by external quality monitoring bodies over the last decade or so, can hardly be said to have been informed by systematic research, or to have been derived from evidence-based policy. Indeed, for the most part, they appear to have been driven by opportunism, political expediency, and a marked lack of trust in higher education.

The proposal was to develop an approach that was reliant on research evidence; what works in the search for continuous improvement of learning and research but also what works in ensuring successful implementation of the improvement activities (Davies, Nutley, and Smith 2000; Newton 1999a, 1999b). There continues to be not only a paucity of evidence on impact but also on implementation.

Taking the case of the United Kingdom: an improvement-led approach is being increasingly reflected in developments in Scotland (QAA 2005) with the development of an 'enhancement-led institutional review' and in the rest of the United Kingdom through an increased emphasis, as was noted above, in the debate about 'enhancement' being given more emphasis than 'accountability' in a mature system where the perception is that accountability is well embedded (Williams 2002). Nonetheless, Brown (2002: 18) argued that while the forces of accountability are strong, "those devoted to improvement, including the promotion of innovation, are fragmented".

In essence, it is not just time for more evidence on the impact of higher education in order to critically evaluate whether the quality process hitherto has been

beneficial or insidious, it is also time to have research evidence underpin the
enhancement approach.

> The present context in the UK is an interesting one. Many institutions are revising their
> quality assurance processes and are releasing considerable energies in support of
> enhancement: institutional learning and teaching strategies have been revised; there has
> been an upsurge of interest in the establishment of educational development units; there
> is a relatively new infrastructure at national level for supporting enhancement; and
> following a major review of Teaching Quality Enhancement, undertaken on behalf of
> the higher education funding council (HEFCE, 2003), a new Higher Education
> Academy has been established. Given that there is also considerable ministerial interest
> in the ways in which higher education is seeking to pursue an improvement agenda, it is
> apparent that quality enhancement has become increasingly important politically.
> (Harvey and Newton 2004: 159)

However, there remains a lack of clear evidence to guide improvement-led
approaches. Despite the declared intention of the British government to encourage
research-led policy, political imperatives often overwhelm research evidence to the
extent that one anonymous civil servant suggested that it is rather less evidence-
based policy than policy-based evidence that characterises government decision
making.

Nonetheless, the contention is that, at all levels – institutional, through national
to international – a research-informed approach to quality evaluation could provide
much needed insights into what makes improvement initiatives work, what the
principal barriers to success are, and how arrangements for quality improvement
might work to the best advantage of all who have an interest in enhancing the
quality of learning and teaching.

To transform quality assurance in the direction of the improvement of the student
experience requires not just adjusted national systems but creating conditions for
bringing about sustained change and improvement in universities. This requires a
more sophisticated understanding of how higher education institutions work. It is
necessary to take account of lessons learned from the close-up study of academics
(Trowler 1998), especially studies of how front-line academics perceive, respond to,
and cope with, quality evaluation (Newton 2000, 2002b, 2003). Increasingly, micro
accounts of the nature of academic engagement with 'quality' are emerging that go
beyond the 'game-playing' and performance of staged review events (as reported
e.g. by Barrow 1999).

To fully understand what is involved in both 'quality evaluation' and 'quality
enhancement' it is, thus, necessary to deconstruct the implementation of quality
assurance processes within the wider context of the activities of academics, the
institutional framework, national frameworks and international developments.
Transforming quality evaluation involves understanding how academics and institutions respond to quality evaluation, how institutions manage the quality improvement enterprise, and how academics themselves engage with improvement practices.

This chapter reasserts the position that national quality evaluation bodies, as well
as institutions, have a responsibility to engage with a research-informed approach to
evaluation and improvement. Indeed, as has been shown, the more academic staff
engaged with national bodies, the less those bodies are associated by them with

'accountability', and the more they are seen as delivering improvement benefits for staff and students (Harvey 2002b; Morris 2003; Harvey and Newton 2004).

4. A FRAMEWORK FOR THE TRANSFORMATION OF QUALITY EVALUATION

The underpinning principle of the transformation is to focus attention on the learner and the learning experience as well as the researcher and the creative research process. The position taken in this chapter remains as before:

> that if we wish to shift the emphasis of quality evaluation to make it transforming, then quality evaluation needs to be reclaimed from opportunistic politicians, trust in higher education needs to be re-established, and attention focused on internal processes and internal motivators. (Harvey and Newton 2004: 161)

Academic communities and quality practitioners alike continue to take, rather than make, the quality agenda, especially where external audit and assessment are concerned. The proposed approach would reverse this trend and seek ways to empower practitioners to make the agenda. This position is also endorsed by D'Andrea (Chapter 9) and by Rosa and Amaral (Chapter 8).

The transformation proposed here takes as its initial reference point Figure 1 ('external evaluation'), which depicts the major approaches, rationales, objects, focal points, and methods used in external evaluation. An alternative framework is suggested (Figure 2), which draws on the model proposed in Harvey and Newton (2004).

The deconstruction, above, of the preponderant form of external quality assurance reveals how processes hijack and mystify quality as part of a politically motivated, ideological, compliance structure. It disempowers the academic community, forces them to respond to bureaucratic requirements, imposes judgments based on perfidious views and questionable performance indicators and stifles creativity to the extent that, as part of the academic process, 'quality' no longer has anything to do with academic endeavour: knowledge creation and student learning. (This is also a process often replicated at institutional level.)

Even improvement-led approaches remain imbued with an ideology that distrusts the academy. The alternative to the predominant approach (Figure 1), which is controlled top-down and by 'external' forces (be it an external agency or an external monitoring unit within an institution), is as follows:

First, the approach (Figure 2) is premised on the notion of self-regulation, is improvement-led, and is research-informed.

Second, although audit and external examining have potential for a research-informed approach (Figure 2), the proposed framework emphasises a research-informed perspective and capability, which is a dimension currently absent from external quality evaluation.

Third, as noted above, the object is the creative/improvement process itself: the learner and learner output or outcomes and the researcher and research outcomes. In short, the framework fixes on the transformative moment.[8]

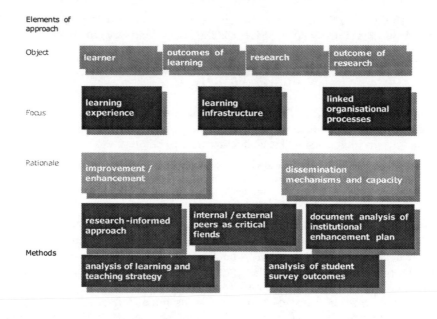

Figure 2. External evaluation: Alternative research-based framework. (Harvey and
Newton 2004)

Fourth, the learning experience and learning environment, and any organisational
processes that impinge upon them, provide a key focus for evaluation of the
transformative process. Evaluation cannot be reduced into a checklist of individualised
components, however overarching and far-reaching these may be. Thus, although the
transformation process is enabled by:

- a shift from teaching to learning
- the development of graduate attributes
- the appropriateness of assessment
- a system for rewarding transformative teaching and learning facilitation
- providing transformative learning for academics
- an emphasis on pedagogy
- an institutional climate supportive of responsive collegiality
- establishing linkages between quality improvement and learning (Harvey
  1997)

this is not a checklist that has to be accomplished. Transformation is a holistic
process, not reducible to independent elements and the above are indicative of the
institutional metamorphosis that is necessary, but not necessarily sufficient, to
enable the transformative moment.

Fifth, the underpinning rationale is improvement and through a shift in discourse to improvement we can capture a deeper meaning, that of improving the critical creative/reflective process, that is at the heart of learning and knowledge creation. Here, in essence, the proposed framework is more insistent on improvement that enables the transformational moment, rather than improvement in more general terms.

Sixth, the compliance and verification elements of conventional forms of external quality evaluation are replaced by an improvement focus, since this is not a system for the inspection of provision. It was initially proposed that the focus of the improvement-led approach to external evaluation would not be provision but a university's 'institutional quality enhancement plan' or 'learning and teaching improvement strategy' (Figure 2), and its systems and mechanisms for the identi-fication and dissemination of good practice (Harvey and Newton 2004: 162). The revisited framework would, in the light of the deconstruction of the quality assurance process, prefer an evaluation process contingent on the pivotal creative moment. However, pragmatically, at least in the first stage of a shift to a research-informed improvement approach, it is probably necessary to concede an interim stage: the framing of an improvement agenda.

Seventh, the self-improvement agenda approach is premised on self-regulation. The institutional plan, or equivalent, would be used as the focal point for external quality monitoring, but on the basis of external input being that of a 'critical friend' or 'external consultant'. Elements of this are present in the approach adopted by the innovative "Joint Nordic Project", established through the Nordic Quality Assurance Network (NOQA) to promote best practice in quality enhancement, and which has made significant progress towards an open, genuinely interactive, and transparent approach to identifying good practice in improvement initiatives (Omar and Liuhanen 2005).

Eighth, as has been made clear throughout, a key requirement is that evaluation should be research-informed. Accordingly, while members of an external evaluation team would include both pedagogic expertise and professional experience of quality evaluation, the team would be required to have appropriate expertise in the area of research-informed approaches to learning and teaching. Mere 'amateur' opinion, based on cursory review of documentation or casual observation of facilities or even the learning process, will not provide adequate insights into the improvement agenda, let alone the transformative moment. Clearly, achieving the right specification for the kinds of expertise required entails further deliberation. However, given the growth of distinct 'communities of practice', in the United Kingdom and elsewhere, in 'quality enhancement' and 'pedagogic research' this does not present insurmountable challenges.

The key issue is what is the evidence that informs the evaluation?

> The [improvement] 'plan' would incorporate self-evaluation of both quality and standards matters. The latter might draw on external examiner reports and student performance data; the former would reference evidence from student surveys. Where an institution is fully taking up the challenge of self-regulation, the institutional plan might also provide a timetable for the internal review and audit of all aspects of the operation of the institution, including learning and student services. This would enable a focus on how the institution itself reviews the learning infrastructure and the wider processes that impact on the student experience. There may also be merit, from a funding point of

> view, in what Yorke (1994) has termed learning development (or 'DevL') funding.
> Here, the level of support awarded might reflect the nature and merits of the
> 'institutional enhancement plan', with the strategic development of student learning
> being encouraged through institutions using their enhancement planning as a basis for
> bidding over a time frame of, say, three years. The success or progress of the plan
> would be subject to external evaluation under the overall model proposed here. (Harvey
> and Newton 2004: 162–163)

This may, at first glance, appear to be a rather subtle development over and
above what external agencies currently require from institutions or subject groups.
However, it privileges looking forward rather than back and requires the *evidence
base* upon which forward planning is based. The upshot is an evaluation of planning
proposal rather than an evaluation of provision per se. The original proposal noted
two distinctive features of this framework.

> First, is the extent of its evaluative focus on the ways in which an institution, through its
> enhancement planning or learning and teaching strategy, is making progress in its
> efforts to embed mechanisms for enhancing student learning and to identify and
> disseminate good practice in learning, teaching, and assessment. (Harvey and Newton
> 2004: 163)

On the face of it, this still has two major drawbacks. The first is that the
improvement-plan approach still places emphasis on bureaucratic compliance –
albeit one that is more in the control of the institution or the academic group. The
second drawback is that although the improvement-plan approach fits more readily
with ongoing review and development processes it does not necessarily facilitate a
deconstructive enquiry that explores the transformative moment. The improvement
plan alone operates at a level above that of fundamental enquiry into how students
learn, how researchers work and what could be done to improve the learning/
creative moment (i.e. transformative moment).

However, the framework provides an entry into a more fundamental review of
the transformative moment through its second feature: the institution's use of both
internal and external research and project work in the area of learning and teaching
enhancement. It provides an opportunity for an institution to demonstrate how it is
making use of the resources and activities of national, regional and international
bodies with responsibilities and expertise in the area of learning and teaching
enhancement, and of 'communities of practice' such as subject associations or
professional bodies. The framework is also sufficiently flexible, potentially, to be
able to accommodate other objectives relating, say, to employability, and how a
university is addressing specific aspects of regional economic agendas.

In this respect, the evidence on the nature and practice of learning (and by
extension research) communities provides an opportunity to explore and evaluate the
transformative process.

So, in a nutshell, the proposal is for continuous forward planning supported by
clear research-based evidence that the proposals would improve the transformative
learning and knowledge creation process (the transformative moment). The key
question for evaluators would be: How do you know that what you are planning to
do in your setting is likely to improve how students learn or how researchers create
knowledge?

This does not mean that each institution or group of academics has to answer this with fundamental research of their own. On the contrary, reinventing wheels should be kept to a minimum: there is more than enough 'not invented here' syndrome in the area of learning development. Harvey and Newton (2004: 164), for example, proposed "a searchable database" of "cases of good practice, worthy of dissemination". However, that does not mean that ready-made answers can be imported without consideration of the context into which they are going. Examples of ill-considered adoption of fads and fashions abound, from management practices, adoption of teaching techniques such as problem-based learning to installation of generic learning environments and the shift to semesterisation. None of these approaches solve anything per se. However, in the United Kingdom, for example, there is a wealth of information and practice on the improvement of the curriculum, assessment and the student experience within the new Higher Education Academy and its constituent elements (such as the LTSN Subject Centres and Generic Centre). A key consideration, therefore, is to use research to identify 'what works' at this university, in this or that subject area, in respect of improving the quality of learning and teaching, and the evidence used to illustrate this.

Finally, ninth, this improvement-led approach requires not only enquiry into structures, mechanisms and procedures, but a clear cycle of action involving delegated responsibility to the institution by the external quality evaluation agency, and also within the institution to subject department and programme level, thus reflecting the 'self-regulatory' principle. Clear information flows, both vertically and horizontally, are also required.

So, why should institutions take the not-inconsiderable step of adopting a research-based approach to improvement? At the moment they are investing considerable resources to comply with external requirements but with minimal and poorly targeted or documented pay-offs. Indeed, the UK Cabinet Office's Better Regulation Task Force, in its report "Higher Education: Easing the Burden" (2002: 7), indicated that "PA Consulting put the annual cost of what it referred to as the 'accountability burden' on HEIs at £250m". Moreover, in his discussion of quality assurance in higher education in Germany, Federkell (2005) points to the vast bureaucracy and cost of running even one cycle of programme accreditation in a higher education system that now has some 30,000 programmes. If each is subject to a three-day visit by a team of four reviewers the cost of the 360,000 reviewer days would be in the region of €250 million. In an accreditation system that is scheduled on a five-year cycle it is hardly surprising that Federkell reports that only 527 programmes have been accredited to date! Be that as it may, the general point is that the nature, extent and longevity of compliance-linked improvement are elusive and the resources expended tend to be written off or accounted for by short-term changes or dealing with reviewer comments, often at a senior level without impinging on the transformation at the learner/teacher or research interfaces. Expending effort on researching what is effective in transforming learning and research and linking it to improvement agendas is a more attractive use of resources, usually involving a longer term commitment but one with continuous improvement impact.

5. CONCLUSION

In this chapter fundamental questions have been posed about the nature and ubiquity of quality assurance, and also the essence of quality itself. It has been argued that quality assurance has thrived on the illusion that quality is intrinsically linked to regulatory frameworks and monitoring processes. The familiar debate around the assumed tension between 'accountability' and 'improvement' was revisited but the argument put forward here is that this tension is illusory and the frequently referred to dichotomy conceals as much as it reveals. The heart of the approach adopted here is a deconstruction of existing dominant approaches to quality assurance and a reconstruction of an alternative, research-informed approach.

There is an argument, perhaps, that the framework proposed here is only applicable to mature systems that have the accountability processes in place; indeed, that this process reflects heavily the UK environment. This is a moot point. The focus on the essential transformative nature of quality, rather than fitness-for-purpose glosses that conceal quality behind quality assurance processes, is something that can be applied in new systems. Indeed, the Swedish National Agency started out with an approach that privileged an audit of improvement processes but was inter alia distrusted by politicians who wanted more ostensive accountability and forced a change of direction.

The original paper summarised the approach thus:

> Such a model incorporates meaningful and supportive dialogue between an external review team and the institution, in contrast to the usual practice in external audit and assessment which routinely involves 'game playing' and artificial exchanges based around an institution defending a position. The focus of evaluation and dialogue is on internal processes, and an underlying intention of the overall methodology is to secure a shift in quality management ideology and practices away from attempts at impression management and controlling appearances, towards encouraging a focus on 'bottom up' driven innovations, cross-institutional cooperation and communication, and a strategic approach which is integrated and focused around the theme of the enhancement of learning and teaching. (Harvey and Newton 2004: 163)

While the above still obtains as a medium to facilitate the review process, the revised approach makes a more fundamental contribution to the debate about quality evaluation. It places even more emphasis on grasping the essential quality of a programme, research project or institution and identifying the means, informed by research, to ensure improvement of the learning and creative process.

It is acknowledged that there remain as yet unresolved questions around how the approach outlined here might be operationalised, and the circumstances and driving forces which could lead to its adoption. These issues are recognised as needing consideration and further work, though they remain beyond the scope of this present chapter. The purpose of this chapter has been to identify the nature and shape of a paradigm shift which many involved in the quality evaluation debate increasingly recognise as being desirable.

NOTES

1   In some countries, notably the United Kingdom, the term enhancement has grown up as an alternative to improvement. In practice, the two terms are used interchangeably. To improve means to make things better or to ameliorate. To enhance means to make larger, clearer or more attractive. Enhancement, thus, has connotations of changing appearance, making quality look better, whereas improvement has connotations of delivering a better service. In that case this chapter prefers the term improvement and uses that except where referring to use made by others of the term enhancement.

2   The original paper (Harvey and Newton 2004) undertook a review and critique of existing systems of higher education quality review. It mapped the approach, object, focus, rationale and methods of existing approaches to quality assurance. It noted that accountability, compliance and, in some countries, control are much more frequent rationales for external monitoring than improvement. The paper argued for more evidence-based research to inform quality evaluation policy, although noting a relative paucity of research, especially on impact. The paper had, as its clarion call, the assertion that "if quality evaluation is to be transformed to make it transforming it is time to reclaim quality evaluation from opportunistic politicians, re-establish trust in higher education and focus attention on internal processes and motivators". The paper raised fundamental questions about both impact and the methodology for assessing impact. It asked "What is the evidence of the impact of quality assurance on higher education quality?" and suggested that there was a lack of serious independent research on impact and that what there was brought into question inquisitorial approaches to quality assurance. It argued that transformation of quality assurance is necessary to ensure that quality assurance is itself a transforming process for those involved in the student learning experience and proposed a model for the transformation of external quality evaluation.

3   Quality assurance used to have a narrower meaning, referring principally to auditing processes rather than assessment, accreditation or standards checking, but since most of these processes in practice tend to use much the same methods, the term assurance has become a catch-all term. In some writings, this term has been replaced by 'monitoring' to encompass the variety of procedures (see Harvey 2004–2005). It is notable that the International Network of Quality Assurance Agencies in Higher Education includes agencies that undertake assurance, assessment and accreditation.

4   Harvey and Newton (2004) explore this initial 'model' in much greater detail.

5   Much of the remainder of this section draws on the discussion of accountability in the *Analytic Quality Glossary* (Harvey 2004–2005).

6   Strain'd in this quote is short for constrained, that is, there are no constraints on the quality of mercy.

7   Portia is telling Shylock (the moneylender who wants his pound of flesh) that mercy must be freely given, and is inviting him to show mercy to the merchant.

8   Moment, in this sense, refers not so much to an instant of time but a particular point in time when the physical notion of 'moment' (the engagement and impact of forces) and the consequential notion of moment (having important effects or influence) are combined into a momentous event of engagement and critical reflection and reconceptualisation. Thus a transformative process, changing one's understanding, manifests in self-realisation or a research output.

REFERENCES

Barrow, M. "Quality Management Systems and Dramaturgical Compliance." *Quality in Higher Education* 5.1 (1999): 27–36.

Better Regulation Task Force. "Higher Education: Easing the Burden." London: The Cabinet Office, 2002.

Brown, Roger. "A Case of Quantity Over Quality." *Times Higher Education Supplement*. 9 August, 2002, 18.

Campbell, C. and C. Rozsnyai. *Quality Assurance and the Development of Course Programmes*. Papers on Higher Education Series. Regional University Network on Governance and Management of Higher Education in South East Europe. Bucharest: UNESCO-CEPES, 2002.

Davies, H.T.O., S.M. Nutley, and P.C. Smith. *What Works? Evidence-based Policy and Practice in Public Services*. Bristol: The Polity Press, 2000.

Doherty-Delorme, D. and E. Shaker. *Missing Pieces II: An Alternative Guide to Canadian Post-secondary Education*. Provincial Rankings: Where Do the Provinces Stand on Education? Ottawa: Canadian Centre for Policy Alternatives, 2000/2001, http://www.policyalternatives.ca/publications/ pub4.html.

Eco, U. *The Role of the Reader*. Bloomington: Indiana University Press, 1979.

Federkell, G. "The Dynamics of Quality Assurance in German Higher Education." Paper presented at the Seminar Dynamics and Effects of Quality Assurance in Higher Education – Various Perspectives of Quality and Performance at Various Levels, Douro, October, 2005.

Frederiks, M.M.J., D.F. Westerheijden, and P.J.M. Weusthof. "Stakeholders in Quality: Improvement or Accountability in Quality Assessment in Five Higher Education Systems." In Goedegebuure, L.C.J. and F.A. van Vught (eds). *Comparative Policy Studies in Higher Education*. Utrecht: Lemma, 1994, 95–126.

GUNI (Global University Network for Innovation). *Accountability*. 1 June, 2003, http://www.guni-rmies.net/news/default.php?int_theme=44&tpgPage=3.

Harvey, L. *Critical Social Research*. London: Unwin Hyman, 1990.

Harvey, L. "Continuous Quality Improvement: A System-wide View of Quality in Higher Education." In Knight, P.T. (ed.). *University-wide Change, Staff and Curriculum Development*. SEDA Paper 83, Birmingham, UK: Staff and Educational Development Association, 1994, 47–70.

Harvey, L. 'Quality Monitoring and Transformative Learning: Changing International Trends and Future Directions." *Proceedings of the INQAAHE Conference: Quality Without Frontiers*, South Africa, 24–28 May 1997.

Harvey, L. "Quality Assurance in Higher Education: Some International Trends." Keynote presentation to Higher Education Conference, Oslo, 22–23 January, 2002a.

Harvey, L. "The End of Quality?" *Quality in Higher Education* 8.1 (2002b): 5–22.

Harvey, L., "Accreditation: perspective from institutions." Keynote at the ENQA Conference, Rome, 13-15 November, 2003.

Harvey, L. *Analytic Quality Glossary*. Sheffield: Quality Research International, 2004–2005, http://www. qualityresearchinternational.com/glossary/.

Harvey, L. and D. Green. "Defining Quality." *Assessment and Evaluation in Higher Education* 18.1 (1993): 9–34. Also Harvey, L. and D. Green. "Qualität definieren." *Zeitschrift für Pädagogik*, Special Issue (2000): 17–39.

Harvey, L. and P. Knight. *Transforming Higher Education*. Buckingham: Society for Research into Higher Education and Open University Press, 1996.

Harvey, L. and M. MacDonald. *Doing Sociology: A Practical Introduction*. London: Macmillan, 1993.

Harvey, L. and J. Newton. "Transforming Quality Evaluation." *Quality in Higher Education* 10.2 (2004): 149–165.

HEFCE (Higher Education Funding Council for England). *Teaching Quality Enhancement Committee: Final Report*. Bristol: HEFCE, 2003.

IDRA (Intercultural Development Research Association). *IDRA Newsletter*. May 2002, http://www.idra.org/ Newslttr/2002/May/Bradley.htm.

Lewis, D.R., T. Ikeda, and H. Dundar. "On the Use of Performance Indicators in Japan's Higher Education Reform Agenda." *Nagoya Journal of Higher Education* (2001): 1.

Marx, K. *Das Kapital*. Trans. Samuel Moore and Edward Aveling, ed. Frederick Engels. Moscow: Progress Publishers, 1975 (1887).

Middlehurst, R. and D. Woodhouse. "Coherent Systems for External Quality Assurance." *Quality in Higher Education* 1.3 (1995): 257–268.

Morris, C. "Towards an Evidence-based Approach to Quality Enhancement: A Modest Proposal." 2003, http://www.ltsn.ac.uk/genericcentre/index.asp?docid=20033.

NCAHE (National Commission on Accountability in Higher Education). *Overview*. State Higher Education Executive Officers (SHEEO), 2004, http://www.sheeo.org/account/comm-home.htm.

Newton, J. "External Quality Monitoring in Wales (1993–1998): An Evaluation of the Impact on a Higher Education College." *Assessment & Evaluation in Higher Education* 24.2 (1999a): 215–235.

Newton, J. "Implementing Quality Assurance Policy in a Higher Education College: Exploring the Tension Between the Views of 'Managers' and 'Managed'." In Fourie, M., A.H. Strydom, and J. Stetar (eds). *Reconstructing Quality Assurance: Programme Assessment and Accreditation*. Bloemfontein: University of the Free State Press, 1999b, 4–51.

Newton, J. "Feeding the Beast or Improving Quality?: Academics' Perceptions of Quality Assurance and Quality Monitoring." *Quality in Higher Education* 6.2 (2000): 153–162.

Newton, J. "Views From Below: Academics Coping With Quality." *Quality in Higher Education* 8.1 (2002a): 39–61.

Newton, J. "Evaluating the Impact of External and Internal Quality Monitoring: Perceptions and Responses of Front-line Academics." In Gnaman, A., D. Bradbury, and A. Stella (eds). *Benchmarks and Performance Indicators in Quality Assessment: The Indo–UK Perspective.* New Delhi: Sterling, 2002b, 135–172.

Newton, J. "Implementing an Institution-wide Learning and Teaching Strategy: Lessons in Managing Change." *Studies in Higher Education* 28.4 (2003): 427–441.

Omar, Pirjo-Liisa and Anna-Maija Liuhanen (eds). *A Comparative Analysis of Systematic Quality Work in Nordic Higher Education Institutions.* Helsinki: Nordic Quality Assurance Network in Higher Education, 2005.

PA Consulting. *Better Accountability for Higher Education: Summary of a Review for the HEFCE.* Report August 00/36. London: Higher Education Funding Council for England, 2000.

QAA (Quality Assurance Agency for Higher Education). *Our Work in Scotland.* QAA, 2005, http://www.qaa.ac.uk/scotland/default.asp.

Trowler, P. *Academics Responding to Change: New Higher Education Frameworks and Academic Cultures.* Buckingham: Society for Research into Higher Education and Open University Press, 1998.

Vroeijenstijn, A.I. *Improvement and Accountability, Navigating Between Scylla and Charybdis: Guide for External Quality Assessment in Higher Education.* London: Jessica Kingsley, 1995.

Vroeijenstijn, A.I. and J.A. Acherman. "Control-Oriented Versus Improvement-Oriented Quality Assessment." In Goedegebuure, L.C.J., P.A.M. Maassen, and D.F. Westerheijden (eds.). *Peer Review and Performance Indicators: Quality Assessment in British and Dutch Higher Education.* Utrecht: Lemma, 1990.

Williams, P. "Anyone for Enhancement?" *Higher Quality*, 11, November 2002, http://www.qaa.ac.uk/news/higherquality/hq11/default.asp.

Yorke, M. "Enhancement-led Higher Education?" *Quality Assurance in Higher Education* 2.3 (1994): 6–12.

BJØRN STENSAKER, MARIA JOÃO ROSA,
AND DON F. WESTERHEIJDEN

CONCLUSIONS AND FURTHER CHALLENGES

The intention with the current book has been to study the regulation, translation, and transformation of quality assurance from a number of perspectives and by different approaches. By doing so we have underlined the multifaceted nature of quality assurance and the many interests associated with the concept.

Three common elements have, nevertheless, emerged from the different perspectives and approaches utilised to study and analyse quality assurance in higher education:

- judged by its effects and impacts, quality assurance is not yet optimal – better processes and/or mechanisms can lead to improvements;
- defining 'quality' remains a problem, although it did not stop this volume's contributors from analysing it;
- a plurality of critical analyses is required – there is no advocacy of certain quality assurance models or policies, there is a balanced analysis of different methods used for assuring quality, there is no forced consensus around certain approaches or perspectives but fortuitously much complementarity, and finally there is not the idea that 'one size fits all'.

This final chapter intends to further develop these common elements, by calling the reader's attention to some of the most interesting ideas expressed by the authors during the 2005 Douro Seminar and that underlie all chapters in this volume. It is also our intention to go through unresolved issues and challenging questions that constitute interesting issues surrounding quality and quality assurance in higher education. We will start by reviewing the contributions to the book.

1. BRIEF SUMMARY OF THE CHAPTERS' CONTRIBUTIONS

The present volume is built around three parts that focus on the regulation, translation, and transformation issues surrounding higher education's quality assurance after the turn of the century.

In the first part of the book, regulatory issues concerning quality were at the centre of our attention. The chapters by Blackmur, Dill, and Westerheijden all discussed the issues: How are quality issues currently regulated? What are the strengths and weaknesses of the current regulatory regimes? How could the regulatory approaches be improved? In all three chapters we are reminded that

D.F. Westerheijden et al. (eds.), Quality Assurance in Higher Education: Trends in Regulation,
Translation and Transformation, 247–262.
© 2007 Springer.

quality assurance is not an obscure, inconsequential issue in higher education, but rather the prime issue in current higher education policy making around the world. Quality assurance is the policy instrument that deals most directly with the 'primary processes' in higher education: education and research.

In the chapter by Blackmur, it is emphasised that we are often too imprecise when talking about quality. As he rightly argues, public regulation is about regulating the *qualities* of higher education, not *quality* understood as a single and easily grasped entity. In a similar vein, Blackmur maintains that we perhaps should take one step back when starting to analyse what we perceive as quality problems, and that many states seem to overlook certain basic choices when dealing with them. What sort of problems should be solved by using public or private means? What is the proper role of governments in such issues?

The basic discussion offered by Blackmur is followed up by Dill and Westerheijden in Chapters 3 and 4 of Part I, respectively. Dill, focusing on the potential and problems associated with market approaches for regulating quality, shows how market competition has influenced higher education in the United Kingdom and the United States over the last decades. Reviewing available evidence, Dill points to the fact that market competition has some built-in side effects that do not necessarily support the quality of higher education. Not least, it is shown how market competition is increasing costs associated with higher education, and that this might even affect institutional teaching and learning activities in a very negative way. In this way, Dill develops a case for supporting some degree of public intervention when dealing with quality issues.

However, public intervention may be easier said than done. By linking quality issues to the ongoing Bologna process in Europe, Westerheijden shows how higher education issues currently are heavily intertwined with economic policy making and the challenges many states face when it comes to handling issues relating to the improvement of public sector performance and effectiveness. Within this perspective, quality issues are part of the new public management agenda invading every policy area in developed countries. The dangers associated with these links are that governments might turn their attention to certain administrative and organisational solutions without critically asking whether these measures actually address and solve the current policy challenges associated with the Bologna process. As Westerheijden concludes, it is not evident that the current European quality assurance initiatives will lead to a more harmonised and transparent higher education area.

Given the difficulties experienced concerning both market coordination and government regulation in the quality area, an obvious question is whether governments and researchers have managed to develop good enough analytical schemes for grasping the essence of the perceived quality problems in higher education, and, in particular, the translation involved when policies are to be implemented within the sector. In Part II of the book, Stensaker, Ewell, and Perellon each offer different theoretical and methodological approaches for analysing quality, hence they point to the many tools available to provide a more multifaceted understanding of quality.

In his proposal for a more sophisticated conceptual framework for analysing quality, Perellon in Part II of the book reminds us of some of the insights higher education research gained from policy implementation studies in the past two decades. By drawing on Premfors (1992) and Sabatier (1993), he structures his policy analysis approach around questions such as the objectives, control, areas, procedures, and uses related to quality assurance. This structure then enables him to identify some of the dynamic factors surrounding the current quality debate. The list of potential actors, processes, and characteristics of higher education then offered should be useful for analysing not only quality issues, but also a range of other policy problems and challenges in higher education. As Perellon points out in his conclusion, this framework should be especially useful for analysing issues concerning potential convergent or divergent developments within the sector.

Stensaker also offers us a highly structured approach for analysing how quality has been introduced to higher education. Inspired by current studies on the diffusion and translation of management ideas in organisational studies in general, attention is drawn to the symbolic aspects of quality assurance, and how fads and fashions should be taken into account when analysing translation processes within the sector. Stensaker also points out that the concept of translation provides us with a more realistic understanding of the processes taking place when ideas are put into practice in higher education than the term 'implementation' does. In this way, Stensaker emphasises that values, norms, and cultures are important factors to take into account when analysing the sector.

Through his detailed and rich analysis of the translation processes surrounding quality assurance in the United States, Ewell then develops a more historical approach to understanding how the concept of quality has evolved in that country during the last 30 years. This approach shows us the value of paying attention to history and the legacy of the past when new ideas and policies are developed. In many ways Ewell's approach is a reminder of how small developments over time are aggregated until reaching a point when there is a need for breaks and new directions. But Ewell's approach is also an example of how higher education researchers construct history and in this way make it more meaningful and easy to comprehend. By doing so, Ewell at the same time develops testable proposals for further increasing our knowledge on the effects of various design issues concerning quality assurance.

Finally, in Part III of the book, attention is directed to the transformational aspects of quality assurance. In the chapters by Rosa and Amaral, D'Andrea, and Harvey and Newton, we learn more about the effects of quality assurance in higher education and, not least, why we sometimes have difficulties in tracing concrete 'transformations' of all initiatives taken in this area. In the chapter by Rosa and Amaral, we are reminded that quality assurance has its origins outside higher education, and that external definitions and concepts concerning quality have infused this sector. Their study of an application of the EFQM Excellence Model at the institutional level also shows that such more standardised models can be relevant to higher education if implemented with consideration for the inherent characteristics of the sector. Not least, it is illustrated how important institutional leadership is when introducing external ideas and concepts into higher education institutions (similarly in Csizmadia 2006).

However, governmental and managerial attempts to adjust and customise quality assurance into higher education institutions have not always succeeded, as D'Andrea points out in her analysis. Through conceptualising quality assurance as a learning process, she shows how external quality reviews are not always in accordance with current theories on learning, and that there are several missing links between current macro-level quality review processes and micro-level attempts to improve teaching and learning. In her conclusion, D'Andrea especially points out that there is need for a more developed theoretical basis for external quality reviews.

The mismatch experienced between macro-level initiatives in quality assurance and micro-level experienced needs is further explored by Harvey and Newton. Noting the rather disappointing results of the many governmental initiatives concerning quality assurance, they argue that it is time to consider a different approach to quality assurance – an evidence-based one. At the core of their approach is the idea that accountability and improvement are not pure opposites, but may walk hand in hand as accountability indeed also can be reached through well-documented and research-informed improvement activities enabled through a meaningful dialogue between evaluators and those evaluated. Not least, it is proposed that evaluation activities should be more focused on reviewing plans for quality enhancement at the institutional level than examining the provision, as is often the practice today.

2. CENTRAL MESSAGES AND FINDINGS

As already stressed, despite the many approaches and perspectives utilised for studying and understanding quality assurance, there are common messages and findings that can be distilled from the book.

First, what all chapters in this book implicitly emphasise is that we should *broaden the analytical approaches* when analysing quality issues in higher education. Quality is not a secondary issue in the sector, but a concept that addresses some of the basic and classical questions in higher education: quality is essentially a question about the effectiveness and efficiency of the sector as a whole. Hence, as pointed out by Blackmur, Dill, and Westerheijden, regulatory issues should be a core theme when analysing quality. However, in practice, many studies linked to this field have only addressed the area of quality assurance understood rather narrowly as the design, implementation, and partially the effects of external evaluation schemes in higher education (see e.g. Westerheijden, Brennan, and Maassen 1994; Brennan and Shah 2000; Schwarz and Westerheijden 2004; Rosa, Tavares, and Amaral 2006). Even though the current book also deals with quality assurance issues, the authors in many of the previous chapters defined quality assurance in a broader way, including in their analyses the links between international and national contextual developments, translation issues, and institutional reactions and responses. This multi-level approach has allowed us to contextualise the design and organisation-focused debate usually surrounding quality assurance, and ask critical questions relating to when and why governments should intervene in this area, the processes involved in 'spreading the gospel' about quality, or even asking whether or not the whole area of quality assurance should be transformed.

Second, as illustrated by a number of contributions in the book, the impact of different national contexts on the implementation of public policy in the quality area seem more recognisable than before. *Adapting the concept of 'translation'* instead of 'implementation' is perhaps the most noticeable indication of this. This in turn extends our understanding beyond the unfortunate dichotomy between homogenisation and diversification that is often linked to quality issues. Even though the contributions in this book identify many similarities surrounding quality assurance, emphasising *translation* reminds us that the starting point for addressing quality assurance is related to a particular (national) context (see e.g. Frazer 1997). Although socio-economic restructuring, internationalisation, and globalisation of education markets, together with the emergence of the knowledge-based society, have influenced higher education development, the fact is that higher education institutions operating within specific national frameworks have their own dynamics and address challenges based on their own positions (with their own strengths and weaknesses). Hence, even the Bologna process might not lead to the homogenisation and transparency intended in the quality area, as Westerheijden concludes in Chapter 4. Evidence from the United States reported in Chapter 6 by Ewell also shows significantly different approaches between the states of the United States when it comes to how quality assurance policies have been put into practice, and, as Rosa and Amaral point out in their contribution, there is evidence that significant translation processes are quite common phenomena also at the institutional level. A final point supporting the importance of the specific national context is the fact that policy action within the quality area differs significantly between states: where some were early innovators (see e.g. Ewell's chapter), others were latecomers in this field – so late, in fact, that we could not secure their contributions to this book.

A third finding throughout the book is the *significant lack of precision* when governments and other agencies address quality issues in their policy making. This lack of precision is related not only to decision makers' formulations of what they perceive as quality problems, but also to a lack of specific objectives within implemented initiatives. As shown in the chapters by Perellon, Ewell, Blackmur, and also Stensaker, decision makers have actually allowed for much of the confusion and debates in the quality area. In a more positive vein, not unusual in policy analysis, we can of course also argue that this lack of precision has led to a smoother translation process into the sector than would have been possible otherwise: ambiguity has its uses as a 'lubricant' in translation processes. In this way, the different actors have had the opportunity to influence locally how quality should be defined (explicitly or implicitly), and add meaning to the implemented measures. Still, within higher education research, trying to define quality during the last 20 years has been one of the longest-lasting activities – starting in the mid-1980s (Ball 1985) – without leading to a finer-grained conclusion than the agreement on the relative aspects of the concept (Harvey and Green 1993). With these arguments in mind, one could, of course, argue that both governments and higher education institutions had a strong interest in not defining quality too explicitly, and that this might provide at least a partial explanation for the somewhat unclear understanding of the core concept. For both politicians and institutions within the sector, precise definitions also increased the chance of being held accountable for the results and effects of the measures taken. As illustrated by D'Andrea and Harvey and Newton we are currently left, therefore, with very little hard evidence of what all the bustle has been about for the last 20 years. A further consequence of the ambiguity may have been that with the ensuing problems related to what exactly to measure if definitions and goals remained vague, one may understand why methodological issues concerning how impact studies should be conducted have been one of the most problematic themes in evaluative research in higher education.

Even though governments as a rule have been vague in formulating their expectations, this has not stood in the way of the development of relatively uniform organisational solutions as to how quality assurance should be implemented. A fourth finding is therefore supporting early observations of a 'general model' for quality assurance in higher education (Van Vught and Westerheijden 1994). However, given the many policy instruments (legal, economical, informational, or organisational) available to policy makers, what this book shows is that it is first and foremost the *organisational approach* that can be associated with quality assurance initiatives in higher education. We could therefore argue that the 'general model' is not so much about the content or the aims of the procedures associated with evaluation (how to perform self-assessments, external assessments, etc.) as it is about understanding it as a description of the dominant place 'organisation' has had as a governmental tool during the last 20 years (see also Neave 1988). Whether we talk about evaluations (either in the form of audits or accreditations), intermediate bodies, or new quality assurance systems at the institutional level, we still end up with organisational solutions. As Blackmur reminds us, there are other instruments and approaches that could have had a more prominent role. Our knowledge as to why this has happened is still far from satisfactory, but this book has pointed to some factors that seem important: fashion and policy copying (see e.g. the chapters by Stensaker, Ewell, and Perellon) undoubtedly play a role, but equally the links between general new public management reforms and the field of quality assurance should not be underestimated (as shown by the chapters of Westerheijden, Harvey and Newton, Rosa and Amaral or Dill).

A fifth and recurrent finding in the book is the recognition of the problems associated with *quality assurance and its relationship to institutional learning and institutional behaviour* in higher education. As especially highlighted by Harvey and Newton, D'Andrea, and also Dill in their respective chapters, there is much evidence of a mismatch between intended effects and implemented measures at the institutional level. An interesting aspect here is that this mismatch goes for both public and private initiatives in quality assurance. In the public sphere, quality assurance has focused on the performance dimensions of higher education (see Blackmur), with accountability as an underlying factor (see Westerheijden), while in the private sphere, and especially related to publicised ranking systems, there is a tendency to emphasise academic reputation where this construct is often taken as a substitute measurement for quality (see Dill). Harvey and Newton and also D'Andrea substantiate how such schemes have led to ritualism and tokenism at the institutional level. This leads them to question the usefulness of such external quality assurance from an institutional perspective, and to their pleading for a transformation of the mode related to how quality should be regulated. This argument has been quite broadly supported over the years by other studies advocating a stronger focus on institutional characteristics and functioning when designing quality assurance schemes in higher education (see e.g. Harvey and Knight 1996; Dill 2000; Stensaker 2003).

3. UNRESOLVED ISSUES AND CHALLENGING QUESTIONS

Even though many themes and national settings have been examined in the current book, we are still far from answering all questions surrounding quality and quality assurance in higher education. As such, we – as many before us – end up with numerous questions and further challenging research problems concerning future analysis. A selection of these issues is presented below in random order.

First, does it matter if regulation of quality is public or private? If so, which option is most effective? We know that both forms of regulatory frameworks are associated with problems concerning either government or market 'failure', but what is, at the end of the day, the relative advantage or disadvantage of going for either public or private solutions in this area? While Blackmur in Chapter 2 argues for utilising a public choice perspective in such situations, both Dill and Westerheijden (Chapters 3 and 4) question the ability of regulators to arrive at rational and objective solutions. A particular problem here is, not least, grasping the complexity of institutional behaviour and the often intricate problems concerning cross-subsidisation between education and research and lack of information (Dill and Soo 2004).

Second and related to the above, questions concerning the costs associated with quality assurance have not really been addressed properly. This goes not only for the direct costs associated with evaluation activities per se, but also studies related to the relative benefits of quality assurance compared to other ways to secure and improve quality. The few studies available (see e.g. Alkin and Stecher 1983; PA Consulting 2000) suggest that the resources related to these activities are considerable both in the United States and United Kingdom. And given the new public management agenda of increasing public sector efficiency as well as its effectiveness, we need not be very 'clairvoyant' to expect an increasing focus on this issue in the years to come.

Third, another spin-off question concerning the fundamental choices related to how best to regulate, control, or improve quality would be to study the impact of the different tools available. As noted earlier, organisation has been a preferred instrument in many national quality assurance schemes in the past, but there are indications that this view might change. The emergence of qualification frameworks in higher education could, on the one hand, be said to be yet another instrument linked to the organisation instrument, but it could, on the other hand, be interpreted as representing a shift towards more legally oriented instruments in the sector. As Brunsson et al. (2000) have argued, such standardisation of higher education's outputs by putting them into the terms of qualification frameworks, may be an alternative instrument for controlling and coordinating complex relationships and situations characterised by mutual dependence between various actors. A question for subsequent study is whether the emergence of qualification frameworks is a sign of the steering models in (European) states turning back to a (renewed) model of state control – do we witness the rise of the 'neo-Weberian' state here (Pollitt and Bouckaert 2004), with its reaffirmation of the state's role and its rule through (administrative) law, but shifting its focus to meeting citizens' needs and wishes? Alternatively, we can point to the 'Model of State Interference' (Kraak 2001) to explain this new form of control by the state. Being unable to adequately steer autonomous institutions when implementing market approaches for competition, "the State resorts sporadically to extraordinary measures that attempt to force reality to conform to its wishes when the institutional framework model does not produce the results desired by political actors" (Teixeira, Rosa, and Amaral 2004: 306).

Of special interest for higher education is the question of whether increased standardisation of quality assurance would affect the use and role of expert knowledge when reviewing quality. Even though the peer review mechanism, in one form or another, is part of most quality assurance schemes at present (Van Vught and Westerheijden 1994), this should not be taken for granted. Standardisation towards a large-scale scheme – possibly a European-wide accreditation scheme – may turn peers (respected colleagues with whom evaluated academics may discuss their education) into administrators or even inspectors (who from a position of power come to check compliance with standards and criteria). In a sense, this change takes us back to the question of the lack of trust in higher education and its institutions: academics may no longer be trusted sufficiently by external stakeholders – the neo-Weberian state in particular – to judge the quality of teaching programmes. On the other hand, just labelling something a 'standard' does not necessarily mean a similar outcome or effect (Prøitz, Stensaker, and Harvey 2004; Stensaker and Harvey 2006).

In the fourth place, we need to question what exactly we study when analysing quality assurance. As emphasised in a number of chapters in the book, quality assurance has been poorly defined by politicians, but also rather under-analysed from a theoretical perspective. In sum, this has led to considerable methodological challenges when analysing the concept which is probably the main reason for the current paucity of methodologically sound impact studies in this area. The conclusion that quality assurance is 'translated' into higher education, recognising the ability and skills higher education institutions often demonstrate when adapting to public policy making in the sector, can of course also contribute to overlooking the possibility that organisational change can be caused by factors not controlled for in the analysis. As Rosa and Amaral argue in their analysis of the application of the EFQM model, we should not overlook the possibility that a reason for the relatively successful adaptation that they found, is that the 'rough edges' related to this model have been 'sanded down'. But how much change in a concept can be allowed before we are actually analysing something else? Only a theory – which as we said is still lacking – can say when 'the same' is 'really different' (Lieshout 1983). Of particular interest here is to further investigate what individual teachers experience as implemented quality assurance mechanisms, and how they perceive the changes experienced (see also Newton 1999; Westerheijden, Hulpiau, and Waeytens 2006).

In the fifth place, related to the previous point, we also need to know more about how quality assurance as an idea and concept is spread internationally. As shown in this book, there are obvious political and economic (cf. the chapters by Westerheijden and Perellon), and cultural and global (cf. the chapters by Stensaker, and Rosa and Amaral) forces driving the process. But what are the interrelationships between these forces? Do these drivers reinforce each other towards a single solution, or do they open the policy design space up for more diversity in approaches, and also for possibilities for national and institutional translations? Two sub-themes are of special interest here. First, there is a need to more thoroughly analyse the reasons for the spread of particular measures within quality assurance. Do we witness policy copying on a large scale (as e.g. with accreditation schemes or through the use of the open method of coordination in the EU, which is based on benchmarks and indicators), symbolic adaptation or specific national agendas underlying the process (Schwarz and Westerheijden 2004)? Second, as addressed in this volume by Perellon, how do quality issues relate to other pressing issues on the higher education agenda such as internationalisation, and the interplay between higher education and the surrounding society, etc.?

Finally, relating to other higher education research, what are the relevant methods and approaches for instigating change in higher education? What are the levers that stimulate improvements in teaching and learning? As Stensaker (2003: 152) puts it, there is a "need for a critical review of what the impact of external quality monitoring is on higher education". So far most impact studies have concentrated on the effectiveness of quality systems rather than on "the impact that the process has had on, for example, the learning experience, pedagogic development, or the nature of research outcomes" (Harvey and Newton 2004: 154). In this book, Harvey and Newton, Rosa and Amaral, and also D'Andrea emphasised the need for more studies on the micro-level examining various perspectives and designs for improving teaching and learning (see also Westerheijden, Hulpiau, and Waeytens 2006). But finding evidence on the impact of quality assessment processes is made difficult by several factors, including methodological problems such as the difficulty to isolate the effects of assessment from those of other processes impinging on higher education (Stensaker 2003; Harvey and Newton 2004; Carr, Hamilton, and Meade 2005), the task being further complicated by, for example, the complex nature of higher education institutions (Weusthof 1995; Askling 1997; Brennan 1997; Stensaker 2003). Over the years, many studies on quality assurance have been remarkably decoupled from more traditional studies within pedagogy, learning theory and more anthropological approaches to grasp the essence of higher education. Recent developments within the sector, for example the creation of the Higher Education Academy in the United Kingdom, and an increasing interest to link structure and action – or, to be more specific, organisation and learning – are therefore interesting as future areas for research (see e.g. D'Andrea and Gosling 2005).

4. QUALITY, QUO VADIS?

New functions have emerged for quality assurance. The old, one might almost say, eternal, questions of regulation, accountability versus improvement, or the quest for the ultimate definition of the quality concept remain. Yet in the changing context characterised by increasing internationalisation and globalisation, and by shifting costs from states to individuals (e.g. the introduction or substantial increase of tuition fees), quality assurance is acquiring a new balance of functions: communicating information about qualities to prospective students is maybe the most important direction of change. Quality assurance acquires new 'neighbours' as policy instruments in that process; particularly now that much attention is placed on the relationship between quality assurance and ranking.[1] The body of literature on report cards of higher education institutions and of study programmes is rapidly increasing. The previous attitude of sceptical dismissal that seemed to dominate the higher education community (Bowden 2000; Clarke 2002; Schatz 1993; Yorke 1998) is giving way to making use of rankings and 'report cards' to inform and attract prospective students – still sceptical due to the shaky methodology of most report cards (Duffy and Cary 1999; Gottlieb 1999; Van Raan 2005). Quality information is part of some report cards (Dill and Soo 2005; Van Dyke 2005). Both quality assurance and report cards are becoming associated with institutional marketing – an emerging area for most higher education institutions. Quality assurance in that perspective becomes an instrument in 'branding' of higher education institutions (Bélanger, Syed, and Mount 2006; Usher and Savino 2006).

In many Western states, the student market is changing from a sellers' market with sheer unlimited demand from growing cohorts of youngsters, growing proportions of whom were attracted to higher education, to a buyers' market with shrinking cohorts of whom almost all with sufficient talent are already in higher education. Three responses seem to dominate reactions in these states.

First, higher education institutions search for new 'pools' of students. Beyond the traditional, young adults who study on campus, full time, the numbers of mature learners are increasing. They are often persons who did not enter higher education immediately after secondary school ('second chance' learners – a temporary 'pool' given the increasing participation rates) or who return to higher education for additional training after some years of gaining work experience ('lifelong learners'). Delivery of study programmes to these mature learners typically is more varied in methods and timing; as a consequence, part-time studies with 'blended' modes of learning (including distance education through online means but also face-to-face teaching) are becoming more prominent in many more higher education institutions than before. Mature learners may often act more like 'informed consumers' than young students, so that communicating a study programme's qualities to these prospective learners is becoming more relevant from the institutional perspective. This development represents a challenge in that many of the quality assurance schemes operating today have a focus on the traditional ways of providing higher education, in which students are assumed to be young (ca. 18–24 years of age), studying full time, and on campus. There is a need to develop more flexible and adaptable information systems on quality (report cards based on suitably adapted quality assurance schemes?) to cater for this increased diversity.

Second, higher education institutions in states with shrinking traditional demand for higher education try to increase their market share, both among traditional and new 'pools' of students, in competition with other higher education institutions nationally. In brief, the competition in the student market is growing. As we mentioned, this is likely to create a strong link between quality assurance and institutional branding efforts, which may also create new challenges for the accountability function of quality assurance. In a more competitive market, trust and legitimacy may become more important as a means to stand out from the rest: credibility is probably the prime message that a brand carries. How quality assurance schemes can fulfil a function in this new game of trust and legitimacy, while maintaining their traditional balance of trust between states and higher education institutions which remains necessary for their acceptance as a steering instrument in public policy, will become a major challenge.

And third, higher education institutions are transgressing national borders much more consciously than previously. Internationalisation is no longer an academic hobby horse, but has become a dire necessity to attract students from abroad. This is another 'pool' of students, and in many cases an especially attractive one, as foreign students often pay (substantially) higher tuition fees than national ones – or in the European Union, higher than EU citizens. This tendency increased or perhaps even created the competition among higher education institutions globally. This development will most likely raise questions about the cultural sensitivity of quality assurance and also create new tensions as national objectives related to higher education are confronted with emerging international conceptions about quality standards.

These three reactions have been stimulated by many states' governments, for – as far as we can see – mainly three reasons. One has to do with states stimulating the development of the knowledge economy, implying amongst other things that a higher proportion of the labour force trained at the higher education level is seen as a national need. Another reason for governments stimulating competition among higher education institutions is that in current political discourses this supposedly contributes to the improvement of quality of education. In the eyes of politicians, a probably not unimportant side effect of stimulating higher education institutions to enter the marketplace is that through higher education institutions earning additional income on the market, the claims of higher education on the state budget may be reduced. In this way, the second reason blurs into the third, namely, that states see in higher education an option for benefits in international trade competition. Potential benefits may seem large at this moment for Western countries with well-developed higher education systems in the face of fast-growing demand for higher education in emerging countries, especially in South and South-East Asia. But with those countries building up their own higher education capacities just as they have built up their industrial capacities (growth rates of higher education in countries like China are as unmatched as those of the Chinese economy as a whole), this is bound to be a temporary 'solution' for maintaining higher education capacity in the Western world; the more so, as countries such as China, India, Malaysia, and other Asian nations are the market for South-South higher education trade.

Higher education institutions in many countries, in sum, have many reasons to communicate their quality in a much more emphatic way than before to all their prospective students. And, equally, as competition in markets and quasi-markets for research contracts, service teaching, etc. is increasing too, higher education institutions have ever more reasons to include other stakeholders and clients in their communication efforts. It looks likely, therefore, that quality, report cards and branding are becoming another 'unholy trinity'.

Experiences with quality assurance both in Europe and the United States would seem to indicate that the increased marketisation of higher education does not mean a decrease in regulation. Perhaps the contrary: while the amount of bureaucratic ex ante control may have been reduced, the regulation of the quality assurance schemes – defining at the higher education system level what to evaluate, how and with what consequences, which results in regulation by higher education institutions with respect to by-laws, quality protocols etc. – has led to substantial re-regulation. As the three contributions in Part I show, the introduction of quality assurance has not solved the power questions underlying relations in higher education systems – though it did change the powers and possibilities of the actors involved. Yet it remains difficult to assess who are the winners or losers in the power game. It is debatable whether quality assurance leads to increased 'professionalisation' of higher education, or whether this is yet another process involved in the perceived '(re-)bureaucratisation' of the sector. Related to this, there is also a debate over how quality assurance changes the administrative–academic interface in higher education, blurring the former boundaries between these actors with respect to responsibilities and authority over education and research. As pointed out by Amaral, Fulton, and Larsen (2003), managers today see themselves as essential contributors to the successful functioning of the contemporary university, while a decade ago they were "very much expected to operate in a subservient supportive role to the academic community" (Amaral, Fulton, and Larsen 2003: 286) and even resented being called 'managers' (Westerheijden 1997). What is clear, however, especially from the chapters in Part III, is that it proved very difficult to use quality assurance to empower the teaching and research staff at the work-floor level, or the students. Much of quality assurance is a game between policy makers, quality assurance agencies, institutional managers, and quality professionals. It seems that the institutional consequences of quality assessment have not yet contributed much to actual improvements in teaching and learning or to transforming the student learning experience (Harvey and Newton 2004; Rosa, Tavares, and Amaral 2006).

If the previous paragraph has validity, the question becomes whether the quality assurance game affects the work-floor level of higher education. Is there truth in what we would like to call the 'inner life thesis', that is, the thesis that there is a disparity between the policy world (of policy makers, quality assurance agencies, institutional managers and quality professionals) and the 'chalk-face' world of teaching and research staff in higher education institutions with a very limited 'trickle down' of policy concepts into the still highly autonomous 'inner life' of academe with regard to teaching and research? In brief, does quality assurance help quality improvement? The answers given to this question in the chapters by Rosa and Amaral, D'Andrea, and Harvey and Newton seem to indicate that there is an impact on the 'inner life', but at the same time that there is much room for improvement – to use a quality assurance cliché self-referentially.

This room for improvement leads to the final question we want to raise here: What does this book mean for the further development of quality assurance in higher education? It was hinted above that new routes may have been opened in recent years and that they set new challenges for quality assurance schemes. Where these will lead is yet unknown. New translations and transformations will be required, which in turn will uncover new problems, but also new vistas. Maybe three main directions can be distinguished, in theoretical terms, some of which are inspired by casting a glance at patterns in biological evolution.

One option is that we see an 'arms race' develop. With higher education institutions becoming ever more ingenious in (outwardly) complying with quality assurance exigencies while shielding their 'inner life' to an increasing extent, external quality assurance schemes need to become ever 'tougher' or 'sharper' to remain effective; further spread of accreditation, and of ever more inquisitive approaches to it, are logical next steps in this 'arms race' scenario.

Another option is that the development is not linear, but results in a 'random walk'. Starting from the same premise that higher education institutions become ever more ingenious in (outwardly) complying with any existing quality assurance scheme while increasingly shielding their 'inner life', external quality assurance schemes need to change regularly but in a random fashion to avoid or minimise such undesirable strategic behaviour, without necessarily becoming 'tougher'. Changes of indicators due to methodological considerations by the quality assessment agencies, or as a result of political priorities, may be enough to keep quality management in higher education institutions 'on its toes', never getting the chance to become a routine that can be left to quality professionals. At a different level, when looking into the history of quality assurance there are also indications that 'random walk' is a relevant metaphor for the ideological shifts in quality assurance often resulting from new governments coming into office. As long as governments keep changing, the possibility remains that such effects are also likely in the future.

Finally, and more optimistically, there is the scenario of the 'next generation': endogenous developments in a benign situation are hypothesised to lead to closure (i.e. to the 'solving') of increasingly sophisticated problems, demanding increasingly sophisticated quality assessment schemes. This is the thesis behind Jeliazkova and Westerheijden's (2002) work, but to date it lacks independent corroboration, because the political drivers seemed to always override such inherent developments. Harvey and Newton (Chapter 10) plead for a better focus of external quality assurance schemes on certain goals, enabling 'slimmer', 'lighter touch' arrangements. The return, in the United Kingdom, to institutional audits after the 2001 revolt of the Russell Group universities, may have been an early effort in this direction. Switzerland recently moved in the same direction and current discussions in some European countries, such as Germany and the Netherlands, to move towards varieties of institutional accreditation to reduce the burden of the current programme accreditation schemes, seem to indicate that a tendency may be developing at least in Europe along this third scenario.

A factor not considered in these three theoretical scenarios, which take the borders of the higher education system as a given, is the internationalisation or globalisation of higher education. Cross-border provision of higher education – though to a large extent not directly affected by the free trade principles of the WTO and GATS (Vlk 2006), if only because it also includes, for example, joint degrees by public higher education institutions – requires quality assurance arrangements that transcend the borders of higher education systems. Forums are discussing these issues; quality assurance agencies especially in Europe are experimenting with options for them. But for definitive answers it is yet too early.

'Quo vadis?' – where goest thou? – was the question addressed in this last section. Obviously, we do not know the answer to which route quality assurance is taking. We just know that the road is still under construction.

NOTES

1   As Cremonini, Westerheijden, and Enders (2006) emphasised, "The term 'Report Card' is preferable to 'ranking', because ... what is needed to inform (prospective) students is an overview of elements that help them make a reasoned choice, which is multi-dimensional and subjective. [A report card] pretends to do no more than that – give information about a number of elements or dimensions. 'Ranking' on the other hand is inherently a uni-dimensional and often 'objective' (in the sense of: same for all) list of higher education institutions or study programmes ordered from 'best' to 'worst'".

REFERENCES

Alkin, M.C. and B. Stecher. "A Study of Evaluation Costs." In Alkin, M.C. and L.C. Solmon (eds). *The Costs of Evaluation*. Beverly Hills: Sage Publications, 1983, 119–132.

Amaral, A., O. Fulton. and I.M. Larsen. "A Managerial Revolution?" In Amaral, A., V.L. Meek, and I.M. Larsen (eds). *The Higher Education Managerial Revolution?* Dordrecht: Kluwer Academic Publishers, 2003, 275–296.

Askling, B. "Quality Monitoring as an Institutional Enterprise." *Quality in Higher Education* 3.1 (1997): 17–26.

Ball, C. *Fitness for Purpose*. Guildford: SRHE/NFER-Nelson, 1985.

Bélanger, C., S. Syed, and J. Mount. "The Make up of Institutional Branding: Who, What, How?" Paper presented at the 28th Annual EAIR Forum, Rome, 30 August – 1 September, 2006.

Bowden, R. "Fantasy Higher Education: University and College League Tables." *Quality in Higher Education* 6.1 (2000): 41–60.

Brennan, J. "Authority, Legitimacy and Change: The Rise of Quality Assessment in Higher Education." *Higher Education Management* 9.1 (1997): 7–29.

Brennan, J. and T. Shah. *Managing Quality in Higher Education: An International Perspective on Institutional Assessment and Change*. Buckingham: Society for Research into Higher Education and Open University Press, 2000.

Brunsson, N., B. Jacobsson, and Associates. *A World of Standards*. Oxford: Oxford University Press, 2000.

Carr, S., E. Hamilton, and P. Meade. "Is it Possible? Investigating the Influence of External Quality Audit on University Performance." *Quality in Higher Education* 11.3 (2005): 195–211.

Clarke, M. "Quantifying Quality: What Can the *US News & World Report* Rankings Tell Us about the Quality of Higher Education?" *Education Policy Analysis Archives* 10.16 (2002).

Cremonini, L., D.F. Westerheijden, and J. Enders. "Disseminating the Right Information to the Right Audience: Cultural Determinants in the Use (and Misuse) of Report Cards." Paper presented at the CHER 19th Annual Conference, Kassel, Germany, 7–9 September, 2006.

Csizmadia, T. *Quality Management in Hungarian Higher Education: Organisational Responses to Governmental Policy.* Enschede: CHEPS, University of Twente, 2006.

D'Andrea, V.M. and D. Gosling. *Improving Teaching and Learning in Higher Education: A Whole Institution Approach.* Buckingham: Society for Research into Higher Education and Open University Press, 2005.

Dill, D.D. "Designing Academic Audit: Lessons Learned in Europe and Asia." *Quality in Higher Education* 6.3 (2000): 187–207.

Dill, D.D. and M. Soo. "Transparency and Quality in Higher Education Markets." In Teixeira, P., B. Jongbloed, D.D. Dill, and A. Amaral (eds). *Markets in Higher Education: Rhetoric or Reality?* Dordrecht: Kluwer, 2004, 61–85.

Dill, D.D. and M. Soo. "Academic Quality, League Tables, and Public Policy: A Cross-national Analysis of University Ranking Systems." *Higher Education* 49.4 (2005): 495–533.

Duffy, B. and P. Cary. "Dissension in the Rankings: *US News* Responds to *Slate*'s 'Best Colleges' Story." *Slate.* 7 September, 1999.

Frazer, M. "Report on the Modalities of External Evaluation of Higher Education in Europe: 1995–1997." *Higher Education in Europe* 22.3 (1997): 349–401.

Gottlieb, B. "Cooking the School Books: How *US News* Cheats in Picking its 'Best American Colleges'." *Slate.* 1 September, 1999.

Harvey, L. and D. Green. "Defining Quality." *Assessment & Evaluation in Higher Education* 18.1 (1993): 9–34.

Harvey, L. and P.T. Knight. *Transforming Higher Education.* Buckingham: Society for Research into Higher Education and Open University Press, 1996.

Harvey, L. and J. Newton. "Transforming Quality Evaluation." *Quality in Higher Education* 10.2 (2004): 149–65.

Jeliazkova, M. and D.F. Westerheijden. "Systemic Adaptation to a Changing Environment: Towards a Next Generation of Quality Assurance Models." *Higher Education* 44.3/4 (2002): 433–448.

Kraak, A. "Policy Ambiguity and Slippage: Higher Education under the New State, 1994–2001." CHET Commissioned Paper, 2001, http://www.chet.org.za/papers.asp.

Lieshout, R.H. "Kleine methodologie voor de vergelijkende politicologie." *Acta Politica* XVIII.3 (1983): 307–328.

Neave, G. "On the Cultivation of Quality, Efficiency and Enterprise: An Overview of Recent Trends in Higher Education in Western Europe, 1986–88." *European Journal of Education* 23.1/2 (1988): 7–23.

Newton, J. "An Evaluation of the Impact of External Quality Monitoring on a Higher Education College (1993–98)." *Assessment & Evaluation in Higher Education* 24.2 (1999): 215–235.

PA Consulting. *Better Accountability for Higher Education: Summary of a Review for the HEFCE.* Report August 00/36. London: Higher Education Funding Council for England, 2000.

Pollitt, C. and G. Bouckaert. *Public Management Reform: A Comparative Analysis.* 2nd edn. Oxford: Oxford University Press, 2004.

Premfors, R. "Policy Analysis." In Clark, B. and G. Neave (eds). *Encyclopedia of Higher Education.* Oxford: Pergamon Press, 1992, 1907–1915.

Prøitz, T.S., B. Stensaker, and L. Harvey. "Accreditation, Standards and Diversity: An Analysis of EQUIS Accreditation Reports." *Assessment & Evaluation in Higher Education* 29.6 (2004): 735–750.

Rosa, M.J., D.A. Tavares, and A. Amaral. "Institutional Consequences of Quality Assessment." *Quality in Higher Education* 12.2 (2006): 145–159.

Sabatier, P. "Policy Change over a Decade or More." In Sabatier, P. and H. Jenkins-Smith (eds). *Policy Change and Learning.* Boulder: Westview Press, 1993, 13–39.

Schatz, M. "What's Wrong with MBA Ranking Surveys?" *Management Research News* 16.7 (1993): 15–18.

Schwarz, S. and D.F. Westerheijden (eds). *Accreditation and Evaluation in the European Higher Education Area.* Dordrecht: Springer, 2004.

Stensaker, B. "Trance, Transparency and Transformation: The Impact of External Quality Monitoring on Higher Education." *Quality in Higher Education* 9.2 (2003): 151–159.

Stensaker, B. and L. Harvey. "Old Wines in New Bottles? A Comparison of Public and Private Accreditation Schemes in Higher Education." *Higher Education Policy* 19.1 (2006): 65–85.

Teixeira, P., M.J. Rosa, and A. Amaral. "Is There a Higher Education Market in Portugal?" In Teixeira, P., B. Jongbloed, D. Dill, and A. Amaral (eds). *Markets in Higher Education: Rhetoric or Reality?* Dordrecht: Kluwer Academic Publishers, 2004, 291–310.

Usher, A. and M. Savino. "One Size Fits All: Global University League Tables." Paper presented at the 28th Annual EAIR Forum, Rome, 30 August – 1 September, 2006.

Van Dyke, N. "Twenty Years of University Report Cards." *Higher Education in Europe* 30.2 (2005): 103–125.

Van Raan, A.F.J. "Fatal Attraction: Conceptual and Methodological Problems in the Ranking of Universities by Bibliometric Methods." *Scientometrics* 62.1 (2005): 133–143.

Van Vught, F.A. and D.F. Westerheijden. "Towards a General Model of Quality Assessment in Higher Education." *Higher Education* 28.3 (1994): 355–371.

Vlk, A. *Higher Education and GATS: Regulatory Consequences and Stakeholders' Responses.* Enschede: CHEPS, University of Twente, 2006.

Westerheijden, D.F. "A Solid Base for Decisions: Use of the VSNU Research Evaluations in Dutch Universities." *Higher Education* 33.4 (1997): 397–413.

Westerheijden, D.F., J. Brennan, and P.A.M. Maassen (eds). *Changing Contexts of Quality Assessment: Recent Trends in West European Higher Education.* Utrecht: Lemma, 1994.

Westerheijden, D.F., V. Hulpiau, and K. Waeytens. "Lines of Change in the Discourse on Quality Assurance: An Overview of Some Studies into What Impacts Improvement." Paper presented at the 28th Annual EAIR Forum, Rome, 30 August – 1 September, 2006.

Weusthof, P. "Dutch Universities: An Empirical Analysis of Characteristics and Results of Self-evaluation." *Quality in Higher Education* 1.3 (1995): 235–248.

Yorke, M. "*The Times*' League Table of Universities, 1997: A Statistical Appraisal." *Quality Assurance in Education* 6.1 (1998): 58.

Higher Education Dynamics

1. J. Enders and O. Fulton (eds.): *Higher Education in a Globalising World.* 2002
    ISBN Hb 1-4020-0863-5; Pb 1-4020-0864-3

2. A. Amaral, G.A. Jones and B. Karseth (eds.): *Governing Higher Education: National Perspectives on Institutional Governance.* 2002   ISBN 1-4020-1078-8

3. A. Amaral, V.L. Meek and I.M. Larsen (eds.): *The Higher Education Managerial Revolution?* 2003   ISBN Hb 1-4020-1575-5; Pb 1-4020-1586-0

4. C.W. Barrow, S. Didou-Aupetit and J. Mallea: *Globalisation, Trade Liberalisation, and Higher Education in North America.* 2003   ISBN 1-4020-1791-X

5. S. Schwarz and D.F. Westerheijden (eds.): *Accreditation and Evaluation in the European Higher Education Area.* 2004   ISBN 1-4020-2796-6

6. P. Teixeira, B. Jongbloed, D. Dill and A. Amaral (eds.): *Markets in Higher Education: Rhetoric or Reality?* 2004   ISBN 1-4020-2815-6

7. A. Welch (ed.): *The Professoriate.* Profile of a Profession. 2005 ISBN 1-4020-3382-6

8. Å. Gornitzka, M. Kogan and A. Amaral (eds.): *Reform and Change in Higher Education.* Implementation Policy Analysis. 2005   ISBN 1-4020-3402-4

9. I. Bleiklie and M. Henkel (eds.): *Governing Knowledge.* A Study of Continuity and Change in Higher Education – A Festschrift in Honour of Maurice Kogan. 2005
    ISBN 1-4020-3489-X

10. N. Cloete, P. Maassen, R. Fehnel, T. Moja, T. Gibbon and H. Perold (eds.): *Transformation in Higher Education.* Global Pressures and Local Realities. 2005
    ISBN 1-4020-4005-9

11. M. Kogan, M. Henkel and S. Hanney: *Government and Research.* Thirty Years of Evolution. 2006   ISBN 1-4020-4444-5

12. V. Tomusk (ed.): *Creating the European Area of Higher Education.* Voices from the Periphery. 2006   ISBN 1-4020-4613-8

13. M. Kogan, M. Bauer, I. Bleiklie and M. Henkel (eds.): *Transforming Higher Education.* A Comparative Study. 2006   ISBN 1-4020-4656-1

14. P.N. Teixeira, D.B. Johnstone, M.J. Rosa and J.J. Vossensteijn (eds.): *Cost-sharing and Accessibility in Higher Education: A Fairer Deal?* 2006   ISBN 1-4020-4659-6

15. H. Schomburg and U. Teichler: *Higher Education and Graduate Employment in Europe.* Results from Graduates Surveys from Twelve Countries. 2006
    ISBN 1-4020-5153-0

16. S. Parry: *Disciplines and Doctorates.* 2007   ISBN 1-4020-5311-8

17. U. Teichler: *Careers of University Graduates.* Views and Experiences in Comparative Perspectives. 2007   ISBN 1-4020-5926-4

18. M. Herbst: *Financing Public Universities.* The Case of Performance Funding. 2007
    ISBN 1-4020-5559-5

19. P. Maassen, J.P. Olsen (eds.): *University Dynamics and European Integration*. 2007
     ISBN 978-1-4020-5970-4

20. D.F. Westerheijden, B. Stensaker and M.J. Rosa (eds.): *Quality Assurance in Higher Education*. Trends in Regulation, Translation and Transformation. 2007
     ISBN 978-1-4020-6011-3